The Shaping of *The Dynasts*

THE SHAPING OF *THE DYNASTS*

A Study in Thomas Hardy

WALTER F. WRIGHT

UNIVERSITY OF NEBRASKA PRESS · LINCOLN

Publishers on the Plains

UNP

Copyright © 1967 by the University of Nebraska Press
Library of Congress Catalog Card Number 67–19159

Manufactured in the United States of America

To Allyson

Acknowledgment

A rapidly increasing number of scholars have contributed to our present understanding of Hardy; those whose conclusions are most immediately pertinent are mentioned in the appendix. I wish particularly to express my appreciation to Professor Harold Orel for reading the manuscript. For the use of books in the Hardy Memorial Library I am indebted to the trustees of the Hardy estate, for the use of the manuscripts of *The Dynasts* to Mrs. H. O. Lock and Dr. E. W. Mann, of Dorchester, and to the British Museum. Quotations from *The Dynasts, The Early Life of Thomas Hardy, The Later Years,* and Hardy's other works are by courtesy of Macmillan and Company, Ltd.

The study was facilitated through a year's leave of absence made possible by the Woods Fellowship in the Humanities, and it was made the more pleasant by the many kindnesses of Mr. R. Peers, Miss M. Samuel, and their associates at the Dorset County Museum. From A. B. W. and S. E. W. I have received much help and encouragement.

Introduction

Thomas Hardy preferred to think of himself as, first of all, a poet, and his epic-drama is his poetic magnum opus. It is not better than his finest prose work, but it epitomizes his world view after he had secured from the philosophers the metaphorical structure for expressing what he had long felt to be true. The following pages are concerned with what went into the shaping of the poem.

The first chapter, which draws heavily upon unpublished materials in the Dorset County Museum Memorial Library, treats of the influences upon Hardy's thought. His autobiography, his notebooks, and the marginalia in the books which he read reveal his preoccupation, through the decades, with the eternal questions presented first in the novels and short poems and then in *The Dynasts*.

Continuing to make use of unprinted sources, especially underlinings and marginal notations, we are occupied, in Chapter 2, with Hardy's education as a poet. Though he himself wrote little about the art of literature, he was by no means unlettered in literary theory. He studied carefully the works of other poets and of such critics as Wordsworth and Coleridge. In his reading of poetry he thought as a poet, and he was always in search of instruction.

The Early Life and *The Later Years* contain several references to a prospective ballad or epic on the Napoleonic Wars. The notebooks and other documents in the Memorial Library extensively supplement these allusions. The full evidence—discussed in Chapter 3—reveals how important the subject was as a focus for Hardy's study long before the actual composition of the poem was begun.

Far more than any of his other major works, the epic-drama is concerned with actual fact. In it one sees the poet starting with the life of man as recorded in the pages of history and interpreting and transforming ephemeral incidents to create from them the eternal substance of art. In short, the growth of the poem is a record of a poet's adventure as he explored hundreds of events and from them attempted to extract truths about the nature and fate of mankind. To develop a feeling for the infinite variety of forms in which truth presented itself to Hardy's imagination requires the examination of numerous specific details. Hence, Chapter 4 treats of what Hardy found, where he found it, and how he transmuted it into a work of art. Naturally, such a study, though only sampling the total and concentrating on the most typical examples, is of chief interest to a student of Hardy who is well acquainted with both *The Dynasts* and the incidents and personages conspicuous in the Napoleonic Wars. Hopefully, however, any reader of Hardy will find in it recurrence of themes and artistic perspectives similar to those which he has encountered in the novels or lyric poems.

Finally—in Chapter 5—we come to the poetic process as demonstrated in the recasting of lines in the manuscripts and in the final revisions for the printed text. It is here that we see Hardy at work, both as craftsman and as poet ruminating upon the ironies of life. With thousands of examples in the manuscripts, pretense at completeness would be futile. The chapter can only endeavour to designate the major characteristics and to suggest the riches which await anyone who may have the good fortune to examine the manuscripts themselves.

Contents

A picture section follows page 146.

THE SHAPING OF *THE DYNASTS*

N.B.: (* * *) in quotations from Hardy indicate an editorial deletion; suspension points (...) indicate that the ellipsis occurred in the original.

CHAPTER ONE

Impressions of Reality

THE INFLUENCE OF OTHERS

When the first of the three parts of *The Dynasts* appeared, January 13, 1904, Hardy was sixty-three years old.[1] He had begun, however, to contemplate a work of epic range with Europe as its scene as early as 1874, and he had settled on the tragic view which dominates his dramatic epic before he wrote "Hap," at the age of twenty-five or twenty-six. There was, indeed, a consistency in Hardy's sensation of life which continued until his death in 1928: Man lived in a Universe which did not foster his aspirations; he was doomed to the commission of folly and to suffering; and his fate was both poignant and aesthetically meaningful. This impression supplies the undertone from the earliest poems and prose attempts to the poetry written in the 1920's.

It is impossible to say when Hardy first became aware of a given philosophic concept; it is also unsafe to designate the source of various metrical techniques. The fact that Hardy marked a passage in a book or copied in one of his notebooks an extract encountered in his reading does not ensure his having been struck with its novelty. Rather, since many similar passages were checked, it is apparent that he often singled out familiar modes of expression of equally familiar ideas.

Nevertheless, in trying to establish what went into the origin and the making of *The Dynasts* one is reminded that Hardy was dependent on his predecessors. Though he was much more original as an author than in the restoration of churches, his hints came from his reading in literature and philosophy. Even in "Hap" he was not an unlettered

[1] The first issue of *The Dynasts | A Drama of the Napoleonic Wars, | in Three Parts, Nineteen | Acts & One Hundred and | Thirty Scenes | by* Thomas Hardy | Part First was dated 1903, but, for copyright considerations the title page was cancelled and one bearing the date 1904 was substituted. Part II is similarly dated 1905 and 1906. Part III appeared in 1908. Cf., Richard L. Purdy, *Thomas Hardy: A Bibliographical Study* (London: Oxford University Press, 1954).

poet, for his serious study in English poetry, in the Bible, and in the classics had begun in early youth. By 1903 he had immersed himself in nineteenth-century thought, repeatedly reread the classics, and become acquainted with current German philosophy. If no single lines in *The Dynasts* are more profound than many from his twenties, the poem is nonetheless an edifice made possible only by long years of study and the meditation which it encouraged.

For a general impression of Hardy's reading the most immediate sources are *The Early Life of Thomas Hardy* (1928) and *The Later Years of Thomas Hardy* (1930), published under the name of Mrs. Hardy, but almost entirely autobiographic.[2] In organizing his life history with the aid of old notes, Hardy named authors and books, sometimes in mere lists of his reading, with no attempt at completeness.[3] His fragmentary account is useful mainly to suggest some of the authors he most valued when he recalled his intellectual adventures and to help in determining at what time in his life he read them.

The other primary sources—apart from allusions in his works—are the books from his library, his notebooks, and other papers now in the Dorset County Museum Memorial Library. After her husband's death Mrs. Hardy assisted in selecting books most treasured by Hardy, especially those which he had annotated, though a few of the latter, including copies of classical authors, were not retained.[4] It is to be presumed that he had made use of some of the voluminous list of books which were sold, but one dare not equate possession with reading.[5] In most of the books in the Memorial Library there are underlinings,

---

[2] Cyril Clemens, in *My Chat with Thomas Hardy* (Webster Groves: International Mark Twain Society, 1944), p. 26, remarked that in 1925 Hardy told him: "Well, I intend to write my autobiography through my good wife. Each day I slant my memoirs, as though my wife were writing them herself. After she has copied the day's stint on the typewriter, we hold a discussion, and she makes invaluable suggestions which are almost immediately incorporated in the text." Evelyn Hardy considers the last four chapters Mrs. Hardy's work, based, of course, on Hardy's notes.

[3] Some of the notebooks, in accord with Hardy's request, were burnt after his death; others were dispersed. Those remaining are in the Thomas Hardy Memorial Library.

[4] Some of the books were examined by W. R. Rutland while they were still at Max Gate; others are among books from Hardy's library now in the Colby College collection.

[5] Numerous titles in the sales catalogues are of sets, running to many volumes. In the Memorial Library there are uncut volumes, and it appears that late in life

marginal markings, and scattered short comments. In a very few instances the annotations are dated, some volumes have a date on the flyleaf, and in several others the year of publication defines the earliest limit of Hardy's reading. With help from the autobiography and from documents yet to be noted, one can conclude that Hardy had read most of the works before 1908, when the third part of *The Dynasts* was published, and usually well before 1903. As for the others, including books printed after 1908, one finds in Hardy's annotations of them the same preoccupations that shaped *The Dynasts*.

His own library did not, of course, furnish Hardy all his literary and philosophic stimulation. In the manuscripts in the Memorial Library are extracts, sometimes in Hardy's own original handwriting, taken from books and magazine articles. Most of these are dated, at least approximately, and others are headed "from old notes written before 'The Dynasts.'" A few of the quotations are from books Hardy eventually owned. Some are identified as copies of earlier notes, and the fact that Hardy had copies made shows the importance he attached to them.

The markings in the Memorial Library volumes include exclamation points and negative annotations. Almost all, however, are of passages with which Hardy found himself in accord as a poet, whatever he may have thought of the writer's philosophic tenets. He required of such authors as Dante, Wordsworth, and Tolstoi, whose theology or philosophy he could seldom accept, that their sensation of life be in some respect true to his own experience. The manuscript notes nearly always quote views harmonious with Hardy's own. A very few times he cited reviews which damned a book's arguments, and in rare instances he quoted only to condemn. These examples, though scant in number, confirm what could otherwise be assumed, that Hardy was putting all authors on trial as he read them. He concurred with such philosophers as Schopenhauer and Hartmann because of what he brought to them. And yet—and particularly from these two authors— he took something additional that justified his copying their words.

Though Hardy would, of course, have maintained with Spenser that form and substance are ultimately inseparable, he marked numerous passages in his books because of what they said, and in his

---

Hardy accumulated the complete works of writers in whom he had previously read selectively.

literary notes he copied long prose excerpts for their ideas. What were these philosophic concepts or impressions which attracted him?[6]

In defending his work, including *The Dynasts*, Hardy maintained that any theology in it was of ancient heritage, though modified in the light of modern thought. Often in the nineties and afterward he was attacked for the gloom which enveloped his characters and for his non-Christian premises. Hardy protested that, if anything, he should be called "churchy." When young he had taught Sunday school; in checking his notes he found particular allusion to his Bible reading in 1870; "In Time of 'The Breaking of Nations'" takes its title from the fifty-first chapter of Jeremiah, and there are scores of biblical echoes in the novels and the other poems. Most certainly, however, passages in the Scriptures meant something to him which was not narrowly churchy at all, at least in the modern sense. Rather, they asserted the eternal recurrence of suffering and the inevitability of death. Some of the most bitter feelings in *The Return of the Native* and in *Jude the Obscure* are clothed in language or in rhythms of the King James Version.

So it is that in a memorandum of 1899 or later headed "Pessimism" Hardy wrote, "Was there ever any great poetry which was not pessimistic?" and he continued from memory, "'All creation groaneth' +c / 'Man that is born of woman' +c / 'Man dieth and wasteth away' +c T.O. / 'I go hence like the shadow that departeth' +c (+ other Psalms)."[7] "Is that pessimism," he queried, "+ if not, why not? The answer would probably be because a remedy is offered. Well the remedy tarries long."[8] Here, and elsewhere in the Bible, was a stark recognition of the relentless sequence of pain and death. The Bible, Hardy admitted, offered a hope; but, unglossed with optimistic interpretation, the lines quoted did not. For that matter, "After-Courses" in *The Return* held out a rather conventional hope, and the concluding chorus of the Pities in *The Dynasts* a more thoughtful one:

[6] In the preface to *Tess of the D'Urbervilles* Hardy insisted that a novel is "an impression, not an argument"; in that to *The Dynasts* he stated that the "doctrines" uttered by the Intelligences were "but tentative."

[7] From Romans 8:22; Job 14:1 and 14:10; and Psalms 109:23.

[8] Memoranda, I. Whenever the notebooks are paginated, the page will be cited. Otherwise the date or approximate date readily identifies the location.

But—a stirring thrills the air
Like to sounds of joyance there
That the rages
Of the ages
Shall be cancelled, and deliverance offered from
the darts that were,
Consciousness the Will informing, till It fashion
all things fair!

But at least of the ills narrated in the epic it could equally be said that the remedy tarries long.

The tone of *The Dynasts* varies. After the mad fever of the battles there descends a quiet of exhaustion and desolation, and there are panoramic views in which soldiers are lost wanderers on the face of an indifferent or seemingly hostile earth. Such scenes are reminiscent of the Psalms, of Ecclesiastes, of the Book of Job, and of the lamentations of the homeless. Hardy's "It" was not the God of either Testament, despite his quoting a line from the Magnificat and, with a change of context, fitting it to his own impersonal Will:

To Thee whose eye all Nature owns,
Who hurlest Dynasts from their thrones * * * .[9]

The mortal passions in his poetry, however, could be found in both Testaments. As he restudied the biblical narratives he was reconfirmed in his bitterness—and his compassion.

Hardy's education at Dorchester included Latin and French. With this foundation, he records in his autobiography, he "took up Greek" when about sixteen years old. Though he notes that he later discontinued Greek tragedy except for "fragmentary" study, his remark must refer to reading in the original; for he made use of specific passages in his novels and in *The Dynasts*. As one might expect, too, in the works of English poets, particularly Arnold and Swinburne, he got at second hand—and sometimes in distorted form—Greek philosophy and the Greek feeling for tragic myth. His primary preoccupation was philosophic, indeed essentially religious, as he was concerned with man's relation to the gods. Hardy's problem in accepting the Greeks is defined in two of several passages which he marked in his copy of Gibbon. Where Gibbon discusses the worship of Greek

[9] After Scene. In a footnote Hardy gives the Greek original from Luke 1:52.

deities in the time of Julian, Hardy put a double line ($\parallel$) by "and the pleasing enchantment produces an imperfect and momentary assent of the imagination to those fables which are the most repugnant to our reason and experience." [10] On the same page he underlined and marked in the margin "instead of an indivisible and regular system, which occupies the *whole extent of the believing mind,* the mythology of the Greeks was composed of a thousand loose and flexible parts . . . ." Gibbon makes a distinction between the proper reading of Homer and the later theology built on the Olympian myths, but what struck Hardy was the looseness of the system. The Greeks could speak of Zeus, of Moira; but their individual gods had some freedom, and man was both a victim of the gods and a being responsible for his actions. [11] Hardy was seeking a theology which would be inclusive, and he came nearest to achieving it in monistic determinism. And yet his own sensation of life required several gods and, at significant moments, free will.

Hardy appears to have been acquainted with most Greek literature. He specifically mentions Plato, he owned Thucydides and Aristotle— among twenty-five unspecified volumes mentioned in the sales catalogue, he read in the original of the *Iliad,* and he wrote Sapphics. It was Pindar and, much more, the three tragic dramatists, however, whose pathos came to him across the centuries—an eternal spirit in avatars unendingly new.

Among several pages of quotations made in 1876 from Mahaffy's *Social Life in Greece,* Hardy included Mahaffy's unqualified praise of Aeschylus: "*No modern theology* has developed higher + purer moral notions than those of Aeschylus + his school, developed afterwards by Socrates + Plato, but first attained by the genius of Aeschylus . . . . He shows the indelible nature of sin, + how it recoils upon the 3^d + 4th gen^r.—thus anticipating one of the most marked features in Xtian

[10] *The History of the Decline and Fall of the Roman Empire,* II, chap. 23, 509, in the seven-volume 1853 edition of Bohn. There is no indication of the date of annotation.

[11] A. P. D. Valakis remarks that for Aeschylus man was in the "clutches" of Moira: there were "impassable bars against which human nature does battle." But there was also a universal progress toward "divine justice . . . moral cosmos . . . righteous consummation." Valakis adds that Hardy's Will is not Moira. He naturally finds the comment of the Pities at the end closest to Aeschylus, as it "reminds us of the Aeschylean idea of moral evolution" ("The *Moira* of Aeschylus and the Immanent Will of Thomas Hardy," *The Classical Journal,* XXI [March, 1926], 431–442).

theology."¹² With his nineteenth-century education in Darwinian science, Hardy could not, like Aeschylus, label an act a sin, but he was convinced of its recoil upon the generations. In his English copy of *Prometheus Bound* Hardy made extensive markings; and in the Greek version beside "Kratos kai Bia" he wrote, "This might be called the Will."¹³ As late as 1903 Hardy copied a page from an introduction to *The Choephori*.¹⁴ His most famous indebtedness to Aeschylus is, of course, near the end of *Tess of the D'Urbervilles*, the Buckley source of which reads, "In truth hereafter the president of the immortals shall have need of me."¹⁵ Had the epitaph on Tess appeared in *The Dynasts*, it could appropriately have been assigned to the Spirit Ironic. It is this Mephistophelean commentator who, in the After Scene of the epic, adapts lines from *The Choephori* to propose the unanswerable question:

> As once a Greek asked I would fain ask too,
> Who knows if all the Spectacle be true,
> Or an illusion of the gods (the Will,
> To wit) some hocus-pocus to fulfil?¹⁶

"*What is fatality.* Sophocles made it clear that the characters of men constitute their fatality * * * . *Our actions*—Each act, as it has had immeasurable antecedents, will be fruitful of immeasurable consequents; for the web of the world is ever-weaving"—in 1876 Hardy copied these pronouncements from J. A. Symonds' *Studies of the Greek Poets*.¹⁷ In so far as he was already inclined toward determinism he would have given less emphasis to character; and yet, when he later conceived of the Immanent Will, he could permit Napoleon's character, while an expression of it, to constitute the Emperor's fatality. The image of the web is at least suggestive of the network imagery in *The Dynasts*.

¹² Literary Notes, I, 61.

¹³ William R. Rutland, *Thomas Hardy: A Study of His Writings and Their Background* (Oxford: Blackwell, 1938), pp. 34 ff. Neither the Dindorf *Poetae Scenici Graeci* (1841), where the notation appears, nor the Bohn Library translations by Theodore A. Buckley of Aeschylus, Sophocles, and Euripedes—once at Max Gate—are in the Memorial Library.

¹⁴ Literary Notes, II, unpaged.

¹⁵ *Prometheus Bound* (1849), verse 169; first noted by Carl Weber, "Thomas Hardy's 'Aeschylean Phrase,'" *The Classical Journal*, XXIX (April, 1934), 533–535.

¹⁶ Identified by Hardy in a footnote.

¹⁷ Literary Notes, I, 69 and 71.

Having begun to read Sophocles at about the same time as he began Aeschylus, Hardy continued to turn to him for oracular pronouncements. He marked his own copy extensively.[18] In a journal entry made at the British Museum, July 24, 1889, he quoted a few words of the Greek from *Oedipus Tyrannus*, verse 1365, and added in parentheses, "'and if there be a woe surpassing woes, it hath become the portion of Oedipus'—Jebb. Cf. Tennyson: 'a deeper deep.'"[19] In an entry of March 1, 1897, he jotted down the motif for a poem—"make a lyric of the speech of Hyllus at the close of the *Trachiniae*." In reproducing the note Hardy added, "It does not appear that this was ever carried out."[20] The gods of Sophocles are anthropomorphic; Hyllus blames them for unashamedly observing the suffering of men, their own offspring, which stems from the folly of the gods themselves. In the chorus of the Spirits after Nelson's heroic death, the Spirit of the Pities speaks of "Necessitation," and continues:

> A life there was
> Among these self-same frail ones—Sophocles—
> Who visioned it too clearly, even the while
> He dubbed the Will "the gods." Truly said he,
> "Such gross injustice to their own creation
> Burdens the time with mournfulness for us,
> And for themselves with shame."[21]

Actually, Sophocles would not have equated his gods with the unconscious force of which Hardy tried to conceive and which he called "It." But Hardy's own characters, be they mortals or, like the Spirit of the Pities, aspects of human thought, feel in anthropomorphic ways.[22] If philosophically the gods of Sophocles are not the Will, poetically here and in several other instances the Will itself is like the gods, for it ceases to be impersonal and perpetrates injustice against its own creation.[23]

[18] Rutland, *Thomas Hardy: A Study*, p. 39.

[19] *The Early Life*, p. 289.

[20] *The Later Years*, pp. 58–59.

[21] Hardy identified his source in a footnote, I, 5, iv.

[22] Hardy has both a Spirit of the Pities and Chorus of the Pities, and similarly choruses for the other Spirits. For simplicity one can speak of Pities, Years, etc.

[23] In *The Return of the Native*, Book First, chap. 7, Hardy had employed Greek mythology in suggesting that, had Eustacia been among the Olympians, there would have been the same whimsical meting out of fortune as now.

Hardy had certainly read Pindar's odes early in his study of the classics. The numerous markings in the 1895 translation by Myers, now in the Memorial Library, indicate that he was singling out felicitous statements of thoughts and passions that had appeared in his own novels and poems. When he marked them cannot be determined, although a passage to be noted later hints of a date before 1903.[24] Many of them emphasize the bewilderment inherent in our human predicament and the bitterness of disillusionment with fate. Typical is a passage which follows the account of Theron's touching the "pillars of Heracles," which is, of course, for Pindar a symbol. Hardy drew a line beside the words with which the ode concludes: "Pathless the things beyond, pathless alike to the unwise and the wise. Here I will search no more; the quest were vain."[25] Marked with double lines is a typically Hardian lament—"Now this they say is of all griefs the sorest, that one knowing good should of necessity abide without lot therein."[26] In the tone of *The Dynasts* is a passage marginally lined in the last paragraph of the ode "For Midas of Akragas": "But if there be any bliss among mortal men, without labour it is not made manifest: it may be that God will accomplish it even to-day, yet the thing ordained is not avoidable: yea, there shall be a time that shall lay hold on a man unaware, and shall give him one thing beyond his hope, but another it shall bestow not yet."[27] The entire sentence might serve as comment on various scenes in Hardy's epic. As for its conclusion— one remembers how much beyond Napoleon's hopes follows the breaking out of the sun at Austerlitz; and one recalls, too, that, when the Emperor at Borodino hails as a good omen the "sun of Austerlitz," he is already fated to disaster in the wastelands of Russia.

Euripedes is less prominent than Aeschylus or Sophocles in Hardy's works. Yet there is a significant comment in the first volume of Hardy's set of Euripedes. After quoting Swinburne's disparaging criticism: "It is far easier to overtop Euripedes by the head and shoulders than to come up to the waist of Sophocles or the knee of Aeschylus," Hardy rebutted, "An old opinion but not true."[28]

[24] *Infra*, p. 114, n. 50.
[25] "For Theron of Akragas," *The Extant Odes of Pindar*, trans. Ernest Myers (London, 1895), p. 13.
[26] "For Arkesilas of Kyrene," in *ibid.*, pp. 78–79.
[27] *Ibid.*, p. 104.
[28] Rutland, *Thomas Hardy: A Study*, p. 35.

In *The Trojan Women* Hardy marked Hecuba's prayer to Jove: "Whoever thou art, hard to be known even by conjecture, Jove, whether thou art the necessity of nature or the mind of mortals, I pray to thee."[29] Hecuba's is the very same philosophic bewilderment with which Hardy was beset in *The Dynasts*.

In his 1904 translation by Gilbert Murray of *The Hippolytus* Hardy put lines beside about twenty verses of a chorus. More pertinent are two marked passages near the beginning. In the first the huntsman queries, "How deems't thou of the Gods? Are they the same?" and Hippolytus replies, "Surely: we are but fashioned on their frame."[30] Since Hardy had, of course, read the play in earlier years, one can recognize in these lines, together with the image of Prometheus in chains, the type of thinking which led him, in *The Return*, to call the heath-dwellers—and all mankind—"fettered gods of the earth."[31] Pitt and Nelson and Napoleon, and indeed the common soldiers in *The Dynasts* are fashioned on godlike frames, and they, too, are in chains. The second passage, spoken by the huntsman, could be recited before every battle in the poem: "What the Gods ask, O Son, that man must pay!" (p. 8).

The influence of Roman thought upon Hardy is overshadowed by the Greek. He records having read several books of the *Aeneid*, some Horace, and some Ovid about 1856. In July, 1865, he mentions having again read Horace, and he remarks of the winter of 1865 that "the following note continually occurs: Read some more Horace."[32] Among the marked passages in his 1859 Bohn edition of Horace is "the jarring harmony of things," which phrase or its Latin original—*concordia discors*—Hardy altered in the After Scene to "the chordless chime of Things."[33]

Part of Hardy's reading of the Latin classics was in an anthology *Thoughts from Latin Authors*, which gave both the original and a translation. Volumes II and III are in the Memorial Library, with "T. Hardy 1864" on a flyleaf. Conspicuous among the marked

[29] *Ibid.*, p. 44.

[30] Euripedes, *The Hippolytus* (London: George Allen), p. 7.

[31] *The Return of the Native*, Book First, chap. 3. Echoes of the sentiment can be found repeatedly in the novels.

[32] *The Early Life*, pp. 36, 64, 69.

[33] *Epistles* i. 12, *The Works of Horace*, trans. C. Smart. The copy is now in the Colby College library.

passages are several from Lucretius. Hardy put double lines beside an attack on superstition. He used a single line by the verses "O miseras hominum . . . ," translated:

> Blind, wretched man! In what dark paths of strife
> We walk this little journey of our life.[34]

And he underlined the famous "Cui tantum in vitâ restet transire malorum," on how an infant falls naked, bloody, and crying from the womb, "a fit presage for all his coming ills." [35] From the excerpts Hardy could not have got a coherent account of the argument of Lucretius. Indeed, the parallels between the philosophies of the two men are only of a general kind. But there is poetic passion in the Latin words, and Hardy could subscribe to their pessimism. In his own works one is sometimes reminded of Lucretius.

Similarly Hardy could find verses in the writings of Vergil that lamented human ills. He marked with double lines "Nusquam tuta fides . . . .":

> Faithless is earth, and faithless are the skies:
> Justice is fled, and truth is now no more.[36]

Perhaps as important as the Roman authors themselves in shaping Hardy's concept of Roman religion was Gibbon's discussion of the transition from worship of the pagan gods to the new Christianity. Almost all Hardy's marks in the seven-volume Bohn edition of Gibbon are in Volumes II and III, particularly Chapters 23, on the apostasy of Julian from an early, wholesome Christianity, and 28, which narrates the triumph of the Christians over the pagans at Rome and their own later reconversion to the practices and superstitions they had presumably overthrown. Hardy marked with double lines "by a strange contradiction he [Julian] disdained the salutary yoke of the gospel, whilst he made a voluntary offering of his reason on the altars of Jupiter and Apollo" (II, 509), and with a single line a reference to the new Platonists, who pretended, "by disengaging the soul from her material bands, to re-unite that immortal particle with the Infinite and Divine Spirit" (II, 514). It was the superstitions, whether traditional Roman, neo-Greek, or fourth-century Christian, that caught his

[34] *On the Nature of Things* ii. 23.

[35] *Ibid.* v. 223. Hardy's library included the 1851 Bohn prose translation of *On the Nature of Things,* now in the Colby College library.

[36] *Aeneid* iv. 373.

interest. As a monist Hardy ought to reject all three types, but he himself had a feeling for premonitions; and he made use of superstition, more often pagan than Christian, in his own narratives—including Napoleon's spectral warning in *The Dynasts*.

As a poet Hardy could go to Vergil, to Lucretius, to Ovid, or to Catullus for an impassioned expression of human anguish;[37] and, though he found many other good things in Horace, it is significant that he singled out for the After Scene "concordia discors." In philosophy he was closest to Lucretius, though with nineteenth-century thought between them.

Certainly Hardy found comfort in the fact that the ills of mankind had been recognized and endured with fortitude from the times of the Hebrews, Greeks, and Romans. Crass casualty might shape the individual destiny, and yet Hardy saw fit to copy in his autobiography a quotation he had made December 31, 1885, from Marcus Aurelius: "This is the chief thing: Be not perturbed; for all things are according to the nature of the universal." [38]

Despite the philosophic abyss between them, Hardy was at one with Dante in his sensation of human suffering, and the Italian poet gave him in heightened intensity what he looked for in his reading of literature, from the Greeks down to his own generation. We have only his copy of the 1882 edition of *The Inferno*, in the original with a parallel translation,[39] though he had, of course, become acquainted with Dante long before. His Italian was self-taught, but quite sufficient for him to read in the original, and his extensive underlinings—mainly in the early pages—are now of it, now of the translation, sometimes of both. Typical are "the eternal pain"—"nell' eterno dolore" (Canto III, l. 2); "Della valle d'abisso dolorosa" (IV, l. 8); "The anguish of the people who are here below, on my face depaints that pity, which thou takest for fear"—"L'angoscia delle genti . . . ." (IV, ll. 19–21); "*There is* no greater pain than to recall a happy time in wretchedness"—"Nessun maggiore . . . ." (V, ll. 121–123); "I am in the Third Circle, *that* of the eternal, accursed, cold, and heavy rain" (VI, ll. 7–8, marked with double marginal lines); and "the

[37] His copy of the 1887 prose translation of *The Poems of Catullus and Tibullus*, by Walter K. Kelly, is in the Colby College library.

[38] *The Early Life*, p. 231.

[39] *Dante's Divine Comedy: The Inferno, A Literal Prose Translation*, trans. John Carlyle (London: George Bell and Sons, 1882).

queen of everlasting lamentation"—"Della Regina dell' eterno pianto" (IX, l. 44). Hardy could comprehend the suffering of the damned and the desolation of Hell.

Perhaps anyone would have been struck by "Who is that, who, without death, goes through the kingdom of the dead?" (VIII, l. 85). Significantly, Hardy underlined it and marked it and the original with double parallel lines. He must have found it easy to identify himself with Dante. There are images and moods in the heath scenes in *The Return* (1878), which were influenced by earlier readings of *The Inferno*,[40] and, of course, the supernatural pattern of *The Dynasts* is in the same tradition as Dante's poem. Its determinism is quite different, and yet it is pertinent that Hardy twice marked "where what is willed can be done" (III, ll. 95–96; V, ll. 23–24), which, at least in tone, makes God the absolute determiner of destiny. As with the Greeks, Hardy could make ample accommodations to find in Dante's theology a place for something akin to the Will.

In English literature Shakespeare was, of course, the most important source of inspiration for Hardy, though the influence was less precise than that of some others. The general resemblances of scenes in both the novels and *The Dynasts* to the low-comedy situations in Shakespeare and the dialogue of soldiers in *Henry IV* and *Henry V* are at once apparent. The numerous markings of words and phrases for stylistic qualities in the 1856 edition of Shakespeare in Hardy's library reveal the thoroughness of his reading.[41] There are even scattered annotations of an elementary factual nature, such as the insertion of the date, August 7, 1485, in *Richard III*. Hardy was obviously concerned to have a clear sense of the relationship of the action in every play.

What is of most importance at the moment is that, in reading Shakespeare, Hardy was from the beginning preoccupied with tragic themes and sentiments. As a boy he loved the plots of Shakespeare's tragedies.[42] In a note of September 6, 1896, he remarked, "Finished reading *King Lear*. The grand scale of the tragedy, scenically, strikes

[40] "Then the whole black phenomenon beneath represented Limbo as viewed from the brink by the sublime Florentine in his vision, and the muttered articulations of the wind in the hollows were as complaints and petitions from the 'souls of mighty worth' suspended therein" (*The Return of the Native*, Book First, chap. 3).

[41] *The Dramatic Works of Wm Shakespeare* (10 vols.; London: Bell and Daldy, 1856).

[42] *The Early Life*, p. 31.

one, and also the large scheme of the plot." [43] Among the passages
Hardy marked in Shakespeare is a lamentation in *Pericles*, III, i, which
we have already encountered in other forms among the Greeks and
Romans, and which one can match in many lines in Hardy:

> O you gods!
> Why do you make us love your goodly gifts
> And snatch them straight away?

In *Henry V*, I, ii, Hardy marked, "Tombless, with no remembrance
over them," and in the margin he added, "cf Sappho."

Inevitably he was intrigued by comments relevant to determinism.
Since in Schopenhauer he found the argument that at moments in
history there could be free will, it would be interesting to know when
and with what opinion he marked in *Julius Caesar*, I, ii, "Men at some
time are masters of their fates." Certainly he found support for his own
view of life in the commentary on *Twelfth Night* by William Watkiss
Lloyd and in somewhat parallel remarks by Lloyd on *Antony and
Cleopatra*. Of Viola, Lloyd wrote, "After her first exertion of will . . .
she simply allows herself to be carried along by the stream of time and
events, which answer to her confidence by floating her at last to
happiness" (III, 480). Hardy put a line by this and also by "Cleopatra
. . . is as much a subject of impulse, and the passion that is born of the
circumstances, and the moment, as the doting Antony" (X, 335).
Impulse, not being controlled by intellect, was, of course, in Hardy's
final philosophy, a direct expression of the Will. Hardy also marked
Lloyd's "the fated superiority of the cool and steadfast gamester for
power, over the ardent and dissipated [Antony]" (X, 338). Whether
or not Shakespeare would fully have accepted Lloyd's making
Octavius a gamester whose casts are fated to succeed, the interpretation
would arrest Hardy. Napoleon, in *The Dynasts*, is unable to leave the
gambling table. His luck is often good, but, whether it is good or bad,
the Emperor chooses to believe that he is a man of Destiny.

In his autobiography Hardy included lists of his reading taken from
his notes of 1887 and 1890. These, together with the lists and quotations in his notebooks, show that he was familiar with the major
works of western Europe and with all the well-known writers of
England from Chaucer to his own time. He obviously valued the books

---

[43] *The Later Years*, p. 54.

for many reasons. The annotations in the Memorial Library copies, however, show variations of the pattern we have already noticed.

In his edition of the poems of Surrey and Sackville, Hardy singled out for his only marking "How No Age Is Content," which laments the loss of youth and joy and the universal restlessness in life.[44] Some of his marks in his Dryden, autographed with the date 1866, are casual identifications, but there are double lines by "And peace itself is war in masquerade" (*Absalom and Achitophel*, Part I, l. 752).[45] One is reminded that in *The Dynasts*, except that men are not at the moment being killed, there is no lessening of strife during the diplomatic sparring and intrigue which fill the intervals of peace. In the 1897 edition of Vaughan some of the marginal lines and all the underlinings seem inspired by the artistry of Vaughan's phrasing. Yet Hardy was impressed by the very quality in the poetry which he himself could not find in life. There was in Vaughan a sufficient recognition of turmoil, but there was also a quiet acceptance. By "The Retreate" Hardy noted, "Cf Wordsworth's Ode," and by "Corruption," "Cf Wordsworth's Ode on Immortality." We are certainly not to suppose that Vaughan resolved Hardy's doubts, but we must remember that Hardy called himself churchy. What Vaughan could achieve through religious meditation is not unlike the peace that settles on Hardy's battlefields when, after the carnage, the curtain of night descends.[46]

Hardy's debt to Milton is, for the most part, something that one feels as he turns from one great epic to an epic drama and senses resemblances in subject and in tragic tone. The possible influence in diction will concern us later. In the 1865 Halifax edition of Milton, autographed by Hardy in 1866, there are several underlinings of words,

[44] *Poetical Works of Henry Howard, Earl of Surrey, Minor Contemporaneous Poets, and Thomas Sackville, Lord Buckhurst* (London: Griffin, n.d.).

[45] *Poetical Works* (Halifax: Milner and Sowerby, 1865).

[46] Henry Vaughan, *Sacred Poems and Pious Ejaculations* (London: George Bell and Sons, 1897).

Tucked inside the cover of a biography of Hardy in the Memorial Library is a five-and-one-half-page carbon copy of notes by Hardy, dated September 17, 1922. Among the corrections of the author's errors is the comment: "In dwelling on Hardy's view of the world, the grave, etc., it is curious that a certain kinship with Donne is not noted." It would be perilous to attribute any given sentiment to Donne, but with Hardy's own acknowledgment to guide one, it is not difficult to find an affinity in the preoccupation with death and the refusal to gloss its harshness.

and beside Satan's "Better to reign ..." Hardy has jotted, "Cf Mormons + Indians." Significantly, the only mark in *Samson Agonistes* is a check beside the third line of Samson's cry:

> God of our fathers! what is man,
> That thou towards him with hand so various,
> Or might I say contrarious,
> Temper'st thy providence through his short course
> Not evenly, as thou rul'st
> The angelic orders, and inferior creatures mute,
> Irrational and brute?

For Hardy consciousness by its very nature brought a feeling of contrariness. Whatever the god to whom one prayed or the Will which one's reason conceived of, the heart of man would still sense a cosmic injustice. In the 1864 Routledge, Warne, and Routledge edition of Milton's *Poetical Works*, autographed "T. H. 1865," the same notation appears on Mormons and Indians, and there are numerous markings, primarily of diction and imagery. Two, however, are concerned with Milton's attempt to reconcile foreknowledge and free will. Hardy marked with double marginal lines

> ... they themselves decreed
> Their own revolt, not I; if I foreknew,[47]
> Foreknowledge had no influence on their fault,
> Which had no less proved certain unforeknown.
>
> (Book III, p. 62)

And by

> To whom the great Creator thus replied:
> "O Son ..."   (Book III, p. 70)

Hardy commented, "The difficulty of reconciling Freewill and Omnipotence very apparent here." It was a difficulty which he himself was destined never to escape. His Will is not Milton's biblical God, and for Hardy there is no possibility of a Paradise to be regained. Yet the Will impels whether man chooses or not, and at the same time the scores of individualized mortals in *The Dynasts* normally assume free will. And though in an evolutionary Universe nothing has been lost to be recovered through the sacrifice of Christ, there is an assertion by

[47] Characteristically, Hardy annotated "if" with the footnote "though."

the Pities of a hope of melioration of the human lot. In one sense Hardy was as far from Milton as from Dante; but the feeling of loss of a happier state was eternal, whether man was called Adam or a fettered god of the earth, whether he was to remember in exile his fortunate estate in Eden or to recall his glad days in Wessex while awaiting death on the alien plain of Vitoria.

Hardy was well acquainted with eighteenth-century English literature, and he acknowledged particularly the influence of Fielding.[48] In the development of his philosophy, however, the literature of the age had little influence. It was in the works of the Romantics that Hardy found the primal questions reasserted. Whether journeying in harmony with the early nineteenth-century poets, as he certainly was with Keats and usually with Byron, or coming out some distance from them, as with Wordsworth and Shelley, he felt the imprint of their words. Since Keats raised no issues which were philosophically controversial for Hardy, he could admire his poems for their beauty and pathos, and he wrote an unreserved tribute to Keats. Byron was of importance for Hardy more for his tone than for any originality of thought. In 1924 Hardy copied from Morley the remark that Byron was penetrated "with the distinctively modern scorn + aversion for the military spirit, + the distinctively modern conviction of its being the most deadly of anachronisms."[49] In the questionings and retorts of the Spirits Ironic and Sinister, both the bitterness and the rhythms are indeed often Byronic, and Hardy drew on Byron for the revelry at Brussels.

Wordsworth was inevitably a major prophet with whom Hardy had to reckon. It has been suggested that Hardy's view of Wordsworth changed with the years from a general acceptance to explicit revolt, but this oversimplifies. At no time in his mature life could Hardy subscribe to a belief in "Nature's holy plan."[50] On the other hand, in no work, including *Jude the Obscure* and *The Dynasts,* could he have written so feelingly of the relation of man and Nature had he not been a student of Wordsworth.

[48] Cf., the carbon copy of September 17, 1922; also letter of November 20, 1895, in *The Later Years,* p. 42.

[49] Memoranda, II.

[50] "Some people would like to know whence the poet whose philosophy is in these days deemed as profound and trustworthy as his song is sweet and pure, gets his authority for speaking of 'Nature's holy plan'" (*Tess of the D'Urbervilles,* chap. 3).

As with Milton, Hardy marked numerous passages in Wordsworth for the diction and imagery. He also noted those which epitomized Wordsworth's thought. In the 1864 edition,[51] which Hardy purchased by 1873, he underlined or otherwise marked in "Tintern Abbey": "The still sad music of humanity," "A presence that disturbs me," and "Knowing that Nature never did betray / The heart that loved her." He put X's or lines by several sonnets dealing with liberty, by the entire sonnet "Written in London, September 1802," and by the first ten lines of the sonnet "I dropped my pen . . . ," written while Wordsworth was attacking the Convention of Cintra. In "Elegiac Stanzas Suggested by a Picture of Peele Castle in a Storm" Hardy underlined and marked with double lines "A deep distress hath humanised my Soul."

In the 1896 edition[52] Hardy again marked "The still sad music of humanity." and "A presence . . . ," though his main use of the set appears to have been confined to the Preface to the *Lyrical Ballads*. In Walter Raleigh's *Wordsworth* (1903) appeared a crucial statement: "Pain and evil, as Wordsworth saw them, did not shake his faith in the law of happiness" (146). The first word of Hardy's annotation is illegible; the second is "Why?"

These key annotations, supported by others, give the clue to both Hardy's acceptance and his discontent with Wordsworth. Hardy found no law of happiness in the natural world or spiritual. In his view of Nature he could allow for nothing beneficent. But as he explicitly stated in *The Return*, man could sense a fellow feeling in Nature; for the thinking man of the late nineteenth century the mood would, of course, be that of Egdon Heath or a moor. More important, however, was the "still sad music of humanity" and the fact that distress would humanize the soul. This is the kind of music that has filled the ears of the Pities; it is the distress that has prepared them to ignore the logic of Years and the taunts of the Spirit Sinister to affirm the reality of compassion in a world gone mad.

There is no copy of Shelley in the Memorial Library, but Hardy knew his poetry well. In 1887, for example, he recorded that while in Italy he thought a good deal about Browning and Shelley.[53] The

[51] *The Poetical Works of William Wordsworth* (London: Routledge, Warne, and Routledge). The volume is autographed "Thomas Hardy 16 Westbourne Park Villas," where Hardy lived 1862–1867 and again 1870–1873.

[52] Wordsworth, *Poems* (8 vols.; London: Macmillan).

[53] *The Early Life*, p. 252.

contrast between the aerial spirit in much of Shelley and the earth-treading realism in much of Hardy is at once apparent. When, as in *The Dynasts*, however, Hardy moved into the realm of figurative representation of human thought, he not only remembered the art of *Prometheus Unbound*; he allowed his supernatural Intelligences to range a cosmos where the material world fell away and only a spiritual essence remained. In that realm the Spirits debate. With the folly of dynastic struggles unfolding before them and a background in post-Darwinian thought, they cannot agree that the world's great age will begin anew. They have become more sober than Shelley's spokesmen. They are experienced in the grayness and desolation of a scientifically defined universe and some of them have come to doubt the validity of human effort. But Hardy himself would not have called them more imaginative or brilliant in their insights than the figments of Shelley's mind. If they had other ancestors, too, they still owed something to the author of *Hellas, Adonais, Prometheus Unbound,* and *The Revolt of Islam*.[54]

As for the most important of the Continental Romantics, Hardy owned Goethe's *Faust* in the 1860 edition of Hayward's translation, given him by his friend H. M. Moule.[55] The only marks in it are under the heading "Night," immediately after the Prologue in Heaven. Hardy checked "What you term the spirit of the times is at bottom only your own spirit, in which the times are reflected" (pp. 18–19). In a memorandum of June 16, 1875, he noted, "Reading Life of Goethe," and at about the same time he drew on the *Life* to remark, "Goethe's religion was all taken out of him by the Lisbon earthquake."[56] *Faust* presents the same general questions about good and evil that Hardy found elsewhere; and, of course, there are resemblances between Mephistopheles and the Spirits Ironic and Sinister. It would appear, however, that Hardy was not a close student of Goethe's thought and that he saw him from the perspective of his own age of doubt.

Apart from his interest in their craftsmanship, Hardy's response to contemporary authors, both English and foreign, depended much on whether they continued in the traditions of the Romantics or whether,

[54] Edmund Blunden tells of Hardy's great interest in Shelley when he visited Hardy in 1922 (*Guest of Thomas Hardy* [Beaminster: The Toucan Press, 1964]).

[55] *Faust: A Dramatic Poem* (London: Moxon and Co.).

[56] Memoranda, I, and Literary Notes, I, 9.

with or without the influence of contemporary science, they found man's lot inevitably beset with doubt or gloom.

In 1868 he mentions reading Browning; in 1887 he read *The Ring and the Book* and, as we have observed, remarked that he had thought much of Browning and Shelley.[57] There was plenty that the poet could tell him about the usual affairs of a reflective life, and Hardy never cast a book aside merely because of philosophic disagreement. The limit of Browning's influence, however, is summed up in a note Hardy jotted down in July, 1890. While quoting two and a half pages, including part of the prologue to *Asolando*—"and now a flower . . . glory ran"—Hardy commented, "Cf. Coleridge's 'Youth + Age'— But Browning ends with a conventional piece of optimism; while Coleridge is true throughout."[58] Hardy may have respected the portraits of the Rabbi and the Grammarian growing old, but he understood better Eustacia's willingness to give up the wrinkled half of life. Several of his heroes, perhaps most conspicuously Marshal Ney, would gladly have accompanied Childe Roland and would have demanded entrance to the Dark Tower with the same eagerness for new adventure. But Hardy himself would not have shared their naïve confidence, for he could not forget the horror, even in scenes of heroism.

In the Memorial Library copy of *In Memoriam*[59] there are many underlinings and marginal lines, some of the passages being chosen for their imagery and diction, but some because they aptly expressed a thought that appealed to Hardy. One, in stanza 5, having to do with the function of poetry, is doubly lined:

> But for the unquiet heart and brain
> A use in measured language lies;
> The sad mechanic exercise,
> Like dull narcotics, numbing pain.

By the last four lines of stanza 77 appears "Cf Shelley, Adonais Stanza 21," and the first of these lines—"O last regret, regret can die!"—is copied on a fly leaf at the back. There are double lines by the last of

[57] *The Early Life*, pp. 76 and 252. Carl Weber has catalogued allusions by Hardy to Browning in *Hardy of Wessex* (New York: Columbia University Press, 1940), appendix 10.

[58] Literary Notes, II, 30.

[59] London: Henry S. King, 1875.

> Likewise the imaginative woe,
>> That lov'd to handle spiritual strife,
>> Diffused the shock thro' all my life,
> But in the present broke the blow   (stanza 84)

and by

>> And on the depths of death there swims
> The reflex of a human face.   (stanza 107)[60]

Certainly, neither Tennyson nor Hardy equated the negative action of narcotics with the creative act of poetic composition. But they did agree that one use of poetic contemplation was to provide inurement to pain—if only through the identification of its universal nature.

It would appear that Hardy gave Newman a serious hearing, but found him not very rewarding. Some time before 1876 he pasted eight small pages of quotations from Newman in what are now Literary Notes, I. In his 1870 copy of *An Essay in Aid of a Grammar of Assent* he marked several passages. Among them was one of some novelty which he could accept: "Without the apprehension of notions we should for ever pace round one small circle of knowledge; without a firm hold upon things, we shall waste ourselves in vague speculations."[61] Hardy marginally lined the passage and underlined the contrasting terms. But there were limits beyond which he refused to follow Newman's argument. Thus, in "Revealed Religion," he marked the first part of the following key passage and then added an exclamation point—his infrequent, but definitive stamp of dissent:

> so by a like dictate we are not justified, in the case of concrete reasoning and especially of religious inquiry, in waiting till such logical demonstration is ours, but on the contrary are bound in conscience to seek truth and to look for certainty by modes of proof, which, when reduced to the shape of formal propositions, fail to satisfy the severe requisitions of science (407).

In actual practice, Hardy would have had to admit, he often did what Newman recommended, but his ideal was quite opposite; and it was in pursuit of it that he turned to the scientists and philosophers.

The tone of Arnold's writing, in contrast, got full acceptance from Hardy. In the Literary Notes there are numerous extracts from the prose, which appear to have been made during and around 1877;

---

[60] Stanza numbers are here revised for modern editions.
[61] (London: Burns, Oates, and Co.), II, 32.

two run to five pages. The Memorial Library includes the Macmillan editions of the *Poetical Works* (1890) and of *Selected Poems* (1893). In the former is a note beside "Dover Beach": "Sept—1896—/ T. H. / E. L. H." When marking both volumes Hardy was presumably rereading poems already familiar. The sentiments echoed those which he had found among the Greeks, with the added quality of a nostalgia for what Arnold believed some Greeks had known. Hardy put double lines beside laments in Act I of *Empedocles*: "Scarce can one think in calm, so threatening are the Gods," "No title from the Gods to welfare and repose," and "To tunes we did not call our being must keep chime." Pursuing his matter-of-fact way, in "To a Friend" he identified as Epictetus "that halting slave." He also underlined "Who saw life steadily, and saw it whole," and beside "Singer of sweet Colonnus" he marginally added "Sophocles." He put *X*'s by several titles, but perhaps the most revealing are the marginal lines by passages in "Stagirius":

> When the soul, growing clearer,
>   Sees God no nearer;
> When the soul, mounting higher,
>   To God comes no nigher . . . .

and

> From doubt, where all is double;
> Where wise men are not strong,
> Where comfort turns to trouble,
> Where just men suffer wrong;
> Where sorrow treads on joy,
> Where sweet things soonest cloy,
> Where faiths are built on dust,
> Where love is half mistrust . . . .

In Arnold's world-weariness there was a degree of stoicism, but there was also unrest; and it was the protests that struck chords in Hardy, even when, as in "Stagirius," the rhythms were out of tune.

Of all the Victorians Swinburne appears to have appealed most to Hardy. Here there was no stoicism; indeed there was only that restraint which meter and the use of classical motifs supplied. Hardy had no major reservations, however, in his admiration of Swinburne. In the Memorial Library are copies of *Chastelard* (New York, 1866), *Poems and Ballads, First Series* (5th ed.; London: John Camden,

1873), *Bothwell, a Tragedy* (London: Chatto and Windus, 1874), *Songs before Sunrise* (Chatto and Windus, 1883), *Atalanta in Calydon* (Chatto and Windus, 1885), *Poems and Ballads, Second Series* (Chatto and Windus, 1887), and *Atalanta in Calydon and Lyrical Poems* (Leipzig: Tauchnitz, 1901). In *Bothwell* there is one underlining, of "life like death's own shadow" in Act V, scene 13. Many of the marks in the other volumes are of felicitous phrasing—usually of sad themes—but a few passages have special philosophic import. In the 1873 edition, near the end of "Anactoria," Hardy put double lines by "Till fate undo the bondage of the gods."

In *Songs before Sunrise* he marked eight lines of "Prelude," stanza 16, and underlined the last: "Save his own soul he [man] hath no star." He marked several passages in the bitterly anti-Christian "Before a Crucifix," including

> Or are there less oppressions done
> In this wild world under the sun?

and

> What desolate evangel sounds
> A hopeless note of hope deferred?[62]

In the "Hymn of Man" he noted, among other lines, "But God, if a God there be, is the substance of men which is man." And he underlined "Men are the thoughts passing through" the roots of God's heart, that is, through the eternal heart of man. Among his markings in the 1885 edition of *Atalanta in Calydon* he underlined: "Joy is not, but love of joy shall be."

In the 1901 edition the marked lines include, from "The Garden of Proserpine,"

> Whatever gods may be
> That no life lives forever

and, in "A Lamentation," long passages, one more than a page in length, on the suffering of man, which is unrewarded by ultimate

---

[62] Sometime before July 15, 1876, Hardy quoted and paraphrased from Jowett's introduction to Plato about a page on ancient opinions of suicide, including: "For the mere brave endurance of pain as an inevitable evil (the view of Plato, Plutarch, + c against suicide) was substituted the new idea of suffering as the righteous penalty of sin + a kind of reparation for it (the Xtian idea)" (Literary Notes, I, 51–52).

knowledge. Perhaps Hardy chose to emphasize for the rhythm and imagery, yet also for the tragic theme, the lines from "Itylus":

> Thy heart is light as a leaf of a tree;
> But mine goes forth among sea-gulfs hollow
> To the place of the slaying of Itylus,
> The feast of Daulis, the Thracian sea.

In Swinburne there were no answers to the questions which perplexed Hardy. The attacks on Christianity, like Hardy's own, were essentially negative, offering nothing ethically valid in its place. Swinburne's glorification of man, arrogant in tone and unconcerned with ontology, offered little for philosophic speculation. There were poems which in effect defended selfishness and twisted logic to make a virtue of evil. It is unlikely that Hardy was unaware of the sophistry with which Swinburne arrived at solutions when he chose to assert them. There was nowhere, however, a more poignant expression of the eternal sorrow of mortal life. Any attempt at a philosophy that Hardy might make had to begin with the recognition of the feast of Daulis and the realization that only fate could "undo the bondage of the gods."

Among the miscellaneous quotations from nineteenth-century authors in the notebooks are many which bear on the philosophy or the tragic perspective of *The Dynasts*. There is, for example, one-half page from Thomson's essay "A Lady of Sorrow," together with a reference to "The City of Dreadful Night." [63] From *Adam Bede* comes "Sorrow lives in us as an indestructible force . . . passing from pain into sympathy." [64] Five pages of quotations from Zola emphasize the harshness of Nature and of the conditions of human life. The following are typical: "The Voreux pit . . . panting louder + louder with its thick + heavy breath, as if obstructed in its painful digestion of human flesh + blood," and "Some giant belly, capable of digesting a whole people . . . Voracious silence." [65] About four pages, copied by 1876, from a book by G. J. Wood on ants, beetles, and the like, describe beautiful creatures living in the midst of filth or exuding an offensive odor and speak of the use of slaves by ants.[66] Hardy might have found much the same in books on natural science or have learned it from his

[63] Literary Notes, I, 208.
[64] Book of Observations, p. 31.
[65] *Ibid.*, p. 66.
[66] Literary Notes, I, 32–36.

own observation of insects on piles of refuse. Coming upon it in Wood, he must certainly have recognized its philosophic implications for the life of man.

From Leopardi, read in translation, Hardy collected a smattering of observations, usually pessimistic and sometimes quasi-philosophical. One which must have intrigued him, not as a statement of ultimate truth, but at least as a way of viewing things poetically, reads, "the world is only a cerebral phenomenon."[67] Strauss's *Life of Jesus* probably merely reconfirmed Hardy in his dissatisfaction with Christian doctrine.[68] In the course of time he quoted a review in the January 25, 1908, *Nation* that called it "not so much a 'Life of Jesus' as a piece of applied Hegelian philosophy."[69]

Many other quotations in the notebooks from works not primarily philosophic are pertinent to the conception of *The Dynasts*. They are recorded in no particular pattern and usually with no indication of how they contribute to any specific philosophic scheme. Essentially they are fragments of thought collected from here and there and set down because, though parts of something larger, they make by themselves acute observations on an aspect of life.

It is important to keep this fact in mind as one turns to Hardy's use of nineteenth-century science and of formal philosophy. In these fields he read carefully, but the extracts which he copied are, nonetheless, not complete expositions of systems. It was not essential for Hardy to be able to follow to its consequences an idea he found dogmatically asserted by any of the philosophers, and he could borrow freely from more than one without worrying about inherent differences in their perspectives. One must not suppose, of course, that the notebooks contain the entirety of what he discovered of significance in each, but the somewhat heterogeneous excerpts attest to the informal way in which he approached his reading. His quotations amount to nuggets rather more than to veins of ore.

As a student of contemporary scientific thought and of eighteenth- and nineteenth-century philosophers Hardy was seeking both new perspectives and more precise definitions. He liked exactness and

[67] Book of Observations, p. 61. Hardy owned the 1880 French translation by F. A. Aulard, of Leopardi, *Poésies et Oeuvres Morales, Première Traduction*, in three volumes. Cf., Rutland, *Thomas Hardy: A Study*, p. 106.

[68] Hardy owned the 1896 edition of George Eliot's translation, but may well have read an earlier edition.

[69] Literary Notes, II.

accuracy, as demonstrated in his annotations of his reading and in his revisions of *The Dynasts*. If something could be put in chart form or in a list of items, he would so put it. At the same time, he carried in his mind a loose assortment of impressions, and he continued to collect support for these till the end of his life. Consequently, one finds, both in his notes and in his works, a mixture of specific philosophic concepts, phrased succinctly, and what may best be called a feeling of reality.

It is likely that Hardy first became aware of many of his scientific and metaphysical concepts in sources other than the books that originated them. Certain ideas were generally current. Moreover, the nineteenth century often provided only variations of theories going back to the time of Lucretius. Yet there was a conviction, almost a superstition, in the second half of the century, that new scientific observations invalidated traditional beliefs and that a new metaphysics must be discovered. Hardy's Preface to *The Dynasts* takes this point for granted. We should think of the poet, consequently, as living in a milieu where new ideas or new expressions of old ones were pervasive, where, for example, a person who had read little or no Darwin could still know a good deal about Darwinism. In such an intellectual atmosphere Hardy looked into scientific works and read the philosophers or commentaries on them not as a methodical student of science or of metaphysics, but as a poet looking for help in synthesizing his own sensations of reality and in giving them harmonious articulation.

His interest in some writers stretched over his mature life; there were others whom he appears to have read only during a particular period. After *The Dynasts* was in print he continued to make notes on statements which reiterated concepts he had dealt with in the 1870's. Clearly, he did not feel that in his epic, any more than in his earlier poetry and novels, he had finally resolved the issues. In the meantime he was confident enough to go on recording his own impressions in his verses, being committed to living among intellectual uncertainties with the kind of attitude that Keats had called negative capability.

What were the problems on which Hardy sought enlightenment from the scientists and philosophers? They were really not different ultimately from those he repeatedly encountered in literature, but they did come in new contexts. Immediately confronting him was, of course, man's relation to his fellowmen and to the phenomena of Nature as these affected his struggle for survival and his emotions. Inevitably

Passions." The root of the tree is "Intellect, Passions, Will"; and a cross section shows Passions to be at the center. Another sketch makes a tree the Passions, and the vines that wind it about are Intellect and Will, subdivided as before. Underneath, in large letters, is the label "Humanity," and, in small script is the notation "Intellect the *adviser* of P. + W."

The various sketches are, of course, arbitrary and inconsistent. From a psychological point of view the small note, which fits none of them, is of considerable importance. In it Intellect is certainly not one of three roots, though it does presumably help to shape personality and action. Will, on the other hand, is again the equal of the Passions as a force. Like the sketches and charts, the note does not attempt to define Will, to distinguish it from the Passions and Instinct. Yet, though thinking in terms only of the human personality, Hardy must have believed that there was something at work in man that was distinct and could be called *Will*. In his use of the word forty years later he would attempt to encompass this entity in a cosmic context not so much psychological as philosophic.

Some fifteen years after these entries, 1878–1879, in the midst of notes for *The Trumpet Major*, Hardy returned to part of the substance of his charts with the note:

Fourier begins by establishg 3 abstract principles in universal nature from which he derives all things natural + spiritual—

　1st—The passive principle or matter—NATURE

　2d—The active principle or spirit—GOD

　3d—The neutral principle or mathematics—Justice. In human nature he finds the passive principle represented by the 5 senses—the active prin by the 4 affections, the neuter prin by the 3 distributive passions of the soul.[70]

Hardy was still willing to entertain a cramped and arbitrary system which employed metaphorical analogies more verbal than real. This was at a time when he had already produced significant fiction and poetry.

Meanwhile he had been reading Comte. The autobiography speaks of his having done so in 1870 and adds that he had read in the *Positive Philosophy* shortly before 1874.[71] Among his notes of 1876 are some

---

[70] Notes taken for "Trumpet Major," pp. 27–28. The quotation is from the preface by Hugh Doherty to *The Passions of the Soul*, translated in 1851.

[71] *The Early Life*, pp. 101, 129.

thirteen pages, mainly short comments, from Comte. Included are "*An omnipotent being* can have no occasion either for wisdom or goodness," Comte's pronouncement that the Positive Religion possesses "the only laws capable of regulating the Present with a view to the Future on the basis of the Past," the remark that social progress is "like 'a looped orbit,' sometimes apparently backwards, but really always forwards," and the note "*Intellect*—The adviser of activity," which takes one back to the chart.[72] It is not possible to say definitively in what respects Hardy found Comte inadequate. Much depends on what one feels is assumed by Hardy in, for example, any possible bringing of the Will to consciousness at the end of *The Dynasts*. If this requires human effort, as it would appear to do, then to that extent it is in agreement with the Positivists. To that extent, too, the poem is not monistically determinist. In general, however, Hardy could not share Comte's optimism.

In the autobiography Hardy remarked that, when a young man, he had acclaimed Darwin.[73] There is no evidence that he was at any time especially interested in the reliability of Darwin's researches or in that of various other scientific investigations, though there are a few short notes revealing a curiosity about scientific facts. About 1876–1877, for example, Hardy jotted down two pages from Spencer's *Principles of Biology*, much of it a classification of plants and animals, with a quotation from Darwin.[74] Hardy was interested primarily in the implications of scientific theories. Thus, probably in 1876, he had quoted from an article by Theodore Watts in *The Examiner*: "Science tells us that, in the struggle for life, the surviving organism is not necessarily that which is absolutely the best in an ideal sense, though it must be that which is most in harmony with surrounding conditions."[75] It may be

---

[72] Literary Notes, I, 74, 79, 81.

[73] *The Early Life*, p. 198.

[74] Literary Notes, I, 95–98.

[75] *Ibid.*, 41. On pages 93–94 Hardy copied and marked an excerpt from the October, 1876, *Edinburgh Review*, itself a summary of ideas in Caro's *Problèmes de Morale Sociale*. The article deplored Caro's views, but it is obvious that Hardy found them stimulating. He headed the quotation "Modern Schools of Morality," "modern" connoting "Darwinian." In part the excerpt reads:

No distinction of sphere is allowed in passing from the phenomena of nature to the phenomena of will. However refractory these latter phenomena they can only be considered as the last transformation of the great natural forces of light + heat + electricity, passing through the mysterious involvements of

added that Hardy had also accepted the doctrine of Malthus on the growth of population when not inhibited. In his reference to the Malthusian thesis in *Tess of the D'Urbervilles* he interpreted it as a recognition of the plight of mortals in a world where at any level there must be relentless struggle and frustration—where by the very nature of existence the circumstantial will was hostile to man.

As for Darwinism, certain authors whom Hardy respected sought to give an interpretation which was not pessimistic, at the same time that they raised doubts about traditional philosophic theism. Their value for Hardy was perhaps more negative than positive in that they showed him what he must not accept, but gave him no new philosophical instrument with which to build. The major authors were Mill, Stephen, and Spencer.

In a letter to *The Times*, May 21, 1906, Hardy spoke of having heard Mill in 1865; he referred to *On Liberty*, "which we students of that date knew almost by heart," and he called Mill "one of the profoundest thinkers of the last century." [76] The marked passages in Hardy's copy are almost exclusively on political and social matters; Mill was, of course, opposed to tyranny. There is a relation, though general and indefinable, between his statement of principles and Hardy's bitter portrayal of the trampling on human rights by Napoleon and the other European dynasts. An entry of July 1, 1868, in *The Early Life* implies Hardy's having read "Individuality," and we may conclude that he knew Mill's other writings well. As to what he gleaned, we can only observe that certain pronouncements of Mill are directly pertinent to Hardy's own views, particularly on theism. To cite the most relevant from *Nature, the Utility of Religion, and Theism* is to present subjects with which Hardy was preoccupied in both his lyrics and *The Dynasts*. Mill rejected Nature as a moral guide: "the order of nature, in so far as unmodified by man, is such as no being, whose attributes are justice and benevolence, would have made, with the intention that

---

the human nervous system. Conscience merely marks the last step in the upward evolution. It has no independent reality, no distinct laws. It falls with all that depends upon it under the empire of force which rules all nature. Free-will vanishes as a dream, + the moral world in its true aspect is merely the last form + highest potency of the cosmical system.

[76] Article pasted in Hardy's copy of *On Liberty* (London: Longmans, Green and Co., 1867); quoted also in *The Later Years*, pp. 118–119.

his rational creatures should follow it as an example." [77] As to the power of that "being," Mill wrote that if a "Creator assumed to be omnipotent ... bends to a supposed necessity, [he] himself makes the necessity which he bends to" (37); and as to the intent of such a power, he added, "If the maker of the world *can* all that he will, he wills misery ...." Mill's solution was at least equivocal, and yet it accorded with man's natural feeling as to his predicament and his possible improvement of his lot:

> The only admissible moral theory of creation is that the Principle of Good *cannot* at once and altogether subdue the powers of evil, either physical or moral; could not place mankind in a world free from the necessity of an incessant struggle with the maleficent powers, or make them always victorious in that struggle, but could and did make them capable of carrying on the fight with vigour and with progressively increasing success (39).

Mill concluded that man's duty lay in "standing forward a not ineffectual auxiliary to a Being of perfect beneficence."

Thus Mill came out cheerfully, though he had to resort to making a scapegoat of the age-old Necessity. For Hardy such a statement would have been significant in that it did deny some established beliefs. It assumed, however, that evolution represented progress, and it would appear to assume on man's behalf freedom of the will. In "Theism," Mill went so far as to assert that survival of the fittest brought a "slow general improvement" (173) and that the process "afford[s] a large balance of probability in favour of creation by intelligence" (174). He repeated his argument that the designer was not omnipotent or infinite in knowledge, or necessarily moral in intent, but he could still insist that "there is a preponderance of evidence that the Creator desired the pleasure of his creatures" (191).

Yet Mill tendered an idea which Hardy was to find laboriously developed by Schopenhauer—that it was "probable, that in a higher, and, above all, a happier condition of human life, not annihilation but immortality may be the burdensome idea" (122). He also insisted that science depends on monism, with invariable laws. Each event could be from "a specific volition of the presiding Power, provided that this

[77] *Nature, the Utility of Religion, and Theism* (London: Longmans, Green, Reader and Dyer, 1874), p. 25. The first two essays were written between 1850 and 1858; the third, 1868–1870.

Power adheres in particular volitions to general laws laid down by itself" (136). This mixes determinism with anthropomorphism, as Mill's "Power" seems to have definable limitations. It also speaks in a free and easy manner about the volitions of this Power. Here, for Hardy, was to be the crux of the problem.

In a note apparently from the end of 1880 Hardy cites Leslie Stephen's view that, as a consequence of Darwin's research, we can "recognize in society, as in individuals, the development of an *organic structure* by slow secular processes."[78] He considered the opinion of sufficient importance to earn double marginal lines. Just how carefully Hardy read Stephen is speculative. In the *Essays on Freethinking and Plainspeaking*, which appeared in *Fraser's Magazine* and the *Fortnightly Review* and were collected in 1873, Stephen attacked traditional Christianity for its superstitions and, with support from Strauss's *The Life of Jesus*, concluded that, pretending to be Christians, we are really skeptics (Chap. 4). Stephen approved of prayer, but only as it helped one in getting a "deeper sense of our close connection with the interests of the universe" (Chap. 4). Most important was his acceptance of Darwinism, which, like Mill, he interpreted optimistically:

> But if, in a more philosophical sense, belief in God means belief in a "general stream of tendency," Darwinism, so far from weakening that belief, helps us to map out some small part of the stream, though its source and its end be hidden in impenetrable mystery (chap. 3).

In so far as Stephen destroyed he was a stimulus for Hardy, though in *Tess* the novelist demonstrated the sterility of Angel Clare's skepticism. Stephen's affirmation of a belief in a "general stream" still left much to be accounted for.

About 1887 or 1888 Hardy quoted from Cotter Morison's *The Service of Man* (published in 1887), on various views of religion and science. Included was Morison's own quotation of Herbert Spencer on how determinism expresses itself in human thought and action:

> From the universal law that, other things equal, the cohesion of psychical states is proportionate to the frequency with wh. they have followed one another in experience, it is an inevitable corollary that all actions whatever must be determined by those psychical connexions wh. experience has generated, either in the life of the individual, or in that general

[78] *Literary Notes*, I, 153.

antecedent-life of wh. the accumulated results are organized in his constitution.[79]

Since an individual's initial experience could not be exclusively an external matter, as it would be qualified by his psychic state, presumably he was in effect determined by the "accumulated results" of genetic inheritance. Hardy had already assumed such inheritance and was to make use of it in *Tess* and *Jude*. In *The Dynasts* he implied it repeatedly in the comments by the Intelligences about collective man; and as for the psychic determinism of one's own earlier experience, the comments by and about Napoleon assume its truth.

What Hardy found in Spencer's *First Principles*, published in 1862, is, like his knowledge of Stephen, conjectural. Some things he would have found better put than in Mill or Stephen, if only because more judiciously stated. Writing on causation, Spencer noted that one cannot say that a First Cause is "partially independent; since this implies some necessity, which determines its partial dependence, and this necessity, be it what it may, must be a higher cause, or the true First Cause, which is a contradiction." [80] Spencer's term for Power was *the Absolute,* concerning which he quoted Mansel:

> The Absolute cannot be conceived as conscious, neither can it be conceived as unconscious: it cannot be conceived as complex, neither can it be conceived as simple: it cannot be conceived by difference, neither can it be conceived by the absence of difference: it cannot be identified with the universe, neither can it be distinguished from it (41).

Spencer concluded that in rejecting rational attempts to describe the First Cause one came to a belief in "the omnipresence of something which passes comprehension" (45). And in the course of his argument, resorting to semantics, he postulated: "To say that we cannot know the Absolute is, by implication, to affirm that there is an Absolute" (88). This was the "actuality lying behind all appearances" (97). Hardy himself repeatedly came to rest about where Spencer had before him. Yet he was determined to go beyond.

There is one passage in Spencer of special importance quite different in substance. It has to do with the nature of consciousness:

> Besides that *definite* consciousness of which Logic formulates the laws, there is also an *indefinite* consciousness which cannot be formulated.

[79] *Ibid.,* 235.
[80] *First Principles* (London: Williams and Norgate, 1863), p. 38.

Besides complete thoughts, and besides the thoughts which though incomplete admit of completion, there are thoughts which it is impossible to complete; and yet which are still real, in the sense that they are normal affections of the intellect (88).

One cannot, of course, prove that Hardy read this passage, or that, if he did, he was struck by it. But it is concerned with a topic much more extensively developed in Hartmann and wrestled with in various choral lines in *The Dynasts,* particularly in the final scene. Spencer is speaking of the individual consciousness, but it requires only an extension, which he himself did not make, to project the idea into a cosmic context.

There were other thinkers from whom Hardy gleaned reinforcement of his views. Even while writing *The Dynasts* and afterward he seems not to have ignored anything in his reading which restated a pertinent belief or argument. From the December, 1886, *Fortnightly Review* he extracted Huxley's rejection of Dr. Büchner's view, in *Kraft und Stoff,* that there are in the Universe only matter and force. To these Huxley would add consciousness.[81] Of indefinite date after the writing of *The Dynasts,* under the heading *Freedom of the Will,* Hardy quoted from Huxley on Hume:

> Half the controversies about the f. of the w . . . rest upon the absurd presumption that the proposition "I can do as I like," is contradictory to the doctrine of necessity. The answer is: nobody doubts that, at any rate within certain limits, you can do as you like. But what determines your likings + dislikings? Did you make your own constitution?[82]

One cannot establish at what time Hardy read John Morley's two-volume *Diderot and the Encyclopaedists,* of which he owned the 1891 edition,[83] or Morley's two-volume *Rousseau,* of which he also owned the 1891 edition.[84] The second is uncut after Volume I, page 152, but Hardy marked a significant passage near the beginning which is unusually in accord with the feeling for destiny that underlies certain of Napoleon's reflections and other lines in *The Dynasts*: "Destiny thus touches us with magical finger, long before consciousness awakens to the forces that have been set to work in our personality,

[81] Literary Notes, I, 214–215.
[82] Literary Notes, II.
[83] London: Macmillan, with the 1878 preface.
[84] London: Macmillan.

launching us into the universe with country, forefathers, and physical predispositions, all fixed without choice of ours" (I, 10). Of the numerous marked passages in the *Diderot* many are on political and social folly and religious superstition. Typical is the phrase on the Protestant Reformation which Hardy underlined: "that rude Reformation, a medley of superstition and freedom" (I, 179).

More interesting is Morley's pronouncement, marked by Hardy, that we must put morals on a scientific basis, since "man has become as definitely the object of science as any of the other phenomena of the universe" (II, 183). Hardy would not, of course, go nearly so far, but underlying Morley's argument was a belief in an identification of the nature of man with certain characteristics of the Universe. Morley was not saying that to follow Nature was good; such a view would have aroused Hardy's scorn. But Hardy could concur in the search for cosmic unity.

Most important of all Morley's comments is one in which he indicates that he is closely following Diderot. Under the heading *"All phenomena are necessary"* he has remarked that in a storm of dust or a tempest every molecule is present by necessity, and Hardy marked what follows:

> So, again, in the terrible convulsions that sometimes overthrow empires, there is not a single action, word, thought, volition, or passion in a single agent of such a revolution, whether he be a destroyer or a victim, which is not necessary, which does not act precisely as it must act, and which does not infallibly produce the effects that it is bound to produce, conformably to the place occupied by the given agent in the moral whirlwind (II, 172).

Hardy would not have placed Morley on a par with Mill for originality, but he respected him; and Morley's words, coming as a restatement of Diderot, would have pertinence for a writer on a European convulsion. Diderot and Morley distinguished between chance and necessity. Long after writing *The Dynasts* Hardy still blurred the distinction, even as in "Hap." But the determinism intrigued him.

Perhaps it is needful here to remark that neither *The Dynasts* nor any other narrative work of Hardy's must be taken as a mere study in determinism. Were it so, it would have only limited interest. The novels and the epic are to be read as the creations of a man who, in seeking a way through a wilderness of phenomena, was especially attracted to deterministic philosophy and who took from it all the help he could get in trying to establish a fundamental principle. Among several quotations from or on Spinoza in the notebooks, probably in late 1900 or 1901, is "absence of Free-will in man . . . Will + Liberty belong only to God." From an article by Professor C. L. Morgan in the June, 1904, *Contemporary Review*, Hardy quoted a page arguing that determinism in science permits free will in man, since one is free "to act in accordance with the essential nature of the underlying Cause." [85] From the June, 1904, issue of the *North American Review* he quoted the argument of Goldwin Smith in defense of free will. A number of other extracts follow in the notebook on the same question.

In the notebooks there are also scattered entries on science and religion, many of them directly or by implication critical of traditional Christian assumptions. As part of two and a half pages from Mrs. Ward's *Robert Elsmere*, probably recorded about 1888, Hardy included a passage which is of particular interest because of the way he shifted the implication when he used much the same assertion in *The Dynasts*. Mrs. Ward wrote: "Christianity seems to me something small + local. Behind it, around it, including it, I see the great drama of the world sweeping on, led by God." [86] In making use of this Hardy ignored the end of the second sentence. What the Spirit of the Years (I, l, vi) says is merely:

> A local cult, called Christianity,
> Which the wild dramas of the wheeling spheres
> Include, with divers other such, in dim
> Pathetical and brief parentheses,
> Beyond whose span, uninfluenced, unconcerned,
> The systems of the suns go sweeping on
> With all their many-mortaled planet train
> In mathematic roll unceasingly.

From an article by Chesterton in the *Daily News*, March 17, 1906, Hardy excerpted "Paganism is Agnosticism which is sufficiently agnostic to admit the probability of spirits." [87] Hardy commented, "for 'Paganism' read 'Christianity,'" and he then qualified his annotation by inserting above the line "Modern" and completing his note "or Present-day Christianity." The qualification was significant.

[85] Literary Notes, II.
[86] Literary Notes, I, 265.
[87] Literary Notes, II.

While Hardy was searching for a concept that would embrace man and Nature, he rejected emphatically the attempts by the quite diverse theorists Maeterlinck and Nietzsche to find a norm of morality in Nature. In a letter to *The Academy and Literature*, May 17, 1902, Hardy scorned Maeterlinck's view that Nature

> may practice a scheme of morality unknown to us, in which she is just. * * * no profound reflection can be needed to detect the sophistry in M. Maeterlinck's argument, and to see that the original difficulty recognized by thinkers like Schopenhauer, Hartmann, Haeckel, etc., and by most of the persons called pessimists, remains unsurmounted.[88]

In a later paragraph Hardy added that "to model our conduct on Nature's apparent conduct, as Nietzsche would have taught, can only bring disaster to humanity."[89]

If Hardy had read only the authors we have reviewed, he would have had voluminous support for his general view of life, and at least one of his reminiscent comments gives major credit to the nineteenth-century British thinkers, to Hume, and to Comte. In a letter to Helen Garwood, published in 1911, Hardy protested that she overemphasized the influence upon him of Schopenhauer: "My pages show harmony of view with Darwin, Huxley, Spencer, Comte, Hume, Mill, and others, all of whom I used to read more than Schopenhauer."[90]

Yet Hardy did read Schopenhauer and also Hartmann, and *The Dynasts* reflects the reading. At the outset of our adventure into their philosophy as it influenced Hardy we must keep in mind that he was not a systematic student of metaphysics. His references to Hegel and Kant do not imply methodical study, and there is no proof that he worked his way stage by stage through the logic of either Schopenhauer or Hartmann. Rather, he was intrigued by what seemed new

[88] *The Later Years,* p. 97.

[89] Probably in 1898 Hardy quoted from a newspaper article the remark that "Nietzsche's sounder doctrines were put forth during his early life, + that his later utterances were tainted with insanity." His comment: "The latter words are true enough" (Literary Notes, II). In a pencil copy of a letter of 1914 or early 1915 to the *Manchester Guardian* concerning Nietzsche, Hardy wrote: "He used to seem to me (I have not looked into his works for years) to be an incoherent rhapsodist, who jumps from Machiavelli to Isaiah as the mood seizes him, and whom it is impossible to take seriously as a mentor" (Personal notebook).

[90] Helen Garwood, *Thomas Hardy: An Illustration of the Philosophy of Schopenhauer* (Philadelphia: John Winston, 1911).

that would give his imagination scope. The two main discoveries came to be epitomized for him under Schopenhauer's concept—vague and shifting though it was—of the Will and Hartmann's of the Unconscious. He arrived at these discoveries, however, circuitously.

Hardy's perplexity as he read the post-Darwinian writers and found that he could not reconcile them with certain earlier philosophers is revealed in a note of May, 1886:

> Have been thinking over the dictum of Hegel—that the real is the rational and the rational the real—that real pain is compatible with a formal pleasure—that the idea is all, etc., but it doesn't help much. These venerable philosophers seem to start wrong; they cannot get away from a prepossession that the world must somehow have been made to be a comfortable place for man. If I remember, it was Comte who said that metaphysics was a mere sorry attempt to reconcile theology and physics.[91]

With his background in Spencer's agnosticism, Hardy could write, July 1, 1892, "the true thing in itself being still, as Kant shows, beyond our knowledge." [92] But he had already begun to wonder about some disturbing questions; and, if metaphysics was insufficient and the answers were beyond one's knowledge, Hardy nonetheless hoped to find a way of apprehending them.

Though his first significant references to both are apparently from 1886, Hardy was rather well acquainted with Schopenhauer's theories before he turned to the modification of them by Hartmann.[93] His library once included the three volumes of *The World as Will and Idea*, in the English translation by Haldane and Kemp,[94] and *On the Four-fold Root of the Principle of Sufficient Reason*, translated by Mme.

[91] *The Early Life*, p. 234.

[92] *The Later Years*, p. 9. There are a few items on Kant in Literary Notes, none of special consequence.

[93] The most extensive discussions of Hardy's use of Schopenhauer are Garwood, *Thomas Hardy* (Hardy's copy in the Memorial Library has a few marginal lines); and J. O. Bailey, *Thomas Hardy and the Cosmic Mind: A New Reading of "The Dynasts"* (Chapel Hill: University of North Carolina Press, 1956). Cf., also Rutland, *Thomas Hardy: A Study, passim*; Ernest Brennecke, *Thomas Hardy's Universe: A Study of a Poet's Mind* (London: Unwin, 1924); and Carl Weber, "Hardy's Copy of Schopenhauer," *Colby Library Quarterly*, Series IV, No. 12 (November, 1957), 217–224.

[94] Rutland, *Thomas Hardy: A Study*, p. 93, says it was the first edition, 1883. The sales catalogue gives the date 1896 (the third edition). In any event, Hardy could have read an earlier edition.

Hillebrand, 1889.[95] As one would expect, the first references in Hardy's notes are to secondary reports of Schopenhauer's thought. Having found promising suggestions in the summaries, Hardy went eventually to the complete texts; and, although *The Dynasts* owes much to others, there are distinguishing features that are peculiarly Schopenhauerian. What Hardy found is suggested in his notes, but there is much additional in Schopenhauer which is in harmony with the epic.

While reading Sully's *Pessimism,* probably in 1886, Hardy jotted down, "Schopenhauer is regarded as the antecedent of Wagner."[96] In late 1886 he took about two pages on Schopenhauer from the *Revue des deux mondes.* In a paraphrase he wrote, "The system of Sch. is scarcely a system, it is made of pieces of the debris of 20 other systems. His pessimism is exterior or eccentric to his metaphysic." Then, from the original, underlining key words, he quoted the summary comment that Schopenhauer

> dépossède l'intelligence de la royauté qu'elle avait exercée jusqu'alors; et, du principal faisant désormais l'accessoire, il met la substance et l'essence de l'homme dans la volonté. Si nous nous regardons du dehors, ce ne sont pas nos *perceptions* changeantes, nos pensées contradictoires, nos *conceptions* abstraites ou vides; ce sont nos *affections,* ce sont nos désirs, ce sont nos *passions* qui seules constituent notre *moi,* l'identité de notre personne et la continuité de notre individu.

Hardy added in brackets, "The writer goes on to combat the logic of this view of Sch's—also his use of the word Will, when he means Force ... wh. differs however only as the genus differs from the species 'en l'enveloppant.'"[97] Sometime shortly before March 17, 1888, Hardy turned to another general source, the *Encyclopaedia Britannica,* for a statement on Schopenhauer. The key sentences merely give the philosopher's conclusions, without meaningful interpretation:

> True life begins only when we have learnt that happiness is impossible by means of gratifying the cravings of desire.

[95] The latter, Schopenhauer's doctoral dissertation, was bought by Hardy, according to Weber, not long after publication. It is now at Colby College. Colby also possesses Hardy's copy of *Two Essays,* translated in 1889 by Mme. Hillebrand.

[96] Literary Notes, I, 204.

[97] *Ibid.,* 224.

The central principle of pessimism (Schopenhauer's) asserts that in the order of nature, i. e.—so long as the will to live remains unbroken, happiness in the true sense is impossible.[98]

Except for the ambiguous use of the term "force" in Hardy's comment on the article in the *Revue*, there is nothing in these entries to suggest a cosmic Will; it is the will in man that must be transcended. The quotations do bear, however, on human tragedy.

Then, in an entry of May 13, 1891, we come upon six pages from Schopenhauer himself. In a quotation from *Studies in Pessimism*, Hardy again focused on tragedy. His excerpts include the first sentence: "Unless *suffering* is the direct + immediate object of life, our existence must entirely fail of its aim";[99] and again, under the heading "Tragedy," "Only when intellect rises to the point where the vanity of all effort is manifest, + the will proceeds to an act of self-annulment, is the drama tragic in the true sense."[100] Hardy also noted Schopenhauer's identification of man with Nature, which involved his concept of the unconscious: "Everything that is really fundamental in a man, + therefore genuine, works, as such, unconsciously; in this respect like the power of Nature."[101] In *On the Fourfold Root*, which he probably read at about the same time, Hardy found, of course, systematic discussion of Schopenhauer's theories. On page 236 he marked Schopenhauer's claim that the "fundamental truth" of his doctrine, "which places that doctrine in opposition with all others that have ever existed, is the complete separation between the will and the intellect"; to which Schopenhauer added, "I am the first who has asserted that a *will* must be attributed to all that is lifeless."[102]

From an article by the Reverend S. A. Alexander in the *Contemporary Review*, January, 1893, Hardy quoted some optimistic lines, including "in philosophy Schopenhauer has given place to Hegel— the hope of cosmic suicide to the thought of a spiritual society, the vision of that City of God to wh. the race of men is slowly climbing

[98] *Ibid.*, 257.

[99] Literary Notes, II, 37. The translation is that of T. B. Saunders.

[100] *Ibid.*, II, 39.

[101] *Ibid.* Hardy also took from Schopenhauer several comments disparaging to women, including: "Taken as a whole, women are + remain, thoroughgoing philistines, + quite incurable. Hence they are a constant stimulus to ignoble ambitions" (*ibid.*, 42–43).

[102] Weber, "Hardy's Copy of Schopenhauer," p. 223.

nearer. Pessimism has had its day." His comment, "comforting, but false,"[103] implies that by now he had read Schopenhauer with some thoroughness. Yet, seven years later, after October 1, 1900, he still made use of a general source, as the following quotation reveals:

> *The unconscious, automatic, or reasonless Will.* "It is necessary to remember the irrationality [non-rationality] of the Will in Schopenhauer. It includes all processes, from attraction and gravitation to motivation, which last is simply 'causality seen from within' . . . . [The irrational will underlies action which does] 'not proceed from a mental initiative.' Cyclo."[104]

One can only conclude that after he had worked with Schopenhauer's own text and become familiar with his major tenets and terms, in translation, Hardy still needed to refurbish his understanding, even in so simplified a source as a cyclopaedia.[105] What is especially significant is that in this excerpt from 1900, when Hardy was on the threshold of the actual writing of *The Dynasts*, there is a striking difference from the earlier quotations. The Will, here, is unmistakably a cosmic unconscious force; and Hardy's bracketed words show that, in contrast with his earlier focus on the plight of man, a subject on which Schopenhauer offered him little that was new, he is now concerned with the "fundamental truth."

For a more extensive accounting of what Hardy had found we must go to the philosopher himself. In so doing we are confronted with difficulties. Schopenhauer sometimes tells his reader that he will later prove what he now accepts as true, he uses analogies which assume the relationship they purport to substantiate, and his very definition of the Will itself leaves its nature more felt than comprehended. Nevertheless, if we keep before us Hardy's Immanent Will, his lyric identification of man with Nature, his feeling that human life is tragically deterministic, and, finally, the hope of the Pities that the Will itself may eventually achieve consciousness, we can find scores of passages in Schopenhauer—who freely repeats himself—that may well have given Hardy either a clue to a new insight or a novel demonstration of what he was already inclined to believe. If we put a number of Schopenhauer's arguments and postulates together, we get, not a tightly logical system, but some provocative suggestions.

[103] Literary Notes, II, 77.
[104] *Ibid.*, II. Hardy's brackets.
[105] There are later minor references to Schopenhauer in Literary Notes, II.

Quite early in *The World as Will and Idea* he asserts that, though it varies in degree, "understanding is the same in all animals and in all men."[106] Hence there is an inherent kinship of man and animal nature, which reminds us especially of Hardy's coneys and their fellow creatures on the route to Waterloo.

In Book II, "The World as Will," Schopenhauer achieves his most nearly complete distinction between Will and Idea. Here he includes all Nature and tries to define the thing-in-itself:

> Phenomenal existence is idea and nothing more. All idea, of whatever kind it may be, all *object* is *phenomenal* existence, but the *will* alone is a thing-in-itself. As such it is throughout not idea, but *toto genere* different from it; it is that of which all idea, all object, is the phenomenal appearance, the visibility, the objectification. It is the inmost nature, the kernel, of every particular thing, and also of the whole. It appears in every blind force of nature and also in the preconsidered action of man; and the great difference between these two is merely in the degree of the manifestation, not in the nature of what manifests itself (I, 142–143).

Though Schopenhauer sometimes becomes as impassioned as a poet or a prophet, he maintains that he is merely analyzing unemotionally the nature of reality. He insists that he is distinguishing between the thing-in-itself and phenomena—even though he will have repeated occasion to admit that what the Will is can never be known. For Hardy the Immanent Will is much like Schopenhauer's Will in that it appears in every blind force. It differs in that it is not only a subject for intellectual speculation, but a felt presence. Moreover, it is oppressive to the point of tyranny.

As for free will, Schopenhauer calls the human individual a "phenomenon of will":

> Hence arises the strange fact that every one believes himself *a priori* to be perfectly free, even in his individual actions, and thinks that at every moment he can commence another manner of life, which just means that he can become another person. But *a posteriori*, through experience, he finds to his astonishment that he is not free, but subjected to necessity; that in spite of all his resolutions and reflections he does not change his conduct, and that from the beginning of his life to the end of it, he must carry out the very character which he himself condemns, and as it were play the part he has undertaken to the end (I, 147).

[106] *The World as Will and Idea,* trans. R. B. Haldane and J. Kemp (London: Trübner and Co., 1883), I, 26.

Here and elsewhere Schopenhauer seems to define free will as the power to act rather than to resolve or reflect, and so to deny it. In *The Dynasts* the most apparent expression of the Will is in the conditions in which one finds oneself. Thus Napoleon can speak of the tragic concatenation which has brought him to fight Alexander or of his being in the toils of a destiny from which he cannot escape. There is also, however, and especially in the spectral choruses, the implication that the Will operates *through* the minds of Napoleon and others, even when they have a sensation of utter freedom. A passing remark of Schopenhauer's that "the will reveals itself as completely and as much in *one* oak as in millions" (I, 167) accords with Hardy's indication that the expression of the Will in any common soldier is really as significant as its manifestation in generals and armies.

Aware of conflict in Nature and in society, Schopenhauer asserted that it demonstrated "that variance with itself which is essential to the will. Every grade of the objectification of will fights for the matter, the space, and the time of the others" (I, 191). How it could so fight while itself a representation of the Will he did not adequately explain. Nor could Hardy. But the web, or network, or ramification of something like a vast nervous system which Hardy spread out over the map of dynastic Europe is a symbol of a Will which finds expression in the phenomena of cataclysmic violence. The theory is monistic simply because, by definition, the Will is the thing-in-itself and the Idea is only its phenomenal manifestation. The human mind, however, is eternally conscious of the phenomena and hence of a strife which is either pluralistic to an anarchic degree or at best is a Manichaean conflict of good and evil. There are analogies and metaphors in Schopenhauer that are dualistic, and in *The Dynasts* the concept of a single Immanent Will does not free Hardy from the sensation of life as the outward expression of an inherent conflict of plural forces. From this divergence between abstract logic or definition, on the one hand, and his feeling for experience, on the other, sprang his need for a reconciliation, and hence the tension in a poem' that attempts to symbolize both the monistic Will and the plural phenomena, that is, the Idea.

When Schopenhauer turns to the subject of tragedy what he has to say has resemblances to earlier views. He does not, however, regard tragedy in a human life as a culmination; rather it is only a phenomenon that can be transcended. Citing Calderón's "Pues el delito mayor / Del hombre es haber nacido," he comments, "The true sense of tragedy is the deeper insight, that it is not his own individual sins that the hero atones for, but original sin, i.e., the crime of existence itself" (I, 328). Speaking of literary tragedy, he first offers an inclusive definition: "The representation of a great misfortune is alone essential to tragedy" (I, 328). He then distinguishes three kinds. The first, as in *Richard III*, portrays persons of "extraordinary wickedness." The second, as in *Oedipus Rex* and the *Trachiniae*, "and in general most of the tragedies of the ancients" uses "blind fate." But the highest type comes from

> the mere position of the *dramatis personae* with regard to each other, through their relations; so that there is no need either for a tremendous error or an unheard-of accident, nor yet for a character whose wickedness reaches the limits of human possibility; but characters of ordinary morality, under circumstances such as often occur, are so situated with regard to each other that their position compels them, knowingly and with their eyes open, to do each other the greatest injury, without any one of them being entirely in the wrong (I, 329).

Such a definition is, of course, not new. For Schopenhauer, however, it is a corollary of his belief in the "variance with itself which is essential to the will." It is also a sufficient description of the action in *The Dynasts*. Schopenhauer remarks, too, that "the life of every individual, if we survey it as a whole and in general, and only lay stress upon its most significant features, is really always a tragedy, but gone through in detail it has the character of a comedy" (I, 415). Hardy had believed this for many years, but in *Jude* and *The Dynasts* he drove the point home with some bitterness. The Spirits Ironic and Sinister are his spokesmen.

In one respect Hardy's acceptance of Schopenhauer was certainly less than complete. He had no trouble in intellectually perceiving that one ought ideally to transcend the will to live.[107] Put in other terms, this tenet can mean the escaping from consciousness of one's personal self and the turning of life into an adventure in intellectual speculation. But by Schopenhauer's system the actual death of an individual was only the death of a phenomenon,[108] and hence not really a cause for

[107] Cf., *ibid.*, I, 199, 506, 508.

[108] *Ibid.*, I, 354. This becomes somewhat involved, since the Universe exists "only as our idea," and thus for each of us the Universe really ceases with death.

lamentation. For Hardy it had always been and always would be a matter for bitterness and tears.

Schopenhauer began with the assumptions that man was not free and that the thing-in-itself, the Will, was unconscious of its own nature. The unconsciousness was really a question of definition: the Will was subject, not object, and it was inclusive; a subject could not be conscious of its own inclusiveness, but only of an object. As he proceeded, however, Schopenhauer evolved an interesting distinction that permitted freedom for man and self-consciousness for the Will: "Thus in man the will can attain to full self-consciousness, to distinct and exhaustive knowledge of its own nature, as it mirrors itself in the whole world" (I, 371). Despite his remark that the Will manifested itself equally in one oak and in many, he chose to make a discrimination here to allow freedom of will only to some men:

> man is distinguished from all the other phenomena of will by the fact that freedom, i.e. independence of the principle of sufficient reason,[109] which only belongs to the will as thing-in-itself, and contradicts the phenomenon, may yet possibly, in his case, appear in the phenomenon also, where, however, it necessarily exhibits itself as a contradiction of the phenomenon with itself. In this sense, not only the will in itself, but man also may certainly be called free, and thus distinguished from all other beings (I, 371).

Men can be free in the sense that they express a free Will, the thing-in-itself. Who such men might be Schopenhauer had suggested earlier in summarizing what he planned to present: "Yet we shall see in the Third Book how in certain individual men knowledge can deliver itself from this bondage, throw off its yoke, and, free from all the aims of will, exist purely for itself, simply as a clear mirror of the world, which is the source of art" (I, 199). In effect this meant that, among a small number, the artist and, of course, the philosopher might be said to be free. The Will, in short, would become conscious in an individual mind only to lose its consciousness again. Here was a fundamental matter; to conceive of a Will one had to deal with the question of consciousness. For Hardy, however, the answer offered by Schopenhauer seems to have been insufficient. When he let the Pities hope that the Will might achieve consciousness, he was not settling for such

---

[109] Defined in *ibid.*, I, 124, as "merely the form of the idea, the orderly combination of one idea with another."

expression in himself as artist; however wan his hope, it was for a cosmic evolution.

For uncertain help with this issue Hardy went to Hartmann. Helen Garwood, in 1911, wrote that in a letter to her Hardy "speaks of his philosophy being a development from Schopenhauer through later philosophers."[110] These included Hartmann.[111] In drawing from his work Hardy demonstrated his own eclecticism and his willingness to take hints from authors without attempting a full acceptance of their views. There were, indeed, essential discordances between Hardy and Hartmann. To cite an extreme example, the philosopher wrote that it was good to let "inferior races . . . savages" become extinct. Then the superior races would compete for survival, and, though bitter, the struggle would be "*advantageous* for the progressive evolution of the race."[112] Continuing, Hartmann pontificated:

> One must only accustom oneself to the thought that the Unconscious can be led astray neither more nor less by the lamentation of milliards of human individuals than by that of as many animal individuals, if only these torments further *development,* and thereby its own main design (II, 13).

Whereas in Hartmann's system this is a cheerful expression of evolution, for Hardy it would have been as arrogant as anything in Nietzsche. He could not deny that the Unconscious was responsible for torments;

[110] Garwood, *Thomas Hardy,* p. 11.
[111] William Archer quotes Hardy as saying:

> Do you know Hartmann's *Philosophy of the Unconscious?* It suggested to me what seems almost like a workable theory of the great problem of the origin of evil—though this, of course, is not Hartmann's own theory—that there may be a consciousness, infinitely far off, at the other end of the chain of phenomena, always striving to express itself, and always baffled and blundering, just as the spirits seem to be.

("Real Conversations. Conversation I.—With Mr. Thomas Hardy," *The Critic,* XXXVIII [April, 1901], 316.)

Nothing could more misrepresent either Hartmann or *The Dynasts* than this concept of a divine consciousness.

[112] Eduard von Hartmann, *Philosophy of the Unconscious. Speculative Results According to the Inductive Method of Physical Science,* authorized trans. William C. Coupland (London: Regan Paul, Trench, Trübner & Co., 1931), Part II, 12. The first edition of Coupland appeared in 1884; Hardy used the 1893 edition, with the same pagination.

on the contrary he recognized the fact all too painfully—and he found
nothing for rejoicing therein.

By the time he first read Hartmann, Hardy had become interested
in the origin of consciousness. After quoting from an article by
M. J. Romanes, "The World as an Eject," in the *Contemporary Review*,
in 1886, he noted, "Qy. how much complication is necessary to produce
consciousness." [113] In a later entry, apparently of the same year, almost
immediately after his quotation from the *Revue des deux mondes* on
Schopenhauer, under the heading "Hartmann's *Philosophy of the
Unconscious*," is a paraphrase from an article in the *Revue*, the gist
being that the "nucleus" of the philosophy is that which "has formed
the core of all great philosophies, the Substance of Spinoza, the
Absolute Ego of Plato + Hegel, Schopenhauer's Will, +c ...." [114]
It is in 1900 that we again find Hardy making notes on a like subject.
Heading an entry "Consciousness in Nature," he noted from
Chambers' *Biographical Dictionary* that "Schelling in the *Philosophy
of Nature* writings, + in the *World-Soul*, supplements the Fichtian
Ego or Absolute Ego by showing that the whole of Nature may be
regarded as an embodiment of a process by which Spirit tends to
rise to a consciousness of itself." In pencil he added, "cf. Clifford's
Mindstuff." [115] Several pages later, among short quotations and
paraphrases from various writers, he cited Clifford:

> The reality ... wh. underlies what we call matter [i.e. phenomena] I shall
> call mind-stuff ... a molecule of inorganic matter does not possess mind
> or consciousness, but it possesses a small piece of mind-stuff .... When
> the molecules are so combined ... the corresponding elements of mind-
> stuff are so combined as to form ... consciousness. [116]

Clifford's effort to provide a scientific basis for cosmic consciousness
appears to have intrigued Hardy. He had, however, to seek an answer
in metaphysics, and a few entries later he extracted seven pages from
Hartmann, including his note of fourteen years before.

He started with Hartmann's definition: "I designate the united
unconscious will + unconscious idea 'the Unconscious.'" [117] This is
different from Schopenhauer's Will and Idea, where Idea is phenom-

[113] Literary Notes, I, 210.
[114] *Ibid.*, 227.
[115] Literary Notes, II. The reference is to William K. Clifford.
[116] *Ibid.* Hardy's brackets.
[117] *Ibid.*; Hartmann, *Philosophy of the Unconscious*, I, 4.

enal representation, and Hardy copies a reference to Leibnitz's having assumed "unconscious thinking." He is here abridging and paraphrasing from Hartmann himself. In the following extracts he is preoccupied with the function of the Unconscious and the power of consciousness. The concept of an unconscious idea was to elude Hardy, as it is certainly not spelled out in Hartmann. Hardy's significant emendation in the following passage shows that, at least, he redefined it if he did not revise Hartmann altogether. With minor slips and hiatuses, under the heading "God as super-conscious" Hardy quoted:

> Of this unconscious clairvoyant intellig^{ce} we have come to perceive that in its infallible purposive activity, ... it infinitely transcends the halting gait of the discursive reflection of consciousness, ever limited to a single point, dependent on sense perception, memory + inspirations of the Unconsc^s. We shall ... designate this intellig^{ce}, superior to all consc^{ss}, at once uncons^s + *super*-conscious.[118]

Significantly—for he made the same change in *The Dynasts* (I, 5, iv)— Hardy inserted above *purposive* "[? processive]"; and, also of significance, he laconically commented at the end of the quotation, "very obscure." At least the unconscious idea or the Intelligence which possessed it was for Hardy not necessarily purposive.

Nevertheless, he copied another passage which hints at the nature of the freeing of the Idea from the Will, essential to Hartmann's theory:

> Only if the existence of the world was decided by the act of a *blind* will ... only then is this existence comprehensible; only then is God as such not to be made responsible for the same .... But why did not God when he became *seeing*, i.e. his all-wise intelligence entered into being, repair the error? ... Here we are again aided by the inseparability of the idea from the will in the Unconscious . . the dependence of the idea on the will; [and] the whole world-process [i.e. throughout time] only serves the one purpose of emancipating the Idea from the will by means of consciousness.[119]

[118] Literary Notes, II; Hartmann, *Philosophy of the Unconscious*, II, 247. Early in Part I Hartmann had admitted that he could not prove "an aim in nature," but he believed he had shown the direction toward proof.

[119] Literary Notes, II; Hartmann, *Philosophy of the Unconscious*, II, 274. Hardy's brackets.

In the original the last sentence concludes, "in order by the opposition of the Idea to induce the peace of the will." There is a general resemblance in the ultimate effects as envisaged by Hartmann and Schopenhauer. Hardy himself was to speak not of the bringing of peace to the Will, but of the bringing of consciousness to it.[120]

Hartmann permitted the Unconscious power of choice, for, in unusual circumstances, "the direct activity of the Uncon⁸ must display itself . . . , e.g., the incursions of the Uncon⁸ in human brains wh. determine + guide the course of history . . in the direct ᵑ intended by the Uncon⁸."[121] Again Hardy would not have been able to accept *intended*, but he did, of course, conceive of "It" as working through human minds.

In his repetitive way Hartmann came back to a statement of the ultimate condition for man essentially in accord with Schopenhauer's view. Heading his quotation "The goal," Hardy paraphrased, "The world redemption from the misery of volition [i.e., life], a condition being that the yearning after annihilation attains resistless authority as a practical motive."[122]

Early in Part III Hartmann had spoken of three "stages of the illusion"—that happiness has been attained and so can be in "earthly life," that it can be reached in a "transcendent life after death," and that it is "relegated to the future of the world" (III, 12, 79, 94). With at least the last of these in mind, Hardy commented on annihilation as the goal:

It appears that the author does not commit himself absolutely to this conclusion; asserting that, sh^d any believe in a future happiness of the world by evolution + c (wh. he has called the 3^d stage of illusion) the

[120] As J. O. Bailey indicates, Hardy

found in Von Hartmann the concept that consciousness, as well as impulses from the Unconscious, may be a ground for action. Decisions to act may arise from reflection upon sensations and perceptions. Then, as consciousness gains in influence during the processes of evolutionary development, consciousness may come more and more to inform the unreflective Mind and lead It toward meditated action. This conception, radically different from Schopenhauer's, underlies Hardy's meliorism

(*Thomas Hardy and the Cosmic Mind*, p. 92).

[121] Literary Notes, II; Hartmann, *Philosophy of the Unconscious*, II, 359.

[122] Literary Notes, II; Hartmann, *Philosophy of the Unconscious*, III, "137 + c." Hardy's brackets.

principles remain just as valid for those thinkers, since the final goal of the world-development may be concerned positively or negatively. The concession strikes me as weakening his philosophy.[123]

Hardy was not asserting that the concession was wrong. He himself was never willing to do more than entertain the notion that annihilation was a possible goal.

Further along Hartmann turned again to the relation of man to Nature and of both to the Unconscious, and Hardy recorded:

Affinity of ourselves with other products of Nature: transfer therefore the anthropological principia to the rest of Nature ... however, at the stages more removed from man ... more + more strip off Consciousness ... But the unconscious spirit also dwells in him wh. he long admired in silence in ... less developed consciousnesses .... Thus .. Unconscious Will + Unconscious Idea coalesced to form the one universal spiritual world-essence.[124]

Finally, Hardy quoted from one of Hartmann's many summaries:

The Absolute Spirit .. if one may call anything original it must be this unity of Will + Perception, of Power + Wisdom, as we have hitherto called it, the Unconscious ... this One Substance ... Thus .. the apex of our pyramid coincides with the one S. of Spinoza.[125]

There are other passages in Hartmann which remind one of *The Dynasts*, and, since Hardy's excerpts are from all parts of the *Philosophy of the Unconscious*, he certainly read them. The translator refers to the Will as an "immanent cause" (I, 69 *et al.*) and he speaks of an "immanent unconscious teleology" (II, 246). Hardy's "It" is an "immanent Will." Hartmann not only calls the Intelligence clairvoyant, but accepts mystical premonitions and clairvoyance for men; Hardy had a special interest in premonitions. The most important passages, however, have to do with the development and function of consciousness, which, as we have seen, is something beyond what we mean in our ordinary use of the label. Thus, Hartmann writes, "In the Unconscious, Will and Representation [Idea] are united in inseparable unity .... Consciousness is the possibility of the emancipation of the intellect from the will" (II, 55). In an eloquent passage he concludes

[123] Literary Notes, II.

[124] *Ibid.*; loosely quoted from Hartmann, *Philosophy of the Unconscious*, III, 144–145.

[125] Literary Notes, II; Hartmann, *Philosophy of the Unconscious*, III, 196.

that "*the greatest possible attainable state of happiness*" is "*that of painlessness*" (III, 125). This state is, in effect, acceptance of annihilation, as he reveals soon after:

> The logical principle guides the world-process most wisely to the goal of the greatest possible evolution of consciousness, which being attained, consciousness [a purposive activity, not ordinary awareness] suffices to hurl back the total actual volition into nothingness, by which the *process* and the *world ceases*, and ceases indeed without any residuum whatever whereby the process might be continued. The logical element [Hartmann calls the Will logical] therefore ensures that the world is a best possible world, such a one, namely, as attains redemption, not one whose torment is perpetuated endlessly (III, 142).

Despite his pessimism, Hardy did not really want annihilation of the mind of man. What he dreamed of was the elimination of pain; and it is possible that Hartmann's term was in his memory when he suggested the hope that the Will, become conscious, might use a "painless hand" (II, 6, vii). This is a form of negation; but, put in a timeless context, it accords in spirit more with Hartmann's "Third Illusion."

To sort out the distinctions between Schopenhauer and Hartmann —perhaps less realities than matters of definition—the former makes the Idea the phenomenal representation of the unconscious Will and the latter bestows on the Unconscious both will and idea, the idea representing purposive direction though unconscious. Schopenhauer would somehow free the Idea from the Will in individual men; Hartmann would free the unconscious idea universally. Each gives man a function; he is to become free of the Will or of that aspect of the Unconscious which is will. Without indicating the role that man is to play in the transformation, Hardy can only hope that the Will itself will become conscious. It must be admitted, of course, that the Will remains for him—as for the other two—ineffable. For Hartmann, who believed in the inheritance of acquired characteristics, including moral enlightenment, evolution could bring the change. Although Hardy was interested in such a belief, *The Dynasts* makes no explicit use of it. The one thing of which Hardy had already been sure was that evolution was processive. At times he was inclined to believe that it was also purposive.

Whereas Hartmann pretentiously insists that his system is not aimless or pessimistic and then makes annihilation the goal of the attainment of ultimate human consciousness, Hardy poetically follows a different path. He is concerned with the life of the human spirit, not its annihilation. He may fondly meditate the notion that the happiest condition would be not to have been born; he may feel that existence can be indeed miserable. Yet, as he repeatedly noted, there are some good things in it. To detach one's personal self from the will to live and to exist as consciousness was a different matter. This he sought in his self-absorption in his very art itself.

Hardy never completely surrendered himself to either Schopenhauer or Hartmann. In their pages, however, especially when they were passionately eloquent, he found intellectual excitement. If they could no more than the Greeks and others define for him their essential concepts, they caused him to imagine in somewhat new metaphorical terms and to become preoccupied with something that could be called an immanent, unconscious Will.[126]

We must keep in mind that Hardy wavered between alternatives in his search for a cosmic view. When we turn to the revision of the manuscript of *The Dynasts*, we shall find instances. He was equally tentative in writing about the poem. The most important pronouncement on it while it was in progress is a letter of June 2, 1907, to Edward Wright. It must be read in the light of Hardy's use of Schopenhauer and Hartmann; his alteration of *purposive* to *processive*; the words of the Pities, apparently not yet written, expressing hope rather than belief; and a remark in his autobiography that had he foreseen the war he would not have gone so far as to admit of hope.[127] Wright had queried

[126] The importance of Haeckel for Hardy was mainly as reinforcement of his own views. Haeckel summarizes much scientific information, some of it hearsay, and attempts to derive philosophic generalizations from it. Hartmann cited him. McCabe's translation of *The Riddle of the Universe at the Close of the Nineteenth Century* appeared in 1900. Hardy pasted in Literary Notes, II, a long article on it from the *Daily Chronicle* of October 1; the review notes Haeckel's antianthropomorphism. From the *Spectator*, March 14, 1908, Hardy quoted from a review of *Concepts of Monism*: "Monism in the hands of its most eminent disciple Haeckel, is not a philosophic creed of any moment. It is in a large measure based on assumptions as to the unity of mind + matter, the functional relationship of the soul to the body + the mind to the brain, that are accepted by no man of science or psychologist of the first rank." Hardy's comment: "!" As earlier mentioned, in *The Later Years*, p. 97, Hardy quoted a letter to *The Academy and Literature*, May 17, 1902, stating that Maeterlinck's argument that Nature "may practice a scheme of morality unknown to us" did not meet difficulties "recognized by thinkers like Schopenhauer, Hartmann, Haeckel, etc."

[127] *The Later Years*, p. 165.

Hardy's use of "Will" and had suggested "Unconscious Impulse" instead. The reply, in the Memorial Library draft, shows Hardy still unsure of his precise ideas, as he crosses out words and inserts others:[128]

> I quite agree with you in holding that the word Will does not perfectly fit the idea to be conveyed—a vague thrusting or urging [impulse] force in no predetermined direction. But it has become accepted for want of a better * * * .
>
> That the Unconscious Will of the Universe is growing aware of Itself I believe I may claim as my own idea solely—at which I arrived by reflecting that what has already taken place in fractions of the whole (i.e. so much of the world as has become conscious) is likely to take place in the Mass; + there being no Will outside the Mass—that is, the Universe—the whole Will becomes conscious thereby: + ultimately, it is to be hoped, [moral] sympathetic. * * *
>
> This theory, too, seems to me to settle the question of Free-will v. Necessity. The will of a man is, according to it, neither wholly free nor wholly unfree. When swayed by the Universal Will (as he mostly must be as a[n] [infinitesimal] subservient [minor] part of it) he is not individually free; but whenever it happens [rarely, of course] that all the rest of the Great Will is in equilibrium the minute portion called one person's will is free, just as a performer's fingers will go on playing the pianoforte of themselves [or stop] when he talks or thinks of something else + the head does not rule them. * * * [129]

The letter, as can be noted, owes much to Schopenhauer and Hartmann. The concepts of the Will and of the Unconscious are borrowed, as is the view that man is normally swayed by the Will, but that he can at rare moments be completely free. At the same time, Hardy properly insists on a certain amount of originality. It is evident, too, that his philosophy is not fixed once and for all, that he is still working his way through experience as he tries to generalize about it. His penultimate paragraph admits to "accidental discrepancies." As we shall see later, there were minor uncertainties in Hardy's attempt to

---

[128] Crossed-out words are in brackets, and insertions are elevated. Irrelevant variants are omitted.

[129] In a letter to Edward Clodd, February 2, 1908, Hardy added as a postscript: "The idea of the Unconscious Will becoming conscious with flux of time is also new, I think, whatever it may be worth. At any rate I have never met with it anywhere" (Thomas Hardy, *Notes on "The Dynasts" in Four Letters to Edward Clodd* [Edinburgh: The Dunedin Press, 1929]).

visualize the role of each of his supernatural Intelligences. To some extent these involve his dramatization of his essential idea, since each Spirit should represent one perspective for looking at our human predicament. More significant is the fact that, though in *The Dynasts* Hardy reminded himself repeatedly of the monistic role of the Immanent Will, he readily became immersed in the human action, where the immediate impression is often one of free will.

This review of Hardy's reading has taken us from the ancients to the first years of the twentieth century. Its justification must be, as for any poet, the contribution of that reading to his own poetry. What the books did for Hardy was to give him a frame of reference and the means of interpreting with universal implications the tragedy of life as he himself had experienced it. Between 1867 and 1872 he had known tragedy in the most poignant form in his ill-starred love for Tryphena Sparks.[130] If strength of character helped the fated pair to untangle their lives after a misfortune that would have won the compassion of Sophocles, the origin of the tragedy could be imputed only to "crass casualty," which, when it brings ill luck, must inevitably seem to wear a malignant grin. And in the years of unhappy alliance with a wife whose mental confusion began to reveal itself soon after their marriage in 1874, Hardy came to know—and to accept—the bitter dole of fate that only fate itself could end.

Had he been unlettered, Hardy would have cried out in isolation against the malevolence of the gods. As it was, in the poetic lamentations from the Bible and the Greeks to Matthew Arnold and Swinburne he found that pain was the common lot of thinking men, that one's personal tragedy took its place in an unending tradition of human sorrow. Finally, among the philosophers—particularly Schopenhauer and Hartmann—he came to recognize a scheme, however imperfect, in which he could identify that sorrow as inherent and inevitable by the very nature of things.

THE POET'S OWN REFLECTIONS

While making his notations on his reading, Hardy also occasionally jotted down his own philosophic impressions, particularly on the

[130] Cf., Lois Deacon and T. Coleman, *Providence and Mr. Hardy* (London: Hutchinson, 1966). I have also had the assistance of unpublished information. Tryphena is not mentioned in the autobiography.

tragic tone of life. When he began putting together his autobiography he incorporated his notes, and they appear with a freshness and inconsistency that suggests that no attempt was made to reconcile them. Some, for example, take free will for granted, and others are deterministic. Some deal with omens and a Dorset countryman's sensation of the supernatural; others are skeptical. Some attack Christian anthropomorphism, and others substitute a pagan one. For Hardy all were honest and true. At the same time, there is a larger consistency, in that what he felt about the tragedy of our human predicament in 1866 he felt the more deeply as time passed. There is also a gradual introduction of new elements in Hardy's thought in the 1890's as he read more in metaphysics, particularly in the two German philosophers.

It would be unfair to his great prose works, all written before *The Dynasts*, and to several of his best lyrics to say that for sixty years Hardy was preparing to write his epic. Nevertheless, one can trace a development which does reach full expression in the poem.

One of the virtues of Hardy as poet is that he could set down in unqualified terms his immediate sensations. Sometimes a note or poem is nothing more than a record of a feeling that came to him with a sharp poignancy. One such example appears in a memorandum dated October 30, 1870: "Mother's notion, + also mine: That a figure stands in our van with arm uplifted, to knock us back from any pleasant prospect we indulge in as probable." [131] The anthropomorphic nature of the figure is obvious, and despite his later objections to Christian anthropomorphism, Hardy never could and perhaps never wanted to lose the feeling of a personal relation with the shaper of human destiny. Four years earlier, in speaking of "crass casualty," he had conceived of a roller of dice who took equal satisfaction in meting out pleasure and pain, when presumably he could have been partial to man; and in *Tess* (1891) he referred pointedly to the "circumstantial will against enjoyment" (Chap. 43). The many omens in his verse and novels presuppose a world of spirits in which an omniscient power satanically foreshadows the ill luck soon to come. Though years later he was to speak of these supernatural phenomena as the mythology available to a poet,[132] the fact is that they were indispensable metaphors simply because they expressed his direct response to experience.

[131] Memoranda, I.
[132] Letter to C. W. Saleeby, 1915, in *The Later Years*, p. 168.

"I sometimes look upon all things in inanimate Nature as pensive mutes"[133]—this note of May 30, 1877, is a generalization, but the concrete evidence to support it can be found in *Far from the Madding Crowd* (1874), more emphatically in *The Return of the Native* (1878), and in phrases here and there in *The Dynasts*. Much more common in Hardy's poetry is the feeling that the live creatures of Nature are akin to mankind in their capacity for suffering. Though not capable of the bitterness that stems from reflection, they are also not nescient, and only nescience spares creatures from pain. The coneys on the route to Waterloo are typical. Any inclusive philosophy, for Hardy, had to encompass both man and *pensive* Nature.

In a note of May 9, 1881, we find one of several outcries by Hardy against the World order: "The emotions have no place in a world of defect, and it is a cruel injustice that they should have developed in it. If Law itself had consciousness, how the aspect of its creatures would terrify it, fill it with remorse!"[134] The phrasing here is traditional, with *Law* representing *Necessity*, but the image is morally anthropomorphic; and when Hardy came to speak of an Immanent Will he did not really eliminate anthropomorphism. That Will is neutral because unconscious, but from man's point of view its workings are defective.

With the conditions of life inherently melancholy, where lay the value of reflection? For Hardy himself as a creative writer the answer is in a note of April 19, 1885: "The business of the poet and novelist is to show the sorriness underlying the grandest things, and the grandeur underlying the sorriest things."[135] In short, however bitterly one might at moments assert that the worst misfortune was to have been born, there were still godlike recognitions awaiting the percipient mind. If tragedy was inescapable, it was also inexhaustibly entrancing. In a note that at first seems ordinary and conventional, Hardy, in November, 1885, set down his own definition of tragedy: "Tragedy. It may be put thus in brief: a tragedy exhibits a state of things in the life of an individual which unavoidably causes some natural aim or desire of

[133] *The Early Life*, p. 150.

[134] *Ibid.*, p. 192. Cf., also an entry of April 7, 1889: "A woeful fact—that the human race is too extremely developed for its corporeal conditions, the nerves being evolved to an activity abnormal in such an environment * * * . This planet does not supply the materials for happiness to higher existences. Other planets may, though one can hardly see how" (*ibid.*, pp. 285–286).

[135] *Ibid.*, p. 223.

his to end in a catastrophe when carried out."[136] But, while not original, the definition is also not Aristotelian. The "natural aim" need not involve pride, ambition, or any excess. It may, indeed, be most innocent. Again, it may represent the collective folly of mankind; or, on the contrary, that folly may express the circumstantial will that brings the catastrophe. It was something of this latter sort that Hardy had meant in a note of February 16, 1882: "Write a history of human automatism, or impulsion—viz, an account of human action in spite of human knowledge, showing how very far conduct lags behind the knowledge that should really guide it."[137]

In a note of October 20, 1884, Hardy provides a variant on the same theme:

> Query: Is not the present quasi-scientific system of writing history mere charlatanism? Events and tendencies are traced as if they were rivers of voluntary activity, and courses reasoned out from the circumstances in which natures, religions, or what-not, have found themselves. But are they not in the main the outcome of *passivity*—acted upon by unconscious propensity?[138]

He returned to the concept in notes of December, 1886, and February 13, 1887:

> I often view society-gatherings, people in the street, in a room, or elsewhere, as if they were beings in a somnambulistic state, making their motions automatically—not realizing what they mean. * * * I was thinking a night or two ago that people are somnambulists—that the material is not the real—only the visible, the real being invisible optically. That it is because we are in a somnambulistic hallucination that we think the real to be what we see as real.[139]

Nothing could more fully express Hardy's concept than the marching of soldiers from battlefield to battlefield. He was to make much of this in *The Dynasts*, where armies proceed, as if in sleep, toward a meaningless doom.

[136] *Ibid.*, p. 230. October 24, 1892, Hardy commented: The best tragedy—highest tragedy in short—is that of the WORTHY encompassed by the INEVITABLE. The tragedies of immoral and worthless people are not of the best" (*The Later Years*, p. 14).
[137] *The Early Life*, pp. 197–198.
[138] *Ibid.*, pp. 219–220.
[139] *Ibid.*, pp. 241, 243.

But somnambulism would not account for the acuteness of human suffering. A different kind of metaphor was needed for that. Hence the "fettered gods of the earth" of *The Return* (Book First, Chap. 3), and a note of May 28, 1885, on people seen at the Marble Arch: "Some wear jewels and feathers, some wear rags. All are caged birds; the only difference lies in the size of the cage. This too is part of the tragedy." [140] If there was grandeur in the sorriest of things, it came from the fact that, however fettered or caged, however buffeted by the figure in the van, the human spirit was resilient. Thus Hardy wrote in July, 1888:

> Thought of the determination to enjoy. We see it in all nature, from the leaf on the tree to the titled lady at the ball . . . . It is achieved, of a sort, under superhuman difficulties. Like pent-up water it will find a chink of possibility somewhere. Even the most oppressed of men and animals find it, so that out of a thousand there is hardly one who has not a sun of some sort for his soul. [141]

Perhaps the best-known instance in Hardy is Tess's recovery after the death of her child. But even the wretched deserters in the cellar near Astorga have their moments of sunshine before death brings the night. Were there no sun there would be the futility of an automaton's somnambulistic progress toward death. Without the glimpses of celestial brightness there would also be no fear of gray twilight, to be followed inevitably by the black.

Though Hardy had repeatedly gone over the questions of theology, they never lost a sense of newness or a power to disturb. In the late 1880's and the years that followed he still sometimes thought in Christian-Hebraic terminology, and in a Swinburnean manner chided an unjust or thoughtless God. Or, more charitably, accepting a divinity omniscient but powerless, he called on a Cause essentially equivalent to Necessity. From 1888 there are two religious pronouncements which are especially pointed. The Reverend A. B. Grosart had posed the issue of "how to reconcile these [evils] with the absolute goodness and non-limitation of God." To this Hardy replied:

> Mr. Hardy regrets that he is unable to suggest any hypothesis which would reconcile the existence of such evils as Dr. Grosart describes with the idea of omnipotent goodness. Perhaps Dr. Grosart might be helped

[140] *Ibid.*, p. 224.
[141] *Ibid.*, p. 279.

to a provisional view of the universe by the recently published Life of Darwin, and the works of Herbert Spencer and other agnostics.[142]

The statement seems even-tempered, but, read in the light of all Hardy had written, it becomes bitter.

Even more acrid is what appears to have been a motif for a poem. Though no such poem was written, the note, of December 10, 1888, could fit incidents in *Tess* and *Jude*, the general tenor of many a poem before and after 1888, and, above all, much of *The Dynasts*: "He, she, had blundered; but not as the Prime Cause had blundered. He, she, had sinned; but not as the Prime Cause had sinned. He, she, was ashamed and sorry; but not as the Prime Cause would be ashamed and sorry if it knew." [143] The Prime Cause is thus brought to judgment in a court where human values must prevail. Indeed, it is not even allowed the mystic virtues of the Jehovah in Job. Hardy's knowledge of Schopenhauer was still fragmentary, and we cannot equate the Prime Cause precisely with an unconscious Will. Yet it would seem to share its two attributes with it. It is not all-knowing and all-powerful as a Christian God might be, nor yet omniscient and at the same time noninterfering in a world of foreknowledge and free will. It is, on the contrary, nescient—at least of what man suffers—and yet all-powerful. So it is, in short, an amoral force, and yet, in any moral context, it is supremely guilty. In the next few years Hardy's rational metaphysics was to be altered, but his inherent feeling of divine injustice was to remain, ready to burst forth in a cry of anguish or a paean of compassion for suffering mankind.

In contrast, even when recognizing the cruelty of men to one another, Hardy felt that there was affinity among mankind. In a note of March–April, 1890, he sees men not as antagonists, but as parts of one being: "Altruism * * * will ultimately be brought about I think by the pain we see in others reacting on ourselves, as if we and they were a part of one body. Mankind, in fact, may be and possibly will be viewed as members of one corporeal frame." [144] In another rumination, recopied under the heading "From old notes written before 'The Dynasts,'" Hardy let his fancy play with the concept of a "collective personality." With his habitual irony he projected the idea as it would find expression in human conflict:

[142] *Ibid.*, p. 269.
[143] *Ibid.*, p. 282.
[144] *Ibid.*, p. 294.

We—the people = Humanity–a collective personality—(Thus "we" could be engaged in the battle of Hohenlinden, say, + in the battle of Waterloo)—Dwell with genial humour on "our" getting into a rage for "we" knew not what.

The intelligence of this collective personality Humanity is pervasive, ubiquitous, like that of God. Hence, e.g. on the one hand we could hear the roar of the cannon, discern the rush of the battalions, on the other hear the voice of a man protesting, +c—Tit. "Self-slaughter": "divided agst ourselves."

Now these three (or 3000) whirling through space at the rate of 40 miles a second—(God's view).

"Some of your family who" (the We of one nation speaking of the "we" of another)

—A battle. Army as Somnambulists—not knowing what it is for.

—"We were called Artillery" +c "We were so under the spell of habit that" (drill)

It is now necessary to call the reader's attention to those of us who were harnessed + collared in blue + brown . . . .

After a digression Hardy returned to his theme to add: "We will now ask the reader to look eastward with us . . . at what the contingent of us out that way were doing—."[145] Significantly, though he began only with people, Hardy could not exclude the chief sufferers on the fields of battle. The undated note can hardly be taken as a prospectus of *The Dynasts* though Hardy had probably already begun thinking on the subject. But it does indicate his sense of the cruelty inherent in our human predicament, where we slay ourselves helplessly, not knowing what the battle is for.

In the digression Hardy recorded two motifs for possible poems. The one was to be concerned with "the difference between what things are + what they ought to be (stated as by a god to the gods— i. e.—as god's story)." The note for the second poem reads: "I = First Cause—omniscient, not omnipotent—limitations, difficulties +c from being only able to work by Law (His only failing is lack of foresight)." Here we are back nearer to acceptance of our old friend Necessity, which is not conscious, together with a First Cause which is really *not* omniscient since it knows nothing of what it is bringing to pass. Neither poem was written. Certainly the second, if not both,

[145] Memoranda, II. The closeness of these notes in general perspective suggests a nearness in dates. The digression, however, in the Memoranda note is closer to the note below from February 5, 1898.

would have been Manichaean, since the "I" would have been essentially human in its struggle against circumstance and in the blindness of its choice.

April 26, 1890, Hardy set down the bald pronouncement: "View the Prime Cause or Invariable Antecedent as 'It' and recount its doings." In editing he added, "This was done in *The Dynasts*." [146] But the problem was by no means solved by the selection of a neuter pronoun. As late as February 5, 1898, Hardy returned to the concept of a fettered God: "Write a prayer, or hymn, to One not Omnipotent, but hampered; striving for our good, but unable to achieve it except occasionally." [147] In editing Hardy remarked: "This idea of a limited God of goodness, often dwelt on by Hardy, was expounded ably and at length in MacTaggart's *Some Dogmas of Religion* several years later, and led to a friendship which ended only with the latter's death." This is an altogether different view from that implied in "It," at least as the latter was soon to become the Immanent Will of *The Dynasts*.

Perhaps Hardy's dilemma was best stated in two notes. In the first, written more than a year earlier, September 8, 1896, he had confessed to futility in his search for answers: "There are certain questions which are made unimportant by their very magnitude. For example, the question whether we are moving in Space this way or that; the existence of a God, etc." [148] The second, from 1899, suggests that semantics may substitute for the realities in contemporary theology:

> It would be an amusing fact, if it were not one that leads to such bitter strife, that the conception of a First Cause which the theist calls "God," and the conception of the same that the so-styled atheist calls "no-God," are nowadays almost exactly identical. So that only a minor literary question of terminology prevents their shaking hands in agreement, and dwelling together in unity ever after. [149]

Though he was writing of the arguments of others, Hardy was certainly allowing for his own latitude in terminology.

A more important pronouncement, and, indeed, a justification of his own literary preoccupation, appears in a letter written about 1901 and "apparently not sent":

[146] *The Early Life*, p. 294.
[147] *The Later Years*, p. 73.
[148] *Ibid.*, p. 54.
[149] *Ibid.*, p. 82.

My own interest lies largely in non-rationalistic subjects, since non-rationality seems, so far as one can perceive, to be the principle of the Universe. By which I do not mean foolishness, but rather a principle for which there is no exact name, lying at the indifference point between rationality and irrationality.[150]

Here was the defense of whatever perspective, whatever metaphors and symbols, including the supernatural, Hardy might wish to employ for transcending reason in his search for reality, and in his attempt to convey his sensation of it. And in a note, December 31, 1901, which hints of the preface to *The Dynasts,* he wrote:

After reading various philosophic systems, and being struck with their contradictions and futilities, I have come to this: *Let every man make a philosophy for himself out of his own experience.* He will not be able to escape using terms and phraseology from earlier philosophers, but let him avoid adopting their theories if he values his own mental life.[151]

Such were Hardy's attempts to formulate a statement of his metaphysics and to make discriminations. The notes are mere fragments of thought; yet, even when discussing the "non-rationalistic," they represent efforts toward order—not the same order each time, but something resembling the views of others to which Hardy could subscribe.

Meanwhile, Hardy had been working in the same direction as novelist and poet. In his fiction and poetry he could let his imagination wander in the realm of the nonrational; and, though he frequently enunciated abstract philosophic concepts similar to those in his notes, he put them in metaphorical and symbolic contexts that express not mere reasoned conclusions, but the author's feeling for reality. Sometimes the commentary is in terms of Greek tragedy or of Old or New Testament theology with an ironic twist. There may even be defense of a beneficent divine spirit struggling in a Necessitarian Universe. Such symbolism in the 1890's and, indeed, into the 1920's represents only variations on the pronouncements in *The Return* or even of poems of the 1860's.

In "Sine Prole," probably of 1900, for example, the poet, unlike the Hebrews, is pleased that the line of descent that has given him life will end with his death. Modern men

---

[150] *Ibid.,* p. 90.
[151] *Ibid.,* p. 91.

> * * * have been schooled by lengthier vision,
> View Life's lottery with misprision,
> And its dice that fling no prize! [152]

There is here no chance whatever of a lucky cast; it is only a question
of the degree of sorrow the sporting gods may inflict. In "God-
Forgotten," written by 1901, the "Lord Most High" is a conscious
being, capable of participating in a dialogue. He has simply lost
interest in the Earth and can only hope that it has perished. Finding,
instead, that it is "by pangs distraught," he excuses his remissness:

> "Thou shouldst have learnt that *Not to Mend*
> For Me could mean but *Not to Know* * * * ."

Again we have a God who is conscious, but not omniscient. He is also
a merciful God in that he directs his messengers to "put an end / To
what men undergo." [153] Only one end is, of course, possible. It is not a
Schopenhauerian resolution because it is not to be reached through
man's transcending the will to live. The wish for annihilation is a
simple cry of despair. In "The Subalterns," also written by 1901, man's
seeming enemies—the leaden sky, the freezing North, Sickness, and
Death—are but passive expressions of "laws in force on high." Such
poems, and there are many of similar meanings, represent the poet's
direct response to human fate. Against whatever divine power or law
they may be uttered, theirs is the mocking voice of the Spirits Ironic
or Sinister; yet, suffusing every poem, is the unheard music of the
Pities, in soft, compassionate tones.

In one poem, "Nature's Questioning," written by 1898, Hardy
sums up alternative theories as to a First Cause. It is the frame,
however, in which he puts Nature's puzzled musings that gives import
to her words. For Hardy starts not with a theoretical premise, but with
reality as he senses it. Nature is "chastened" and "cowed." In "pool, /
Field, flock, and lonely tree" the poet sees "faces dulled, constrained,
and worn." In the questionings that follow, Nature considers various
philosophic choices. No one of them is the "It" of *The Dynasts*;
and yet one perceives that, were this unconscious force, incapable of

---

[152] *Human Shows—Far Phantasies.* Cf., *The Later Years*, pp. 85–86, for
probable date. Poems for which only the date of book publication is known may
have been written some years before, though the substance of many suggests
composition after about 1890.

[153] *Poems of the Past and the Present.*

jest or foreknowledge, of creating a mechanism or of fighting evil, to be added to the list, it would but make another variant within the frame:

> "Has some Vast Imbecility,
> Mighty to build and blend,
> But impotent to tend,
> Framed us in jest, and left us now to hazardry?

> "Or come we of an Automaton
> Unconscious of our pains? . . .
> Or are we live remains
> Of Godhead dying downwards, brain and eye now gone?

> "Or is it that some high Plan betides,
> As yet not understood,
> Of Evil stormed by Good,
> We the Forlorn Hope over which Achievement strides?"

The images are complex enough. An Imbecility is capable of a jest; the Godhead itself once had but now has lost an intellect; a Manichaean Good works through something akin to Darwinian evolution, but in accord with a high Plan that assures ultimate success. Except for the optimism implied in the Plan, Hardy could and did entertain notions in accord with all three stanzas. And yet he comes out where he entered, baffled after a fruitless search:

> Thus things around. No answerer I . . .
> Meanwhile the winds, and rains,
> And Earth's old glooms and pains
> Are still the same, and Life and Death are neighbours nigh.[154]

Once more there is substance for silent lamentation by the Pities.

There are certain poems and comments in the novels which in their metaphors or imagery are yet closer anticipations of the philosophic language and symbolic images in *The Dynasts*. Among many from the late 1880's and after, a few may be cited as typical.

In *The Woodlanders* (1887), after picturing Marty and Winterborne walking alone in the early morning, apparently isolated for the moment from all other human life, Hardy employs a metaphor that fixes their lot in the universal destiny of mankind: "And yet their lonely courses formed no detached design at all, but were part of the pattern in the

[154] *Wessex Poems.*

great web of human doings then weaving in both hemispheres from
the White Sea to Cape Horn" (chap. 3). In "Doom and She," written
by 1901, Hardy calls the "Mother of all things made" a "World-
weaver." In the dialogue she is characterized as "unlit with sight,"
and Doom is "vacant of feeling." When she wonders whether she has
done well in shaping or should perhaps undo all, Doom cannot
answer her, for he cannot tell joy from pain. So Hardy concludes with
pity for her:

> —Unanswered, curious, meek,
> She broods in sad surmise . . . .
> —Some say they have heard her sighs
> On Alpine height or Polar peak
> When the night tempests rise.[155]

It would be impossible to work out a system of metaphysics that would
fit the poem without some arbitrariness in definitions. And yet the
impression, as distinguished from the argument—to use Hardy's
terms—is realistic. The World-weaver can make patterns; all around
him Hardy saw them. From the days of the Hebrews through the
enduring centuries down to post-Darwinian times the patterns had
been weaving. They were orderly enough, despite the endless variations. But when Hardy reflected on human fate, he found in the
patterns no purpose as men understand purpose. The weaver was ever
busy, but her fingers were unguided by sight. The supernatural pair
do not match any two supernatural beings in *The Dynasts*; but "It"
creates patterns in networks and webs, there are hints of Doom in the
Spirit of the Years, and, of course, the consequence for man is the same.
We have only men's word that the World-weaver sighs, which amounts
to saying that the compassionate part of man's nature finds reason for
such sighing; it was this human quality that Hardy was to personify in
the Pities.

In "He Wonders about Himself," November, 1893, Hardy employs
the term *Will* in what appears to be a Schopenhauerian meaning:

> Part is mine of the general Will,
> Cannot my share in the sum of sources
> Bend a digit the poise of forces,
> And a fair desire fulfil?[156]

---

[155] *Poems of the Past and the Present.*
[156] *Moments of Vision and Miscellaneous Verses.*

The poem is directed to the speaker's beloved and describes his yearning for personal freedom within the Will. If, however, the Will itself were to become altered, one means would, of course, be the concerted efforts of all men. Significantly, Hardy finds no assurance of this. Even for the individual he presents merely a question, with the implication that he has never found evidence for answering yes. The question was still before him as he wrote *The Dynasts,* including the lines of the Pities at the end.

In *Jude the Obscure* (1895), Hardy ranges, as usually in his novels, from bald statement of narrative fact to lyric commentary. Within a few pages near the close of the tragic liaison of Jude and Sue, Hardy represents them as helpless children, seeking futilely for a philosophy that will free them from wretchedness, and finally succumbing to a force less noble than themselves. Their words and Sue's thoughts are really Hardy's.

In her grief after the death of the children Sue cries out: "There is something external to us which says, 'You shan't.' First it said, 'You shan't learn!' Then it said, 'You shan't labour!' Now it says, 'You shan't love.'" Certainly Sue is thinking of the anthropomorphic figure standing in the van. Any theoretical Immanent Will to be conceived by Hardy cannot escape its hostile attributes. Soon afterward Jude laments: "Nothing can be done * * * . Things are as they are, and will be brought to their destined issue." When asked, "Who said that?" he replies: "It comes in the chorus of the *Agamemnon.* It has been in my mind continually since this happened." (Part Sixth, chap. 2).

Then comes a rapid summing up of Sue's philosophic history. She has earlier toyed with being a Roman pagan, and later she has fancied herself a calm, rational philosopher who could believe in a dispassionate First Cause. Now Hardy puts in her mind feelings and half-articulated thoughts which we have found in his notebooks and poems:

> Vague and quaint imaginings had haunted Sue in the days when her intellect scintillated like a star, that the world resembled a stanza or melody composed in a dream; it was wonderfully excellent to the half-aroused intelligence, but hopelessly absurd at the full waking; that the First Cause worked automatically like a somnambulist, and not reflectively like a sage; that at the framing of the terrestrial conditions there seemed never to have been contemplated such a development of emotional perceptiveness among the creatures subject to those conditions as that reached by thinking and educated humanity. But affliction makes opposing

forces loom anthropomorphous, and those ideas were now exchanged for a sense of Jude and herself fleeing from a persecutor (Part Sixth, chap. 3).

Sue will return to her husband as a penance, to placate a vengeful God. She has offended and must pay, and so she submits to an Hebraic-Christian tradition in its most oppressive form. As for Jude, in returning to Arabella and enduring her contempt, he acknowledges "terrestrial conditions" that can only bring suffering to a man of "emotional [and moral] perceptiveness." If we call Sue superstitious, we are only saying that her imagination gives tangible embodiment to Hardy's own thoughts. Moreover, although society and social conventions may at times be the means through which the supernatural force afflicts her, the tragedy is not in man's struggle against mores. Events have happened that leave Sue no alternative to separation from Jude. To continue to live as if nothing had struck them down would have been horrifying. Had Hardy called upon the Spirit of the Years, that dispassionate commentator would have used the language of Schopenhauer rather than of Aeschylus, but the essence of his pronouncement would still have been, "Things are as they are, and will be brought to their destined issue." In short, for Hardy all religious and philosophic perspectives which he could seriously entertain were akin. He merely got a better image for symbolizing his own view when he spoke of something—in this case, a First Cause—which "worked automatically like a somnambulist." He was still to establish certain attributes when he renamed it, in *The Dynasts*, the Will.

In "The Bullfinches," written by 1901, personified Nature is essentially a First Cause, though not omnipotent, and she works somnambulistically:

> Busy in her handsome house
> Known as Space, she falls a-drowse;
> Yet, in seeming, works on dreaming,
> While beneath her groping hands
> Fiends make havoc in her bands.
>
> How her hussif'ry succeeds
> She unknows or she unheeds,
> All things making for Death's taking! [157]

In a poem significantly entitled "The Sleep-worker," also written

---

[157] *Poems of the Past and the Present.*

by 1901, Hardy asks the sleeping "Mother" what she will do when her eyes are opened to "All that Life's palpitating tissues feel":

> Wilt thou destroy, in one wild shock of shame,
> Thy whole high heaving firmamental frame,
> Or patiently adjust, amend, and heal? [158]

Finally, for our purpose, in "By the Earth's Corpse," likewise written by 1901, the "Lord" looks out over a World where all life is extinct, admits his guilt, and repents:

> "Written indelibly
> On my eternal mind
> Are all the wrongs endured
> By Earth's poor patient kind,
> Which my too oft unconscious hand
> Let enter undesigned. * * *
>
> "As when, in Noë's days,
> I whelmed the plains with sea,
> So at this last, when flesh
> And herb but fossils be,
> And, all extinct, their piteous dust
> Revolves obliviously,
> That I made Earth, and life, and man,
> It still repenteth me!" [159]

In hoping, in *The Dynasts,* that the Will, when awakened, will use a painless hand, Hardy was thinking of mending and healing; but in these lines annihilation is the only recourse.

Such were Hardy's philosophic impressions as he prepared to write *The Dynasts.* He was looking for an all-encompassing concept. Yet he still had to think, as indeed he felt, in anthropomorphic symbols and images. There had been no reversal from his earliest acceptance of the Greeks; what he now believed was essentially a refinement upon them. He still needed supernatural spirits to represent his philosophic questionings, and even his Immanent Will could not be divested of anthropomorphic attributes.

In his representation of a deterministic Universe, Hardy recognized the fact that man was capable of moral choice. Indeed, without it man's suffering would be less poignant, for he deliberately accepted suffering

[158] *Ibid.*
[159] *Ibid.*

which might otherwise have been avoided. Jude is a good man, and so is Hardy's Pitt. Tess sacrifices her life for an ideal, and so does Nelson. The shaper of man's destiny, however, seems to be indifferent to a moral sense as it weaves somnambulistically. Theoretically, Hardy should have viewed it as a neutral force, not to be brought before the bar of human justice. "Its" workings should have remained incomprehensible. And yet, from brooding on his own experience, Hardy could not avoid attributing to that ineffable Will a hostile or sporting tendency. It was unweeting; but, were it ever to be informed by consciousness, it ought to alter the patterns it wove—or destroy them. How was its consciousness to be brought about? This question, whose answer Schopenhauer worked out in abstract theory, was to remain for Hardy the impenetrable mystery.

CHAPTER TWO

Hints Toward a Prosody

Beyond elementary instruction in the art of composition Hardy was inevitably self-taught. He had a good education in the Dorchester academy, and he later discussed the classics with Bastow at Hicks's architectural office and then with his friend Horace Moule. His insights into the subtleties of versification, however, came from his private study of the English poets and from desultory reading in literary criticism.

As a boy Hardy knew best the rhythms of ballads, hymns, and country dances. Alternating four- and three-foot lines were to remain his most natural medium, and many of his poems which are not in ballad meter are in kindred forms. Before he wrote *The Dynasts* he had done little in blank verse and not much in heroic couplets, and he had written few sonnets. There are a good many five-foot lines in his short poems, but, except in the sonnets, they are usually preceded or followed by lines of four feet, or three, or even two. Several poems are in four-foot meter, others in three, and still others with two-foot variants from four- or three-foot lines. If one were to read these without attention to the diction and imagery, they would either become singsong or else race ahead in galloping monotony. Hardy, of course, did not read them in so naïve a manner. He heard the words in slow cadences, with long pauses to give even greater slowness. The regular beat of iambic tetrameter or trimeter established only an undertone; it was the departure from it, when a line was properly read, that surprised and captured the ear. Significantly, Hardy found within his short lines more flexibility than he usually managed in continuous pentameter. Not that every poem is entirely successful, for some are strained and artificial; but the ideal was a ballad or ballad-like poem that could be talked.

Two major requisites, which were to become especially apparent in *The Dynasts*, were unusual diction and unfamiliar imagery. When

Hardy read the poets he looked for both. Two of his chief sources of instruction were Milton and Shakespeare, both of whom he studied early and continued to read. In his 1865 edition of Milton,[1] autographed "1866," numerous single words and phrases are underlined. In Book VII of *Paradise Lost* these include "*uttermost convex*," "*tumid hills*," "*conglobing* from the *dry*," "by night *altern*," "*unlightsome* first," and "*corpulence*"; in "The Passion," "*otherwhere*" and "*wannish* white." Characteristic of Hardy's reading methods are annotations in his 1856 Shakespeare.[2] Some are textual queries or emendations which reveal his instinct for word choice. One under-lining and marginal notation in *Timon of Athens*, Act V, scene i, perhaps best illustrates the poetic imagination at work. Hardy under-lined "*black-corner'd* night" and commented, "i.e. Deep shades in every nook + corner." In *Hamlet* he noted unusual expressions that could still be heard in Dorset. As the date "Dec 15 / 1870" appears in *Hamlet* (on page 319 of Volume IX), we can assume that the under-scorings are those of a student seeking hints in technique.

In Act I, scene ii, of the undated edition of *The Tempest*,[3] Hardy underlined "*In the dark backward and abysm of time.*" He marginally lined and, as indicated, underlined

> Thou dost; and think'st it much to tread the ooze
> Of the salt deep,
> To run upon the sharp wind of the north,
> To do me business in the *veins* o' the earth
> When it is *baked* with frost.

In Act II he put triple lines by "He receives comfort like cold por-ridge." In Act IV, scene i, underlinings include "*toothed briars*," "*frail shins*," "So his mind *cankers*," "*aged cramps*," "*pinch-spotted*," and "*printless* foot." The underlinings demonstrate careful reading, and they come on pages which are replete with startling images and metaphors and abound in variety of rhythm. Indeed, Hardy, whose imagination was Spartan, must have found *The Tempest* a fairyland of fancy. He never attempted to match the profusion of images of Shakespeare. He obviously learnt, however, from the richly connota-tive language.

[1] *Poetical Works* (Halifax: Milner and Sowerby).
[2] London: Bell and Daldy.
[3] London: Longman's, Green.

Since Hardy admitted to the influence of Donne, we may suppose that he liked the complex images and the ruggedness of his poetry.[4] A major encouragement toward novel phrasings and irregular rhythms was most certainly Browning, whose poems, as we have noted, he knew well.[5] There was also the example of Barnes. In his 1879 edition of *Poems of Rural Life in the Dorset Dialect*, Hardy underlined and defined words and clarified the syntax. In *The Dynasts*, even more than in the poems which preceded it, one is struck, sometimes jarred, by what contemporary critics regarded as eccentric diction and crabbed verse.

At the same time, however, that Hardy was working to give variety to his rhythms he was marking hundreds of phrases in his books that were graceful and flowing. More often than not they dealt with melancholy themes. Here and there he also singled out eloquent passages on themes that Burke would have called sublime.

In his 1864 edition of Milton,[6] carrying the inscription "T. H. 1865," there are markings of both the sweet and the grand. In *Paradise Lost*, which is unmarked after Book III, the latter preponderate. Hardy liked

> His legions, angel forms, who lay entranced
> Thick as autumnal leaves that strew the brooks
> In Vallombrosa.   (Book I, 301–303)

In the margin he noted, "Cf Virg. Aen VI, 309—Multa in sylvis autumni etc." By "Hell trembled at the hideous name, and sighed" he commented, "Horrible!" And by the description of the gates of Hell he put double lines:

> So wide they stood, and like a furnace mouth
> Cast forth redounding smoke and ruddy flame.
> Before their eyes in sudden view appear
> The secrets of the hoary deep, a dark
> Illimitable ocean, without bound,
> Without dimension, where length, breadth, and height
> And time, and place are lost; where eldest Night . . . .
>   (Book II, 888–894)

[4] In the 1896 edition of *Poems*, edited by E. K. Chambers (London: Lawrence and Bullen), there are no significant markings.

[5] The markings in the 1893 edition are possibly not Hardy's; they are very faint. The book was a gift from Florence Henniker, July 29, 1894. The marks in the 1897 edition are not revealing.

[6] *The Poetical Works* (London: Routledge, Warne, and Routledge).

There are only hints of such vastness in the cadences of Hardy's shorter poems, but there are prose passages descriptive of the heath and of night which rise to measured eloquence. And, of course, in *The Dynasts*, in both verse and prose the imagery and rhythms sometimes remind one of Milton.

Hardy's copy of Spenser [7] carries "16 Westborne Park Villas" on the title page and so was bought not later than 1873. Over a page of "Epithalamion" is lined, part doubly, and at the side appears "E L G," which dates the reading before Hardy's marriage in 1874. Great numbers of passages throughout the book are marked, and in later years Hardy returned to Spenser. [8] Among stanzas which he liked was that in Book I, Canto ix, ending

> Sleep after toyle, port after stormie seas,
> Ease after warre, death after life, does greatly please.

The theme of this would, of course, attract Hardy, but he obviously appreciated the phrasing. At the top of the stanza appears "1. 1. 11," and at the end "22 / 9 / 21." Some of the verses singled out have moderate alliteration, always of interest to Hardy. Typical are the two lines he marked doubly at the end of Book II:

> Let Gryll be Gryll, and have his hoggish mind:
> But let us hence depart, whilest wether serves and winde.

There is no question that Hardy had an ear for Spenser's varied cadences and that he was aware of what could be done with the pauses in the Alexandrine line.

Of the three-volume 1877 edition of Sidney's poems in the Memorial Library only the first has more than incidental marks. [9] Hardy was, of course, not reading Sidney for the first time at the age of thirty-seven or later. His annotations consequently represent his recognition of familiar lines. It was Sidney's art that interested Hardy, and he found ample instruction in *Astrophel and Stella*. In Sonnet 1 he singled out the Alexandrine: "Some fresh and fruitfull showers upon my sunburn'd brain." He marked and underlined the literary advice of

[7] *The Fairie Queene . . . to Which Is Added His Epithalamion* (London: Routledge, Warne, and Routledge, 1865).

[8] He may have returned specifically to the marked part in Book VI on Tristram when he was writing *The Famous Tragedy of the Queen of Cornwall.*

[9] *The Complete Poems* (London: Chatto and Windus).

"Foole, said my Muse to me, *looke in thy heart,* and write." In Sonnet 15 he liked the classical formality of

> You that do search for every purling spring
> Which from the ribs of old Parnassus flowes.

In Sonnet 23 the subject would have caught his attention, but the image and rhythm were in perfect accord: "Whence those same fumes of melancholy rise." And, of course, he marked in Sonnet 31

> With how sad steps, O Moone, thou clims't the skies!
> How silently and with how wanne a face.

In visualizing Hardy reading Spenser and Sidney we must not picture a Jude the Obscure suddenly brought into the presence of courtiers. But we can see him as a poet whose inspiration was closely identified with the countryside of Dorset and the poignant experiences he had undergone. When he read the courtly Elizabethans he had a moral earnestness that made their lines live in his own life, and he was also concerned with their mastery of form.

The poetry of James Thomson also attracted Hardy. In his copy, which is inscribed "T. Hardy 1865," the markings, as might be expected, are much more in "Autumn" and "Winter" than in the other seasons.[10] In "Autumn" he marked doubly line 206, which expressed his own feeling for both Nature and art: "But is, when unadorn'd, adorned the most." He underlined line 212: "And breathes its balmy fragrance o'er the wild," and added the obvious footnote from Gray: "and wastes its sweetness on the desert air." The account of the cruelty of sportsmen would have caught his attention quite apart from any merit of the verse, but it was the imagery and eloquence of the lines that most often impressed him, as in the cosmic gloom and grandeur of "Autumn," lines 1138–1144:

> Now black and deep, the night begins to fall,
> A shade immense. Sunk in the quenching gloom,
> Magnificent and vast, are heaven and earth.
> Order confounded lies; all beauty void;
> Distinction lost; and gay variety
> One universal blot: such the fair power
> Of Light, to kindle and create the whole.

---

[10] *The Poetical Works of James Thomson, James Beattie, Gilbert West, and John Bampfylde* (London: Routledge, Warne, and Routledge, 1863).

In "Winter" Hardy underlined several words and phrases, and he marked lines 988–997 on winds, frosts, and torrents, ending:

> And, where they rush, the wide-resounding plain
> Is left one slimy waste.

The lines, of course, in their vagueness and somewhat stilted rhetoric, are inferior to descriptions which, by his late twenties, Hardy himself was writing. But read slowly, with proper pauses, they demonstrated the flexibility of blank verse. And though he was to wait until he was sixty years of age to try his own pen at it on any serious scale, Hardy was much interested in the form. In employing it for emotive description Thomson supplemented Shakespeare and Milton.

Sometimes, as in James Montgomery's *Greenland*,[11] Hardy seems to have been carried away by the mere roll of the verse. In Canto 3 of that poem he checked and lined both margins of

> O'er rocks, seas, islands, promontories spread,
> The Ice-Blink rears its undulated head.

A few lines further on he similarly marked and doubly emphasized the last two lines of

> With glacier-battlements, that crowd the spheres,
> The slow creation of six thousand years,
> Amidst immensity it towers sublime,—
> Winter's eternal palace, built by Time.

Not uncommonly Hardy's marginal lines and underscoring are frequent in the early pages of a work, then scattered or nonexistent thereafter. Presumably, once he had discovered the essence of the author's style his interest waned. So it was with his reading of Macpherson.[12] In *Cath-Loda, Songs of Selma*, and Book I of *Fingal* there are a large number of underlinings of words and phrases. Typical in *Cath-Loda* is "She throws a broken song on wind"; in *Songs*, "the hill of storms," "calm moon," "windy steep," "sounding rock," "walk through broken clouds, O moon!" and "ye dark-brown years"; in *Fingal*, "a glittering rock. His spear is a blasted pine. His shield the rising moon!" "windy walls," and "whistling heath." We do not know when Hardy read *Ossian* or whether he reread any of it. Naturally, today we are tempted to imagine only a very young person

---

[11] *The Poetical Works* (London: Warne, n.d.).
[12] *The Poems of Ossian* (2 vols.; London: Lackington, Allen, and Co., 1803).

taking the inflated lines seriously, but "dark-brown years" is the kind of phrase that the mature poet would have seized upon.[13]

Much better substance in the same mood awaited Hardy in his 1882 edition of Dante's *Inferno*. As earlier noted, the poet marked a good number of lines in both John Carlyle's prose translation and the original version. Where every verse expressed melancholy and the entire poem was in tune with Hardy's own sensations, it appears that he singled out individual phrases and passages for the felicity of their expression. Thus we find the lines already mentioned by "I am in the Third Circle, *that* of the eternal, accursed, cold, and heavy rain."

We have noticed Hardy's sympathetic reading of the 1875 edition of *In Memoriam*. Besides the lines directly relating Tennyson's sorrow there were others which appealed because of their sound and imagery. Among these, Hardy doubly lined

> And drown'd in yonder livelier blue
> The lark becomes a sightless song (revised as stanza 114);

and he underlined the simply phrased image "the winds were in the beech." As for passages like the first of these, we must not forget that, despite his gloom—his penchant for watching the shadows lengthen on the face of the heath—Hardy was by no means oblivious to the ecstatic. He liked verses which soared upward.

He also appreciated the fragile and wistful, as in his only marking in the 1874, first, edition of O'Shaughnessy's *Music and Moonlight*.[14] He may well have been struck by the rhythmic variations O'Shaughnessy achieved within the limitations of a two-foot line. The verse flits with seeming lightness and yet conveys the haunting loneliness:

> Aloe, I made thee
> A garden to shade thee,
>   Where moonlight is falling,
> Pale, soothful, and sallow;
> And there, with the gleam of thee,
> I, in my dream of thee,
>   Yearn for thee, calling
>   Aloe, my Aloe!

[13] In 1865 Hardy noted that he was reading *Childe Harold* and *Lalla Rookh* (*The Early Life*, p. 64). Again it was the powerful verse and the romantic melancholy that caught his ear. His indebtedness to *Childe Harold* will concern us later.

[14] London: Chatto and Windus.

In Meredith it was again the tragic that attracted Hardy, but also again in lines of subtle beauty. In his 1892 edition,[15] he marked, in Part I of "The Sage Enamoured and the Honest Lady,"

> They held the look whose tenderness condoles
> For what the sister in the look has dealt
> Of fatal beyond healing; and her tones . . .

and the melancholy simile

> As when in a dropped viol the wood-throb moans
> Among the sobbing strings, that plain and chide . . . .

He also appears, from his markings, to have respected Kipling's *Barrack-Room Ballads*.[16] Among the lined passages is one particularly alliterative in "The English Flag":

> Where the sea-egg flames on the coral and the long-backed
>   breakers croon
> Their endless ocean legends to the lazy, locked lagoon.

Alliteration was a basic tool for Hardy, as we shall see in his revisions of *The Dynasts*.

As we have observed, the poetry of Vaughan seems to have been profoundly significant for Hardy. We cannot be sure when he first read him, as his own copy is of 1897. That copy is well marked for its thought and for unusual images. Hardy could not, of course, have written Vaughan's lines, and yet he must have read some of them in a manner that would fit his own. In the first three of "The Lampe" the form is iambic pentameter, but when one departs from the meter by slowing the lines down, he gets an effect not unlike that in Hardy:

> 'Tis dead night round about: Horrour doth creepe
> And move on with the shades; stars nod and sleepe,
> And through the dark aire spin a firie thread . . . .

In these lines, marked by Hardy, passion is restrained by the discipline of art. Hardy himself did not always hold so tight a rein on his own feelings, and he was guilty, too, of the commonplace and even the cliché. But he must have recognized the genius of Vaughan in achieving complete poetic freedom through the mastery of form.

---

[15] *Modern Love, to Which Is Added The Sage Enamoured and the Honest Lady* (London: Macmillan and Co.).

[16] *Barrack-Room Ballads and Other Verses* (London: Methuen, 1892).

It is impossible to assess the relative influence of the various poets on Hardy. He himself, for example, singled out Donne; we know from his notes and other remarks that he liked Arnold; and there are numerous hints of the influence of Shakespeare, Milton, and Browning. There were four other poets, however, who appear to have had a lasting appeal for Hardy. These were Wordsworth, Keats, Shelley, and Swinburne.

We have already noticed Hardy's interest in Swinburne's tragic views. In the vast quantity of marked passages in his poetry almost every line could have been checked for its theme. Yet, since the same perspective is repeated again and again, so that Hardy was not getting a really new philosophic insight in each, we may conclude that the haunting rhythms and the imagery appealed to him. Many of his marginal lines extend for several verses, and they cover almost all those that have become the staples of anthologies. To give examples most likely to have been selected for their poetic art—we find in "Laus Veneris," in the 1873 edition,

> Where tides of grass break into foam of flowers
> Or where the wind's feet shine along the sea . . . ;

in "Hymn to Proserpine," in the same edition, "In the darkness of time, in the deeps of the years, in the changes of things . . .";and in "Memorial Verses on the Death of Théophile Gautier,"

> A new song mixed into the song supreme
> Made of all souls of singers and their might—

beside which Hardy noted, "(Cf Shelley)." [17]

Except that he used alliteration, Hardy's verse is not especially reminiscent of the metric devices of Swinburne, and even the alliteration in Hardy is more abrupt because of the meter. But there was an ache in even such descriptive images as "where the wind's feet shine along the sea." How to capture such preternatural sensations as this was one of the exacting tasks Hardy set for himself. He went about it as a craftsman, and he had some success. In both the spirit world and the vast military ranges of terrestrial Europe he pursued his prey.

The influence of Wordsworth permeated Hardy's work. His 1864 edition is extensively marked; and, though all the lines have philo-sophic import, many are Wordsworth's most poetic and must have

[17] There are other annotations, citing, among others, Wagner, Browning, and again Shelley.

struck Hardy with their music or imagery. In "French Revolution" Hardy doubly marked

> [Not favoured spots alone, but the whole earth]
> The beauty wore of promise, that which sets . . .
> The budding rose above the rose full blown;

as well as the famous last three verses. In "Tintern Abbey" the numerous markings include the marginal lining and underscoring of

> . . . *thy mind*
> Shall be *a mansion for all lovely forms,*
> Thy memory be as a dwelling place
> [For all sweet sounds and harmonies].

Most of the marked passages are in sonnets and odes, but Hardy also studied carefully the lyrical ballads. The simple eloquence of the ballads was an example, not only for his own ballad writing, but for some of the short lines in *The Dynasts*. As for the blank verse and the pentameter of the sonnets, these must be included with the models in Shakespeare, Milton, and the others. Yet it can be added that Hardy and Wordsworth were again and again trying to express similar feelings and that the memory of Wordsworth's verses was always present for Hardy to draw upon.

The Rossetti edition of Keats's poems in the Memorial Library is presumbly of 1872.[18] Because some of the lines marked in *Endymion* are imitative and sentimental, one assumes that Hardy checked them soon thereafter. We know that he continued to have a warm admiration for Keats throughout his life.[19] The notations need not be regarded as defining the limits of Hardy's appreciation. In Book III of *Endymion* there are no marks, and in Book IV only one. It appears again that Hardy was looking for characteristics of style and that he found sufficient examples in the first two books. Among the marked passages are

> Where nested was an arbour, overwove
> By many a summer's silent fingering,

the entire seventeen-line stanza on Nature, beginning "So she was gently glad," ten lines beginning "Alone and sad," and a number of

[18] *The Poetical Works* (London: Moxon). A W. M. Rossetti bibliography gives the date as 1872.

[19] Hardy's poem of tribute to Keats is in the Keats House.

descriptive phrases, some general, some precise. His underlinings include "globes of clover," "temperate sweets," "Quick waterflies," "smothering fancies," "kernel of his hopes," and "eventide of gems." He put a single line by

> There blossom'd suddenly a magic bed
> Of sacred littany and poppies red,

and double lines by

> The loveliest moon, that ever silvered o'er
> A shell for Neptune's goblet.

He also marked, in "Lamia," "That but a moment's thought is passion's passing bell," and, in "Isabella," six lines beginning "And she forgot." In "The Eve of St. Agnes" he doubly lined "As though a rose should shut, and be a bud again"; and he checked the titles of "Ode to a Nightingale," "To Autumn," and "La Belle Dame sans Merci."

As to what Hardy learned from Keats we can only speak conjecturally. In all his writing Hardy tended to stay close to the incident itself, with little embellishment, little choral comment. The action made the point, except for perhaps a few words by the author in his own character. The most striking exception is the description of the heath in *The Return*. The beauty of Keats's odes lay, of course, in the meaning and emotion that the poet built to a climax through many verses. Like Shakespeare, Keats was inventive in summoning up concrete images, and he could build with them for a cumulative effect. Not even in *The Dynasts* did Hardy achieve a comparable mastery. In the choruses of the Spirits, however, he sometimes let his imagination run free, going beyond the action itself to lyric meditation on the nature of things. Insofar as Keats may have had an influence on his art it was in encouraging poetic rumination, the amplification of lyric commentary, the writing of verses not quite so lean.

Since the copies of Shelley's poems were not retained, we do not know what lines Hardy may have singled out.[20] As we have observed, however, Hardy specially noted that he thought much of Shelley when in Italy in 1887. In 1922 he restated his admiration.[21] Again we are left to deduce influences. *Prometheus Unbound*, is, of course, not the

---

[20] The Hodgson sale catalogue lists the two-volume, 1882, edition by Buxton Forman; the Export Book Co., catalogue, the four-volume edition of 1839.

[21] Edmund Blunden, *Guest of Thomas Hardy* (Beaminster: The Toucan Press, 1964).

only work whose form provided hints for *The Dynasts,* and it is not an epic drama of the scope of Hardy's poem. But it does concern itself with cosmic forces, it uses characters who have reality essentially as personifications of thought, and it dramatizes human passions in a manner which is both concrete and thematically symbolic. Choruses and antiphonal responses Hardy could find elsewhere, but they were in *Prometheus Unbound* as well.

In shaping his general pattern Hardy could not help recalling the construction of Shelley's drama. His own work was concerned with mortals performing historical acts, but it was his Spirits who were to observe, speculate, and at least tentatively conclude. Shelley's spirits were concerned with the question of freeing the bound Prometheus from a tyrannical Jupiter; Hardy's were exclusively preoccupied with discussion of a similar issue—the freeing of fettered gods of the earth. Shelley unbound Prometheus; Hardy fondly hoped that the Will would become conscious, for then man would be free. So the theme was in the largest sense identical. The devices, too, were often much alike. Finally there remains an influence as intangible as that of Keats, but different from his because Shelley's poems, even when in the same meter or stanza form, are technically unlike Keats's. One of the bewitching qualities of Shelley's verse is, of course, that it sings. Whatever its form, even that of terza rima or Spenserian stanza, it seems to burst from its confining meter to suggest ecstasy. Now, even as Hardy's imagination did not overflow with concrete images, so it did not easily sing. The poet's instinct was rather to look at the brownness of the heath or at a leaden sky and by a certain doggedness to worry from it a symbol, often ironic, of ancient truth. Hardy was not by nature a revolutionary creator or innovator. His genius was in testing and retesting and modifying what had been given him. Such rumination did not naturally break forth in the rhythms of "To a Skylark," "Adonais," "Hellas," or passages of *The Revolt of Islam* and *Prometheus Unbound.* Yet here and there in *The Dynasts* the fetters do shake loose and Hardy's verse bursts into song. At such moments one almost hears the voice of Shelley.

If the evidence covers only a fragment of Hardy's total reading, it is, nevertheless, sufficiently varied to show his eclecticism. A few of his poems, such as the Sapphics, are imitative exercises. The others use traditional forms as the basic pattern and are experimental within the form. As one reads them, including *The Dynasts,* two Hardys are apparent. One is the poet who, when told that one of his poems was not good, would reply that it was, nonetheless, true. It is the Hardy who needed historical documents for the creation of an epic and who, in revising *The Dynasts*, inserted minor details for the sake of historical precision. This is Hardy the mere craftsman, who studied the poetry of others for hints on imagery and rhythm. It is a matter-of-fact man, thrifty in his art even as he was in his personal life. It is the Hardy who wrote many a competent line and some others that were pedestrian.

The other is, of course, the genius, trained in the craft, but transcending it. It is not, however, a genius working in a cultural void. Rather, it is one so familiar with the voices of Shakespeare, Milton, Wordsworth, Keats, Shelley, and the rest that the essence of their art often infused his verse.

When we turn to Hardy's poetic theory, we are again confronted with fragments. He marked passages he was reading or copied them in notebooks, and now and then he added a comment of his own. Sometimes, as in his letters during and after publication of *The Dynasts*, he expatiated on one or another point. Nowhere, however, did he make a coherent structure of his views. As with his general philosophy, the markings and excerpts do not necessarily mean that Hardy was discovering ideas. In fact, many are statements of theories he had been observing for some time. Yet it can be said that his reading in literary criticism helped to clarify his impressions about the nature of poetry.

We cannot, of course, perfectly establish the chronology of his reading, but the evidence does permit certain conclusions. Hardy did not proceed in any systematic way to study literary criticism. Though he knew Aristotle, for example, we have not only no record of the use of the *Poetics*, but ample evidence from his narrative works to show that he did not take Aristotle for his guide in the construction of his plots.[22] On the other hand, when he came by chance across a discussion of theory, he sometimes studied it most carefully. Indeed, he seems to have been concerned even with elementary matters. Thus in Walker's *Rhyming Dictionary*, dated on the flyleaf 1865, he made numerous additions to the author's list of rhyming words, and on the last page

[22] Hardy's library once included Bohn's Library, 1850, and Butcher's three-volume, 1902, edition of *Aristotle's Theory of Poetry and Fine Art*. Cf., Hodgson sale catalogue.

and back flyleaf he classified sounds and gave a list of kindred ones. He also pasted in sheets on phonetics and penciled notations on them.[23]

In the preface to *Tess*, as we have noticed, Hardy remarked that a novel is "an impression, not an argument." In an undated note, included in his autobiography among items of 1917 and later, he summed up his view of poetry in similar language: "I hold that the mission of poetry is to record impressions, not convictions."[24] If the distinction insists on a poet's being permitted a certain looseness, perhaps inconsistency, in thought, it also allows for the function of the art itself, since the impression is inseparable from the form. In accord with his feeling that a poem is to be experienced as an artistic revelation of life is his interest in Arnold's touchstone theory. Among the passages extracted from Arnold is one, probably of 1886, which, in a mixture of quotation and paraphrase, gives the essentials of the theory.[25] Actually, many of Hardy's poems do assert convictions, but each may be regarded as a piece of stained glass, and the entire window has need for many colours.

While discussing Hardy's philosophy we have, of course, been concerned with the substance of his poems and indirectly with the function of poetry. We have to begin with the view that never to have been born might have been the best lot of all. Then, as in the lines noted in Tennyson and in implications of many others, we find literature serving as an anodyne. But as a poet Hardy, like Tennyson, could not rest with so negative a view. Two of what may be among his earliest notations are concerned with the alchemy by which poetry transmutes pain itself into pleasure. In his 1861 edition of Crabbe, he marked a footnote by Wilson:

> The stream of life flows over a rugged and precipitous channel in the poetry of Crabbe, and we are rarely indeed allowed to sail down it in a reverie or a dream. The pleasure he excites is almost always a troubled pleasure, and accompanied with tears and sighs, or with the profounder agitation of a sorrow that springs out of the conviction, forced upon us, of the most imperfect nature, and therefore the most imperfect happiness of man.[26]

[23] J. Walker, *A Rhyming Dictionary* (London: Wm. Tegg, 1865).
[24] *The Later Years*, p. 178.
[25] Literary Notes, I, 225; drawn from *Introduction to the English Poets*.
[26] *The Life and Poetical Works of George Crabbe*, edited by his son (London: Murray, 1861), p. 378.

A more coherent statement of the transformation appears in a passage Hardy marked in the preface to Coleridge's *Poems,* which carries his signature and the date 1865. Indeed, the argument of Coleridge is an ample justification of almost all Hardy's own poems:

> After the more violent emotions of sorrow, the mind demands amusement, and can find it in employment alone; but full of its late sufferings it can endure no employment not in some measure connected with them. Forcibly to turn away our attention to general subjects is a painful and most often an unavailing effort. The communicativeness of our nature leads us to describe our own sorrows; in the endeavour to describe them, intellectual activity is exerted, and from intellectual activity there results a pleasure, which is gradually associated, and mingles as a corrective, with the painful subject of the description.[27]

Like many other authors of the late nineteenth century, Hardy was concerned with the moral value of literature. Despite his willingness to adjust his fiction to serial publication and his penchant for melodramatic plots, he did seek an honest representation of life. A number of extracts in his notes bear on the subject. Thus, in an account of an address by Morley in 1887 he put double lines by a paragraph on the importance of representing moral truth and human passion.[28] Sometime in 1898 or afterward he singled out a passage in Coleridge on the high calling of the poet: "There is no profession on earth which requires an attention so early, so long, or so unintermitting, as that of poetry; and indeed, as that of literary composition in general, if it be such as at all satisfies the demands both of taste and of sound logic."[29]

In a nineteen-page mixture of quotation and paraphrase from J. A. Symonds' *Essays Speculative and Suggestive,* entered in his notebook in 1891, Hardy was interested in such subjects as realism, idealism, and classicism; and he also included several pages on democratic art, in which Symonds referred to Whitman.[30]

Perhaps his main text, however, was Wordsworth's "Preface." Certainly he had read it thoroughly long before he marked his 1896

[27] *The Poems of Samuel T. Coleridge,* ed. Derwent and Sara Coleridge (London: Moxon, 1859), pp. xv–xvi.

[28] Literary Notes, I, 215–217; taken from the *Daily News,* February 2, 1887.

[29] *Biographia Literaria and Two Lay Sermons* (London: George Bell, 1898), p. 23.

[30] Literary Notes, II, 43–62.

edition.[31] As we shall notice, he agreed with Coleridge on the question of diction. But he marked a host of passages on the function of poetry and the ways of the imagination. To "poetry is the breath and finer spirit of all knowledge; it is the passionate expression which is in the countenance of all Science" he appended a footnote: "briefly = poetry is science become impassioned" (I, 62). He was struck, too, with Wordsworth's statement on the relation of thought and feeling: "For our continued influxes of feeling are modified and directed by our thoughts, which are indeed the representatives of all our past feelings . . ." (I, 50). If it be argued that Wordsworth's definition of his terms here is somewhat loose, that he really does not have two clearly separable activities of the mind, perhaps in that very ambiguity he succeeds in expressing Hardy's own sensation of the relation of thought and emotion, for *thought* meant to Hardy something very like *impression.*

By definition art should be beautiful in the sense of being aesthetically satisfying. Indeed, the recognition of the difference between pain in actual life and the artistic representation of suffering must be a discovery of beauty. If a writer should at all times be preoccupied with the creation of beauty, it must be admitted that Hardy himself had lapses. In some parts of his prose narratives he settled for a mere cranking of the machinery to bring about situations, and at its worst his verse was hardly more than rhetoric for providing information or enunciating a belief. But at his best Hardy perceived that there could be no art without concern for beauty. A good example is his comment on Ibsen. He took about a page and a half from an article in *Literature* of August 17, 1901, which, by implication, commended Ibsen's daring and included a quotation from Shaw saying that he "claims afresh the old Protestant right of private judgment in questions of conduct as against all institutions, the so-called Protestant churches themselves included." Naturally, such words pleased Hardy, and he annotated Shaw with the note "This is excellently put." He continued, however, "But neither writer dwells sufficiently on the fact that Ibsen's defect is a lack of the essentiality of beauty to art. T. H." [32] (In his notations the adding of his initials generally meant "I have so pronounced.") Sometime in 1904 or later, in the introduction to Campbell's *Poems,*

[31] *Poems,* ed. William Knight (8 vols.; London: Macmillan).
[32] Literary Notes, II.

Hardy marked "The poet's function is to mould human speech into new forms of beauty."[33]

There are many other excerpts in the notebooks and marked passages in the books Hardy read that deal with the nature of literary art. In the notebook entries during the eighties and afterward there is much on realism, naturalism, symbolism, and other matters having to do with a writer's perspective and the architectonics of narration. Hardy was reading the literary magazines, including the *Revue des deux mondes*, and, as we have noted, he had some acquaintance with the work of Zola.[34] In a notebook, probably in 1884, he pasted an attack on naturalism which had appeared in the *Revue*.[35] Drawing its examples from Zola's novels and other naturalistic works, the article objected to painful literature and asked that art assist man in escape from Nature. Hardy did not comment, but one suspects that his disagreement with the author was by no means total. Usually he put an exclamation point or a demurrer beside views which he rejected, and in most instances he quoted them only because they reproduced a misconception which he felt to be widespread.

Later he copied over seven pages from an article by E. M. de Voguë, "De la Litterature Réaliste," which had appeared in the *Revue* of May 15, 1886. Voguë deplored contemporary French realism, including the work of Flaubert. Hardy marked for special note: "Since it [realism] does not recoil before ugliness + miseries it must render them supportable by a perpetual overflow of pity. Realism becomes odious when it ceases to be charitable."[36] A few pages later in the notebook is a four-page entry from articles in the *Revue* of October 1 and November 1, 1888, by Brunetière, which again attacks the naturalists, among others. From the Glasgow *Herald* of February 27, 1892, is an item praising Thoreau and Whitman as realists and deploring Zola, Daudet, and Bourget.[37]

[33] *Poems of Thomas Campbell*, ed. Lewis Campbell (London: Macmillan, 1904), p. xxxii.

[34] Book of Observations, p. 66; part of an undated five-page series from Zola. In a letter of November 20, 1895, Hardy wrote, "I am read in Zola very little, but have felt akin locally to Fielding * * *" (*The Later Years*, p. 42).

[35] Literary Notes, I, 185. Since Hardy appears to have read the *Revue* regularly, the entries in the notebooks probably are not long after the date of publication.

[36] Literary Notes, I, 276.

[37] Literary Notes, II, 70.

Hardy's own view of realism, or naturalism—as the two are used interchangeably in the notebooks—is expressed sweepingly in a note of August 5, 1890, which he inserted in his autobiography, and in another of 1891. In the first he wrote:

> Art is a disproportioning—(i.e. distorting, throwing out of proportion)— of realities, to show more clearly the features that matter in those realities, which, if merely copied or reported inventorially, might possibly be observed, but would more probably be overlooked. Hence "realism" is not Art.[38]

An entry from an article by Dowden in the *Fortnightly Review* of November, 1891, must be regarded as an amendment to this pronouncement. Hardy quoted: "The possibility of a 'spiritual naturalism' has been conceived by M. Huysmans." He added, "'spiritual naturalism' nearly defines my own old idea of the principle of novels of the future." [39] If we are to use terms to distinguish such a story as Hardy's "The Romantic Adventures of a Milkmaid" from passages in *Jude*—and much of *The Dynasts*—we find ourselves speaking of realism. But Hardy would never have accepted the standard set by Zola. Art must do more than record or imitate actuality. Its problem was to select and emphasize and to find universality.

What this meant in a narrative work is suggested by a note of February 23, 1893: "The whole secret of fiction and the drama—in the constructional part—lies in the adjustment of things unusual to things eternal and universal. The writer who knows exactly how exceptional, and how non-exceptional his events should be made, possesses the key to the art." [40] Needless to say, Hardy sometimes lost the key. At an unknown time he had doubly lined a passage in the introduction to his 1872 edition of Beaumont and Fletcher, in which the editor, using italics, had complained that the two dramatists founded "their plots and characters on the *possible* instead of the *probable*." [41] He himself sometimes committed the same error.

In turning to history for his subject matter he experienced the danger once again, for, despite his justification of certain of his poems merely on their truthfulness to fact, he knew that from historical

[38] *The Early Life*, p. 299.
[39] Literary Notes, II, 68.
[40] *The Later Years*, p. 16.
[41] *The Works of Beaumont and Fletcher*, with introduction by George Darley (London: Routledge and Sons), I, xxvi.

incidents one must select and modify to reveal the "eternal and universal." As early as 1886 he quoted from T. H. Green's *Introduction to Hume* the remark that one theory of history involved singling out from the "chaos of events a connected series of ruling actions + beliefs." [42] As to the artistic problem confronting an historical dramatist, perhaps the most significant entry is a broken quotation from an article in *Literature* of October 8, 1898, when Hardy was thinking a good deal about the substance that was finally to become his epic. Given as it appears in his notebook, it reads:

> Where the poet is bound by history he can hardly have a real plot with a real dramatic unity . . . . The dramatist instead of one central action is often obliged to content himself with a panorama of shifting scenes . . . . No one who has read a Greek play side by side with one even of Shakespeare . . . . will deny . . . attic tragedian . . . immense advantage. [43]

Hardy commented, "an instance of the *non sequitur*; but suggestive."

The advantage of using history, for Hardy, was that he could feel that what had happened was true. If he were to test his views of human life, he needed the touchstones which he could find in actual events. As for the dramatic unity or, indeed, any coherent relation of a mass of historical fact, Hardy certainly believed that, as a narrator, he was not imposing it from without. Rather, he saw his task as the selection and proper representation of events—what he had called "distorting." If a work of art were to result, the events would, of course, need a frame. The problem would be where to start and to end, and the answer would depend on finding an epoch that appeared to present a beginning, a development, and a sense of finality.

Perhaps major examples for Hardy were the Old Testament stories. He reread them many times, and in a note of Easter Sunday, 1885, he remarked, "But in these Bible lives and adventures there is the spherical completeness of perfect art." [44] Another was certainly the *Divine Comedy*. In his 1882 edition Hardy doubly lined a pair of sentences by J. A. Carlyle, the translator, which summed up Dante's method:

> And it is not so much by what has been loosely called Invention, as by true and clear recognition of the Nature of Things in that age of his, by unerring discrimination of what is significant from what is insignificant,

[42] Literary Notes, I, 205.
[43] Literary Notes, II.
[44] *The Early Life*, p. 223.

and by boundless diligence withal, that he constructs an original and enduring work. In his inmost heart the scattered incidents gradually cohere, and expand, and become a living whole—fit for utterance: the "Sacred Poem" for many years has made him lean.[45]

The biblical stories were, to be sure, vignettes, and Dante was not writing history. Besides, there was more invention in Dante's epic than Carlyle's words imply. But both when he was considering a series of ballads on the Napoleonic Wars and after he conceived of an epic, Hardy saw part of his substance as self-contained vignettes, and, like the *Divine Comedy,* it must be in essence a spiritual history. Its impression of completeness would depend on the finding of dramatic unity in the spirit of an age, with specific historical events serving to open and close the action and specific historical figures to epitomize the variations on the tragic theme.

Even as Dante, however, was writing not merely of the Middle Ages, so Hardy, in both prose and verse, always hoped that the lives of even the little people would cast giant shadows across the generations. Hence he was preoccupied with the symbolic and mythical.

While reading Lewes's *Life of Goethe,* in 1875, Hardy recorded a quotation from Schlegel: "the deepest want + deficiency of all modern art lies in the fact that the artists have no Mythology."[46] Here was a succinct statement of Hardy's own predicament, and he was to re-affirm it in the preface to *The Dynasts.* It was not that a late nineteenth-century poet could not use the gods and mythological legends, but that they would have allegorical connotations which would cramp his thought. Yet a mythology must be felt, not just intellectually comprehended. The problem was to create a new mythical world which would seize the imagination and the feelings. As we have seen, Hardy had from childhood a sense for ghosts, not a mere recognition of what they might morally represent as expressions of the guilt or frustration the living persons had experienced, but a power to feel their presence through an effort of imagination. A new mythology must have a similar immediacy for the imagination. In sensing the actions of a crowd as somnambulistic Hardy was thinking mythologically; and he was not coercing the image, but finding that it forced

---

[45] *Dante's Divine Comedy: The Inferno. A Literal Prose Translation* (London: George Bell and Sons).

[46] Memoranda, I, June 16; under the heading "Modern Art wants," the remark is repeated in Literary Notes, I, 10.

itself upon him. Yet, even as the study of poetry increased one's sensitivity as poet, so one could exert conscious effort to conceive of a universe in new mythical symbols, with the hope that a discovery would result, a discovery so natural that its poetic expression could be shared by one's readers.

Hardy put his problem in intellectual terms in a note of March 4, 1886. What he wrote in reference to the composition of a novel he was to follow to a degree in *The Dynasts*: "Novel-writing as an art cannot go backward. Having reached the analytic stage it must transcend it by going still further in the same direction. Why not by rendering as visible essences, spectres, etc. the abstract thoughts of the analytic school?" To make his thought more precise he continued:

> The human race to be shown as one great network or tissue which quivers in every part when one point is shaken, like a spider's web if touched. Abstract realisms to be in the form of Spirits, Spectral figures, etc.
>
> The Realities to be the true realities of life, hitherto called abstractions. The old material realities to be placed behind the former, as shadowy accessories.[47]

Hardy was not to achieve this effect completely, despite his use of Intelligences and a panoramic network to express the Will, for his actual historical persons normally have a customary reality; but at rare intervals he was to make of material realities shadowy accessories. That is to say, the actual was to become ghostly and the spiritual was to seem physically real. Needless to say, between the abstract conception of the idea in 1886 and its poetical embodiment much imagining and testing in short poems was to take place; and certainly the reading in Schopenhauer and Hartmann was to contribute not alone philosophic theories, but food for the imagination in the creation of the mythology of *The Dynasts*. The point which Hardy had reached by the time he wrote his epic is indicated in his letter to Dr. Saleeby in 1915. After speaking of Bergson as having "rather an imaginative and poetical mind than a reasoner's," Hardy added:

> Half my time—particularly when writing verse—I "believe" (in the modern sense of the word) not only in the things Bergson believes in, but in spectres, mysterious voices, intuitions, omens, dreams, haunted places, etc., etc. But I do not believe in them in the old sense of the word any more for that.[48]

[47] *The Early Life*, p. 232.
[48] *The Later Years*, p. 168.

A believer in the old sense, we may assume, might be startled unexpectedly by a bogie on Egdon Heath. Or, if we remember Hardy's strictures on Christian superstitions, he might conceivably expect to deal personally with emissaries of the Lord. A believer in the modern sense would see in the countenances of living men the souls of those who had died at Walcheren. There was no need to suspend disbelief. One needed rather to use all the powers of the intellect; and then, if inspiration happened to coincide, one might so intensely see that he could indeed say that he believed in what he saw—the spiritual realities.

In an article by Henri de Regnier, "Poètes d'aujourdhui et Poésie de Demain," in the August, 1900, copy of *Mercure de France* Hardy marked, sometimes with double lines, numerous passages on symbolism and on the relation of the new French poetry to life. Among those doubly stressed was Regnier's metaphor on the function of myth: "Un Mythe est sur la grève du temps comme une de ces coquilles ou l'on entend le bruit de la mer humaine. Un mythe est la conque sonore d'une idée." [49] For Hardy in *The Dynasts* the myth was to express the theme, and, in a sense, it also created it. For only as one could see life in the imagery of the myth could he approach its deepest truths. If his myth were itself perfect, he could hear in it the true tones of the human sea.

For the technique of narrative writing Hardy had ample masters. He studied both the plots and characterization in Shakespeare, noting such things as the jump in the action between scenes v and vi in Act III of *Antony and Cleopatra*—"We here leap over a host of important events too suddenly"—and what he considered an inconsistency in Casca's speech in Act I, scene iii, of *Julius Caesar*—"This speech seems hardly to suit the idea of Casca as previously given us." In the several pages of corrections which he made in 1922, to which we have referred, he denied his biographer's statement that he had been influenced by George Eliot: "It was Shakespeare's delineation of his Warwickshire clowns (who much resemble the Wessex peasantry) that influenced Hardy most." This remark applies, of course, not only to the novels but to the Wessex scenes in *The Dynasts* and to other scenes as well, on the battlefields and on the streets of London. In the same corrections Hardy acknowledged a heavy debt to Fielding "(whose scenes and characters are Dorset and Somerset)" and he concluded his remark with "and Scott?" In his Shakespeare a few

[49] *Mercure de France*, XXXV, No. 128, p. 343.

notations concern Shakespeare's rearranging of history, and, of course, Hardy must have found similar examples in Scott. He himself had to telescope and otherwise alter events, as we shall discover in *The Dynasts*. One persistent problem was that of revealing character and, at the same time, advancing plot. In rebuttal of his biographer's assertion that he had learned from Reade and Collins how to convey narrative through dialogue, Hardy retorted, "This as to his dialogues is news to T. H. And, if anybody, it should be surely Dumas père."

In his novels Hardy sometimes moved without psychological motivation from one incident to the next, being little concerned with how a circumstance came about and much with the emotional result. For *The Dynasts* he had a sequence of incidents linked together, as they were part of the career of Napoleon or the opposition to him, but Hardy was again not interested in causal relation so much as in the lyric development of his theme. Thus he had as his total technical problem the telling of a narrative, the revelation of character, the exemplification of a philosophy, and, pervading all these, the symphonic rendering of a world tragedy. In short, his poem would be a dramatic epic, but its ultimate virtue must be lyric. And so we are again returned to Hardy's debt to the poets and the prose stylists, both for inspiration and for instruction. The former might come from Dante or Milton or Shelley, the latter from almost anyone. We have remarked on Hardy's liking for Crabbe. In a note of October 17, 1896, he cited him as the exemplar of a particularly subtle art: "A novel, good, microscopic touch in Crabbe. He gives surface without outline, describing his church by telling *the colour of the lichens.*" [50] Scattered through his notes are entries on style. Probably in 1876, for example, he took almost a page from De Quincey headed "Style." [51] In 1892 he quoted from a review of a translation of the *Bacchae* which called it "perhaps the poet's most finished work." His own study of Euripedes led him to comment, "I quite agree with the above criticism." [52]

Throughout his poetic career Hardy was interested in theories on vowel sounds. In 1901 he copied from a quotation in an article by Brander Matthews:

"The primitive lyrist is almost always exact in the repetition of his vowel. Where he is careless is in the accompanying consonants .... In all early

[50] *The Later Years,* p. 57.
[51] Literary Notes, I, 92.
[52] Literary Notes, II, 76.

European poetry, from The Song of Roland to the popular ballads, the ear was satisfied with assonance, that is, the harmony of the vowel sounds: h*a*t is ass^t to t*a*g" +c.[53]

Hardy had, of course, observed the practice long before in the British ballads. He was perhaps even more inclined toward alliteration, evidently finding in it something of the development and resolution of suspense that is commonly associated with end rhyme. We have hundreds of examples in *The Dynasts*.

In 1907 Hardy quoted three pages from Patmore on various technical aspects of versification and added, "Some of these ideas are suggestive—others doubtful."[54] Other excerpts and paraphrases show that Hardy's preoccupation with the theory of versification continued. In what appears to be an entry of 1922 he quotes Bridges on free verse: "The main effectual difference between the rhythms of the old metrical verse + of fine prose is that in the verse you have a greater *expectancy* of the rhythm . . . + the poet's art was to vary the expected rhythm as much as he could without disagreeably baulking the expectation."[55] Varying the expected rhythm was a delicate task. To a degree Hardy's use of alliteration tended to curtail the variation; novel diction and other jarring devices accentuated it.

All his writing life Hardy sought for an art that would disguise concern for art by giving a feeling of informality to his lines, whether in verse or prose. In his autobiography he reproduced a long note, apparently from early 1875, which focuses on his prose writing—and we must remember that some of the best lines in *The Dynasts* are in prose—but also reveals his conscious intent in his verse. The note itself reads like an exercise in application of the principles it sets forth:

> Read again Addison, Macaulay, Newman, Sterne, Defoe, Lamb, Gibbon, Burke, *Times* Leaders, etc., in a study of style. Am more and more confirmed in an idea I have long held, as a matter of commonsense, long before I thought of any old aphorism bearing on the subject: "Ars est celare artem." The whole secret of a living style and the difference between it and a dead style, lies in not having too much style—being, in fact, a little careless, or rather seeming to be, here and there. It brings wonderful life into the writing:

[53] *Ibid.*, II.
[54] *Ibid.*
[55] Memoranda, II, 26; from the *London Mercury* of November 22.

"A sweet disorder in the dress . . .
A careless shoe-string, in whose tie
I see a wild civility,
Do more bewitch me than when art
Is too precise in every part."

Otherwise your style is like worn half-pence—all the fresh images rounded off by rubbing, and no crispness or movement at all.

It is, of course, simply a carrying into prose the knowledge I have acquired in poetry—that inexact rhymes and rhythms now and then are far more pleasing than correct ones.[56]

In his corrections of 1922 Hardy protested that his biographer had given insufficient attention to his poetry, which was "the work of more years" than his prose, "novels about 27 years; poetry between 28 and 29." He continued: "This disposes of the cuckoo-cry that T. H. being new to poetry expresses himself clumsily in verse, his verse good or bad being, as his long practice would suggest, and the best critics acknowledge, more finished than his prose, except where intentionally rough hewn." The last five words were added to the carbon typescript, and the afterthought is significant.

A technique in which Hardy was least successful is discussed in a note of December, 1887, and in his comment on it as he looked backward when putting it in his autobiography. He quoted Addison on Milton: "In the description of Paradise the poet has observed Aristotle's rule of lavishing all the ornaments of diction on the weak, inactive parts of the fable." In retrospect he added: "And although Hardy did not slavishly adopt this rule in *The Dynasts*, it is apparent that he had it in mind in concentrating the 'ornaments of diction' in particular places, thus following Coleridge in holding that a long poem should not attempt to be poetical all through." [57] Unfortunately, in trying what for him was not nearly so natural a style as it was for Milton, Hardy was frequently guilty of "forcing the note."

He was far more at ease in a totally different style. In recalling his early attempt, *The Poor Man and the Lady*, he spoke of its stylistic indebtedness to Defoe:

the style having the affected simplicity of Defoe's (which had long attracted Hardy ∗ ∗ ∗ to imitation of it.) This naïve realism in circumstantial details that were pure inventions was so well assumed that both

[56] *The Early Life*, p. 138.
[57] *Ibid.*, p. 266.

Macmillan and Morley had been perhaps a little, or more than a little, deceived by its seeming actuality ∗ ∗ ∗ .[58]

It was easy to learn from Defoe, because Hardy's mind tended to work in a naïve, matter-of-fact way. His notebooks and his letters demonstrate this, as do many of the revisions in *The Dynasts*. Sometimes in both the novels and the epic the result is commonplace; sometimes it shows a homely genius.

Naturally Wordsworth's discussion of the language of poetry was of major interest to Hardy. With certain pronouncements he agreed; on others he sided with Coleridge. Long and numerous markings in the 1896 edition, with several notations, show how critically he examined Wordsworth's theories. The Preface reads:

> and it was previously asserted, that a large portion of the language of every good poem can in no respect differ from that of good Prose. We will go further. It may be safely affirmed, that there neither is, nor can be, any *essential* difference between the language of prose and metrical composition.

Hardy comments: "Quite true. The best poetry is, in fact, the best prose, i.e. if the restrictions of rhyme and rhythm were withdrawn, no more direct and clear expression of the thought could be found within the liberty thus gained." But when Wordsworth writes, "If it be affirmed that rhyme and metrical arrangement of themselves constitute a distinction which overturns what has just been said on the strict affinity of metrical language with that of prose," Hardy leaps upon this concession: "It certainly does, and here we come to the weak point of W's argument."

Wordsworth permits only a limited modification from the natural language of men:

> [the poet] will feel that there is no necessity to trick out or to elevate nature: and, the more industriously he applies this principle, the deeper will be his faith that no words, which *his* fancy or imagination can suggest, will be to be compared with those which are the emanations of reality and truth.

Hardy cannot accept what would here seem to be a naturalistic reproduction of actual speech. His rejoinder may not be fair, since Words-

[58] *Ibid.*, p. 81.

worth did allow for selection, and yet it recognizes the fundamental function of the artist; he writes, "theoretically, but powers of expression may be defective in the latter case."

Hardy's next demurrer is much the same. "How, then," writes Wordsworth, "can his language differ in any material degree from that of all other men who feel vividly and see clearly?" Hardy remarks, "But poetry is also *artistry*." Wordsworth continues with the argument that to reach men who are not poets he must use simple language, and Hardy rejects this sacrifice of meaning for the sake of communication with the curt pronouncement, "The reasoning is defective here." Finally, for our purpose, Wordsworth turns to the defense of meter: "why should I be condemned for attempting to superadd to such description [as is possible in prose] the charm which, by the consent of all nations, is acknowledged to exist in metrical language?" To this Hardy appends, "Then why not add also that which exists in 'poetic diction?'"

We do not know how soon after 1896 Hardy made these annotations. We can say, however, that, fully aware of how far Wordsworth himself ranged from his prescription, Hardy wanted to agree as far as he could with him that simple language could express profound feelings, and yet to allow for the esoteric terms which a late nineteenth-century thinker needed to express concepts and sentiments beyond the articulation of common men. Without the learned terms—and we are not referring to the mere ornaments of style—Hardy would have felt helpless to weave together his various strands. Yet the verses in which he explicitly stated his philosophy are more often merely adequate than distinctive. The lyric beauty comes, again and again, clothed in simple language. After the emotion has been heightened and the essence is to be distilled, we find the simplicity of Clym's tribute to the dead Eustacia—"She looks very beautiful now"; Tess's cry of anguish— "Only—don't 'ee make it more than I can bear"; or Rumour's summing up of Napoleon's moral tragedy as he retreats from Waterloo—"He loses his last chance of dying well."

CHAPTER THREE

Genesis of an Epic-Drama—and Aftercourses

In his correction of his inept biographer Hardy wrote, in the third person, "Nobody 'guided him into Wessex.' He had always been there." He could not say that he had always been in the age of Napoleon, even as regarded the few Wessex scenes, and he was to a degree still a stranger when he began to compose *The Dynasts*. But he was also not a late comer. First there had been a natural boyish attraction toward a glamourous age filled with adventure and heroism. In time there developed a recognition that the Napoleonic Wars were a fruitful source for ironic verse. Meanwhile the youthful enthusiasm had led to a semischolarly antiquarian curiosity about specific events, particularly those which had become famous in popular legend. And slowly there was taking shape in Hardy's consciousness a sense that the era represented a vast area of human experience, mainly tragic, which seemed to epitomize the history of the human race.

From his reading Hardy had gathered impressions of the poignant odyssey of mankind. In his own personal life he had proved the validity of what he had read. And increasingly he was becoming acquainted with the theories of the philosophers, which might help to formalize, however loosely, his impressions from his reading and experience.

Eventually he was to recognize the age of England's struggle against the French Emperor as much more than a source of poetic anecdotes. All his impressions and his philosophic speculation were to coalesce in his discovery that the period of conflict provided a coherent, dramatic series of incidents, with a beginning, a middle, and an end. It could hardly be said that he tested his philosophic tenets against the historical events. Rather, he seemed to find them suggested by the very incidents themselves. Involved, of course, were the problems of sorting and searching for meaning and also the creation of an artistic frame-work, and it should be admitted at the outset that, even as in his short ironic poems, Hardy was sometimes to be arbitrary. Nevertheless, in a general sense, fact and philosophic belief were to emerge together in Hardy's consciousness as he strove to interpret the wars of Britain and Napoleon.

The boyish enthusiasm was never to vanish totally. It was to show itself in heroic scenes of adventure; and the names of such gallant heroes as Nelson and Ney were never to lose their glamour; nor was the melancholy charm of Josephine to dim, or the pathetic coquetry of the Prussian Queen. The antiquarianism was to persist; indeed, Hardy would have been thrilled to discover the exact location of the ballroom where the officers danced before they died at Waterloo. And the impish obsession with life's little ironies was to inspire comments ranging from the facetious to the bitterly profound. But above all, the philosophic overview of history was to give to his epic its grand sweep, its illimitable vistas, its cruel pathos, its mixture of hope and doom.

As a boy, at about the same time that he was becoming acquainted with Dryden, Vergil, and other English and foreign classics, Hardy read in his grandfather's copies of *A History of the Wars*, a periodical concerned with the Napoleonic era. In looking back he concluded that his browsings in this work "were the first" to suggest *The Trumpet Major* and *The Dynasts*.[1] At fifteen he began lessons in French, and he eventually possessed a good reading knowledge, so that he suffered no hindrance in the use of French sources when he turned seriously to the study of the Wars.

Sometime after 1865 Hardy marked in an anthology an excerpt translated from Thiers' *Histoire de la Révolution*.[2] A number of entries in his Book of Observations from 1867 or shortly thereafter reveal an unusual interest in French history since the beginning of the Revolution. His citations are often bitter. Quoting and paraphrasing from Carlyle's *The History of the French Revolution*, he noted, "Show the century as a *Hypocrisy*," and again, "Such tugging + lugging + throttling of one another, to divide the joint felicity of man in this Earth."[3] From Hugo he took a summary, ending: "They made the

---

[1] *The Early Life*, p. 21.

[2] "Books from Hardy's Max Gate Library," *Colby Library Quarterly*, Series II, No. 15, pp. 246–254.

[3] Book of Observations, pp. 33, 44.

first relay with Mirabeau, the second with Robespierre, the third with Buonap^te; they are thoroughly exhausted."[4] Part of a long extract from Hugo attacks the restored Bourbons:

> They [the Bourbons] [*sic*] *were surly with the 19th cent^y*. . . . They believed that they were strong because the Empire had been swept away before them like a scene at a theatre. They did not perceive that they themselves *had been brought in* in the same way. They did not see that they also were *in that hand which had taken off* Napoleon.[5]

Hardy's underlining is not to be construed as an endorsement of belief in a Christian God. But it may well have represented the agreement of a determinist who was later to return to the question of Napoleon's destiny. From Hugo, Hardy also gleaned "The Revolution had had its say under Robespierre, the cannon had had its say under Buonaparte."[6] By this time he certainly had detailed knowledge of the course of the Revolution and the Age of Napoleon.

Sometime before June 17, 1868, Hardy recognized the career of Napoleon as a quarry for poetry. On that date he outlined part of a "narrative poem on the Battle of the Nile."[7] The sources of his information on the Egyptian campaign are unknown. In various English histories he would have found a mixture of evidence, making Napoleon out to be an audacious adventurer, inhuman in his treatment of prisoners, and ignorant in leading his soldiers in unfamiliar terrain. If one source was Thiers' *History of the French Revolution*, he would have been able, despite his author's apologies and justifications, to reach much the same conclusion. The naval battle was, of course, famous because it brought Napoleon into his first major confrontation with the valour of Nelson. One important source could have been Southey's *Life of Nelson*, on which Hardy was later to draw. In any event, to judge from his thoroughness in establishing historical facts for *The Dynasts*, we may suppose that, in contemplating a narrative rather than a lyric, Hardy was well informed on the events preceding and during the battle. He was certainly not a casual excursionist who happened on a romantic subject for a poem.

The next identifiable reference to the Wars is the simple note saying that on May 18, 1870, Hardy had been impressed with the "Death of

[4] *Ibid.*, p. 54.
[5] *Ibid.*
[6] *Ibid.*, p. 55.
[7] *The Early Life*, p. 76.

Ney" by Gérôme at the Royal Academy.[8] Sometime that year he went to Chelsea Hospital to talk with veterans of Waterloo.[9] Since his record gives no clue, one cannot tell how much he inquired about the battles of the Peninsula and the Belgian frontier. As he later revealed in *The Trumpet Major,* for which he took notes in 1878–1879, he was much interested in the camp life of soldiers quartered in Wessex during the Wars. In Masson's anthology *La Lyre Française,* annotated "T. Hardy—1872" and probably read immediately, is an *X* by the title of Hugo's "Lui," a four-page effusion on the grandeur of Napoleon. Though noncommittal, the mark is one more bit of evidence that Hardy saw Napoleon himself as a proper subject for poetry.

Then suddenly in a note of March 13, 1874, appears the bold asseveration "Let Europe be the stage + have scenes continually shifting." Cramped in at the bottom of the page is a later notation, "Can this refer to any conception of The Dynasts?"[10] One is puzzled by Hardy's own puzzlement, as the exhortation can hardly refer to anything except his own plans, however nebulous. Moreover, it does cover what he was eventually to do. This is a far greater subject than the Battle of the Nile. It is of epic expanse and implies an action in which Napoleon is to be only one character among many. We must not say that *The Dynasts* herewith assumed any definite theme, still less a form; but Hardy now had a focus for his study of the epoch and at least a guiding principle for his artistic contemplation.

In late September, 1874, Hardy and Emma visited France. In Mrs. Hardy's account it is clear that scenes of major interest were Napoleon's tomb, the Tuileries, and Saint Cloud.[11] On Waterloo Day of the following year Hardy revisited Chelsea and talked with John Bentley, who had been at Waterloo. Not even Wellington could have discussed the details of the battle strategy without recourse to documents, and there is no reason to suppose that Hardy expected from Bentley anything on the manoeuvring of the troops. These he could find in books. But he could get an old soldier's reminiscence of what mattered—the sensation itself of the battle. And his note shows that he got also a story which could have suggested the parting of lovers at Brussels,

[8] *Ibid.,* p. 100.

[9] *Ibid.,* p. 103.

[10] Memoranda, I.

[11] Diary of a Journey to Holland, the Rhine, Black Forest, +c, 1876. The 1874 trip is recorded in the same little book.

for Bentley told him of his love for a girl he had met there and of their eternal separation.[12]

In the same month of June, Hardy recorded what, at the time of sorting his notes, he believed was his first reference to the substance of *The Dynasts*: "Mem: A Ballad of the Hundred Days. Then another of Moscow. Others of earlier campaigns—forming altogether an Iliad of Europe from 1789 to 1815." [13] This is more explicit than the entry of the preceding year; it also suggests a looseness of structure and a confining of historical fact to the items that could be assimilated in the ballad form.

During the next few years Hardy continued to be occupied mainly with his fiction and an occasional short poem. There are references, however, to the idea of a long dramatic work and also, in his note-books, here and there a related entry. The most important notes have to do with the theme or structure, but there are others that reveal Hardy's respect for factual accuracy. A fragment from Macaulay, in 1876 or before, is headed "*All for nothing*" and it continues: "The Seven Years War scarcely surpassed in history for severity + carnage." [14] From Macaulay, Hardy also took the note "*Zenith of Glory*," with his two examples "Fred[k] after the battle of Zorndorf" and "Napoleon after Austerlitz." Such notes do not represent the kind of quasi-systematic historical reading which was immediately to precede and to accompany the composition of the epic. Rather they indicate the types of anecdotes or philosophical observations on war that increased Hardy's sense of the importance of his subject.

In June, 1876, Hardy and Emma visited Waterloo. Mrs. Hardy was not a graphic writer, but she was observing, and her record in her diary gives us some impression of what Hardy saw. Indeed, it was he who directed their steps. What interested both was the contrast between the present fields on June 17, almost the anniversary of the battle, and what the relics in the museum and neighborhood suggested of a hideous day some sixty-one years before. Mrs. Hardy's diary reads:

> It was a lovely day, + plenty of air, even breezes, but hot sunshine—many flowers—a broad expanse of corn fields—rye—no *heights* to be seen—went up the steps + saw all over the field + read the account.

[12] *The Early Life*, p. 140.
[13] *Ibid.*
[14] Literary Notes, I, 4.

Guides were disturbing with their talk then lunched at Hotel—saw Museum—sculls, weapons, hair. . . . Walked to Hougomont—(much crimson clover in the field) Hougomont + wall [?] ruins, low walls to the orchard, buttresses fallen away. . . . Then walked to La belle alliance. . . . Then walked to La Haye Sainte—The largest + best farm house very large courtyard, very large house inside. Young woman ironing in spacious stone room at left—cupboard or a small cellarette opposite front door, as at Kirland. This door had bullet marks—then went down passage to right—one kitchen at right-small iron barred window—*room to left* a small room with small barred window, at the right of this window, in an alcove, or *extension* was *the well*—we looked down deep + black— + many men could be thrown into it. . . . walked back through Mont St Jean + Waterloo—saw house where Victor Hugo wrote the last of Les Miserables. . . . Mont S. J. very quiet—Waterloo, larger [?] houses round cupola church—closed—long walk to station—great fatigue, so ended Waterloo day—Today I am still greatly fatigued + Tom is cross about it. . . .

Mem. From the Lion's Mount the field of Waterloo is spread out from Wellington's position, + Hougomont + the rest seem near; the two armies were so close together—When we got past La Belle Alliance + between it + la Haye Sainte the ground seemed to rise a little at our left—

Hay making going on round us + we walked in a narrow path through the high grain . . . .

Quite worn out with the day at Waterloo.[15]

Mrs. Hardy also included a short note: "Saw the Duchess of Richmond's house—at corner of street like the others long white french windows—to distinguish it, the upper portion of windows are painted pink—."[16] The diary makes explicit Hardy's meticulous care in examining the field and environs. When he came to the scene in his epic he could not depend on his own memory; he had historical sources. But the visit provided touchstones. Used to tracking the steps of his Wessex heroes and heroines, Hardy wanted the feeling of the place. His poem was still unbegun, but a poetic narrative of some kind was brewing.

The date in the journal is confused, but it was apparently soon after their return from Belgium that Mrs. Hardy recorded, "Went this morning to Chelsea Hospital—Had a chat with *Bentley* after the service."

[15] Diary of a Journey to Holland.
[16] This does not, of course, identify the ballroom.

Two of Hardy's notes from 1876 illustrate his habit of picking up
impressions and images. Among some ten pages of extracts from
Mahaffy's *Social Life in Greece* appears: " *The courage* of the Homeric
chiefs was of a second-rate order ... like the courage of the French,
dependent upon excitement ... not that stubborn valour characteristic of the English + German soldier." [17] In any of several books
which he was to use later Hardy could find the same asserted contrast
between the French intoxication with battle and the British phlegmatic
determination—though he would find the former not called second-
rate and he would learn of Wellington's contempt for some of his
men. Mahaffy's opinion, except for the disparaging adjective, was to
remain Hardy's own. It was a few pages later that Hardy recorded
from Symonds the image already noted, which was to reappear in
amplified form in his poem: "the web of the world is ever-weaving." [18]

The structure of the poem was obviously undergoing metamorphoses
in Hardy's speculations. In a note of June, 1877, it was no longer a
ballad or series of ballads: "Consider a grand drama, based on the
wars with Napoleon, or some one campaign, (but not as Shakespeare's
historical dramas). It might be called 'Napoleon,' or 'Josephine,'
or by some other person's name." [19] This implies a tighter framework
than before. It remains vague as to scope, and the entertaining of
"Josephine" for the title is especially strange; for the Empress was
more a sufferer from fate than an agent of it.

The next specific reference to what was by now a serious preoccupation for Hardy is more than a year later. On October 27, 1878,
he again visited Chelsea. He records that he "met a palsied pensioner—
deaf. He is 88—was in the Seventh (?) Hussars. He enlisted in 1807
or 1808, served under Sir John Moore in the Peninsula, through the
Retreat, and was at Waterloo ∗ ∗ ∗ ." [20] The old soldiers spoke of the
horror of the winter retreat to Coruña and of the severity of military
punishments. When he came to write of the deserters near Astorga and
of the desperate journey of the English troops through the snow and
mud, Hardy had printed sources, which were both detailed and graphic.
But it was what a man had remembered for nearly seventy years that
provided the authentic tone.

[17] Literary Notes, I, 56.
[18] *Ibid.*, 71.
[19] *The Early Life*, p. 150.
[20] *Ibid.*, p. 161.

In November, 1880, as noted in his autobiography, Hardy projected a "Great Modern Drama."[21] March 27 of the next year he
returned to the concept of a long ballad: "A Homeric Ballad, in which
Napoleon is a sort of Achilles, to be written." But a few days later he
again thought in dramatic terms: "Mode for a historical Drama.
Action mostly automatic; reflex movement, etc. Not the result of what
is called *motive*, though always ostensibly so, even to the actors' own
consciousness. Apply an enlargement of these theories to, say, 'The
Hundred Days'!"[22] Here we have the first hint of fusion of deterministic philosophy and historical fact. The three notes reveal that
Hardy still had much uncertainty as to the form which the narrative
was to take and even as to its geographic and chronological scope. A
year later, February 16, 1882, appears the ambiguous note already
quoted: "Write a history of human automatism, or impulsion—
viz, an account of human action in spite of human knowledge, showing
how very far conduct lags behind the knowledge that should really
guide it."[23] Since by "Great Modern Drama" and "a historical
Drama" Hardy meant a work on the Wars, we may interpret "a
history of human automatism" not as a study of incidents drawn from
the centuries of human experience, but as a record of some striking
example. So read, the note is a continuation of the train of thought in
the previous one. It may be added that it is philosophically indecisive.
Man is again evidently a deterministic phenomenon, and yet his
present knowledge, if applied to his moral decisions, ought supposedly
to make him free. He is unquestionably, at least in a generic sense,
responsible for his failure to use the means to freedom. In short,
Hardy could not resolve his philosophic difficulty by unreservedly
embracing determinism, and he was to face it again more than twenty
years later.

Meanwhile he continued to collect impressions, some specific, some
general, which illuminated the nature of war. Since he was focusing
on the Hundred Days, he probably concentrated on those parts of the
Napoleonic histories that described them. Sometime before 1881 he
took from Thiers an item which, though not to become conspicuous
in his own poem, concerned a major irony in the Waterloo campaign.
Hardy's version reads: "*Backwards + forwards*, trying to help both +

[21] *Ibid.*, p. 188.
[22] *Ibid.*, p. 191.
[23] *Ibid.*, pp. 197–198.

helping neither—Count d'Erlon—between Ligny + Quatre Bras."[24]
At about the same time, under the heading "*Battle*," he quoted from
the *Daily News*: "Tellenbach, a German officer, who investigated this
matter, concludes that no troops will endure a loss of 36 per cent
without precipitately retiring."[25] Such a statistical analysis would not
affect Hardy's factual reporting of battles, since he would always have
documentary evidence as to what happened; but it was this kind of
general observation which could determine his tone.

In the April–May, 1881, issue of *The Fortnightly Review* was an
article by Herbert Spencer entitled "Political Heads." From it Hardy
took a fundamental observation which was never to be explicitly
stated in *The Dynasts*, but which was the key to much of the action.
His note reads:

> *Successful militancy leads to political power*. Political leadership commonly
> begins with the influence gained by the finest warrior—his activity in war
> generates the subordination of the rest: + therefore the growth of political
> power continues primarily related to the exercise of militant functions.
> e.g. in modern times, Napoleon +c.[26]

An undated note of 1881–1883, from Charles Reade, takes us back
to Emma's diary: "The chronic history of Waterloo field is to be
ploughed + sowed + reaped + mowed: yet once in a way these acts
of husbandry were diversified with a great battle, where hosts decided
the fate of Empires. After that agriculture resumed its sullen sway."[27]

In August, 1883, Hardy met an old man, "P——, whose father, or
grandfather, had been one of the keepers of the Rainbarrow's Beacon,
1800–1815."[28] He was to have other sources for his own account, and
he was to transplant Grandfer Cantle from *The Return* with no change
in characterization. But here again we have evidence of Hardy's concern for any personal anecdote or relationship that might illumine.
His note omits the old man's reminiscences, but Hardy got enough to
justify the note, and presumably in repeating it about forty years later
in the autobiography he was confirming its importance.

[24] Literary Notes, I, 134. The page reference, XX, 71, indicates use of the
English translation by D. F. Campbell, *History of the Consulate and the Empire*
(20 vols.; London: Henry Colburn, 1845–1862).

[25] *Ibid.*, 133.

[26] *Ibid.*, 160.

[27] *Ibid.*, 171.

[28] *The Early Life*, p. 212.

A sweeping generalization from 1885, which Hardy saw no need to qualify when reproducing it in his autobiography, has oblique implications for an historical drama: "History is rather a stream than a tree. There is nothing organic in its shape, nothing systematic in its development. It flows on like a thunderstorm-rill by a road side; now a straw turns it this way, now a tiny barrier of sand that." [29] In his novels Hardy had given some prominence to the fact that a straw or barrier of sand could shift the course of one's life. At the same time he had felt justified in putting a series of incidents within a frame with one climactic incident to provide unity. As we have noticed, he had been searching for a frame for his ballad or drama. His pronouncement is a recognition of the recalcitrance of his materials. He apparently found some encouragement in T. H. Green on Hume, from whom, in 1886, as we saw, he quoted a half page saying that one theory of history required sorting out from the "chaos of events a connected series of ruling actions + beliefs." [30]

From the January, 1886, number of *The Edinburgh Review* Hardy took about a page and a half on Hugo, important both for its interpretation of the French poet's view of human history and for its specific reference to *La Légende des Siècles*: "Hugo's theme is the predestined fate of human existence, the struggle between man + destiny; he insists upon the compulsion of circumstances ✳ ✳ ✳ . It is by La Légende des Siècles that Hugo's epic genius must finally be judged." [31] The author accused Hugo of superficiality. It has been argued that Hardy was indebted to him for the concept of his own epic. A comparison suggests only that general resemblance which might be expected between a grandiose apocalyptic effusion and a poem which, despite its supernatural machinery, was solidly anchored to historical fact. Indeed, we have no proof that Hardy actually read *La Légende*, and certainly it did not give him his initial impetus. But Hugo's determinism may have offered reassurance to Hardy, and this was always welcome.

It was in 1886, too, some eighteen years before Part I appeared, that Hardy first recorded systematic work on *The Dynasts*. The comments we have noted from previous years indicate that he had been dipping into histories and trying to settle on the range and structure of his poem.

[29] *Ibid.*, p. 225.
[30] Literary Notes, I, 205.
[31] *Ibid.*, 203.

Now he was far enough along to have a notion of what he needed to study. From his notes he records: "The remainder of his spare time in London this year appears to have been spent in the British Museum Library and elsewhere, considering the question of *The Dynasts*." [32] In December, 1886, he set down his observation that people could seem "as if they were beings in a somnambulistic state." [33] As should be expected, all the elements that were to make his epic were developing concurrently. He collected factual evidence from historical documents, but he was at all times the poet sensing impressions.

The following spring, 1887, Hardy and Emma went to Italy. In recalling his visit to the Milan cathedral he believed that it was on its roof that he "conceived the Milan Cathedral scene in *The Dynasts*." [34] The two also went to the bridge of Lodi, famous in the early career of Napoleon. "Sometime after the excursion" Hardy wrote his "pleasant jingle" contrasting the oblivion of the battle among present-day dwellers at Lodi and the haunting memory of the old marching tune which the poet brought with him to the scene. [35] The trochees are more suited to the marching song than to a poem, but the juxtaposition of ideas is typically ironic. Those who have never heard of the battle may, by their ignorance, demonstrate the irrelevance of wars, and yet they seem to live humdrum daily lives; and so it is the poet who has the final word:

> And if here, from strand to steeple,
>   Be no stone to fame the fight,
> Must I say the Lodi people
>   Are but viewing war aright?
>
> Nay; I'll sing "The Bridge of Lodi"—
>   That long-loved romantic thing,
> Though none show by smile or nod he
>   Guesses why and what I sing!

How inchoate Hardy's plans still were in 1887 is apparent in his later account:

Another outline scheme for *The Dynasts* was shaped in November, in which Napoleon was represented as haunted by an Evil Genius or Fami-

[32] *The Early Life*, p. 240.

[33] *Ibid.*, p. 241.

[34] *Ibid.*, p. 256.

[35] *Ibid.*, p. 257. Mrs. Hardy recorded events of the journey in a diary, Italy 1887.

liar, whose existence he has to confess to his wives.[36] This was abandoned, and another tried in which Napoleon by means of necromancy becomes possessed of an insight, enabling him to see the thoughts of opposing generals.[37]

Both these designs would have meant a regression from an epic historical scope to a symbolic deification of Napoleon. Historical fact would have had to be subordinated, if not essentially altered, to allow for supernatural vision. The poet who had always been addicted to realistic authenticity in his presentation of events—however romantic his feeling toward them—was meditating cutting the cable which had invariably anchored his imagination to solid earth. For a short poem there would have been no issue, as Napoleon could have ceased to be a mortal and have become merely the vehicle for a poet's speculation; but for a poem of any length the project was, for Thomas Hardy, sensationally daring. Theory would have taken possession and the poem would, indeed, have become an apocalypse. How quickly Hardy abandoned his wild scheme is unknown. What is significant, however, is that, while discarding the ideas as motifs for a long narrative, he did not reject the first one altogether. The insight into the thoughts of others would imply a magic infallibility that would not accord with the vagaries of Napoleon's fortunes. But a genius, or familiar, is a matter of conscience. It was not a severing of the cable to give Napoleon such a visitant, provided that he never was aware of his guest's presence until circumstance had prepared for his coming. The over-all plan was abandoned, but the genius remained to haunt Hardy and, no longer evil, to play a subdued but lyrically convincing role in his poem.

A one-page entry in Hardy's notes suggests that the notion of employing necromancy may have represented only a momentary aberration, for a quotation from the December 12, 1887, number of *The Times* takes us back to a historian's approach to history. The article reported A. J. Balfour's address to the students of St. Andrews. Allowing for whatever sociological usefulness the study of history might offer, Balfour, according to the reporter, stressed its value as a source of "'spectacular' enjoyment." The gist of his argument came forth in impassioned sentences which might well remind Hardy of Gibbon's prose. History, for Balfour, was certainly one of the arts:

[36] For a possible source, cf., *infra*, p. 111.
[37] *The Early Life*, p. 266.

The imagination is moved by the slow unrolling of this great picture of human mutability, as it is moved by the contrasted permanence of the abiding stars. The ceaseless conflict, the strange echoes of long-forgotten controversies, the confusion of purpose, the successes wh. lay deep the seeds of future evils, the failures that divert the otherwise inevitable danger, the heroism wh. struggles to the last in a cause foredoomed to defeat, the wickedness that sides with right, + the wisdom wh. huzzas at the triumph of folly—fate, meanwhile . . . working silently towards the predestined end—all these form together a subject the contemplation of wh. need never weary.[38]

Since Hardy himself was at first to use "purposive" in describing the course of events impelled by the Will, Balfour's overview of history was a remarkably close approximation of his own as it was to unfold in his epic. Certainly Balfour saw historical procession as a dramatic sequence, and his phrasing implies that one can extract from its never-ending stream of incidents a series which can be conceived within a frame. In speaking as a historian he was not talking about some hypothetical end in the illimitable future. He was thinking of episodes which had demonstrated what he believed. The art of the historian consisted in finding a coherence within such divisions of our human past—in short, in establishing a beginning, middle, and end. As for the ironies by which wickedness would support virtue and what he loosely called wisdom could rejoice in folly, here Balfour was putting succinctly a distinguishing quality of Hardy's own thought.

During 1888–1889 there are various notes which Hardy appears to have jotted down with special reference to his projected poem. Thus, as part of a seven-page paraphrase and quotation from his friend John Morley's *Voltaire*, he recorded that Voltaire "was the first influential writer—for the Abbé Saint-Pierre had no influence—who deliberately placed war among retrograde agencies."[39] He also took from Morley and at some time marginally lined "V. did not know how much a man is the product of a system operating on + with the individual pre-disposition." This pronouncement would have borne particularly on Hardy's characterization and contemplated role of Napoleon.

The date of September 21, 1889, represents a milestone. In his autobiography Hardy recorded his note without elucidation: "For carrying out that idea of Napoleon, the Empress, Pitt, Fox, etc., I feel

[38] Literary Notes, I, 231–232.
[39] *Ibid.*, 271.

continually that I require a larger canvas .... A spectral tone must be adopted. ... Royal ghosts. ... Title: 'A Drama of Kings.'"[40] The note is important both for its explicit statement and for its implications. The four names suggest a small canvas, to present Napoleon's marital life and his conflict with England. The "etc.," as well as "that idea," implies vagueness as to what more would be included and as to the form. "Spectral tone" and the reference to ghosts are also vague. The language hints rather of the use of ghosts as in Shakespeare than of the supernatural apparatus of *Faust* or *Prometheus Unbound*. It does indicate that the events of history are to be given an interpretation for which supernatural machinery can be useful.

What the note provides additionally is a clue to Hardy's reading. It would appear that by 1889—if not by 1887, when he considered using an evil genius or familiar—Hardy was acquainted with Robert Buchanan's pretentious work *The Drama of Kings*, of 1871.[41] Hardy was eventually to draw his own title from the original Greek of the Magnificat, and, indeed, "Kings" was a most inadequate description of Napoleon and the Parliamentary leaders of Britain. But it would seem that, coming upon Buchanan's title, Hardy liked it so well that he did not consider the impropriety of borrowing it. In his Epilogue, summing up his closet drama, Buchanan had referred to "these ghosts of Kings," meaning the influences of rulers on human history, and the phrase—not its connotation—evidently caught Hardy's eye. Buchanan had Napoleon call upon his Famulus: "O Famulus—O Spirit—O good Soul / Come close to me and listen ...."[42] His is a docile familiar, but it may have suggested to Hardy in 1887 the use of an evil genius. Hardy's final conception of spectral voices that admonish Napoleon is really closer to Buchanan, since, though in vain, they encourage remorse.

What can Hardy ultimately have got from Buchanan by the time he wrote his own epic drama? From *The Drama of Kings* he could have obtained little or no philosophic stimulation. Though dedicated to Comte as a "Drama of Evolution," the poem is a hodgepodge of ideas,

---

[40] *The Early Life*, p. 290.

[41] Cf., Hoxie N. Fairchild, "The Immediate Source of *The Dynasts*," *PMLA*, LXVII (March, 1952), 43–64. Details in the Memorial Library MS supplement the evidence in the article. One need not agree, however, that *The Drama of Kings* "exerted so strong an influence on Hardy's *Dynasts* that it deserves to be regarded as the immediate source of that work."

[42] *The Drama of Kings* (London: Strahan and Co., 1871), p. 110.

with much talk about God. Two of its three parts concern 1870–
1871 and so had no historical pertinence for the era of the first Napoleon.
Part I leaps about, and it offered Hardy no useful historical information.
Buchanan's Queen of Prussia, for example, unlike Hardy's, berates
Napoleon and Alexander. And though *The Dynasts* contains awkward
lines, it is unlikely that Hardy had much respect for most of Buchanan's
verse.

But Hardy was eclectic. He had a habit of taking what caught his
imagination in whatever surroundings he might find it. He already
knew Goethe, Shelley, and others who had employed supernatural
personages, and, for that matter, Buchanan was an imitator. Nevertheless, the title and the paraphernalia of *The Drama* were suggestive.

Buchanan puts the action of his Prelude in the "Heavenly Theatre,"
with the Lord, Archangels, and Celestial Spectators present, and, as he
states in a note at the end, with Lucifer a "Mystic Devil ... in the
divine service working for good." Admitting indebtedness to *Paradise
Lost*, he has departed little from Milton's retinue, and he has offered a
Christianized Book of Job, with echoes from *Samson Agonistes*,
Prometheus Unbound, and *Hellas*, and here and there a reminder of
Dante. His antagonist is Man himself, as the aspiring spirits are bound
"by Man, not God" (108). This is a concept foreign to Hardy's determinism, and yet not to evidence that could be cited in his works. Though
Buchanan's Napoleon thinks of himself as mastering the "Titan"
—that is, the "Soul of Man"—at the end the Titan has been awakened,
and with help from God there will be "the last laying of these ghosts
of Kings." The concept calls to mind Shelley's depiction of Prometheus
and Demogorgon. It could have been one more reminder to Hardy
that a hint of evolutionary progress might complete his poem.

Buchanan introduced a character named Time, who also calls himself Death, to utter moral lessons and otherwise serve as a chorus.
Though an Epilude and a philosophic note follow, it is Time who
brings the action to a finale in the Epilogue:

> O to see
> The great black Curtain fall, the music cease,
> All darken, the House empty of its host
> Of strange Intelligences who behold
> Our Drama, till the great Hand, creeping forth
> In silence, one by one puts out the lights.

These, among the best lines in the drama, might be expected to catch Hardy's attention, and the word that held him was "Intelligences." At the beginning of his own After Scene, Years, who most resembles Buchanan's Time, initially addressed his companions, "Intelligences, thus the Drama goes."[43] In his Epilude, Buchanan employed a not unusual metaphor: "Last of the fruits of Earth, first of the fruits of Heaven." In the After Scene, Hardy tried as one of two alternative lines "What fruit matures in the Immense?"[44]

The use of heavenly scenes and spectators and the other reminders of a dramatic form, such as the closing of the curtain and putting out of the lights, and perhaps even the rising and falling of the tone of the verse, may have given the poet hints as to how a closet drama could be made to retain both the quality of history and the symbolism of a celestial theatre. As we have remarked, we cannot be sure how much encouragement Hardy got from Buchanan by 1887 or 1889. But by the latter year he was at least aware of the general structure and the devices of The Drama. His final indebtedness is to these and to the choral parts—particularly the Epilogue and Epilude.

In March or April, 1890, as we have observed, Hardy set down the note which, though general in import, has special pertinence for The Dynasts: "Altruism * * * will ultimately be brought about I think by the pain we see in others reacting on ourselves, as if we and they were a part of one body. Mankind, in fact, may be and possibly will be viewed as members of one corporeal frame."[45] The essential element in the frame would be, of course, the nervous system. The idea was still vague, but it was related to the concept expressed in 1876 of a web of the world. Certainly Hardy believed he could interpret social history as if it were the story of one human spirit. If the Napoleonic era were to be dramatized, there must be a way of suggesting unity amid a multiplicity of characters. In his note Hardy has defined his perspective. It is to his credit that, though he did make use of a supernatural network of nerves, he did not preach his theory obtrusively in the action of his poem. We read the separate incidents as we might read them in chronicle histories. Yet, when we think back over what we have read,

[43] Memorial Library manuscript.

[44] Ibid. Hardy modified his version to read: "To what tune dances the Immense."

[45] The Early Life, p. 294.

we are conscious of "one corporeal frame." It would be impossible to demonstrate that Hardy reached his generalization from the observation of human conduct; it may have come to him as a phantom of a sportive imagination. But, in any case, when he finally worked out his epic view of actual history, he did not have to coerce the facts to support his theory. He did reiterate other ideas, but the mere selection of tragic incidents and of human follies substantiated his metaphor of the corporeal frame.

April 26, 1890, as we have noted, Hardy recorded his concept of an impersonal god, though it was not a new idea for him: "View the Prime Cause or Invariable Antecedent as 'It' and recount its doings."[46] The doings that were of interest to Hardy, were, of course, those through the human medium. The adjuration may be only general, but it does fit what Hardy was to maintain in *The Dynasts*. "It" was to impel the frame.

During 1891 Hardy continued to meditate his plan, which he characterized as "A Bird's-Eye View of Europe at the beginning of the Nineteenth Century."[47] He had already visualized a large range of action, but this may represent his first concept of the stage directions that spread great stretches of terrain beneath the reader's gaze. The form of the poem is still amorphous after years of contemplation. Hardy also tried a new title: "It may be called 'A Drama of the Times of the First Napoleon.'"[48]

A note of June 26, 1892, brings us closer to the fusion of historical fact and Hardy's belief in determinism: "Considered methods for the Napoleon drama. Forces; emotions, tendencies. The characters do not act under the influence of reason."[49]

Thereafter we are confronted with a blank until 1896, though comments in *Jude the Obscure* (1895) and in short poems point toward *The Dynasts*.[50] In October, 1896, Hardy again visited Waterloo. His note on the occasion shows both his characteristic concern for precision and his awareness of Time's ironies: "Walked alone from the English line along the Charleroi Road to 'La Belle Alliance.' Struck with the

[46] *Ibid.*

[47] *Ibid.*, p. 306.

[48] *Ibid.*

[49] *The Later Years*, p. 9.

[50] In his 1895 copy of Pindar, Hardy at some time marked: "Of many kinds is the greatness of men; but the highest is to be achieved by Kings" (*The Extant Odes of Pindar*, trans. Ernest Myers [London, 1895], p. 6).

nearness of the French and English lines to each other. Shepherds with their flocks and dogs, men ploughing, two cats, and myself, the only living creatures on the field." [51]

By now Hardy's notion of his poem was beginning to take on the dramatic pattern he was later to follow. It had a new title and major divisions and characters:

> Europe in Throes.
> Three Parts. Five Acts each.
> *Characters*: Burke, Pitt, Napoleon, George III, Wellington ... and many others. [52]

Since, however, Burke died in 1797, it appears that Hardy expected to begin at about the time of Napoleon's ascent to power. He still did not see his subject as it was eventually to become defined.

In a note a few days later, October 17, Hardy reveals that he was still bitter because of the reception of *Jude*, which had been attacked both directly and obliquely for its alleged irreligion. His note applies to certain of his later short poems and also to *The Dynasts*. It justifies turning away from prose to verse:

> Perhaps I can express more fully in verse ideas and emotions which run counter to the inert crystallized opinion—hard as a rock—which the vast body of men have vested interests in supporting. To cry out in a passionate poem that (for instance) the Supreme Mover or Movers, the Prime Force or Forces, must be either limited in power, unknowing, or cruel—which is obvious enough, and has been for centuries—will cause them merely a shake of the head; but to put it in argumentative prose will make them sneer, or foam, and set all the literary contortionists jumping upon me, a harmless agnostic, as if I were a clamorous atheist, which in their crass illiteracy they seem to think is the same thing. [53]

In one or another short poem Hardy was to entertain all three of the alternative descriptions of the Prime Mover—limited in power, unknowing, or cruel. For *The Dynasts* he was to be explicit only in maintaining the second. In so far as he had the epic in mind when he wrote his lament he was conceiving of its action as the manifestation of a Prime Force.

Hardy's notes became fewer after 1896, and, as he indicated in his

---

[51] *The Later Years*, p. 57.
[52] *Ibid.*
[53] *Ibid.*; *Jude* had been treated as an argument.

autobiography, after 1900 nearly ceased. He did record having studied on the subject of his poem during 1898 at the British Museum.[54] Among other pieces of information, he came upon details that suggested "The Peasant's Confession," which he published that same year in *Wessex Poems*. His introductory note to this poem of a French countryman's treachery quotes Thiers' account of Grouchy's failure to succour Napoleon at Waterloo. In 1898 Hardy also wrote the mediocre "Leipzig," in which he showed some familiarity with incidents in the battle of 1813 that sent Napoleon reeling toward France. The fact that both poems, together with the quotation from Thiers, concern the closing events in the Wars suggests that in 1898 Hardy was not working up his materials in chronological order, but was, instead, intensifying his sensation of the conflict, both as it affected the destiny of nations and as it intruded on the private lives of inconspicuous men and women. In short, we are not on the trail of a scholar seeking historical erudition; we are following a poet who wanders around among documents, gathering and modifying impressions. When he finally came to the composition of his poem, Hardy would go back to the same sources and to others, and even while revising his manuscript he would verify facts and make minor corrections. But while he was still meditating the theme and the scope of his action he was likely to see it now from a "bird's-eye" philosophical vantage, now from that of some isolated mortal, illiterate and limited in horizons, but capable of articulating universal passions.

Again, except for the extracts from his reading that bear on *The Dynasts*, there is a gap in the records. Beginning in 1902 we can pick up the traces—sometimes in mere notations of progress, more importantly in an occasional comment, critical or philosophic. In the second half of 1902 Hardy was "working more or less on the first part of *The Dynasts*." At the end of September, 1903, he sent it to Macmillan's and it was in print in December.[55] During May, 1904, Hardy was reading at the British Museum—"probably historic details that bore upon *The Dynasts*."[56] He had completed the second part by September 28, 1905.[57] In June, 1906, he studied again at the British Museum "verifying some remaining details for *The Dynasts*, Part

[54] *Ibid.*, p. 74.
[55] *Ibid.*, pp. 100–101.
[56] *Ibid.*, p. 107.
[57] *Ibid.*, p. 117.

Third." [58] On the "Eve of Good Friday 11:30 P.M.," 1907, he noted, "Finished draft of Part III. of *The Dynasts*," and he completed the final manuscript September 25.[59] In a letter to Edward Clodd, New Year's Eve, 1907, Hardy wrote, "In two or three days I shall have done with the proofs of *Dynasts* III." He had not lost his wry humour: "It is well that the business is over, for I have been living in Wellington's campaigns so much lately that, like George IV, I am almost positive that I took part in the battle of Waterloo, and have written of it from memory." [60] Part III was published February 11, 1908.[61]

At the conclusion of Part I, Hardy appended a table of contents for the next two parts.[62] There is no evidence as to how minutely at this time he had mapped out his projected action. Presumably he expected each scene not only to contribute to his main impression, but to provide variety in tone and novelty in substance. When he finally worked out the details, however, he rearranged a number of episodes, dropped some, and added or expanded several others. In Part II he struck three scenes labeled "Erfurth" and left only oblique reference. If these were to have delineated the intricate diplomacy carried on there, he may have decided that they would prove wearisome. In Part III he omitted Dresden, Cadiz, Vienna, and London.

What he added is more illuminating. Two new scenes at Tilsit and the river Niemen played up the hollowness of reconciliations and gave Hardy a chance to present a fencing match between Napoleon and the charming Queen of Prussia. The palace of Godoy provided both a glimpse of the effete and debauched Spanish Court and some situation comedy in the midst of tragedy. The boudoir of Josephine gave additional prominence to that romantic heroine, who had been singled out in Hardy's earlier plans. Two scenes at Brighton filled in exposition and displayed the frivolity of a titular dynast, the Prince of Wales. A dumb show and a choral lamentation described the debacle of Walcheren, where thousands of inactive soldiers died of fever. An ironic scene in the mad King George III's apartments at Windsor permitted another close-up, as the bird's-eye view gave way to personal tragedy. Part III was opened with a prophetic incident on the banks of the

[58] *Ibid.*, p. 120.

[59] *Ibid.*, pp. 123, 127.

[60] *Notes on "The Dynasts*," pp. 10–11.

[61] Cf., *supra*, Chapter I, n. 1.

[62] Reproduced in Richard L. Purdy, *Thomas Hardy: a Bibliographical Study* (London: Oxford University Press, 1954), pp. 127–128, 131–134.

Niemen. The Moscow catastrophe was expanded to show the isolation in the interior of the Kremlin, where Napoleon should have reached the zenith of triumph. A scene in the open country between Smorgoni and Wilna reiterated the horror of the retreat and added the desertion of his troops by Napoleon. The Battle of Leipzig was expanded from three to five scenes to cover the various stages in this tremendous conflict which ultimately sent Napoleon to Elba. A brief dumb show— the replacement of the tricolour with the Bourbon flag at Bayonne— was a reminder that the conflict in the west, too, had dragged on, to end with demoralization and defeat.

There is one puzzling omission in Hardy's epic. One is not astonished that there is nothing on Ratisbon or that the fiendlike devastation of Ebersberg is passed over in a phrase (II, 4, i). Hardy was forced to economize and he had to choose. But the siege of Saragossa was another matter. The horror of life in the city and the futile heroism of the besieged offered a supreme example of the madness of war and of the sweetness that can flower in its very midst. Many years after his epic had been published—apparently in 1923—Hardy referred to a manuscript which no longer existed: "Rejected Scene or two of Dynasts (Saragossa. St. Petersburg)." [63] There is no guessing what action he may have intended for St. Petersburg, but only the siege would have been relevant for Saragossa. It is possible that he could not fit the episode into his over-all pattern, though he should, indeed, have been willing to make sacrifices to put it in. It is more likely that he had failed in execution. The artistic problem was exacting; the suffering would have to be depicted concretely and to overwhelm the reader, and yet the poet must skirt the abyss of sentimentality.

Such is the external evidence concerning the composition of the poem. The omissions, rearrangements, and expansions, and particularly the rejection of the Saragossa scene reveal the tentative nature of Hardy's architectonics, even when he thought they were settled.

As soon as Part I appeared, Hardy was under attack, both for his philosophic tenets and for his artistic method. His replies to critics and his explanations to friends show how experimental he considered his epic. Indeed, long after Part III had been published he was still wondering about the ending and justifying his concept of a Prime Cause. His comments remind us of his problems as he saw them while at work on the poem. In answer to a review "'The Dynasts': A

[63] Memoranda, II.

Suggestion," in the January 29, 1904, number of *The Times,* he defended his dramatic format: "to write Scene so-and-so, Time so-and-so, instead of Once upon a time, At such a place, is a trifling variation that makes no difference to the mental images raised. ✱ ✱ ✱ The methods of a book and the methods of a play ✱ ✱ ✱ are fundamentally similar." [64]

A *Times* article of February 6, "'The Dynasts' and the Puppets," brought a reaffirmation of the theology sketched in Hardy's preface:

> The philosophy of "The Dynasts," under various titles and phases, is almost as old as civilization. Its fundamental principle, under the name of Predestination, was preached by St. Paul. ✱ ✱ ✱ the only difference being that externality is assumed by the Apostle rather than immanence. It has run through the history of the Christian Church ever since. St. Augustine held it vaguely. Calvin held it fiercely, and if our English Church and its Nonconformist contemporaries have now almost abandoned it to our men of science (among whom determinism is a commonplace), it was formerly taught by Evangelical divines of the finest character and conduct. [65]

Though Hardy insisted that the consequence was the same for men whether one followed the views of St. Paul or of *The Dynasts,* he certainly understated the importance of "the only difference" between them. Even the term *immanence* was sufficiently broad to cover divergent concepts, but both metaphysically and artistically the distinction between any immanent agent and a god who worked externally was essential in his poem. Indeed, his technical problem lay in employing metaphors and supernatural personages appropriate for representing an external being when he was really talking about something altogether different. His poetry, in short, had to be concrete, and yet he was by no means portraying the God of St. Paul.

A few days later Hardy lamented the obtuseness of critics and then went on to explain his difficulty in conveying his theological concept. Sir Henry Newbolt had reviewed *The Dynasts,* and March 13 Hardy thanked him for his sympathetic approach to the poem. He was piqued by the complaints of other reviewers, who had merely pointed out artistic infelicities, which he felt "any child could do." Turning to his

---

[64] "'The Dynasts': A Rejoinder," dated Max Gate, February 2, printed February 5; in Reviews of the Poetry.

[65] "'The Dynasts': A Postscript," dated February 16, printed February 19 in *ibid.*

use of the term "Will," Hardy indicated that he had chosen it for
want of a better:

> But the difficulty was to find another, fit for poetry, which would express
> an idea as yet novel in poetry—that condition of energy between attentive
> and inattentive effort which the scientific call "reflex," "instinctive,"
> "involuntary" action; "unconscious formative activity," etc. "Urgence"
> occurred to me, and I think I used it once, but it seemed scarcely natural-
> ised enough.[66]

March 22 Hardy went over the same ground in a letter to Edward
Clodd. He indicated that he had not planned to publish Part I separately until shortly before he sent it to the publisher. Then he retraced
his argument concerning his use of "Will": "Another word would
have been better if one could have had it, though 'Power' would not
do, as power can be suspended or withheld, and the forces of nature
cannot."[67] Then, perhaps recalling that, in revising his manuscript,
he had sometimes changed his mind on which Spirit should pronounce
a given opinion, he minimized the seriousness of any remaining slips.

June 28, 1904, while defending Tolstoi's "philosophic sermon on
war," in a letter to *The Times*, Hardy obliquely justified his own use of
metaphor and the didactic tenor of his poem. He maintained that any
defect in Tolstoi's reasoning was rendered unimportant by the
"blaze of glory that shines from his masterly general indictment of
war as a modern principle, with all its senseless and illogical crimes."[68]
The indictment assumes at least a modicum of free will. Hardy could
let Years put the responsibility on the Will, but he still had a sensation
of moral choice.

Though in 1896 Hardy had believed that readers would accept in
verse what they would not in "argumentative prose," the reception of

[66] From the typed extract in the Memorial Library, taken from Sir Henry
Newbolt, *The World as in My Time* (London: Faber and Faber, 1932), pp.
282–299. The reviews of *The Dynasts*, preserved in Reviews of the Poetry, tell
more about their authors than about Hardy. One must, in charity, remember
that Part I gives only one third of a total work and that readers were not in a
position to do much more than discuss the apparatus and the phrasing. Consequently, the reviews of Part I range from cautious approval to denunciations of a
genius for imposing on his admirers. The response to Part II was generally
favourable, and some of the reviews of Part III were mawkishly adulatory.

[67] *Notes on "The Dynasts,"* p. 7.

[68] *The Later Years*, p. 107.

Part I disillusioned him. In sending Part II to Newbolt, February 9, 1906, he wrote that his "art (whatever it may be worth) unhappily is or will be, made the scapegoat of its philosophy in many quarters—although the latter is advanced as 'tentative' only." [69] Hardy did have a valid claim against those reviewers who, angry with determinism, condemned him out of hand. His apologetic lament, however, is no defense against a legitimate examination of the philosophic tenets of his poem. What it does imply is that, as always, he saw himself as first of all a poet. Whatever he might try to do in Part III, or have already attempted in Part II, to harmonize the divergent metaphorical connotations, he would not sacrifice his poetic sensation of experience. He continued, nevertheless, to be disturbed, as we have seen in the letters to Edward Wright, June 2, 1907,[70] and to Edward Clodd, February 2, 1908, in which he tried to explain what he meant by the Will. In his letter to Clodd he defended the meliorism of the ending: "Yes: I left off on a note of hope. It was just as well that the Pities should have the last word, since, like *Paradise Lost*, *The Dynasts* proves nothing." [71]

Sometime later Hardy reportedly told Newbolt that the ending had been influenced by his and other comments on Parts I and II: "He told me that my first article [on Part I] had convinced him of [his] injustice to 'the Will.'" Referring to the ending, Hardy, according to Newbolt, continued, "those concluding lines are my acknowledgment of the criticism of two or three of my friends—you are one of them, and I am glad that the message has reached you." [72] One could assume that Hardy's words to Newbolt represent more than mere politeness. If so, they conflict with his letters to Wright and Clodd, in which he took personal responsibility for the meliorism. So again we are reminded of the tentative nature of his conclusions.

After the text had appeared in print, Hardy did not consider it final. A letter of January 16, 1909, to Newbolt indicates an uneasiness about the execution and even a dissatisfaction with the subtitle: "As for the diction, to which you allude, a great deal of it is as good as I could make it, but I had periodic frights lest I should never live to finish the book—when alas! I rattled along too hurriedly." The title had read: "The Dynasts / A Drama / Of the Napoleonic Wars / In Three Parts,

[69] Typed extract from Newbolt, *The World as in My Time*.
[70] *Supra*, p. 54.
[71] *Notes on "The Dynasts*," p. 13.
[72] Typed extract from Newbolt, *The World as in My Time*.

Nineteen / Acts, & One Hundred And / Thirty Scenes." Hardy wrote
Newbolt: I have thought of

> A mental drama
> A vision drama
> A closet drama
> An epical drama, etc.

or "A Chronicle poem of the Napoleonic Wars under the similitude of a
drama," but I cannot decide.[73]

For the 1910 edition Hardy was to strike the reference to acts and scenes
and to end with the subtitle "An Epic-Drama / Of the War with
Napoleon." The shift implied the prominence of England.

Two pronouncements show Hardy some years later still brooding
on the philosophic perspective of his epic. In writing his autobiography for 1914 he was concerned about the ending:

> He said he would probably not have ended *The Dynasts* as he did end it
> if he could have foreseen what was going to happen within a few years.
> Moreover, the war gave the *coup de grâce* to any conception he may have
> nourished of a fundamental ultimate Wisdom at the back of things.[74]

He must have recognized that to blame the war was to admit to lack of
imagination and to ignorance of the long succession of devastations in
human history, for he added that his view had been similar before. Of
course, he sensed more keenly now a horror immediately and
inescapably present.[75]

Before the war had ended Hardy recorded yet another bitter note:

> I might say that the Good-God theory having, after some thousands of
> years of trial, produced the present infamous and disgraceful state of
> Europe—that most Christian Continent!—a theory of a Goodless-and-
> Badless God (as in *The Dynasts*) might perhaps be given a trial with
> advantage.[76]

[73] *Ibid.*

[74] *The Later Years*, p. 165.

[75] During the war Hardy was influenced by the patriotism of the time. August
28, 1914, he mentioned to Clodd that "everybody seems to be reading *The
Dynasts* just now—at least so a writer in the *Daily News*, who called me this
morning, tells me." In response to the interest he helped prepare a dramatic
version, which was produced by Granville Barker November 25, 1914. For it
Hardy wrote a prologue and an epilogue of no artistic merit, *The Dynasts: The
Prologue and Epilogue*, privately printed.

[76] *The Later Years*, p. 175. The note is from 1917.

There is here no hint of any awakening of the Will. Nevertheless, in subsequent editions Hardy let his ending stand.

Finally we have the preface which Hardy wrote in December, 1927, for a projected French translation.[77] The last paragraph starts with a gesture of tolerance for Napoleon, but soon develops into yet another plea by Hardy to be treated as an artist:

> Napoléon est un personnage particulièrement adapté à être traité par le dramaturge comme une marionnette du Destin: en fait lui-même s'est souvent regardé comme tel; et comme tel peut-être pouvons-nous lui pardonner certaines de ses erreurs et de ses ambitions, en attendant que dans l'avenir nous puissions en arriver à tout lui pardonner * * *. En tout cas les compatriotes de Descartes sauront apprécier cette théorie [monism] comme système dramatique, même s'ils ne l'acceptent pas en tant que philosophie.

The fact was that if determinism would not explain experience as we sense it, neither could complete freedom of the human will. Hardy felt that he had dealt with his historical evidence honestly. He had, at times, argued, of course, but even the arguments conflicted; and in the very conflict itself was the substance for poetry. For poetry could present life as it was apprehended by the imagination. Not that the imagination could not err, but it was less fallible than mere reason and less limited. Indeed, in the midst of intellectual incertitudes one could still aspire toward imaginative truth. And to the extent that he was successful he would be concerned not with a philosophic argument, but with an *impression*.

[77] The copy in the Memorial Library is so dated and signed by Hardy. The preface appeared in *La Revue Nouvelle* (1928), pp. 40–41.

CHAPTER FOUR

The Substance

It was all very well to meditate philosophic questions in the abstract, but Hardy's feeling for reality always prevailed. His desultory reading in history confirmed his impression that he could find in it the substance for poetry. During his years of browsing he could be satisfied with general evidence and with anecdotes that illuminated the plight of mankind. When he came to working out the scenes of an epic poem, however, he found himself in need of a vast quantity of precise information. An epic could not be a string of lyric passages commenting on major incidents in the Wars or generalizing about the tragic ironies of war.

Another poet might have been contented to use the generic features of Napoleon's career or of the conflict of the nations and to build thereon a mixture of narrative and dialogue which would presumably catch the spirit of the times. Indeed, this is all that Hugo had attempted in his *Légende*, with its glimpses of great epochs; and Buchanan had needed only a rough acquaintance with history for his *Drama of Kings*. But Hardy was of a different temperament from either. In his novels he did invent geography and alter actual landscape for his convenience, but he also liked authenticity and precision. He was capable of flights of imagination, but he appreciated the difference between "about a mile" and "a mile and a quarter," between a morning in early May and 9:00 A.M., May 7, between rear and right rear on a battlefield, and between "officers" and a list of officers by name and rank. He could improvise dialogue, but he felt more secure when he knew some of the very words which, according to those present, had been spoken.

So it was that Hardy had to do more than gather general impressions. In his concern for authenticity and verisimilitude he came to read not very systematically, but extensively. The vagaries of his reading appear when, for example, evidently having used Napier's

History of the War in the Peninsula and in the South of France, he bought a set of his own and, without cutting the pages, marked a few passages where the pages were open. They appear even more when one examines the works on which he was willing to rely. If we allow ourselves for the moment a bird's-eye survey, not of history, but of Hardy's historians, we are astonished by the range.[1]

At the one extreme is an adventure story by Méry in which the romancer, depending on secondary sources and using his imagination, drew a brief graphic picture of a scene at Trafalgar. Not greatly different is *War and Peace,* from which Hardy gleaned a few descriptive details, either imaginary or based on Russian sources which he could not himself consult. About as fictional are the purportedly scholarly accounts of the Reverend George Gleig, a Christian apologist whose naïve moralizing should have revolted Hardy. At or near the other end of the scale are documents which are either primary sources or secondary ones which a modern historian would be contented to use. Such are the reports of the Parliamentary debates, the military dispatches, the accounts in the *Morning Post* and *Morning Chronicle* of the Royal family at Weymouth, and Beatty's eyewitness story of the death of Nelson.

Between the extremes are the histories which are themselves drawn from memoirs, dispatches, and letters, or based on other, more specialized histories. Sometimes these agree so completely that there is no determining which Hardy employed as a source. Sometimes, too, as the manuscript reveals, having initially stayed close to his author, he later so rewrote a passage that the finished version might seem to have come equally well from some other account. Of the historians nearly all are partisan, Lanfrey especially so; or argumentative, Napier quite scornfully so. But one work which is both partisan and argumentative is also, in a way, an eloquent tragedy. Hardy could not have accepted the justifications which Thiers offered for certain ruthless acts of Napoleon and his generals, nor did he share his passion for the glory of France. But he recognized the grandeur of the twenty-volume *Histoire du Consulat et de l'Empire.* He also put his trust in its accuracy, for in certain instances, having noted parallel descriptions of events, he rejected the alternative for Thiers'.

Instead, however, of anticipating our story with general evaluations,

[1] Cf., also Emma Clifford, "Thomas Hardy and the Historians," *Studies in Philology,* LVI (1959), 654–668.

we can best concern ourselves with what Hardy confronted as he worked his way from scene to scene. In addition to those in the Over-world there are 131 scenes. On the basis of substance and technical artistic problems, however, this great number fall into a few essentially homogeneous groups.

For a person born in 1840 none of the incidents between 1805 and June of 1815 could be called familiar. There was an intriguing strange-ness about the entire epoch. Yet the events that took place in England were, of course, less removed from Hardy's own experience than were those on the mainland of Europe. Stories had come down to him from the years when invasion threatened, and he could also feel that what he observed around him in his own time was not altogether unreliable in offering analogies with the past. Closest of all in spirit were the scenes in Wessex and in the London streets. Somewhat more distant were the Parliamentary debates; these have not changed much in tone or relevance over the decades, but Hardy was not a student of the debates of his own time. About equally unfamiliar were the activities of British statesmen and of King George III and the Prince of Wales. For all these British matters Hardy had to go to the documents for authentic information. But he could also trust his impressions, however acquired, of the tenor of life in earlier England.

Completely foreign, on the other hand, was the history of diplomacy and intrigue. For this Hardy was dependent wholly on books. The record of attempted negotiations between the warring powers, of edicts, of reversal of alliances, and of the machinations within the French government itself was long and intricate. In those histories which discussed politics it was scattered in fragments in various chapters. Using the sources which Hardy employed, one would find much difficulty and tedium in trying to sort out the pieces and fit them together. Even more troublesome for Hardy was the fact that they were definitely not the normal stuff of poetry.

Also foreign to Hardy were the strategy and tactics of war. Here he was again entirely dependent on what he could glean from books. After a while, of course, he became familiar with the principles involved, and, as we have noted, could almost feel that he had been present at Waterloo. But the battles were of divers kinds in a variety of climate and terrain, and Hardy had sometimes to reconsult his sources to verify or add details. With minor exceptions the battle scenes can be grouped under major campaigns—the struggle at sea, with its climax at Trafalgar; the Peninsular seesaw; the comic opera of horror in Germany and Austria; the disastrous invasion of Russia and the even more disastrous retreat; the terrible slaughter at Leipzig; the giddy downward spiral of Napoleon's fortunes, ending with his journey to Elba; and the Hundred Days, culminating in the Wood of Bossu.

Within the scenes given over mainly to battles or their aftermaths there are other elements not so unfamiliar to Hardy the novelist. It took an act of imagination to enter the mind of a common soldier, and Hardy had practiced well. Nevertheless, he welcomed whatever printed bits he could find that provided touchstones, as in the withdrawal toward Coruña and the flight from Moscow. With much more evidence concerning such officers as Nelson and Wellington, and Villeneuve and Ney, or the wives of Napoleon and the Queen of Prussia, Hardy had to be careful not to contradict the essential historical facts. Yet, while following his sources, sometimes to the letter, he was always on the watch; and, when he could, he gave his own accent to the recorded words, and he took responsibility for motives where these were lacking or obscure.

Permeating his entire epic, of course, was the presence, actual or felt, of Napoleon. After all, Hardy's subject matter was the Napoleonic Wars. It was the enigmatic Emperor who, of all individual men, most strikingly exemplified for Hardy the workings of the Will. These workings, however, were shrouded in ambiguity. Hardy had the benefit of thousands of pages on Napoleon, sometimes giving his very words, written or spoken, in the reminiscences of persons whose veracity there was no need to question. What made the records fascinating was the baffling complexity and inconsistency of the portrait; and it was a not dissimilar puzzlement that beset Hardy when he thought of good and evil, of the sublime and the petty, which seemed to emanate from the unconscious Will.

The Microcosm That Is Wessex

From the threat of invasion to Waterloo—this was the ten-year epoch from which Hardy finally chose to draw his evidence. Within that chronological frame, with a very few earlier incidents for background, he concluded that he could present the essence of the turmoil among the nations and tell a tragic story with a beginning, a middle, and an end—a tragedy which would represent the human manifestation of the Will.

Having established in the Fore Scene, set in the Overworld, the tenor and philosophic implications of his play, Hardy began the action among mortal men. Where should such a vast array of incidents begin—a series of events that would cost hundreds of thousands of lives? In his novels Hardy had made a corner of Wessex a microcosmic epitome of the Universe. What started as a small matter in an inconspicuous home became heroic in its overtones. In *The Dynasts* he again decided to begin in Wessex. Looking down upon a "ridge in Wessex" between Dorchester and Weymouth, the Spirit of the Years identifies the forthcoming story with the life of every Englishman:

> Hark now, and gather how the martial mood
> Stirs England's humblest hearts.   (I, 1, i)

Though his reply is in a derisive tone, the Spirit Sinister indicates Hardy's artistic plan: "Ay; begin small, and so lead up to the greater. It is a sound dramatic principle."

It happened that Wessex, or more specifically Weymouth and its environs, was a microcosm of no little appropriateness for Hardy's epic. King George came there with the Royal retinue, so that socially, on each of his visits, it was transformed into a miniature London; statesmen conferred with him there, and decisions affecting the nations were made at Gloucester Lodge, overlooking the bay. During the Wars the fields to the north became an important training ground for soldiers, and, though not a major one, the port was engaged in naval traffic. Like the rest of the south coast, it was regarded as a possible debarkation site for Napoleon's army. And, of course, if Hardy were to dramatize what March, 1805, meant to the average Englishman, he could best draw on a region about whose traditions and manner of speech he possessed special knowledge.

Some things he knew from having lived in Dorset and having talked with persons who were there during the threatened invasion. But he had also gone to the printed documents. In the Memorial Library, as we have observed, is a notebook headed "B^{sh} Museum / Notes / taken for 'Trumpet Major' / + other works of time / of Geo III— / in / (1878–1879—)." For his novel Hardy wanted information on costumes, mores, and typical events during the years 1803–1805. Having no certainty as to what might finally be relevant, he leafed through the *Morning Chronicle* and *Morning Post* and other contemporary sources, jotting down in his notes whatever seemed to illuminate the age. Not all his items are dated, and the origin of some is unidentified. They cover activities of the Royal family at Weymouth, information on military dress and training, examples of local customs and beliefs, rumours of invasion, and an assortment of details that might help in giving verisimilitude to a scene.[2]

A few items may be singled out because they reveal Hardy's method in borrowing. He had heard, from childhood, the tales of the beacons which were to warn the countryside when "Boney" set foot on the Channel coast. A note of February, 1871, reads "Whiting (son of the man who kept Rainbarrow's Beacon)."[3] In the notebook Hardy collected a number of references to the fear of invasion in 1803,[4] but for *The Trumpet Major* he needed to know also about 1804. Hence, we find in the notebook: "N.B. The autumn of 1804 was one of alarm at the expected invasion, equally with 1803, though perhaps not to such an intense degree. So that the beacon-firing $+c$ may be in either year."[5] By the time he wrote *The Dynasts* he was able to extend the period to have a firing in the summer of 1805. After the fire has been lit on Rainbarrow one countryman complains, "Nine times has my rheumatical rest been broke in these last three years by hues and cries of Boney upon us" (I, 2, v).

A pair of entries show Hardy's problems in getting authenticity. Having dropped back to 1801, he recorded—apparently from the July 4 issue of the *Morning Chronicle*: "On Wdn^y morning two privates [corrected to "private $+$ corporal"] of the York Hussars were shot on Bincombe Down W^t. W."[6] His note describes the execution, but gives no indication that the men were Germans. Further along is a second entry in which, after noting sources to explore for more information on military costume and discipline, Hardy added a query: "Any descrip^n of York Hussars—Are they same as German Legion."[7] Obviously he had come separately on both names and as yet knew very little about the Hussars. Before he quit he managed to find

[2] The notebook consists of Volumes I and III.

[3] Memoranda, I.

[4] Notes taken for "Trumpet Major," I, 17.

[5] *Ibid.*, I, 44. Cf., also Emma Clifford, "The 'Trumpet-Major Notebook' and *The Dynasts*," *The Review of English Studies*, New Series, VIII (1957), 149–161.

[6] Notes taken for "Trumpet Major," I, 13–14.

[7] *Ibid.*, I, unnumbered, upside-down page.

sufficient facts to narrate the execution in "The Melancholy Hussar."
In writing *The Dynasts* he evidently remembered his own initial confusion and so included a specific identification: "The troopers now
passing are the York Hussars—foreigners to a man, except the
officers—the same regiment the two young Germans belonged to who
were shot here four years ago" (I, 2, iv). As one reads the passage he
has the illusion that Hardy is casually tapping a reservoir of knowledge
for local colour. If he rereads it after completing the Peninsular
Campaign and Waterloo, he may also perceive in the seemingly
gratuitous reference to the execution a hint of the discipline which
contributed to the British success, a discipline indispensable for the
efficient killing of one's fellowmen.

An item in the notebook, evidently from the *Morning Post*, reads,
"1805 Feb. The Abergavenny, East Indiaman, went down off Portland
Bill." At some time Hardy learned that the captain was Wordsworth's
brother. How much he came to know about the event itself is conjectural. But again, for verisimilitude, he needed facts as they would
appear to a contemporary, and so we read in *The Dynasts*: "That
wide bay on the right is where the 'Abergavenny,' Captain John
Wordsworth, was wrecked last month" (I, 1, i). This was not to be
the last time that Hardy was to build with limited knowledge the
illusion of easy familiarity.

Not all the historical facts in the Wessex scenes are traceable to
their sources, but enough are to reveal Hardy's eclecticism. Most of the
purely local matters have parallels in the notebook. Among the references to the effect on Weymouth of the King's arrival is one from the
Morning Post in 1805: "Weymouth July 13. In a great bustle for
several days past with the prepar^ns for recept^n of R. family. Numbers
sat up all night to be gratified with the sight of the arrival of the
R. F." [8] With such guidelines Hardy felt free to open the terrestrial
action by having one coach passenger, in March, 1805, comment,
"There seems to be a deal of traffic over Ridgeway, even at this time o'
year," and to have a second reply, "Yes. It is because the King and
Court are coming down here later on. They wake up this part rarely!"
(I, 1, i).

In the midst of such locally derived conversation Hardy could
interpolate remarks drawn from quite different sources. Thus, in scene
one, a passenger expresses what was one opinion of the time—"I

[8] *Ibid.*, I, 28.

much doubt his [Napoleon's] intention to come at all"—and after the
invasion army has left Boulogne King George, no longer afraid,
questions Pitt:

> Was it his object to invade at all,
> Or was his vast assemblage there a blind?   (I, 4, i)

Now, in Capefigue's ten-volume *L'Europe Pendant le Consulat et
l'Empire de Napoléon* (Paris, 1840), Hardy had marked the first lines of
the King's address to Parliament, in which, after reviewing Napoleon's
preparations, he continued, as translated, "mais il n'a fait aucune tentative pour mettre à exécution ses menaces réitérées" (V, 203). Hardy
had also looked into De Bourrienne's memoirs, in which the author
insisted that the activities at Boulogne were a mere feint.⁹ Hardy did
not agree, but he considered the question sufficiently controversial
to deserve his two allusions; again he wanted to be accurate to the
spirit of the age.

In the first scene, also, Hardy began a practice he was to use repeatedly, that of tucking in references to matters of diplomacy, in this
instance the King's refusal to answer an overture from Napoleon until
he had consulted the Continental powers. Such general information was
available in almost any history. But while giving the essential, yet
unpoetic facts, Hardy still kept before him his local historical scene.
So it is that a passenger who helps inform the reader also reflects the
tone of the time with his oath "Damn my wig, sir * * * ." And for this
we go back specifically to the notebook—"Oath of the period 'Damn
my wig,'"—from the *Morning Chronicle*, October 11, 1805.¹⁰

The second Wessex scene (I, 2, iv) has much from the notebook.
It includes the King's review of the troops, more on the fear of invasion
and of the possible abduction of the King and Queen, and additional
local colour. In the notebook there are numerous brief references to the
spectacle of the Royal reviews, and two entries are of particular
importance. An account from the *Morning Chronicle* reads:

> Sept 20 [1805] Grand field day of the regiments in camp, before his
> majesty, under the command of the Dk. of Cumberland. The line ex-
> tended from Ridgeway Hills to Upwey, + on to the Bridport Road. It

⁹ L. A. F. de Bourrienne, *Memoirs of Napoleon Bonaparte* (4 vols.; Rev. ed.;
New York: Crowell, 1885), II, 207.
¹⁰ Notes taken for "Trumpet Major," I, 11.

reached upwards of three miles. The hills were covered with carriages +
spectators. The artillery made a very grand appearance. The Lord
Chancellor, Ld Mulgrave, Count Munster, Mr. Pitt + Mr. Villers
accomp^d his M.[11]

Further along is an item from the *Morning Post*: "Wey^h July 14
[1805]. H. M. inspected camp . . . . Her M + 3 of the Pc^sses went in a
coach drawn by 6 cream cold. horses, + the other 2 P^csses in another
drawn by 4."[12] In *The Dynasts* Hardy fused these accounts. His scene
takes place in July on a "ridge-like down." From further reading for
The Trumpet Major he knew that the regiments consisted of "artillery,
cavalry, and infantry, English and Hanoverian." Under the Duke's
command, they constitute "a vast military array, which extends three
miles, and as far as the downs are visible." Pitt and Villers, of the
September party, are not present, but Hardy had established the
presence of the others at the July review or else was willing to assume
it. The horses have been further identified: "In a coach drawn by six
cream-coloured Hanoverian horses Queen Charlotte sits with three
Princesses; in another carriage with four horses are two more Princesses." It was safe to add to the Royal party "many other luminaries
of fashion and influence."

In a note from *The Adventures and Recollections of Colonel Landman*
we find "6. a. m. The Queen in the street—a little old woman, small
black silk bonnet, + the remainder of her person covered by a short
plain scarlet cloth cloak."[13] Hardy could not use the entire description,
but he preserved a vivid touch with "her red cloak and pattens."

It is evident in the notebook that Royal reviews, Royal walks and
rides, and Royal visits to the theatre were always newsworthy, but
most exciting of all was the possibility of abduction. On the protection
of the King and the flurry that developed the night he was late at the
theatre Hardy combined two sources. From the *Morning Chronicle,*
with the dateline September 12, 1804, he quoted:

Not only the frigates + other armed vessels are everynight posted in a
line across the mouth of the harbour [corrected to "bay"], but two lines of
centinels [*sic*], one at the water's edge + another behind the Esplan^de
occupy the whole harbour ["bay," as above] after 8 every night. The
King's guard mounts every night round Gloucester Lodge, + outlying

[11] *Ibid.*, 9.
[12] *Ibid.*, 29.
[13] *Ibid.*, 46.

pickets are so stationed on the hills round the town as to command the
harbour. There is besides a battery of 6 24 pounders on the point of the
Mole ["Nothe?" superimposed] which commands the entrance, + a
camp of flying artillery on the opposite shore, consisting of twelve 6
pounders + several howitzers. Added to this a camp of four thousand
men horse + foot within a few minutes march.[14]

From the *Gentleman's Magazine* of 1806, Hardy gleaned an account
of the nocturnal ado August 22, 1805, that is, some five weeks after
his scene. Excerpts read:

about 11 the Royal Family went on board the Yacht. In the evening all
were in the greatest anxiety for their safety till 10 o'clock. * * * At 7 the
Theatre was filled; + by half past 7 the audience began to express considerable anxiety to know the cause of their non arrival; when Mr. Hughes
informed them that the Royal Family had not returned from their cruise;
+ as the Yacht did not appear in sight he offered to proceed with the
play; but this was opposed by the audience. The Manager repeated this
offer but the audience would wait. It being 10 when they landed their
Majesties sent to inform the Manager they should not attend. * * * The
cause of their being so late was the Yacht having fallen in with the home-
ward-bound West India fleet which being a novel + grand sight engaged
the attention of the Royal Family for three hours.[15]

In drawing from both reports Hardy was again concerned with the
sense of immediacy. His characters revel in the excitement that the
threat of invasion has brought and they are proud of the might of
England. As the Third Spectator heightens the facts it is obvious that
for him Weymouth is the hub of the military universe:

'Twould be no such joke to kidnap 'em as you think. Look at the frigates down there. Every night they are drawn up in a line across the
mouth of the Bay, almost touching each other; and ashore a double line
of sentinels, well primed with beer and ammunition, one at the water's
edge, and the other on the Esplanade, stretch along the whole front.
Then close to the Lodge a guard is mounted after eight o'clock; there be
pickets on all the hills; at the Harbour mouth is a battery of twenty four-
pounders; and over-right 'em a dozen six-pounders, and several howitzers.
And next look at the size of the camp of horse and foot up here.

Except for "primed with beer and ammunition," which needed no

[14] *Ibid.*, 15–16.
[15] *Ibid.*, III, 26–27.

documentation, this represents a novelist's rewriting of a journalist. The First Spectator replies:

> Everybody however was fairly gallied this week when the King went out yachting, meaning to be back for the theatre; and the time passed, and it got dark, and the play couldn't begin, and eight or nine o'clock came, and never a sign of him. I don't know when 'a did land; but 'twas said by all that it was a foolhardy pleasure to take.

As his note reveals, Hardy did know when the King's party landed, but his Spectator's narrative has the flavour of contemporary gossip.

The Second Spectator quickly puts the King in his proper role when he admits that with his loss "we should have nobody to zing to, and play single-stick to, and grin at through horse-collars, that's true. And nobody to sign our few documents. But we should rub along some way, goodnow." This is based on a note from the *Morning Chronicle* dated October 1, 1805, which reads, "Details of the single stick + c in Mr [or "Mrs.] B's field." [16] In I, 4, i, Hardy returns to the local entertainment. The King tells Pitt that the stage outside the window is "a type of all the world. * * * At six o'clock this evening there are to be combats at single-stick to amuse the folk; four guineas the prize for the man who breaks most heads." A juxtaposition of the passages shows what Hardy could make of his bit of knowledge. The first, like the other scenes which present common folk, whether in Wessex or elsewhere, is reminiscent of Shakespeare. Superficially it is low comedy; but, within the metaphorical framework, it gives a Dynast and a west-country fellow equality under the Will. When the King himself takes up the subject, with an obvious allusion to Shakespeare, the breaking of heads for amusement becomes a symbolic epitome of Hardy's theme. Had the Spirit Sinister been present, he could have said no more.

To a reader of the novels the scene in mid-August on Rainbarrow's Beacon (I, 2, v) may sound as if it sprang full blown from Hardy's imagination. Yet in the midst of the caricature and whimsy identifying Private Cantle of the Bang-up-Locals and his neighbours Hardy used fragments from the printed page. The function of the scene is to reiterate the fear of invasion. Few historical facts were needed. But if beacons were to be fired, Hardy wanted everything authentic. In his notes is a letter from Lord Dorchester, October 12, 1803, indicating

[16] *Ibid.,* I, 10.

the possible invasion of the Isle of Wight and instructing in the pro-
cedure to be followed at the beacons:

> I have to beg of you that you will give directions for an assembly of
> fagots, furze + other fuel, also straw to be stacked + piled on the
> summit of Badbury Rings, so as the whole may take fire instantly + the
> fire be maintained for two hours. The general direction if you will take
> the trouble of the execution is that this beacon may be fired whenever the
> beacon off St Catherine's (Christ Church) is fired to the eastward, or
> whenever the beacons on Lytchet Heath or Woodbury Hill, are fired to
> the westward, but not from the demonstration of any coast signal.[17]

There are minor discrepancies in Hardy's version, which may well
have drawn also from some oral account,[18] but his second fire is to be
kept "burning for two hours." For the fun of it, Hardy has not
another beacon nor even a coast signal provide the alarm, but the
gleam of fishing-fleet oars in the moonlight.

A note from the *Morning Chronicle* of August 14, 1805—"Sudden
apprehension of invasion at Dover, Deal, +c, a tremendous firing
having begun"[19]—accounts for Mrs. Cantle's "we've been troubled
with bad dreams, owing to the firing out at sea yesterday"; and perhaps no more was needed for the Second Pedestrian's later remarking:

> All yesterday the firing at Boulogne
> Was like the seven thunders heard in Heaven
> When the fierce angel spoke.

Stories of Napoleon's monstrous habits were legion, but Hardy
gave a local twist by bringing in the Cerne Giant. Even on this well-
known Wessex character he had seen fit to make a note September 12,
1890, describing how the giant had "threatened to descend upon
Cerne + ravish all the young women on a particular night, + to kill
the young men next day" and so had been waylaid and slain. He
"lived somewhere up in the hills, was waited on by wild animals, used
to steal the farmers' sheep, eating one a day."[20] Hardy was probably
truer to local legend in implying a more dreadful diet. With an air of

---

[17] *Ibid.*, 4.

[18] In a footnote Hardy describes remains of the hut by the beacon and adds,
"The two keepers themselves, and their eccentricities and sayings, are tradi-
tionary, with a slight disguise of names."

[19] Notes taken for "Trumpet Major," I, 12.

[20] Memoranda, I.

authority Mrs. Cantle affirms that Boney "lives upon human flesh, and has rashers o' baby every morning for breakfast—for all the world like the Cernel Giant in old ancient times!"

In one passage Hardy drew on family history. The Old Man invites his friends in for "a drop o' sommat" and boasts of having "housed eighty tubs last night." This bit of lawlessness is based on Hardy's grandfather's smuggling between 1801 and about 1805: "He sometimes had as many as eighty 'tubs' in a dark closet * * * each tub containing 4 gallons."[21]

The irrational and essentially automatic lighting of the beacon and the ensuing flight of a multitude inward from the coast are again, on the surface, quaintly amusing. But they are also somnambulistic manifestations of the workings of the Will. The smuggling is only one of several reminders that life goes on as little changed as possible. There may be a great war somewhere and the sons of neighbours may be dying to save the country, but one may still cheat the Exchequer for a little profit.

Scene I, 4, i, in autumn, 1805, is a conversation between the King and Pitt. Since it takes place at Gloucester Lodge, Hardy put in some local description. Among other details, he included on the esplanade a "fashionable crowd." There is nothing unusual about this; it could be assumed. And yet it is indicative of Hardy's reliance on authentic sources that he had noted from the *Morning Chronicle*, "Sept. 9 [1805] 'The grandest esplanade this season.' (The King rides early almost every morning)." The parenthetical half of his entry, with hints on the same page and elsewhere in his notes, justified his having the King ask Pitt to join the Royal party the next day "for a ride on the Ridgeway, and through the Camp on the downs."

From the *Morning Chronicle* of September 5, 1805, Hardy quoted, with interpolation:

> Weymouth, Sept 3. . . . Capt. Hardy, Ld. Nelson's Captain, was waiting the return of his majesty [from riding on horseback, early accomp^d. by Dukes of York, Cumberland, + Cambridge, from which ride he returned soon after 9 o'clock] + had a long convers^n. with him.[22]

The parenthetical details show Hardy's methodical ways; he might need them, and so he put them in. He happened not to have use for

[21] *Ibid.*, I, March 22, 1871.
[22] Notes taken for "Trumpet Major," I, 7.

them in *The Dynasts*, but he did fit in a reference to the visit of his ancestral relative, who lived at Portisham, nearby.

The main item of statecraft in the scene is Pitt's futile request to include Fox and Grenville, of the Opposition, in the government. For this there were various possible sources, all known to Hardy. In Roseberry's *Pitt*, in the margin beside the record of Pitt's attempt, Hardy wrote, "Summer, 1805." [23] In Fitzgerald's *Life of George the Fourth* was a vivid account of the King's hatred of Fox. [24] The essence was also in Gifford's *A History of the Political Life of the Right Honourable William Pitt* (1809), III, 729–730, and in Stanhope's *Life of the Right Honourable William Pitt*, III, 355, *et al.* Hardy did what he could to enliven his exposition by calling heavily on metaphor. In his climactic line he was still close to his source—"Rather than Fox, why, give me civil war!"

Scene I, 5, vii, after the Battle of Trafalgar, narrates plans for Nelson's funeral at St. Paul's and ends with a commemorative "new ballet," "The Night of Trafalgár." But in between we have what purportedly happened to the spirits with which Nelson's body was preserved. In Beatty's version a leaguer was "filled with brandy." This was once drawn off and replaced, and since the body had absorbed some of the brandy, wine was added at Gibraltar. The "Victory" arrived at Spithead five weeks later. [25] Since Beatty was Hardy's primary source for the death of Nelson, he knew the official version. But he was fascinated by the popular one, which went very differently. The First Boatman lowers his voice as he tells it: "And grog ran short, because they'd used near all they had to peckle his body in. So—they broached the Adm'l!" But, as Hardy was so often to remind his reader, the mind adjusts to anything; and so the Boatman, with the utmost propriety, bespeaks the Admiral's approval: "So he was their salvation after death as he had been in the fight. If he could have knowed it, 'twould have pleased him down to the ground! How 'a would have laughed through the spigot-hole: 'Draw on, my hearties! Better I shrivel than you famish.' Ha-ha!"

[23] Lord Roseberry, *Pitt* (London: Macmillan and Co., 1892), p. 252.

[24] Percy Fitzgerald, *The Life of George the Fourth including His Letters and Opinions with a View of the Men, Manners, and Politics of His Reign* (New York: Harper and Brothers, 1881), pp. 38 ff.

[25] William Beatty, *Authentic Narrative of the Death of Lord Nelson with the Circumstances Preceding, Attending, and Subsequent to That Event* (London: Cadell and Davies, 1807), pp. 62 ff.

So we have, in one scene, the tribute to be paid to a great national hero, whose life was to become a romantic legend, one of many songs in the English tradition of topical ballads—to be sung either before or after a round of drinks—and a piece of grotesqueness, presumably apochryphal in origin, but destined to live as a jocular phrase. For Hardy human existence was not infrequently a mixture of the grand, the merry, and the grotesque.

The last Wessex scene, III, 5, vi, laid in Dorchester, introduces, by way of the coach guard from London, the news of Napoleon's return from Elba. It also benefits from Hardy's antiquarian interest in popular tunes and songs; casual annotations in his books attest to the extent of that interest. Here, besides alluding to "Lord Wellington's Hornpipe," which must be quite new, and to "When War's Alarms," he offers a lament by a maiden whose lover has gone to war.

The motif for the scene, however, is the burning of Boney in effigy, which, we learn from the guard, has a moral equivalent in London; where, for "one shilling; children half-price," he can be seen on horseback "hung up with his head downwards." The scene is thoroughly pagan. In the tradition of low comedy from Shakespeare to Dickens, a rustic feels cheated because Boney himself is not to be burnt; and the vicar chides him for imagining that "we should be so inhuman in this Christian country as to burn a fellow-creature alive." Coming after all the slaughter in previous scenes and in the midst of the cowardly bloodthirstiness in the present one, the vicar's pious syllables need only a shift in intonation to fit the Spirit Sinister. Even the vicar is so disturbed at the sudden news of the Emperor's return that he starts to swear, but recovers to finish, "Dear me—dear me! The Lord's will be done." When the effigy has blown up and the crowd has dispersed, the vicar "stands musing."

One is reminded of the weird shadows cast by the bonfire on Egdon Heath in *The Return* and of folk cruelty in *The Mayor of Casterbridge*. These are comics acting out their antics on Durnover Green. Except that the persons have changed whose effigies are to be consumed by fire, the same incident has remained unaltered throughout the centuries. Men have done this sort of thing not by free will, but as if they were somnambulists. There is a fantastic madness in the nocturnal ritual— the more fantastic in that it is an act of futility and frustration. The men and women are fettered gods who can get some kind of catharsis only by performing like demons around a bonfire in Hell.

The Wessex scenes are, in short, the work of a thinking craftsman. Hardy had picked up, during a lifetime, odd bits of knowledge which seemed to illuminate human nature. He added authentic facts from the newspapers and books, so blending them into the dialogue as to disguise their extraneous nature. And in the fusion which resulted he achieved an effect which, on the surface, had a quaintness of local colour a century removed from the moment of composition. But beneath that surface were all the elements of his total drama—the pride, the folly, the dignity, the pettiness, the inclination toward merriment which seemed to animate humanity, and the undercurrent of thoughtless cruelty and tragedy. He began small, but he let the "web of the world" grow ever larger. His last Wessex scene, after all the campaigns have been fought except the one already on the horizon, is a partial measure of how it has been spun. None of the supernatural spirits comment on this scene, but, except for the love song, its genius is the Spirit Sinister.

Pandemonium

Since decisions affecting peace and war were commonly questioned and defended in Parliament, it was appropriate to tell what went on in the House of Commons. But Hardy did not settle for short summaries. He used outsiders to tell what occurred at one session, but he gave overlong abridgments of two others as they would have been heard on the floor. His reasons can only be conjectured. The democratic debate in I, 1, iii, does contrast with the dictatorial letter of Napoleon quoted in scene ii. It also shows both Pitt and Fox in action—the one at the head of government, the other soon to replace him. Hardy was, of course, aware of the reputation of Parliamentary debate as a mélange of seriousness and wit. In his copy of Roseberry's *Pitt* he marked with double lines the comment that, in Pitt's address of May 23, 1803, and Fox's reply the next day the House of Commons "heard the highest expression of English eloquence" (p. 237). It happened that the debate of March 6, 1805, was also a good example. If Sheridan was pacemaker, the Prime Minister himself was his equal, and Fox and others were worthy competitors. To capture the tone of their eloquence, perhaps to embellish it, was a challenge. Having said this, we must admit that Hardy's success was by no means complete.

In his notes for *The Trumpet Major*, Hardy quoted excerpts from

the *Morning Chronicle* of June, 1804, on the second reading of a bill
for the "defence of the country." Fox had spoken for an hour and a
half against it, but it had passed 221 to 181.[26] The full title as recorded
in Cobbett was: "An act for establishing and maintaining a permanent
additional force for the defence of the realm, and to provide for aug-
menting his Majesty's regular forces, and for the gradual reduction of
the militia of England." [27] It was called the Patent Parish Bill because
of "penalties assessed on parishes for deficiencies under the act"
(col. 634). The responsibility for recruitment, in short, lay with the
parishes, and it was argued that the act would substantially increase the
military force.

Unfortunately these elementary facts are obscured in Hardy's
version. After the Recording Angels have indicated that England has
no support from allies, that her own plans are "poorly defined," and
that, though ill, Pitt has consented to try to bring order and energy to
the struggle, we suddenly hear Sheridan supporting repeal of "Mr.
Pitt's Patent Parish Pill." Unless we ourselves have followed Hardy's
peregrinations, we do not know what Sheridan is talking about, and
at the end of the debate we are still not entirely in daylight. What we
do observe is a display of pyrotechnics, with much *ad hominem*
ridicule and a modicum of sense. But if we go back to Cobbett, we
learn that in the original there really was a good deal of the latter,
which the wit ornamented, but did not obscure.[28]

To trace in detail what Hardy left out or added would be tedious
indeed. A few examples, however, will indicate how he employed his
sources.

In Cobbett, Sheridan gives the title of the bill and calls it "Mr.
Pitt's parish defence bill," with no attempt at alliterative punning. He
then indulges in elephantine humor: "When I gave my notice of this
motion, I could not help observing, that it appeared to excite some

---

[26] Notes taken for "Trumpet Major," III, June 9, 1804.

[27] *Parliamentary Debates*, III, col. 52.

[28] Pitt's speech is paraphrased and quoted in John Gifford (pseud.), *A History
of the Political Life of the Right Honourable William Pitt* (3 vols.; London:
Cadell and Davies, 1809), III, 744, and in *The Speeches of the Right Honourable
William Pitt in the House of Commons* (4 vols.; London: Longman, Hurst, Rees,
and Orme, 1806), pp. 403 ff. The latter has one phrase used by Hardy that is not
in Cobbett. The editions of the speeches of Fox (1815) and Windham (1812)
do not include this session; that of Sheridan's (1816), though apparently also
used by Hardy, is less close than is Cobbett's.

surprise on the part of some gentlemen opposite; a surprise not
unmixed with marks of disapprobation of a nature not the most
orderly" (col. 725). This loses all pretense of humour in Hardy:

> The ministerial countenances, I mark,
> Congeal to dazed surprise at my straight motion.

Thereafter, for a number of lines, Hardy departs from Cobbett by
both omitting and expanding. Finally in Cobbett we reach Sheridan's
zenith when, having insisted that the act has supplied few men, many
of them vagrants, he becomes especially derisive:

> Where the right hon. gentleman's own influence was particularly directed,
> 11 men were procured, all of whom deserted; and in that particular
> district where his own authority and popularity are so abounded, where
> all the people admire him as a general, as much as they venerate him as a
> politician and a statesman, I mean the Cinque-ports, the spot of his own
> residence, he has contrived so far to stimulate martial policy as to have
> been able to raise one man! ac ille leo est! I wish we could get a look at this
> extraordinary man. He must be a very Hercules (cols 732–733).

Hardy condenses and changes the wording, but with loss of wit:

> In Ireland, where the glamouring influence
> Of the right honourable gentleman
> Prevails with magic might, *eleven* men
> Have been amassed. And in the Cinque-Port towns,
> Where he is held in absolute veneration,
> His method has so quickened martial fire
> As to bring in—one man. O would that man
> Might meet my sight! (Laughter.) A Hercules, no doubt,
> A god-like emanation from this Act * * *.

The original of Sheridan's speech is long, with some rambling and
reiteration; so, too, is Pitt's reply. Much of Hardy's paraphrase of the
latter amounts to a complete rewriting of salient points. But he lifted
from late in Pitt's rebuttal an animadversion on Sheridan as wit.
Putting this only a few lines after the latter's facetious attack, he may
have intended to give the victory to Pitt. In *The Speeches* we find:

> The honourable gentleman seldom condescends to favour us with a
> display of his extraordinary powers of imagination and of fancy; but
> when he does come forward, we are prepared for a grand performance.
> No subject comes amiss to him, however remote from the question before
> the house. All that his fancy suggests at the moment, or that he has

collected from others—all that he can utter in the ebullition of the moment—all that he has slept on and matured, are combined and produced for our entertainment. All his hoarded repartees—all his matured jests—the full contents of his commonplace book—all his severe invectives—all his bold, hardy assertions—all that he has been treasuring up for days, for weeks, and months, he collects into one mass, which he kindles into a blaze of eloquence, and out it comes altogether, whether it has any relation to the subject in debate or not.[29]

Here the Hardy paraphrase is possibly as good as the original:

> Each device
> Of drollery he has laboured to outshape,
> (Or treasured up from others who have shaped it,)
> Displays that are the conjurings of the moment,
> (Or mellowed and matured by sleeping on)—
> Dry hoardings in his book of commonplace,
> Stored without stint of toil through days and months—
> He heaps into one mass, and lights and fans
> As fuel for his flaming eloquence,
> Mouthed and maintained without a thought or care
> If germane to the theme, or not at all.

For the speeches of Windham, Whitbread, and Bathurst, Hardy improvised freely, but also sometimes came back close to the text. Thus "when they had struck a dreadful blow in some quarter"[30] became

> till some black blow
> Be dealt by them in some undreamt-of quarter.

If Hardy here followed a method demonstrated in the manuscript of Part III, he first wrote down Cobbett's own words and then between the lines wrenched the prose into verse. It is not the best way to achieve poetic grace. In pranking Bathurst's rather ordinary argument, Hardy turned "who had conducted this business" (col. 772) into "who would inter this corpse-cold Act"; "what new scheme of military defence should be adopted" became

> how to frame
> A finer trick to trounce intrusive foes,

[29] *The Speeches of Pitt*, IV, 416–417.
[30] Whitbread's speech, *Parliamentary Debates*, III, col. 770. Cobbett uses both quotation and paraphrase.

which was then followed with a Miltonic repetition: "To whom such trick against intrusive foes * * * ."

Quite baffling are the five lines from Fuller, who was probably little more than a name to Hardy. Fuller disapproved of Windham's arguments, yet was going to vote "for the repeal, from the impossibility of carrying the act into execution." Hardy covers only the objection to Windham and lets Tierney, who favours repeal, so interpret the speech.[31] Possibly, like the rest of us, Hardy took incomplete notes and afterwards guessed wrong. In Tierney's speech "unless you can get men to work cheaper than they find it to be their interest or inclination to do" (col. 773) became the Shakespearean imitation:

> binding men
> To serve for less than service proves it worth.

The original of Fox's speech has caustic lines, but Hardy intensified its sarcasm by omitting other parts and expanding simple statements into rhetorical periods; thus his last twelve lines match about two-thirds as many in Cobbett. The last three illustrate the tinkering involved. Cobbett gives us "which the partiality of friendship can possibly consider as the mark of an enlarged and vigorous mind" (col. 779). Hardy reads:

> Which all the partiality of friendship
> Can kindle to consider as the mark
> Of a clear, vigorous, freedom-fostering mind!

In Sheridan's concluding speech Hardy again slipped by misreading a pronoun reference in Cobbett. The last few lines are his own.

To what do the speeches add up? We remember how Milton permitted his fallen angels to discuss philosophy and then pronounced their erudition vain knowledge. We are tempted to conclude the same about the debate of 1805, but Hardy does not want us to do so unqualifiedly. It is true that Pities protests that, "if each decision work unconsciously," they have changed no votes; and Years, translating a vote of 127 for repeal to 267 against as "Ins as Ins and Outs as Outs, remain," endorses this view. But meanwhile Rumour has suggested that

---

[31] *Ibid.*, III, col. 773. Hardy does not identify Tierney as ex-Treasurer of the Navy, hence identified with those obliquely criticized in Pitt's bill.

There may react on things
Some influence from these, indefinitely,
And even on That, whose outcome we all are.

Also, Hardy ended Pitt's speech on a lofty note, and Years gives us a prophetic eulogy on Pitt. It would appear that Hardy hoped that his readers would be impressed with the debate. But the failure to identify the issue and also the less-known participants, the emphasis on witty invective which becomes repetitive, and the rhetorical metaphors all tend to make the pages read like an exercise in declamation. And the scene does not qualify under Aristotle's theory that one can enliven the lesser parts of a narrative with ornamental language.

In II, 5, iv, Hardy aimed at advancing the narrative through dialogue and at the same time giving a feeling of what the war meant to Englishmen. Members of a club in St. James's Street, some well in their cups, gossip about the divorce of Josephine the previous December, and before the scene ends they are informed by Sheridan that Napoleon will wed Maria Louisa of Austria, thus cementing an alliance with a former enemy. Neither fact is altogether new. During their narration Hardy gives a disconnected review of recent debates, in which the Opposition has attacked the Government for inefficiency in the use of war resources, for its failure in Spain, and especially for the disaster at Walcheren. The substance bears only a loose resemblance to the debates of late March, 1810.[32] At the closest we have, in the *Debates*, Burdett's "The ministers ought to be called to an account very different from a mere censure of that House and the officers ought to be tried by Courts Martial" (col. 405) and, in Hardy, Ward's "Do his Majesty's Ministers expect censure? Not a bit. They are going about asking in tremulous tones if anybody has heard when their impeachment is going to begin." Contrasted with I, 1, iii, the scene has an informal naturalness. Like the scenes in Wessex, it brings together a variety of topics and shows how each lingers for a moment or two in men's minds before giving way to something new. The divorce, ill fortune in Spain, disaster at Walcheren, Gower's Parliamentary repartee, the prospective Franco-Austrian marital alliance—of such is a club man's daily newsfare composed.

The last Parliamentary debate, III, 5, v, is presented by Hardy in the same dramatic manner as his first. It took place April 7, 1815, after

[32] *Ibid.*, XVI, March 26 ff.

Castlereagh, now Foreign Secretary, had read the March 13 declaration denouncing Napoleon for his return from Elba. The Treaty of Vienna had already been signed March 25, but the news had not yet reached London. In a rambling, repetitive speech Castlereagh defended a proposal of April 6 that would commit England to readiness to support the allies. The gist of the debate, as reported in Hansard, was that opponents felt that Castlereagh was too belligerent, that Napoleon's return was an internal matter for France, and that the proposal should be amended to urge pacific negotiations.

In abridging Hardy stayed rather close to the original, often merely taking out a phrase and inserting an equivalent. In Hansard, Castlereagh, for example, says that England "must either embark in a war, in conjunction with the other continental Powers, or it must, in conjunction with them, adopt measures of military precaution, sufficient for its protection under the present circumstances."[33] Hardy gives us

> two alternatives,—of war
> In concert with the Continental Powers,
> Or of an armed and cautionary course
> Sufficing for the present pucker of things.

Castlereagh concludes,

> That ... we shall with the utmost zeal and alacrity, afford the requisite assistance to enable his Royal Highness to make an augmentation of his Majesty's forces by sea and land, and to adopt all such measures as may be necessary for its accomplishment (col. 435).

Hardy coerces this into uninspired meter:

> That we, with zeal, will speed such help to him
> So to augment his force by sea and land
> As shall empower him to set afoot
> Swift measures meet for its accomplishing.

In the original Castlereagh's speech is neither clear nor orderly. In contrast, though overlong, Hardy's abridgement is both. Consequently, in Hardy, the witticism of Whitbread, who favours peaceful ways, loses much of its original contextual aptness. Hansard gives us

> if he thought with the hon. baronet who preceded him, that there was anything like ambiguity of sentiment in the speech of the noble lord

[33] *Ibid.*, XXX, col. 432.

(ambiguity of expression was inseparable from the speeches of the noble lord), he might be content to vote for the Address (col. 441).

Hardy adorns this only slightly:

> Were it that I could think, as does my friend,
> That ambiguity of sentiment
> Informed the utterance of the noble lord
> (As oft does ambiguity of word),
> I might with satisfied and sure resolve
> Vote straight for the Address.

Hardy breaks off the debate without giving Ponsonby's rebuke to Whitbread for his appeasement: "but he wished to inform his hon. friend (in perfect good nature) that he was not quite such a fool, but he could understand what had been submitted to them without his assistance" (col. 463). Without this sting, which ends the debate, the scene lacks a conclusion. Once again, as in I, 1, iii, we are given a glimpse of the kind of activity that went on in the halls of government. But the vote to sustain Castlereagh is of no consequence anyway, since the decision has already been made at Vienna to restore the Bourbons.

In all his Parliamentary debate Hardy's focus is on the byplay between gentlemen of eloquence. They represented one facet of the life of the time. Hardy appears to have respected the speakers, who, after all, included the statesmen responsible for the sturdy determination of England. Except for the remarks of Pities and Years, he made no gesture to place them in the role of puppets subservient to an Immanent Will. Yet each does play only a fixed role; each parrots his party's line. If there is freedom to be witty, there is still no meaningful display of free will. Indeed, one cannot find evidence to support Rumour's belief that these debates will have any influence on "That, whose outcome we all are."

PITT, FOX, THE KING, AND PRINNY

Though the policies of government were invariably debated in Parliament, the weight of their execution bore primarily, of course, upon the Ministry, with symbolic and sometimes actual participation by the Monarch. In the later years of the Wars no statesman rose to distinction as head of the government. In the beginning, from before Hardy's epic took up the story, the burden of foreign affairs rested

Part of Hardy's Napoleonic Library

a stable

/ So that ~~the~~ peace ~~shall carry this guarantee~~

but when we conclude peace it shall carry this guarantee
with it — it shall bring an end to the evil influence that Russia
has exercised on the [affairs of Europe for the last 50 years!

short midsummer
The night ~~gets~~ darkens. They all make their bivouacs, & sleep.

Spirit of the Pities.

ripped
voice
mouths
☐ Something is tongued afar.

☐ What do I hear afar? I trace dim lines after.

Spirit of the Years

The Russian proclamation ~~~~ the breeze?
rides

A wild ~~~~ in the wind.

Napoleon's brain

[Against our Empire "For long we have ~~observed~~ the hostile proceedings of the French Emp.

towards Russia but we always entertained the hope of avoiding

hostilities by measures of conciliation: but seeing that all our efforts
are without success we have been compelled to assemble our armies

Still we hoped to maintain peace by resting on our frontiers in
a defensive attitude, without committing any act of aggression.

All these conciliatory measures have failed. The Emperor Nap.

by a sudden attack on our troops at Kowno has declared war.

Seeing therefore that nothing can induce him to remain at peace,
all left for us is to invoke the succour of the Most High, & oppose
our forces to the enemy. I need not remind the officers & soldiers
of their duty; to excite their valour; the blood of the brave Sclavonians
flows in their veins. Soldiers, you defend your religion, your country,
or your liberty. I am with you. God is against the oppressor!"

Spirit Ironic

~~Ha!~~ "Liberty" is queant, & pleases me!

They look across at the long straight causeway from the Ranstadt-Gate at the N.W
corner of the town.
& the bridge over the Elster beyond).

Third Citizen.

The Emperor rode over the battlefield yesterday — gloom, regret, inaction.
Had an interview with Meerveldt whom he had taken prisoner. Spent
the rest of the day in his tent . . . . . was gazeled. caelen.

Citizen.

He was out late last night at the Reudnitz Seubouny, & called
round on his marshals, not getting home till the small hours. 7h.
Past midnight he ordered his horse: rode to Bertrand at Lindenau, then
to Ney at Reidnitz . . at last he returned to his tent at Stetteritz.
He bivouacked at Probsthayda . . 1h?

First Citizen.

Last night I saw, the two columns appear on the Dresden Road
and then, anon. He already stout arrives of Schw? Were stationed more
the ranks of the army of Schwarz soon thickened undoubtedly. I deemed
from here just before dark, Bernadotte's army came. hemming in
in on the north still more thoroughly. The horizon glowbred with a
thousand fires. The circle was shut round as the unyielding circle

As it grows lighter they gaze and define the armies.

Citizen.

Those lying between Connewitz & Dölitz are the right wing of Murat
Out there's Napoleon's centre at Probstheida where he bivouacked — Those
this way his left wing with Ney — forming the north between Paunsdorf &
Gohlis. Poniatowski, Augereau, Victor, & the rest
Thus you see they are skilfully drawn up set behind villages with cannon
ranged in front of them: and every patch of copse is filled with riflemen.

The heavy sky has begun to clear with the coming of the morning. The sun
bursts out, — the previously dark & gloomy masses glitter in the rays.

Page 109 of the rough draft

Napoleon's Return from Elba, after Steuben

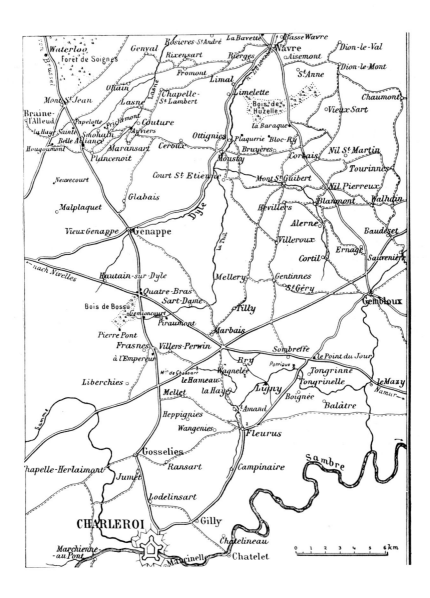

Map of the Belgian Campaign

Napoleon and Queen Louisa at Tilsit, after N. S. F. Gosse

Sir Thomas Picton, after the portrait by H. R. Cook

Marshal Ney, after the portrait by Gerard

mainly upon Pitt and, after his death, upon his able opponent, Fox. In the background was George III, whom Hardy brought forward for the purposes of tragic irony; and playing a very minor political role was the Prince of Wales, whom Hardy, with no great injustice, turned into a Shakespearean comic on a par with the London clubmen.

Nelson and Wellington were, of course, the traditional British heroes, and Hardy concurred in honouring them. Pitt, though remembered as a statesman, lacked the glamourous history of Nelson and the obvious success of Wellington. But for Hardy it was Pitt who most represented the genius of England. Wellington had the patience to persevere and a dogged determination to win, in which there was no place for fear. For Hardy he was an admirable man, but devoid of that complexity which makes an interesting hero in literature. Life was a rather simple matter for the great general. Nelson had for Hardy a much greater appeal because of the melancholy that made him indifferent to death. The world-weariness which Hardy identified with him was not unlike that in some of his own poems. But Pitt, who entered Parliament at twenty-one and at twenty-five was the most powerful man in England, was yet more complex than Nelson. His work had no possibility of glamour. Much of it was as tedious as Wellington's building of his fortress at Torrès Védras, and within his own lifetime it appeared futile. There were no moments to match Trafalgar or Waterloo. Pitt worked long hours trying to influence actual or potential allies and to invigorate moral and financial support at home. He accepted the conditions of debate, even to crossing foils with Sheridan in a duel of wit. He pleaded with an unimaginative monarch and gracefully acquiesced when refused a coalition cabinet so essential for the cause. Without self-pity, he never cried out, as did Hardy, against the injustice of the Universe. And yet he suffered both for his own mistakes in judgment and for the mistakes of England and her allies; and, broken by the strain, he went to a premature death at forty-six. The portrait which Hardy managed to give in a series of vignettes is, of course, incomplete, and yet it shows why Pitt was for the author of *The Return* and *Jude* the most fascinating of all his heroes, the man whose sense of tragedy stemmed from his profound awareness of the nature of things.

Apart from the debates, Hardy had three principal sources for the career of Pitt. He owned and marked extensively Lord Roseberry's *Pitt*. Certain of his lines more closely agree with John Gifford's

History of the Political Life of the Right Honourable William Pitt; and he went to Stanhope's *Life of the Right Honourable William Pitt* for part of I, 5, v, and probably for James Stanhope's "minutes" on the last days of Pitt. Though at the time of writing he had, of course, to check his authorities for dates and notable phrases, Hardy was solidly informed on his subject and could select incidents and borrow or invent words that best represented the greatness of Pitt as a human being.

He knew that in early 1804 Pitt had pleaded with George III for three hours to accept Fox and his political friends in the Ministry. The trip to Weymouth in 1805 (I, 4, i) was therefore a desperate resort. As if in passing, in Pitt's audience with the King, Hardy indicates the arduous task he has undertaken in cementing alliances and providing British arms and men. When his Monarch dismisses his request and turns the subject to trivial affairs, Pitt accepts the defeat with the decorum repeatedly described in Gifford and Roseberry.

The ultimate source of part of I, 4, vi, at Spring Gardens, is a few lines in the First Earl of Malmesbury's *Diaries and Correspondence*. Since Hardy has one or two facts not in the biographies, he evidently examined the original. Starting with Pitt's inability to believe that Mack could have surrendered at Ulm, Malmesbury continues:

> But on Sunday, 3rd November, he and Lord Mulgrave came to me in Spring Gardens about one o'clock, with a Dutch newspaper, in which the capitulation of Ulm was inserted at full length. As they neither of them understood Dutch, and as all the offices were empty, they came to me to translate it, which I did as well as I could, and I observed but too clearly the effect it had on Pitt, though he did his utmost to conceal it.[34]

Except for reading "morning," Hardy merely expanded Malmesbury. He has Pitt walk away "disquietedly," and lets Malmesbury be his own spokesman on the catastrophe at Ulm: "His labour's lost; and all our money gone!"

Pitt's next appearance, I, 5, v, is after the news of Trafalgar, when a bystander says he "looks hearty as a buck," the implication being that his courage has sustained him. Toasted at the Guildhall, he gives all credit to his countrymen:

> England has saved herself, by her exertions:
> She will, I trust, save Europe by her example!

[34] *Diaries*, edited by his grandson (London, 1844), IV, 340.

As noted by Rutland, these stirring words are almost verbatim from Stanhope (III, 364).

Then comes the yet greater blow of Austerlitz. Roseberry, whom Hardy follows, writes: "Melville and Ulm had borne heavily on Pitt; Austerlitz killed him" (256). Hardy did not fit in an allusion to Pitt's loyalty to his friend Melville, but in I, 6, vi, at Shockerwith House, he captured the effect of Austerlitz. Roseberry gives it briefly:

> Tradition says he was looking at a picture gallery when he heard the furious gallop of a horse. "That must be a courier," he exclaimed, "with news for me." When he had opened the packet he said, "Heavy news indeed," and asked for brandy. . . . He then asked for a map, and desired to be left alone.

Upon examining a map when he had returned home, he said, according to Roseberry, "Roll up that map . . .; it will not be wanted these ten years" (256).

Hardy made the most of his clues. Perhaps he went further than Roseberry justifies in making Pitt unusually perceptive in judging a work of art and quoting with ease from Churchill's *Characters*, but he knew that Pitt was a man of cultivated tastes. More important, Hardy saw in Roseberry's account the sanity that a great statesman had retained in spite of the burdens which were crushing him. The evil of war is epitomized when, at the moment of Pitt's conversation on the wonders created by civilization, the news is borne him at a gallop that that civilization is being ravaged in a senseless act of barbarism. Long before he wrote the scene Hardy had learned that the names of obscure points on the map of Europe had suddenly become household words because the terrain and the proximity of armies had destined them for fame. Such a place was Austerlitz, for which even a British statesman needed a map. And using poetic license, Hardy compressed chronology to include Pitt's weary pronouncement:

> Roll up that map. 'Twill not be needed now
> These ten years! Realms, laws, peoples, dynasties,
> Are churning to a pulp within the maw
> Of empire-making Lust and personal Gain!

Of all men whom he hated, Napoleon hated most William Pitt; but he could not despise him as he later despised Frederick and Alexander. Pitt hated Napoleon as evil incarnate. Unless his words are apocryphal, his "ten years" was prophetic.

For Pitt's death (I, 6, viii) Hardy apparently drew on all three biographers and at the same time invented dialogue and made minor changes in chronology. Roseberry's account of the death is a short summary, but, in Pitt's meeting with King George at Weymouth, Hardy had made use of Roseberry's earlier comment that the King at some time "went so far as to say that he should prefer civil war to Mr. Fox" (241). To drive home the seriousness for Pitt of the King's obstinacy Hardy now had Farquhar repeat his words: "Rather than Fox, why, give me civil war!" In Stanhope was an extract from his father's minutes, written January 26, 1806, three days after Pitt's death, and Hardy's version is close to this. Stanhope, for example, gives Pitt's words: "East; ah! that will do; that will bring him quick." [35] Hardy reads:

> When I said "East," he answered "That is well!
> Those are the breezes that will speed him home!"

Most famous, of course, were what Stanhope gave as Pitt's last words: "Oh, my country! how I leave my country!" (III, 391). To fit his iambic meter Hardy merely dropped the "oh"; he could not improve the lament.

The death of Pitt comes near the beginning of Hardy's action. The vignettes, however, give a perspective for the judging of men's motives, and they remind us that courage is found not only in the excitement of battle. Pitt's was a lonely ordeal. He was caught up in the web of circumstance; and yet, if at moments the human will were to assert its freedom, as Hardy had concluded with Schopenhauer that it sometimes could, then in the midst of defeat, with his world apparently spinning toward destruction, Pitt at moments exemplified free will—not by reshaping events, but by transcending them.

For Pitt only the defeat of Napoleon could ensure peace. Fox, on the contrary, was willing to make concessions. His position was delicate because when he became Foreign Secretary England had commitments to allies. Nevertheless, he worked with remarkable patience, and, though his attempts were futile, he won Napoleon's admiration. In his memoirs of the Emperor at St. Helena, Count Las Cases reproduces Napoleon's diatribe against Pitt and then continues with his praise of Fox: "As to Fox, one must not look for his

---

[35] *Life of the Right Honourable William Pitt* (London, 1879), III, 391; "him" refers to Pitt's emissary, Lord Harrowby.

model among the ancients. He is himself a model, and his principles
will sooner or later rule the world." [36] Perhaps even more remarkable
was George III's reversal. Fitzgerald speaks of the King's "bitter
hatred to Fox which, as was well said, in time became 'a rankling
ulcer.'" [37] But he later records from Grey Bennett's diary the
reconciliation in 1806:

> Fox, at his first interview, made a speech, in which he said he had been
> misrepresented, and yielded to no man in attachment to constitution for
> his Majesty. The King agitated, and said, "I believe you, Mr. Fox. I
> know you to be a man of honour, and thank you for what you have said"
> (427).

Hardy could not afford to develop the portrait of Fox in any fullness,
but there was one incident in his career which perhaps revealed him at
his best and provided a contrast with Napoleon. Reserving for the
following scene a summary of Fox's diplomatic attempts, Hardy gave
an entire scene, II, 1, i, to his rebuke of a volunteer assassin. The source
was a letter from Fox to Talleyrand March 6, 1806. It gained fame in
later years, and among histories in which it appeared were Capefigue's
L'Europe Pendant le Consulat et l'Empire de Napoléon (1840) and
Coquelle's *Napoléon et l'Angleterre,* 1803–1813, translated in 1904,
at the very time Hardy was beginning Part II.[38]
  In his letter the Foreign Minister summarized Gevrillière's plot:

> the scoundrel had the impudence to tell me, that to secure the peace of all
> the reigning houses it was necessary to do away with the leader of the
> French, and that a house had been hired at Passy for this purpose, whence
> this dastardly project could be executed with certainty and without any
> risk.

Hardy built this into many lines. His most interesting concern the
temptation. Having rejected the title of assassin, the Frenchman
justifies his offer:

[36] M. J. E. Las Cases, *Mémorial de Sainte Hélène. Journal of the Private Life and
Conversations of the Emperor Napoleon at Saint Helena* (4 vols.; London, 1823),
IV, 97. Cf., also B. E. O'Meara, *Napoleon in Exile; or, A Voice from St. Helena*
(2 vols.; London, 1822), II, 121.
  [37] *The Life of George the Fourth,* p. 40.
  [38] *L'Europe Pendant le Consulat* (Paris), VI, footnotes, 157–159; *Napoléon et
l'Angleterre* (Paris), pp. 82–83 (French original, pp. 90–92).

> My knowledge of your love of things humane,
> Things free, things fair, of truth, of tolerance,
> Right, justice, national felicity,
> Prompted belief and hope in such a man!

In the letter Fox wrote, "I am not ashamed to admit to you, who know me, that I was much embarrassed to find myself in conversation with a declared assassin." Hardy transforms this as a reply to Gevrillière's compliment:

> Sir, your unconscienced hardihood confounds me,
> And your mind's measure of my character
> Insults it sorely. * * *
> I have been led to prattle hopefully
> With a cut-throat confessed!

Finally, after ordering the man detained, Fox does remark, in some puzzlement:

> The man's indifference to his own vague doom
> Beamed out as one exalted trait in him,
> And showed the altitude of his rash dream!

As late as 1915 Hardy was to paste in his notebook an item on assassination—stating that the German War Book endorsed it.[39] Napoleon, as Hardy well knew, had allegedly employed assassins. Fox's comment, which is entirely Hardy's own, condemns the practice, whatever the motives. It may be said that his solution oversimplifies, since, once war itself is accepted, distinctions as to the relative morality of tactics become blurred. Nevertheless, the decisiveness of Fox in rejecting the Mephistophelean argument when the Will seemed to be impelling men toward barbarism is not alone a mark of his own greatness. If the hope of the Pities is to be justified—if the Will is to be rendered conscious—it may be only through the humanity of a Fox that the awakening can take place. It is the Pities who, in the next scene, about six months later, pronounce his epitaph:

> He was the friend of peace—did his great best
> To shed her balms upon humanity;
> And now he's gone! No substitute remains.

[39] Memoranda, I.

For his glimpses of George III, Hardy used the *Morning Post* and *Morning Chronicle*, Fitzgerald's *Life of George the Fourth*, and unidentified sources. The first two gave him the record of the King's activities at Weymouth; Fitzgerald helped with characterization and probably was the source of a few lines in II, 6, v, at Windsor. Any of several memoirs or histories could have told Hardy of the King's grief after the death of the Princess Amelia, his piety during his madness, his pleasure during those years in being accorded the recognition due a king, and his love of his subjects.[40]

By definition George III was a dynast, and therein lay the irony which demanded compassion. Though severely restricted as a constitutional monarch, he did have the power to interfere in such important matters as the formation of a cabinet. Yet by 1805 he was not altogether unlike King Lear. The labours of government were to be conducted by others while the King rode out to review the troops or watched his subjects grin through horse-collars. In his political partisanship, including his hatred of Fox, he was less a being above the melee than a common, frustrated mortal. And the courtly formality of his letters to the Prince of Wales could not disguise the anguish of an ineffectual father dealing with a hostile son.

To climax his portrait of the Monarch, Hardy chose a scene early in June, 1811, soon after the madness had returned. For one detail he may have drawn specifically on Fitzgerald, who speaks of Dr. Willis' having been called back to Windsor and adds, "At the sight of the doctor he gave a piteous shriek: 'Oh! John Willis again! God help me!' and fell on the ground in a fit" (477). Hardy reads, "(Finding Dr. Willis is among them he shrieks.) 'O, they are going to bleed me—yes, to bleed me!'"

In this scene George is reminiscent of Lear during and after his madness, and Hardy clearly intended the insanity to provide a commentary on the hurly-burly of the action beyond the walls of Windsor. A band outside is celebrating the victory of Albuera, oblivious of the carnage that has supplied it; and, to cheer the King by treating him as responsible for the good fortune, Halford congratulates him on "this glorious victory you have won." It is in such lines as his reply that Hardy is most at home and consequently at his best:

[40] All these, which are shown by Hardy, appear, for example in John H. Jesse's *Memoirs of the Court of England, The Life and Reign of King George the Third* (5 vols.; Boston, n.d.).

> He says I have won a battle? But I thought
> I was a poor afflicted captive here,
> In darkness lingering out my lonely days,
> Beset with terror of these myrmidons
> That suck my blood like vampires! Ay, ay, ay!—
> No aims left to me but to quicken death
> To quicklier please my son!—And yet he says
> That I have won a battle! O God, curse, damn!
> When will the speech of the world accord with truth,
> And men's tongues roll sincerely!

Hardy cannot resist pointing the moral, as a Gentleman remarks, aside:

> Faith, 'twould seem
> As if the madman were the sanest here!

The preceding scene has ended with a dirge by the Pities for those slain at Albuera, in which are repeated the cruel lines—

> Hide their hacked bones, Earth!—deep, deep, deep,
> Where harmless worms caress and creep.

Now, even before they have withdrawn from the presence of the tormented King, Halford is in a hurry to get back to town for a party at Mrs. Siddons', and Dr. Baillie is looking forward to a gala at Vauxhall; and the Prince Regent, so Baillie tells us, is "grumpy" at having to postpone his fête. Between these pieces of news from far and near we learn that the King is to be bled until he is unconscious so that, hopefully, he can regain his reason and reenter, if only fitfully, the world of sane men.

As a historical figure the King is much less important than Pitt or Fox in Hardy's epic. He does little to shape the action, and that little is negative. Nevertheless, in a tradition from the days when the judges ruled in the land he is a royal tragic protagonist. And in the light of Hardy's theme, where the best fate would be to have the Will become conscious, he exemplifies the second best—for man to sink into nescience.

"*When King* Geo IV went to the theatre during the Queen's trial a man in the gallery called out 'Where's your wife Georgie?'"— Hardy must have been familiar with anecdotes about the fourth George before he copied this note from Greville's memoirs in 1876 or before. Also from Greville he noted, "*Coarse jokes* of Geo IV at Brighton pavilion after dinner" and "*Geo IV*'s (hallucination) 'He thinks that he led the heavy dragoons at Salamanca.'"[41] While collecting background for *The Trumpet Major* Hardy jotted down the note: "Papers [M. Post?] [*sic*] for 1805 also contain a chronicle of the Prince of Wales's doings at Brighton. (In July he has a touch of gout)."[42]

It was inevitable that the Prince Regent should find a minor place in *The Dynasts,* and it was not unreasonable that Hardy should heighten the comedy of his at times fatuous existence. Changing the occasion to several years earlier, Hardy transformed his first note from Greville to open his own Opera-House scene, III, 4, viii: "Prinny, where's your wife?" calls a voice from the gallery. Hardy may also have picked up impressions from C. H. Gifford's *History of the Wars,* Volume II.[43] Though commenting only generally on the entertainment of Alexander and Frederick at the opera, Gifford has a detailed description of the elaborate festivities in honour of their visit to London. Whatever other sources were available to Hardy, the main authority was Fitzgerald's *Life of George the Fourth.*

Fitzgerald has his own moral tone. He disapproves of the Prince's betting on low sports, such as races of geese versus turkeys, and he is glad when he pours vast sums into horse racing instead. But the portrait he exposes is pathetically comic. George is an engagingly disingenuous egoist, who only wants to be admired by society and to be pampered by women. Yet he is officially humiliated by his father because of his debts and associates. He is involved in a petty feud with his royal spouse; and in the rivalry of the other women he resembles an enormous doll, torn and buffeted as they contest, not over him, but over the position his rank may confer on them. For a poet with an ironic bent his career was abundantly grotesque.

The first scene in which the Prince has a part, II, 2, iii, at the Marchioness of Salisbury's, reminds us that political alliances—this time between England and Spain—are conducted by envoys far

---

[41] Literary Notes, I, 37–38; from Fulke Greville, *The Greville Diary,* under dates of February 7, 1821; December 18, 1821; and November 9, 1829.

[42] Notes taken for "Trumpet Major," III, 18.

[43] *History of the Wars Occasioned by the French Revolution, from the Commencement of Hostilities in 1792, to the End of the Year 1816* (2 vols.; London, 1817). The history is item 293 in the Hodgson sales catalogue. Gifford was one of Hardy's sources for I, 4, v, and may have contributed to various scenes. Sometimes, though less extensive than other accounts, his are as inclusive as Hardy's own.

removed from the suffering of the people they represent. The Prince is
an outsider, depending on rumour, yet imagining himself at the very
center of policy making. War, for him, is a simple game, and the mere
voting of fifty millions will rid Spain of Napoleon. Hardy was free to
invent the dialogue, which is in the spirit of Fitzgerald. At his next
appearance, at the Royal Pavilion, II, 4, vi, George is almost dignified
and rather eloquent. There has been a great victory at a place "long
unknown," and so he exhorts his guests to find partners and make
merry till dawn. With the music in the background, one is reminded
of Dryden, for none but the brave deserve the fair; and, as we have
just learned, Englishmen have been supremely brave at Talavera.
In the following scene, in the assembly rooms, the Prince's eloquence
climaxes in a prediction of new victories—at Walcheren. Now, it was
known that Sheridan had helped his Royal Highness with his composition. Hardy gave the dramatist credit for his speeches as well; so
that, ironically comic as they are in the context of human anguish,
they are yet more ludicrous coming from a ventriloquist's puppet.

The inability of George III to accommodate his illness to the
convenience of his son was a vexation. As Fitzgerald tells the story,
the Prince "had now determined to exhibit such a gala to the country
as would make his name celebrated," and for the June 19, 1811, fête
at Carlton House he spared "nothing that could contribute to the
display of magnificence or state" (502). Among the numerous details
that Hardy could use were the "cutting and jostling among the fine
ladies to be in at the fête," the sending of invitations to the dead, a
rumour of the King's death that initially caused a postponement, and
especially the activities of the Prince's "wives." Caroline had been
excluded and, because seating was to be by rank, Mrs. Fitzherbert
was to come only as a private person. According to Fitzgerald neither
came. Caroline "made a jest on the matter, declaring she was like an
archbishop's wife, who does not partake in her husband's honours"
(505). Hardy altered the phrase for his meter and caught the spirit of a
good many pages of his source by adding, "Funny me" (II, 6, vi). As
for Mrs. Fitzherbert, Fitzgerald reports that either that evening or the
next she went to Devonshire House, where, "in passing through the
rooms, she saw the Prince and Lady Hertford in a tête-à-tête conversation, and nearly fainted . . .; but, taking a glass of water, she recovered and passed on" (506). Hardy knew that neither had come to
the fête, but he needed them; consequently, the Spirit Ironic, arguing

that curiosity would win out over dignity, pronounces, "So deem them here." Taking the Devonshire incident as his guide, Hardy let the now flustered Prince refer to Mrs. Fitzherbert in a context that unintentionally reflects on her virtue:

> There have been such damned mistakes made in sending out the cards that the biggest w—— in London might be here. She's watching Lady Hertford, that's what she's doing. For all their indifference, both of them are as jealous as two cats over one tom.
>
> *Somebody whispers that a lady has fainted up-stairs.*
>
> That's Maria, I'll swear! She's always doing it. Whenever I hear of some lady fainting about upon the furniture at my presence, and sending for a glass of water, I say to myself, There's Maria at it again, by God! (II, 6, vii).

By a shift in chronology Hardy has had the rumour of the King's death arrive at the fête itself, eliciting from the Prince, "Dead? Then my fête is spoilt, by God!" The report is unfounded, but with the new shock, he can only lament, "God, I begin to loathe the whole curst show!" Hardy could not end Part II on so minor a theme and so brought in the Spirits to narrate some current history and to philosophize. Including in his world-view what has just been acted out before us, Years sums up:

> No less through regal puppet-shows
> The rapt Determinator throes,
> That neither good nor evil knows!

But Pities, nevertheless, ends on a note of hope.

Caroline is either an actual or a felt presence throughout many pages in Fitzgerald. Having introduced her at the fête, Hardy brought her back as a cause of misery for her husband about three years later. Here, in the scene at the Opera-House (III, 4, viii), he telescoped incidents to catch the essence of the Royal conflict. The occasion was June 11, 1814, when the Prince was host to the King of Prussia and the Emperor of Russia. We have noted the antedating of the remark in Greville. Hardy also took freedoms with Fitzgerald. Recounting the affair, the biographer had the Princess decline to accept the applause of the pit, with the comment, "My dear, Punch's wife is nobody when Punch is present." To this Hardy added only the intensive, *himself*. But in Fitzgerald when the Prince bows to the audience and his greeting is interpreted as for the Princess, she does not return it; in Hardy she starts a comedy of misunderstanding on the part of the

Emperor, accompanying her act with her broken English "Mine God, then; I will bow too!"

In speaking of "these domestic broils" of 1813, Fitzgerald provides a charming illustration of the Prince Regent's relative values: "Some one descanting, in his presence, on the victories of Lord Wellington 'in the north,' he burst out, after his favorite style: 'D——n the north, and d——n the south, and d——n Wellington; the question is, how am I to be rid of this d——d Princess of Wales?'" (577). Since Hardy changed the circumstances, he altered the terms, but not the spirit: "Oh, damn the peace, and damn the war, and damn Boney, and damn Wellington's victories!—the question is, how am I to get over this infernal woman!" To Fitzgerald's description of the Princess' leaving the Opera-House Hardy added a few flourishes, including "Three cheers for a woman wronged!"

The giving of a little recognition to the Prince Regent could be justified on historical grounds. It can be defended more validly for its pertinence to Hardy's theme. The Will acts without consciousness, but through human minds. If it is to become conscious, human effort will possibly assist in the awakening. Along with Frederick and Alexander, the Spanish monarchs, the clubmen, some persons in Wessex, and others scattered about western Europe, the Prince represents the inertia that must be overcome. The point could be made, to be sure, in less space than Hardy allotted. As to why he let the Prince so much occupy the stage—well, Hardy was a gloomy man, but he had, nevertheless, a certain zest for humour.

DIPLOMACY, STRATEGY, AND POUNDS STERLING

Hardy selected among battles and the machinations of statesmen with an eye to his theme. But he had to suggest the political and military milieu in which events took place. Before a given battle there were fencing manoeuvres, involving lesser battles, and there was sometimes an attempt to co-ordinate the strategy of several armies. Meanwhile, during both the fighting and the brief cessations, the diplomats were scurrying about Europe, most often having started from London or Paris. Half promises were made, understandings were assumed on the basis of earlier treaties made in other circumstances, documents were signed which were ambiguous as to key issues, an agreement with one nation was interpreted in the light of one or more agreements with others. Allies were suspicious, even contemptuous of one another, and alliances shifted. At one time England was at war with Spain; soon the two countries were together fighting France. Again, England attacked Denmark, a natural ally. Francis of Austria fought against, then with, and once more against France. After their armies had slaughtered each other Alexander became Napoleon's admiring friend—and the invasion of Russia soon followed. While the Emperor was at Elba dissension among his enemies threatened a new alignment, with France wooed as an ally. Money flowed from London, to be wasted on the Continent, duchies and princedoms were created or changed hands to satisfy petty vanity, recriminations afflicted the allies, and bitter rivalry obsessed Napoleon's generals.

All these manifestations of confusion and of the overweening ambition of dynasts were substance for Hardy's epic. They demanded illustration, and this Hardy could sometimes offer in scenes given over to single examples. But he had also to provide transition and to give the context in which his highlighted actions occurred. To do this authentically was by no means easy.

In the works which Hardy can be proved to have consulted there is a great deal on the preliminaries to the major campaigns, and, especially in Thiers, a fair amount on financial conditions, civilian and military morale, and diplomacy. Hardy's problem was to determine the essential impressions and to choose specific facts which would succinctly dramatize them. We must remember that he was not a historical scholar, but a poet. Though he did read thousands of pages, he was always seeking the symbolic detail. At the same time, though he was willing to telescope or otherwise modify events for artistic convenience, he valued historicity. He would have been willing to surmise Balboa's thoughts; but, had he mistakenly attributed them to stout Cortez, he would have been aggrieved by the error.

As we follow Hardy's tracks—the markings in his books, the notes, both in the manuscript and in the printed text, and the similarities of phrasing that indicate his sources—we sense the task that confronted him. A striking example concerns the events which led up to Trafalgar. Thiers, Hardy's primary authority, reviews the complex manoeuvres of the French fleet during the preceding months and discusses Napoleon's relations, through emissaries, with Villeneuve. But the information is mixed with other matters and presupposes acquaintance with earlier chapters of the monumental work. Thiers develops one aspect of his subject and then another, and it is difficult or even impossible to establish a precise chronology as one turns from one train of incidents to a parallel one. If Hardy consulted Gifford at this point, he found him yet more frustrating; and others, such as Lanfrey, only dipped in here and there, with no pretense of completeness.

Elsewhere in Thiers and the other historians the discussion of a given stage in the relationship of the nations involves allusions to previous treaties and the obscure activities of specific diplomats. To untangle these and understand what is being said one must go back at least to the Peace of Amiens, three years before *The Dynasts* begins. Starting with that treaty of March 27, 1802, which was intended to redistribute lands among the European powers, but which became only a hollow instrument, one would need to tie together a network of events and, indeed, to write his own history. Hardy's interest did not extend so far as that. As he told Collins, "Some of [the histories] were very long and not very good. You may be sure I have not read them since." [44] Even in the authors whom he liked Hardy must have found it irksome to run down elusive facts. The consequence was that he sometimes narrated details whose full meaning was apparently unknown to him, and in a few instances he did confuse facts.

Illustrative of the discrepancies are lines in scenes I, 3, i and II, 1, ii. In Gifford (I, 453) Napoleon is shown not to have been offended by a letter from Mulgrave rather than one in the name of George III himself. Hardy, in contrast, represents him as petulant:

> My knock at George's door
> With bland inquiries why his royal hand
> Withheld due answer to my friendly lines,
> And tossed the irksome business to his clerks * * * .

Scene II, 1, ii, "The Route between London and Paris," is almost exclusively a summary of fruitless negotiations between Napoleon and Fox. According to Rumours, England has insisted on making Russia a party to any agreement, but France has refused and then "secretly with—Russia plights her troth!" In Coquelle the story is much more intricate, involving Sicily and revealing that Napoleon yielded on the question of Russia's participation. Moreover, "plights her troth" is too strong a term, since Russia still had ties with Prussia

---

[44] Vere H. Collins, *Talks with Thomas Hardy at Max Gate* 1920–1922 (New York: Doubleday, Doran, 1928), p. 43.

and was soon to fight France. The patient efforts of Fox, through Yarmouth, to achieve peace and the subsequent attempt by Lauderdale are only obliquely hinted as Hardy focuses on the disillusionment of Fox. His account conveys a very different impression from Coquelle's,[45] and it demonstrates the vexations in trying to dramatize whole chapters of political history. On the other hand, its rapid recitative of the futile bargaining fits the tone of a world spiraling downward to disaster.

How Hardy picked up background information which could be interpolated here and there is revealed in some of the marginal linings in his books. In Capefigue (V, 213), he doubly scored "Le théâtre des mouvements diplomatiques de l'Europe était Londres, d'où partaient toujours les inspirations du continent." In Thiers, Lanfrey, and elsewhere he would have found scattered passages of similar import. From these he built his general impression of the dominant role of England. In I, 1, v, "London. The House of a Lady of Quality," a scene indebted also to Thiers (V, Book 21) and Lanfrey, Hardy dramatized Capefigue's words. A lady serves as spokesman:

> The chequerboard of diplomatic moves
> Is London, all the world knows: here are born
> All inspirations of the Continent—＊＊＊.

Among the considerable number of markings in Lanfrey several bear on diplomatic intrigue. Two concern plans in January, 1805, for a coalition against Napoleon (III, 275). Hardy may previously have read about the origins of the coalition, but he was now pinning down information which might prove useful. Since his own work starts with events a few months later, this became background material, to be summarized in I, 1, v. Most of the scene is intended to supply the reader with some notion of the diplomatic activity that has occurred, and a Minister reviews the terms of the coalition as if they were fresh news in London. Though the sources of Hardy's information were scarcely more extensive than his own account, he succeeded in leaving the impression of drawing on a bountiful stock of diplomatic knowledge.

Another marked passage (III, 405) describes the economic bondage of Prussia to England. Hardy drew on it for Napoleon's repeated

---

[45] *Napoléon et l'Angleterre*, p. 91 ff. It is slightly closer to P. Lanfrey, *Histoire de Napoléon Ier* (5 vols.; Paris, 1876)—in the Memorial Library.

animadversions on England's use of gold to enslave her allies. He marked Lanfrey's unqualified pronouncement: "Au fond son grand objectif n'avait pas cessé un instant d'être l'Angleterre, parce qu'il sentait avec raison que là se trouvait le vrai foyer des résistances continentales" (IV, 114).[46] This summary, which precedes Lanfrey's narration of events at Tilsit, epitomizes Hardy's own view of Napoleon's fury against England, most bitterly expressed at Berlin and Tilsit (II, 1, vi and viii).

In Roseberry's *Pitt* (156 ff.) Hardy marked a series of condemnations of political Europe after the Revolution. Included was the simple statement "Europe was rotten." Roseberry went on to illustrate, country by country, and Hardy followed him with his pencil.

To what extent Hardy used *Oeuvres de Napoléon Bonaparte*[47] is conjectural. Here was a most convenient source of documentary evidence, as it contained the bulletins issued from Napoleon's headquarters. The French historians drew from them, and Hardy demonstrates familiarity with them. They provided firsthand proof of Napoleon's hatred of England; indeed, the passage in Lanfrey was ultimately, if not directly based on them. In one instance Hardy merely paraphrased the most important anti-British bulletin of all, the "Décret constitutif du blocus continental—En notre camp impérial de Berlin, le 21 novembre, 1806."[48] It announced that England was to be barred from Continental ports, to be blockaded at home, and to have her ships confiscated at sea. In II, 1, vi, the "voice" of the Emperor reels off the details, which are hardly more than a rearrangement of the original document.

These are but a few glimpses of Hardy conning his books. The Memorial Library provides a goodly number. One sees the poet searching for both the impression and the concrete fact, sometimes marking something which seems obvious, noting an occasional phrase for its sweeping pronouncement, and again seizing on a complete document, as with the Berlin decree and the proclamation outlawing Napoleon upon his return from Elba. But in examining what Hardy made of the pages of information on diplomacy and the general political and military conditions one senses at all times the hurry of the

[46] Unmarked passages in Lanfrey roughly match Hardy's dramatization of Napoleon's attempt to divide the allies (I, 6, v) and of his betrayal of Turkey (II, 1, viii).

[47] In 5 vols.; Paris, 1821.

[48] *Ibid.*, IV, 112–115.

poet, eager to have done with the complexities and to achieve a conclusion. For the reader of limited background some of Hardy's allusions must remain almost totally obscure. A reference to Amiens, to Erfurt, to Lunéville is but the naming of a treaty or a manifesto, not a description of its substance. Yet, if such a reader will accept the urgency of Hardy's style as evidence of their importance, the names become resounding echoes of tragic dynastic events. No, Hardy was not a scholar, and yet, even in the morass of diplomatic intrigue and counterintrigue, he had a feeling for essential truth.

Melancholy Trafalgar

Almost ten years of warfare were to succeed the defeat of the French and Spanish ships at Trafalgar. Had Nelson lost, there would still have remained sufficient naval strength to withstand any invasion threat. Besides, Napoleon had withdrawn his army from Boulogne and won a victory at Ulm before the loss at sea. But the decisive victory of England was, nevertheless, significant. Whatever boasts Napoleon might later make, as in his Berlin decree, he was henceforth virtually defenseless against British devastation at sea and the transporting of men and supplies to the Continent.

Trafalgar had long been a symbol of the heroic spirit of Britain, and for Hardy it had additional significance because its tone had been set by the opposing admirals. As he read on the events leading up to the battle—and his major text, as he stated, was Thiers[49]—he discovered that he had not one hero, but two. Thiers' protagonist is Napoleon, and yet in vignettes he sometimes enters sympathetically into the tragic dilemmas of others. One such is Villeneuve. Thiers introduces the French admiral as "bon soldat et bon citoyen." Having described his discouragement at the condition of his men and his vessels, he builds up to a sense of despair: "son âme, tendue par le désespoir, souhaitait le péril, presque la défaite . . . ." Finally, after the flagship, "Le Bucentaure," is out of action, Thiers employs the simple epithet "l'infortuné."[50] For Hardy this gallant, melancholy figure was

[49] "Through this tangle of intentions the writer has in the main followed Thiers, whose access to documents would seem to authenticate his details of the famous scheme for England's ruin" (footnote to I, 2, ii).

[50] L. A. Thiers, *Histoire du Consulat et de l'Empire* (20 vols.; Paris, 1845–1862), VI, 132, 142, 161 and 162. Hardy also used the English translation, which will be cited only when there is evidence that he drew from it.

perhaps even more appealing than Nelson. The English admiral was an epitome of the Byronic tradition. Villeneuve was a romantic, too, but he was also a precursor of the post-Darwinian age—a man who could be valiant in his certainty of defeat, and whose despair sprang not from his own failure, but from the nature of the Universe.

For Hardy the Trafalgar episode became a rigorous artistic challenge. He had to give enough paraphernalia to lend magnitude to the incident, then to dramatize a battle which was not only violent but technically complex, to drop the curtain suddenly on the fury and descend to the cockpit for the memorable phrases of the dying Nelson, and then to avoid anticlimax in bringing all to a close with the suicide of Villeneuve.

The preliminaries are, by themselves, of little interest, and yet without them the great scenes would lose in stature. It is enough to know what the issues and basic facts were and how Hardy used them to amplify his story. Napoleon's strategy consisted of leading the British navy to desert the Channel in following Villeneuve to Martinique, after which the full strength of the French and Spanish Atlantic fleets would return to protect the crossing from Boulogne to England. De Bourrienne (II, 207) denied that an invasion was intended, and W. M. Sloane, whose four-volume *Life of Napoleon Bonaparte* (1901), Hardy used for later incidents, insisted that the invasion was only a threat to keep England from attacking on the Continent.[51] But Hardy accepted the traditional view, for which there was extensive evidence in Alison;[52] Capefigue, whom he cited in a footnote to I, 3, i, drawn from a footnote in *L'Europe*, V, 172; and, of course, Thiers.[53] In I, 1, ii—"Paris. Office of the Minister of Marine"

[51] *Life of Napoleon* (London: Macmillan, 1901), II, 214. Count Miot de Mélito, in his *Memoirs* (2 vols.; London, 1881), I, 581, says that Ireland may have been the invasion goal.

[52] Archibald Alison, *History of Europe from the Commencement of the French Revolution in 1789 to the Restoration of the Bourbons in 1815* (20 vols.; London, 1847–1848). There are few marks in Hardy's copy. He may well have bought the set after using another.

[53] John S. Memes, *Memoirs of the Empress Josephine* (New York, 1844), p. 233, reports, only to reject it, Napoleon's own denial of intent to invade. Claude-François Méneval, *Napoléon et Marie-Louise. Souvenirs Historiques* (3 vols.; Paris, 1843), I, 126, speaks of the practice in embarking and disembarking and insists that everything was ready for sailing. O'Meara, *Napoleon in Exile*, I, 349–350, says that Napoleon expected to invade and to secure demo-

—Admiral Decrès reads a letter of instructions from Napoleon which sums up the general strategy. It is founded on no single passages in the histories, but is a composite of a series of letters by Napoleon, Decrès, and Villeneuve, and, even more, of the record of what actually happened.

Scene I, 1, iv—"The Harbour of Boulogne"—describes the extensiveness of the preparations and the rehearsals. It prepares for a second scene at Boulogne, I, 2, iii, which, to judge from a date given in *Oeuvres,* took place in early August, 1805.[54]

Between these two scenes we have been given a significant introduction to Napoleon in a detached event for which Hardy prepared in the Parisian scene. The Emperor's coronation at Milan was historically important because, as Memes noted—and Hardy agreed—the Austro-Russian coalition was "mainly caused by his assumption of the Lombard crown." [55] Hardy also wanted the coronation in order to demonstrate Napoleon's regal arrogance and to hint of the tragic tenor of what was to come.[56] For the scene, I, 1, vi, Hardy has details not in Thiers, Gifford, or Memes, who describe the event. The words with which the Emperor grasped the crown, however, were well known and, with variation, appear in all three.[57] Hardy omitted the anticlimactic crowning of Josephine, but added a reproach from Pities, whispered into Napoleon's ear. So we have the first manifestation of an equivalent of Buchanan's Famulus. Hubris and something akin to the Eumenides have thus already appeared.

In I, 2, iii, we are brought into Napoleon's presence for the first time in his capacity as general. The scene matches Thiers only in its

---

cratic support in London. Hardy knew all three gossiping accounts. Napoleon's words in I, 2, iii, may have their source in O'Meara:

> Descend on London, and the while my men
> Salute the dome of Paul's I cut the knot
> Of all Pitt's coalitions; setting free
> From bondage to a cold manorial caste
> A people who await it.

[54] *Oeuvres,* I, 13 ff. Napoleon visited Boulogne, August 2.

[55] *Memoirs of the Empress Josephine,* 303.

[56] As we have noted, Hardy believed that on the roof of the Cathedral of Milan, in 1887, he "conceived the Milan Cathedral scene." "Conceived of a scene" would be more accurate.

[57] In Memes, *Memoirs of the Empress Josephine,* "Dio mi l'ha data—guai a chi la tocca" (302).

major direction. Its intent is twofold—to review naval activities and the political situation in Europe and to show Napoleon as a military strategist. If we had only this evidence, we should admire the brilliance with which he plots in some detail the immediate steps for freeing the Channel for his invasion while outlining, as an alternative, the successive overthrow of Austria and Russia. He is, indeed, planning moves well ahead in his game of chess. Already, however, in the preceding scene, we have learned that the ships on which he is depending are "rotten." So we have the first evidence of the Nemesis that will bring his downfall. He cannot be everywhere, and he cannot conceive of weaknesses where he needs strength. Soldiers under his personal command, as Hardy knew, had seemed to perform miracles. What he was expecting from Villeneuve—not to win, but to delay the enemy for twenty-four hours—was, so far as Napoleon could tell, a reasonable performance, not a miracle. Napoleon, the general, was to have perhaps average luck over the years in relying on his officers, but he was to wait in vain for Grouchy at Waterloo. So we now have, not a full-length portrait of the Emperor, but certain major characteristics which fit him into the pattern of ancient tragedy. As the picture is developed it will take on nineteenth-century connotation.

Meanwhile, in I, 2, i—"The Dockyard, Gibraltar"—we have been introduced to Nelson, and in I, 2, ii—"Off Ferrol"—we have met Villeneuve. These scenes, together with I, 3, i—"Boulogne. The Château at Pont-de-Briques"—pick up background history, but more especially they focus on the world-weariness of the two admirals. As for the history, most of it is in Thiers, scattered over many pages, in the bitterly anti-Napoleonic Lanfrey, in Capefigue, as Hardy's footnote recognized, and among others, in Southey.[58] Again, however,

---

[58] Collingwood's warning that the French will probably attack Ireland would appear, for example, to come from Southey's *Life of Nelson* (New York, 1871), p. 279. Southey also suggests that the voyage to the West Indies was a mere ruse. In Notes taken for "Trumpet Major," III, 16, Hardy had quoted from the *Morning Post*, May 2, 1805: "It is suspected by gov^t that the enemy meditates some serious designs upon Ireland." In addition to the intricate account in Thiers and Lanfrey on Napoleon's dissatisfaction with Villeneuve and tentative plans for relieving him, Hardy may have had an essentially primary source in *Memoirs of the History of France During the Reign of Napoleon Written at Saint Helena and Published from the Original Manuscripts Corrected by the Emperor* (7 vols.; London, 1822). Drawing on "Book of Instructions and Orders. Navy. Instructions for Admiral Villeneuve" for August 13 and 15, 1805, its summary is close to remarks of Napoleon in I, 3, i.

as with the record of diplomatic activity, it was not what amounts to recitative that seriously interested Hardy. The naval strategy he presents is naturally oversimplified and, even so, in part obscure. But in the midst of events his two heroes begin the last act in their tragic dramas.

Hardy had certainly read other accounts of Nelson's life besides Southey's, but the portrait he offers preceding Trafalgar can be traced to Southey, where he found far more than he could use. The interest for us lies in the subtle alteration in tone with which he put his colours on his canvas.

Southey is both moral and pious. He treats Lady Hamilton respectfully, but deplores not only her alienating Nelson from his family ties, but her totally unromantic meddling in affairs of state. The most notorious instance was her encouraging a hasty court-martial of Caraccioli to please the Neapolitan Court:

> Doubtless, the British admiral seemed to himself to be acting under a rigid sense of justice; but, to all other persons, it was obvious, that he was influenced by an infatuated attachment—a baneful passion, which destroyed his domestic happiness, and now, in a second instance, stained ineffaceably his public character (181).

A few pages earlier Southey has summed up Nelson's feelings and inserted his own moral interpretation:

> this most unfortunate attachment ... brought with it its punishment. Nelson was dissatisfied with himself; and, therefore, weary of the world. This feeling he now frequently expressed. "There is no true happiness in this life," said he; "and in my present state I could quit it with a smile."

Southey then quotes a letter to Nelson's "old friend Davison": "Believe me, my only wish is to sink with honour into the grave; and when that shall please God, I shall meet death with a smile." The letter continues with much more of the same, verging on sentimental self-glorification (176–177). But Southey indicates that, when he was called to take command, Nelson regained the enthusiasm which he had lost years before. In an entry in his journal he accepted the possibility of death, but wrote first, "May the great God, whom I adore, enable me to fulfil the expectations of my country! and if it is His good pleasure that I should return, my thanks will never cease being offered up to the throne of His mercy" (284). In short, the love affair of Southey's Nelson lacks the glamour of Antony's. It brings a penitence which wins his biographer's sad approval, and then yields to a new excitement when Nelson has an opportunity to be every inch a sailor once again.

Hardy's Nelson as he talks with Collingwood is a retouched portrait. Though he will fight bravely, he has not been lifted from his depression. It was consistent with Hardy's view of life that he should remain melancholy till the end. As for his sins, they are private ones, whose

> unworded censure * * *
> Makes all my public service lustreless,

and Lady Hamilton is a figure of romance:

> I fear I am much condemned
> For those dear Naples and Palermo days,
> And her who was the sunshine of them all! . . .
> He who is with himself dissatisfied,
> Though all the world find satisfaction in him,
> Is like a rainbow-coloured bird gone blind,
> That gives delight it shares not. Happiness?
> It's the philosopher's stone no alchemy
> Shall light on in this world I am weary of.—
> Smiling I'd pass to my long home to-morrow
> Could I with honour, and my country's gain.

The parallels of phrasing in the two versions are obvious, but the differences are significant. In Hardy we have a lover who is perhaps even more a Lancelot than an Antony; and instead of an author of conventional pious platitudes in a journal written as for posterity, we have a poet and something of a philosopher.

Yet Hardy made a distinction between his melancholy Englishman and his disillusioned Admiral of the French Fleet. In I, 3, i, at the Château, Decrès contrasts them. Though he is defending his friend, he is in part Hardy's spokesman. In the scene off Ferrol, Villeneuve has revealed both his courage and his humanity:

> Yet I would die to-morrow—not ungladly—
> So far removed is carcase-care from me.
> For no self do these apprehensions spring,
> But for the cause * * *.
> I'll not command a course so conscienceless.
> Rather I'll stand, and face Napoléon's rage * * *.

Now, having spoken tribute to Villeneuve's patriotism, Decrès continues:

> Yet no less
> Is it his drawback that he sees too far.
> And there are times, Sire, when a shorter sight
> Charms Fortune more. A certain sort of bravery
> Some people have—to wit, this same Lord Nelson—
> Which is but fatuous faith in one's own star
> Swoln to the very verge of childishness,
> (Smugly disguised as putting trust in God,
> A habit with these English folk); whereby
> A headstrong blindness to contingencies
> Carries the actor on, and serves him well
> In some nice issues clearer sight would mar.
> Such eyeless bravery Villeneuve has not;
> But, Sire, he is no coward.

It is the French Admiral who, in lines appropriated from Méry's novel, is to speak the epitaph of the heroes at Trafalgar:

> How hideous are the waves, so pure this dawn!—
> Red-frothed; and friends and foes all mixed therein.[59]

(I, 5, iii)

These are really the sentiments of the Pities, uttered by a victim of the Will.

When the battle is over and the Admiral is alone at Rennes, Hardy lets him describe himself with the epithet bestowed on him by Thiers—"Unfortunate Villeneuve." A paraphrase of the ancient lament—"Better, far better, no percipience here"—three lines from Lanfrey of thankfulness that he has no child to "groan beneath the burden of my name," [60] and a final "ungrateful master; generous foes; Farewell!"—these words and determined stabs with a dagger end the days of one who in the moil of an active life has remained a poet.[61] There is no

[59] François J. P. A. Méry, *Trafalgar* (Paris, 1865), p. 9: "La mer si joyeuse le matin, était hideuse à voir, elle roulait d'horribles épaves dans une écume rouge, elle engloutissait les blessés et les rejetait cadavres à sa surface . . . ." Méry's novel is only briefly concerned with Trafalgar. Hardy may have been led to it by the title.

[60] Hardy quotes the original in a footnote.

[61] O'Meara in *Napoleon in Exile*, gives us what he states was Napoleon's version—that after his defeat Villeneuve studied anatomy to determine the location of his heart; then he placed a large pin at the proper spot, "shoved it in

allusion to recent scientific or metaphysical thought, and the wish for impercipience is classical. Yet, by intensifying ever so slightly the shading in the portrait given him by Thiers and Lanfrey, Hardy has presented a man of late nineteenth-century sensibility. Of all the characters in his epic Villeneuve has a spirit most attuned to the voice of the Pities, and Hardy lets this Spirit murmur his epitaph:

> May his sad sunken soul merge into nought
> Meekly and gently as a breeze at eve!   (I, 5, vi)

Indeed, Villeneuve is in philosophic outlook most like the poet himself.

Before this lonely scene, where a man is confronted with the essence of percipience and the thought of its annihilation, the great battle has been fought, with its climax, the death in victory of Nelson.

Hardy's borrowing on Trafalgar reveals his usual eclecticism.[62] As we have indicated, the major source for things French was Thiers. Certain manoeuvres, including the intervention of the "Redoubtable" to protect the "Bucentaure" are most fully described in Brenton.[63] Interpasses of ships and the sunshine on the sails (I, 5, i) are indebted to Alison. Villeneuve's sentiments before the battle are closest to Lanfrey. His exhortation to his men to board the "Victory" is from Méry. Nelson's praise of Collingwood is in both Brenton and Southey. And the scene of Nelson's death is, of course, from the famous account by his surgeon, Beatty. Among details which do not appear in the printed sources is the rescue of the naked wife of the captain of the "Achille" (I, 5, iv). Since there were many women on the ships, one may agree with Rutland that Hardy drew on local traditional stories. The grotesquerie of the "mermaid" is the kind of merriment that accentuates the uncivilized horror of the scene.

---

to the head, penetrated his heart, and expired" (I, 56–57). Either Napoleon or O'Meara is confused about the initial directive to the Admiral, for the exiled Emperor is quoted: "for I had ordered him not to sail, or to engage the English." He is said to have added, "He need not have done it . . . as he was a brave man, though possessed of no talent." There was also a rumour that Napoleon had had Villeneuve assassinated; Southey believed it. Hardy antedated his scene and so indicated in a footnote.

[62] Cf., also W. R. Rutland, *Thomas Hardy: A Study of His Writings and Their Background* (Oxford: Blackwell, 1938), pp. 304 ff.; and "The Sources of 'The Dynasts,'" *Times Literary Supplement*, November 13, 1937, p. 866.

[63] Edward P. Brenton, *The Naval History of Great Britain from the Year 1783 to 1836* (2 vols.; rev. ed.; London, 1837).

From the histories Hardy got the stirring signals, first from Villeneuve—

> Each captain, petty officer, and man
> Is only at his post when under fire—

and next—"England expects every man will do his duty." To such gallant words he added, adapting from Méry,

> We'll dash our eagle on the English deck,
> And swear to fetch it!

And, as we have seen, he took also from Méry the graphic lines on the madness of the waters.

There are small discrepancies among Hardy's sources as to what happened on the quarter-deck of the "Victory." He must have known, too, that there were divergent reports of Nelson's last words. There was, for example, the November 7, 1805, edition of *The Times*, a special gazette, from the Admiralty Office, quite different from Hardy's version.[64] For his own account of events on the quarter-deck Hardy drew on Beatty, who was not present, and somewhat more on Brenton, who, like Southey, depended in part on Beatty. For the death scene in the cockpit he trusted Beatty. He must have recognized that even Beatty's eyewitness report had adapted actual events to the ideal; to this he would have said amen. Even when he himself was drawing heavily on Beatty, Hardy innovated in arrangement, proportion, and tone to shape things yet closer to the ideal. Indeed, as Rutland has remarked, some of the best lines are entirely his own. Thus, knowing that love of country was, first of all, love of one's own home and countryside, he let Captain Hardy reminisce to Nelson about things "down Wessex way." This was the same sentiment that, with an ironic twist, he was to use for a deserter thinking of home at Astorga.

The famous "Kiss me, Hardy," and "Thank God, I have done my duty" fitly mark the death of a hero. In the chorus of Spirits that follows, Hardy restates his philosophic themes. Quoting the *Trachiniae*, Pities laments the suffering endured by Nelson just before death. To Years he protests:

> But out of tune the Mode and meritless
> That quickens sense in shapes whom, thou hast said,
> Necessitation sways!   (I, 5, iv)

[64] In his Notes taken for "Trumpet Major" (III, 29 ff.), Hardy quoted extracts from the *Morning Chronicle* on Trafalgar.

He is chided by the older Years in lines that remind one of Hardy's
reading from Lucretius to Hartmann:

> Nay, blame not! For what judgment can ye blame?—
> In that immense unweeting Mind is shown
> One far above forethinking; prócessive,[65]
> Rapt, superconscious; a Clairvoyancy
> That knows not what It knows, yet works therewith.—
> The cognizance ye mourn, Life's doom to feel,
> If I report it meetly, came unmeant,
> Emerging with blind gropes from impercipience
> By listless sequence—luckless, tragic Chance,
> In your more human tongue.

After yet another lament by Pities that man was not permitted to
remain without "cognition," the Chorus of the Years implies a
teleological hope:

> O heap not blame on that in-brooding Will;
> O pause, till all things all their days fulfil!

For all who have died at Trafalgar and for Villeneuve the Will has
offered no hint of what time may fulfil. For them death is final, and
they have accepted its certainty only because, though fettered, they
have transcended the Will which has impelled them. The fact that their
lives have constituted but a moment in the humanly inconceivable
duration of the Universe magnifies the poignancy of their fates.

It represents no anticlimax to turn back from the prose and poetry
of Hardy to the pages of Thiers. Here and there in the Trafalgar scenes
the English poet had taken his facts from his French history, but he
was drawn to it most of all by its poetic eloquence. So we may conclude this act in Hardy's drama with what amount to choruses in
Thiers. The first sums up the battle itself: "Jamais plus grande scène
d'horreur ne s'était vue sur les flots" (VI, 172). The second, from a
graphic sentence almost a page in length, completes the episode:
"et le chef vaincu projetant le suicide comme seul refuge à sa douleur,
telle fut, nous le répétons, cette fatale bataille de Trafalgar, avec ses
causes, ses résultats, ses tragiques aspects" (VI, 181). On the causes
and results Hardy, because of the limitations of his epic form, was at a

---

[65] *Prócessive* replaced "purposive" after the 1910 edition. But "purposive"
did not mean teleologically omniscient.

disadvantage. The two writers were alike great on the sublime proportions of the tragedy.

PATHOS IN THE PENINSULA

The war in the Peninsula was secondary for Napoleon to that in the
east. The forces in a given battle were much smaller, and the Emperor
normally tried to manage the strategy through his lieutenants. Yet the
struggle was important, as he could hold France itself only by pre-
venting attack from the west. As for the British, until Napoleon's
abdication in April, 1814, though their money helped elsewhere, their
armies were committed mainly in Portugal and Spain.

Hardy, of course, recognized the military value of the campaign.
More significantly, he found in it varied evidence for his theme. The
British officers and common soldiers were no braver than others;
indeed, the armies all over Europe had their share of stragglers,
deserters, pillagers, drunkards, and other desperate men; and Wellington evidently felt that he was especially afflicted with the dregs of
mankind. In Roseberry's *Pitt* Hardy had marked:

> "The French system of conscription brings together a fair specimen of
> all classes; our army is composed of the scum of the earth," said the Duke
> of Wellington, with more accuracy than gratitude. So it was, and so it was
> treated . . . it was scourged and bullied and abused as if outside humanity
> (159).

But Hardy knew the British soldiers better than the others; he felt
closer to them as men. Freezing to death was the same, whether in
Spain or Russia, but sometimes Hardy could find in the Peninsular
campaign a special quality akin to that of Wessex life in his novels.
He tried, of course, to do justice to other aspects of the campaign.
Directly or obliquely they all illuminated the lot of suffering humanity
—foolish and heroic—impelled by the unconscious Will.

The first scene is in February, 1808, as sixty thousand French
soldiers file up the mountain passes not far from Bayonne. This is
some twenty-eight months after Trafalgar. The next-to-last scene
brings us again near the border November 10, 1813, and the final one
records the symbolic lowering and raising of flags April 28, 1814,
once more at Bayonne. On the canvases Hardy paints for us to typify
those six years we are present at the burial of Sir John Moore, we hear

Picton swearing, as we shall again at Waterloo, we follow a widow searching for her slain husband, and we see soldiers shaking hands with enemies during a lull from exhaustion of battle. We also become aware that, despite his low opinion of them, Wellington's men win against superior strength and that there is in the General himself an un-glamourous attention to tactics and a perseverance that in the stretch of fighting during the long summers and winters will somehow prevail.

Hardy's major source was, again, Thiers. It is in this portion of the *Histoire* that Thiers' authoritarian perspective is most apparent. He was later to deplore the career of Napoleon because of his misuse of power, but he took for granted that men must be subjected to the discipline of a firm government. In his narration of the Napoleonic usurpation in Spain he condemned as barbarism the killing of French soldiers by the civilians, but the retaliatory executions were, for him, only a natural consequence. Allowing him his bias and also his willingness to accept Napoleon's statistics, which undernumbered both the French forces in a battle and the losses incurred, Hardy could still trust him for the panorama of the campaign. He also made some use of Alison; and, although he often differed from Napier, he studied his maps and watched for special details.[66] Alison cites a great number of sources, but most of them are secondary, and he seems to have had access to few French documents unseen by Thiers. He contrasts with the latter in having a strong Christian piety which leads him to find God's will being carried out where Hardy finds only the impulsion of the Will, but he is careful and judicious in his evaluations. Napier is argumentative when not outright irascible. He scolds Thiers for using the "yellow" books, "concocted to mislead friends and enemies," instead of the original "green" ones. Having been criticized for his first edition, he appended to his revision a set of justificatory notes in which he calls Alison an enemy of Sir John Moore; and in an appendix he damns Robinson's *Memoirs of Lieutenant-General Sir Thomas Picton*, possibly because Robinson was one of his critics. Besides these three, Hardy used James Moore's biography of his brother, perhaps also his *Narrative of the Campaign*,[67] probably Lanfrey and Robinson,

[66] Hardy's 1892 edition of Napier is uncut, but has annotations of maps and other marks. Hardy had evidently also used another copy.

[67] James Carrick Moore, *The Life of Lieutenant-General Sir John Moore, K. B.* (2 vols.; London, 1834); and *A Narrative of the Campaign of the British Army in Spain, Commanded by His Excellency Lieut-Gen. Sir John Moore, K. B.* (2nd ed.; London, 1809).

and, at least once, Wellington's *Dispatches*.[68] One has to qualify sometimes in attributing sources since, as we have noted, much the same account appears in two or more and Hardy further obscured his indebtedness in his adaptations. In addition, he had, of course, miscellaneous information. He picked up anecdotes and the common soldier's impressions of battle from Bentley, he must have seen the originals or reproductions of paintings, including Goya's, and he could transplant some things from one time or geographical location to another. For example, in Notes taken for "Trumpet Major" he has descriptions of the equipment and clothing of British soldiers, apparently from the *Regulations for His Majesty's Forces* (1788–1793), and of priming and loading, from the platoon manual; sketches of soldiers, from the *Soldier's Companion*; one of their attire, from the *Regulations* for 1786; and others of the coat of Captain Absolute in the Haymarket performance of *The Rivals*.[69] Since he was meticulous on such matters, he may well have verified his facts for 1808–1814.

Before we see the French columns with their guns and baggage winding up the Pyrenees and spreading out on the Spanish plains (II, 2, i—"The Pyrenees and the Valleys Adjoining"), we have seen others leaving Boulogne in similar trains and have been present at Ulm and Austerlitz. It is winter, but the progress is orderly. At the Spanish strongholds the armies are given a hesitant welcome, but there is no fighting. So it was that Hardy, drawing generally on Thiers, pictured the new assertion of Napoleon's seemingly overwhelming force. The Emperor's star is ascendant. What is to follow is first one, then another small reverse, which by slow attrition in six long years will deny his role of one chosen by the gods to reshape the destiny of the Peninsula.

But before turning to the battles themselves Hardy interposed scenes of a quite different nature. The first concerns a night of comic horror which helps to explain the initial success of the French in Spain. Through the intrigue of Napoleon's emissaries Ferdinand had been persuaded to accept French aid in deposing his father and destroying the power of the Favourite, Prince Godoy. In each of the histories the story is brief, with emphasis on the political machinations.

---

[68] *The Dispatches of Field Marshal the Duke of Wellington During His Various Campaigns in India, Denmark, Portugal, Spain, the Low Countries, and France from 1797 to 1818* (13 vols.; London, 1838).

[69] Notes taken for "Trumpet Major," I, 33–37.

From them Hardy could have learned only in a general way of the liaison between the lustful Queen and the Prince of the Peace. He would have found that Godoy was forced to hide in a storeroom of his palace at Aranjuez, that his mistress Doña Josefa Tudo was evidently there, that his own wife, who certainly was present, was uninjured by the mob, and that the elegant home was ransacked. The sources used by Alison, including Toreno's *Historia del Levantamiento*, are no more informative.[70] Hardy's initial unfamiliarity with the situation at the Spanish Court is implied in his underlining "Prince of Peace" in Alison and noting in the margin "i.e. Godoy" and five pages later underlining "Godoy" and noting "(Prince of the Peace)" (XI, 296 and 301).

For his own Scene II, 2, ii—"Aranjuez, Near Madrid. A Room in the Palace of Godoy, the 'Prince of Peace,'"—which took place March 17, 1808, Thiers offered more than Alison, both on the licentiousness of the Queen and on the mob violence.[71] But there are two kinds of substance in Hardy that are not in the histories. One is a description of the rich furnishings of the room. Hardy's phrasing, however, is so generic that it fits any elegant Spanish apartment and so may come from his general fund of knowledge. The second is pure invention. Thiers indicates that the Queen was not with Godoy; instead, she was frantic to learn what had become of him. And, of course, no one was present to report any dialogue between the Prince and his mistress or his wife. Here Hardy enjoyed free play in depicting a gallant dealing first with a doting Queen, then a girlish mistress, and finally a neglected but protective wife. Mixed with the comedy is evidence of the popular support of Ferdinand, that is, of France, but with a warning from the people's leader:

> We have saved our nation from the Favourite,
> But who is going to save us from our Friend?

So dynasts fall, to be replaced by new.

In the following scene—"London: The Marchioness of Salisbury's"—we learn that the Spanish envoys consider Napoleon's meddling an "act of cheatery" and hence are asking England for aid. The next—"Madrid and Its Environs"—a dumb show, is based on general impressions in Thiers and probably others. Gifford, for ex-

---

[70] Alison's account is in his *History of Europe*, XI, 325 ff.
[71] *Histoire du Consulat*, VIII, 352, 505–507.

ample, remarks that "in all the towns and villages through which Joseph passed on his way to the capital, a sullen silence prevailed" (I, 600). Thiers says that he entered Madrid on July 20, 1808, "au milieu d'une froide curiosité," and that he found there "comme ailleurs une répugnance vraiment désésperante à s'approcher de sa personne" (IX, 118). Drawing on his general background and being willing to heighten effects, Hardy describes an arrival in pomp and splendour through streets whose houses are closed. The proclamation that Joseph is King of Spain is "received in silence."

After Trafalgar, Hardy's battles were to be on land. In II, 2, v— "The Open Sea between the English Coasts and the Spanish Peninsula"—however, he represented the magnitude of the transport of soldiers to the Spanish and Portuguese harbours. Wellington sailed with ten thousand men from Cork on July 12, 1808, and others followed from Channel ports. The scene enabled Hardy to give an impression of the logistics in the maintenance of the armies in Spain. He did not record Wellington's acrid complaints of lack of supplies, but he did later make clear the destitution in a straggler's excuse at Coruña (II, 3, iii).[72] In his ocean scene, too, Hardy took the opportunity to enumerate the names of officers. Like Homer, he found poetry in the cataloguing of names. Even though he had no occasion later to individualize some of the officers, his initial introduction gave them a familiar status on their reappearance.

In a sense these are orientation scenes. They lack the poignancy of those to come. Yet Hardy did make them relevant for his theme, and in those at the Palace and at Madrid he gave rein to the spirit of irony that was always with him. For though not the designated spokesman, it was the Spirit Ironic that described the initial welcoming of an oppressor and then the vanity of Joseph's triumphal passage through the empty streets of Madrid.

With a design that called for a great number of battles, Hardy had to avoid monotony and to build to climaxes. Among encounters that he played down was that of Wellington against inferior infantry but superior cavalry at Vimiero (Hardy's spelling), August 21, 1808 (II, 2, vii). Almost all his facts are in Alison; Napier provided a map, as for all the Peninsular battles; and, of course, Hardy also studied

[72] Hardy marked Napier's own attack (IV, 102) on the politicians for not supplying equipment at the siege of Badajos in March, 1812. Thiers (XI, 442 ff.) refers to Wellington's bitter letters to Castlereagh on the lack of provisions.

Thiers. As described by Alison (XII, 113–115) the contest was indeed savage. His report is actually more moving than Hardy's dumb show because, in sacrificing detail, Hardy also sacrificed magnitude. The same comment can be made on other occasions, especially in the contrast of Hardy with Thiers. Even four or five pages of impassioned prose and verse in Hardy could not equal the effect of twenty or thirty equally heightened pages in Thiers. But the poet could, nevertheless, stamp his trademark of irony on the slaughter at Vimiero. A small river, the Maceira, flowed through the valley. Hardy writes, "Close by the carnage the little Maceira stream continues to trickle unconcernedly to the sea."

Alison contrasts the French and English soldiers. The former could hope, at least to some extent, for promotion; few of the English officers were commissioned from the ranks. Pay was low and discipline was enforced with the lash. Yet Alison finds the English soldiers better cared for than any others. In a note he quotes Foy, who says that at the end of a day's march the French fighter hustles about to find water and cook his meal. The English, in contrast, after a moderate exertion sits down to await food and instructions. When deprived of his routine he commits excesses. But Foy adds:

> [He] is not brave at times merely; he is so whenever he has eaten well, drunk well, and slept well. Yet their courage, rather instinctive than acquired, has need of solid nutriment; and no thoughts of glory will ever make them forget that they are hungry, or that their shoes are worn out (XII, 24–25).

With this Hardy agreed. His two scenes of demoralization near Astorga (II, 3, i and ii) and the recovery before Coruña (II, 3, iii) make the point.

In the winter of 1808–1809 Sir John Moore was retreating, and morale always declined during a retreat. The army was also burdened with disorganized Spanish soldiers and a multitude of peasants, who cluttered the roads. James Moore speaks of the "half-naked and unfortunate peasants." [73] Of the stop beyond Astorga he writes: "before moving off next morning, [Moore] sent parties to drive out the stragglers from the houses; but many of the intoxicated were uncontrollable; and neither threats nor warnings of danger could make them quit their quarters." [74] Napier gives an equally desolate picture

---

[73] *A Narrative of the Campaign*, p. 186.
[74] *The Life of Moore*, p. 198.

(I, 311–319), and Thiers stresses the drunkenness, pillaging, and desertion in spite of Moore's rigorous punishments, including execution (IX, 516 ff.). He sums up the degradation: "car cette armée, qui ne se soutient que par la discipline, en la perdant par la fatigue et la précipitation, perdait tout ce qui la rend respectable" (IX, 517).

Hardy had all the evidence he needed. His genius translated numbers into individual men. His drunken deserters hiding in the straw in a cellar and thinking of lust in the midst of dying women are as close to the mere animal level as men can become. Their unconscious humour is on a plane with Caliban's. Hardy keeps their portraits free of sentimentality and he does not moralize, but he inserts touches which provide a perspective. In his sleep one soldier mumbles the directions for loading his weapon, in words based on the platoon manual Hardy had read. Indeed, these men have fought. Meanwhile, outside the cellar other soldiers are dragging themselves along in a semblance of order, though tomorrow some of these will be drunken deserters, too. And if he is not a philosopher, the second deserter is something of a poet. He remembers singing at the "Adam and Eve" in Bristol, and he can characterize the merriment as "a romantical thing enough." It is the fatigue of war that has brought men to this disintegration on New Year's Day. In three lines the Spirits conclude the scene. The Spirit Ironic speaks first: "Quaint poesy, and real romance of war!" Such is Hardy's own sentiment; but so, too, is the reply of the Pities:

> Mock on, Shade, if thou wilt! But others find
> Poesy ever lurk where pit-pats poor mankind!   (II, 3, i)

Napoleon was briefly at Astorga, and in his second scene (II, 3, ii) Hardy gives him a long soliloquy and then a conversation with Soult to narrate what has been happening elsewhere and what is now afoot. His adaptation of sources is illustrated by his use of Bulletin 23 from the Army of Spain—Astorga, January 1, 1809. It reads, in part: "Fox ou même Pitt, n'auraient pas commis de telles fautes. S'engager dans une lutte de terre contre la France . . .; c'est, pour l'Angleterre, pousser la folie jusqu'à ses derniers excès; c'est être avide de honte." [75] Hardy converts this into blank verse:

> Nor Pitt nor Fox displayed such blundering
> As glares in this campaign! It is, indeed,
> Enlarging Folly to Foolhardiness
> To combat France by land!

[75] *Oeuvres*, IV, 367.

In two lines Hardy refers to what he once intended to make into a scene:

> Then, too, there's Lannes, still sweating at the siege
> Of Sullen Zaragoza as 'twere hell.[76]

Drawing from controversial reports in his sources, Hardy pictures Napoleon as revealing an "unhealthy face and stoutening figure." He will make more of this later. It fits with Years's concluding remark that the Emperor is "turning from his apogee." The lines on Zaragoza help show why. So does the following scene, "Before Coruña."

As he goes on from his report on the nadir of the British army's morale to describe the battle of January 16, 1809, Napier writes: "It has been well said, that a British army may be gleaned in a retreat but cannot be reaped; whatever may be their misery the soldiers will always be found clean at review and ready at a fight" (I, 319). Hardy puts it: "Yet they are the same men, suddenly stiffened and grown amenable to discipline by the satisfaction of standing to the enemy at last" (II, 3, iii). Even after their leader has been mortally wounded, his words "Forty-second, remember Egypt" strike chords in two weapon-less stragglers and send them again into the melee.[77] But the special quality of the scene is in the last recorded words of Moore himself. The original eyewitness accounts by Captain Hardinge and Colonel Anderson are reproduced in James Moore's *Narrative* (220–225). In using the authentic records Hardy made some changes. He re-arranged the order of Moore's statements, omitted Anderson and Stanhope, making Hope the auditor of words addressed to them, and, more significantly, heightened the tone.

There was, as Hardy knew, a difference among historians as to Moore's wisdom as a general. To counter this, Hardy let him justify his action and also lament his ill luck. The portrait by Hardinge and Anderson is indeed noble, but Hardy went even further. It was on the advice of others that Moore decided to be carried on a blanket instead of in a waggon; Hardy has him decline the waggon in generosity to its wounded occupant. His sword was entangled between his legs, but he requested that it leave the field with him. Hardy has its pommel "thrust into the wound" and lets his hero comment, "One hurt more

---

[76] There will be other short references, for example, in II, 3, iii, where the dying Moore speaks of the city's "holding out heroically."

[77] Moore said, "Highlanders . . . ." Hardy gave them their official designation.

matters not." Two lines are reproduced almost verbatim, but with a striking change in effect. Anderson wrote, "I hope the people of England will be satisfied!—I hope my country will do me justice!" Hardy added two dashes:

I hope that England—will be satisfied—
I hope my native land—will do me justice!

The pauses admit of doubt.

One passage has a curious interest. According to Anderson, "After some interval he said, 'Stanhope [Captain Stanhope, third son of the Earl and nephew of Pitt]—remember me to your sister.'" Hardy expands this:

If I must die
Without a word with Stanhope, ask him, Hope,
To—name me to his sister. You may know
Of what there was between us?

When the Reverend John Oliver asked for further information on the last line, Hardy wrote, February 6, 1911: "I am sorry to say that I cannot remember the particulars on which the passage * * * was based—further than that it related to some love-affair between Sir John Moore and Stanhope's sister. You will probably be able to ascertain the facts from the Life of Moore." [78] His correspondent would have looked in vain. Once more Hardy had imaginatively augmented his source.

Three short paragraphs in the *Narrative* describe Moore's burial at daybreak as enemy firing begins. In II, 3, iv—"Coruña. Near the Ramparts"—taking his cue from "the funeral service was read by the chaplain," Hardy, of course, ended the service with words of Christian hope. Only from his statements elsewhere would one know that his own sentiments agreed with the first words of the service, from the fourteenth chapter of Job, "Man that is born of a woman hath but a short time to live, and is full of misery."

The two-day battle, July 27–28, 1809, at Talavera was one of the most important in Spain, with more than fifty-thousand British and Spanish forces under Wellington against at least as many French. It ended with the allies scant victors, too exhausted to pursue. All the histories stress the ferocity of the contest, and in II, 4, iv and v—

[78] Carl Weber (ed.), *The Letters of Thomas Hardy* (Waterville: The Colby College Press, 1954), pp. 85–86.

"The Field of Talavera"—Hardy draws a gripping picture of the seesaw butchery. But again he seized upon one event, recorded in Lanfrey and Napier,[79] but most fully in Alison, who emphasizes the respect of one courageous man for another:

> The extreme heat of the day now for a few hours suspended the combat .... Meanwhile, the troops on either part, overcome by thirst, straggled down in great numbers to the streamlet which ran in the bottom of the ravine which separated the two armies. Not a shot was fired, not a drum was beat; peaceably the foemen drank from the opposite banks of the same rill; and not unfrequently the hands which had so recently been dyed in mutual slaughter, were extended and shaken across the water in token of their mutual admiration of the valour and constancy displayed on both sides (XIII, 243).[80]

Hardy begins with hardly more than a rearrangement of Alison's words: "The combat flags, and is suspended." What follows is precisely Alison's canvas, but the tone is changed. Heroism and respect are implied; but Pities, the Spirit Ironic, and finally the Spirit Sinister are the interpreters:

> What do I see but thirsty, throbbing bands
> From these inimic hosts defiling down
> In homely need towards the little stream
> That parts their enmities, and drinking there!
> They get to grasping hands across the rill,
> Sealing their sameness as earth's sojourners.—
> What more could plead the wryness of the times
> Than such unstudied piteous pantomines!

These words of compassion from Pities remind one of "The Man He Killed." Dated 1902, the poem ends:

> "Yes; quaint and curious war is!
> You shoot a fellow down
> You'd treat if met where any bar is,
> Or help to half-a-crown."

For a thinking man the interlude, to be succeeded by unremitting enmity, only intensifies the irony of war. Mankind must be either stupid,

[79] In Napier he put a bookmark at II, 178–179, on the battle. In Thiers, XI, 160, by the heading "Mort du général Lapisse" he put the knowledgeable annotation "Qy was not Marlot also slain?"

[80] The original source was Marshal Jourdan's MS.

cursed, or helpless; and the Spirit Ironic chooses the third alternative:

> It is only that Life's queer mechanics chance to work out in this grotesque shape just now. The groping tentativeness of an Immanent Will (as grey old Years describes it) cannot be asked to learn logic at this time of day! The spectacle of Its instruments, set to riddle one another through, and then to drink together in peace and concord, is where the humour comes in, and makes the play worth seeing!

Again, there were three alternatives. The Will might remain unconscious and man's lot continue unchanged. It might achieve consciousness and his destiny become meliorated, a possibility with which Hardy was to end his poem. But we must remember that Hardy could never rid himself of the feeling, of ancient heritage, that man would have been more fortunate not to have been born. And so the Spirit Sinister completes the chorus: "Come, Sprite, don't carry your ironies too far, or you may wake up the Unconscious Itself, and tempt It to let all the gory clock-work run down to spite me!"

From Greville's *Diary* Hardy made a note: "*Buonaparte* had not the patience requisite for defensive operations (said Wellington."[81] Hardy knew that the French soldiers grew restive when idle and that the Emperor sought to keep momentum, turning quickly from one victory to the next battle. The glory of France—much emphasized in Thiers—and the hope of reward stirred the French as they prepared to fight. English soldiers could also become bored in a strange land, with a monotony of hardship and none of the familiar activities that gave them excitement and importance at home. But Wellington valued defense, and the monument to his strategy was the fortifications at Torrès Védras. His men had fought and would fight again, but, as Thiers noted, the mere presence of his forces on the coast of Portugal was a threat to the French; and so he withdrew his men from potential battles for the tedious labours of building the massive fort.

Napier provides a map and describes the outer line as twenty-nine miles long, the middle and main one as twenty-four, both lines from the Tagus to the coast (III, 38 and 45). Thiers speaks of 152 redoubts and 700 pieces of ordnance.[82] Lanfrey estimates that the fortifications sheltered more than 75,000 soldiers—about 30,000 of them British—and another 32,000 nonmilitary men (IV, 84–85). Wellington began

[81] Literary Notes, I, 38; the *Greville Diary*, I, 71.
[82] Cf., *Histoire du Consulat*, XII, 320–416, for the full description.

the lines in early October, 1809, and they required more than a year to build. All three historians indicate Masséna's amazement upon discovering their vastness. The life within had some of the restrictions of a town besieged.

In II, 6, i and ii—"The Lines of Torrès Védras"—Hardy describes the lines on a winter day in 1810. They are still not quite completed when Masséna searches for a weak place. Again there is a characteristic Hardy touch. As the British soldiers enter the fortification we read, "Beside one of the roads two or three of the soldiers are dangling from a tree by the neck, probably for plundering." Hardy could take for granted this bit of local colour.[83] The very construction of Torrès Védras was an imposition of discipline. Contrary to a soldier's natural impulses, it was, nevertheless, sound strategy, which in a war of attrition would have the best chance to prevail.

Hardy's narrative of the battle, May 16, 1811, at Albuera, scene II, 6, iv, is very much a composite, as no one of his usual sources comes near to supplying all the facts. In Volume III of Napier there is a bookmark at pages 170–171, where a section on Albuera ends and a new chapter begins. Hardy accepted Napier's figures on the unbelievable loss that left only 1,800 of an initial 6,000 in the sector on the hill (III, 170). Napier speaks of serious fighting for four hours and of a loss of 7,000 allies and 8,000 French killed or wounded. Gifford, with Beresford's own report as his source, describes the field as "literally covered with dead, lying in heaps in every part" (I, 741). Only Thiers (XII, 687 ff.) treats Albuera as a minor battle, which in terms of consequences perhaps it was. Alison gives credit to Hardinge's advance for saving the day (XIV, 251), and Hardy seems to concur. Napier and Gifford speak of the heavy rain that fell soon after the fighting started.

Hardy had been describing the devastation of battle after battle, and he had somehow to give a newness to what he calls "the most murderous struggle of the whole war." In the narration he emphasized the closeness of the combatants, "discharging musketry in each other's faces." But more importantly, he rang variations on his themes. Comparable to the unconcerned stream at Vimiero are the "birds in

[83] In a Dorset newspaper in 1964 were printed the reminiscences of a soldier who had climaxed his career at Waterloo. He had been flogged and he took punishment for granted. But he had never been flogged for cowardice, for which, to his satisfaction, another soldier had been soundly beaten and disgraced.

the wood," who, "unaware that this day is to be different from every other day they have known there, are heard singing their overtures with their usual serenity." Hardy mentions no downpour, but, instead, after the carnage, makes a thing of sweetness accentuate the horror: "Hot corpses, their mouths blackened by cartridge-biting, and surrounded by * * * limbs and viscera, accumulate on the slopes, increasing from twos and threes to half-dozens, and from half-dozens to heaps, which steam with their own warmth as the spring rain falls gently upon them." With no dialogue of mortals, the Spirit of the Pities gives the dominant tone. Its first observation mingles compassion and irony:

> On earth below
> Are men—unnatured and mechanic-drawn—
> Mixt nationalities in row and row,
>   Wheeling them to and fro
> In moves dissociate from their souls' demand,
> For dynasts' ends that few even understand!

And the Chorus of the Pities concludes the scene with the lines from which we have already quoted:

> Hide their hacked bones, Earth!—deep, deep, deep,
> Where harmless worms caress and creep.—
> What man can grieve? what woman weep?
> Better than waking is to sleep! Albuera!

For the maimed in body and the seared in spirit the working of the unconscious Will still leads without alteration to misery. But for those whose dirge is being chanted the half-prophecy of the Spirit Sinister at Talavera is in a sense confirmed. For them the "gory clock-work of the show" has, indeed, "run down."

In Napier (IV, 252–253) Hardy drew arrows on the map of Sala-manca and marked a half page on the fording of the Santa Marta during a violent thunder storm that killed "many men and horses." As Napier tells the story—

> to a military eye there was nothing more imposing than the close and beautiful order in which the soldiers of that noble light division were seen by the fiery gleams to step from the river to the bank and pursue their march amidst this astounding turmoil, defying alike the storms and the enemy (IV, 262).

In Napier (V, 181), as noted by Rutland, Hardy got his picture of Mrs. Dalbiac following her husband on a charge; he had, of course, long known that women were commonly at fields of battle.

When he read Thiers, Hardy already had some knowledge of the events, for he twice corrected "Pakenham" to "Pack" and in the margin noted that Picton was "temporarily under Pakenham" (XV, 97). He also marked a long passage on the "graves conséquences" of this battle of July 22, 1812 (XV, 99). Neither Wellington nor Marmont planned an encounter, but the armies found themselves too close, and fighting on a small scale led to total involvement. As Thiers sums it up—

> Telle fut cette funeste et involontaire bataille, dite de Salamanque ou des Arapiles, qui eut pour l'armée anglaise des conséquences fort imprévues, car elle lui procura une victoire inespérée, au lieu d'une retraite inévitable, et commença, comme on va le voir, la ruine de nos affaires en Espagne.

In III, 1, ii and iii—"The Ford of Santa Marta, Salamanca" and "The Field of Salamanca"—Hardy accepted Thiers' interpretation, and he returned to it when giving Napoleon's reaction upon hearing the news at Borodino. It was, in short an important contest, in which great slaughter occurred—one in which Wellington characteristically waited and then countermanoeuvred. As an example of efficient slaying it presented no novelty.

But for Hardy the variety of things ironic and pathetic was infinite. Nature this time is not indifferent or unaware. Hardy transformed Napier's storm into a supernatural manifestation:

> While marching men come, band on band,
> Who read not as a reprimand
> To mortal moils that, as 'twere planned
> In mockery of their mimic fray,
> The skies fling flame.

These superstitious sentiments of the Chorus of the Pities hardly accord with the concept of an unconscious Will, but then, Pities usually describes things less as they fit into Hardy's philosophy than as they seem to a feeling spectator.

The haphazard nature of collecting intelligence about the enemy and the inefficiency in liaison among one's armies was to be most amazingly demonstrated in the Waterloo campaign, especially by the

French. In Hardy's dramatization at Salamanca a peasant tells Mrs. Dalbiac, an officer's wife, that the Spanish have withdrawn their garrison at the bridge at Alba. She tells a sergeant, who relays the message. It finally reaches Wellington too late; there was no point in telling him sooner, since the story was too absurd for belief. Of course, Hardy heightened the romance with a Cassandra in a man's world, but he did no injustice to the military mind.

The wife of a Captain Prescott had brought her children to Spain, and after the battle she was to find the body of her dead husband on the field. Hardy added a footnote that he had been unable to trace her subsequent fate and, in 1909, revised it to say that a descendant had reported her remarriage and eventual death at Venice. Some ten thousand were killed or maimed at Salamanca, but what one remembers is the captain's widow searching the field of slaughter. Given the responsibilities which Wellington must carry out, we need not condemn him if with his pity he mixes vexation:

> Well, I'm damned sorry for her. Though I wish
> The women-folk would keep them to the rear:
> Much awkwardness attends their pottering round!

Statistically the General is in the right. Hardy, in contrast, was haunted by the image of the widow "wandering to and fro."

Mankind, however, as Hardy knew, is incorrigibly resilient. The Prince of Wales is not present to lead a victory celebration, but the local populace has cause for dancing and merry-making till midnight. Irony, pathos, and again irony—of such stuff, felt Hardy, man's life is made.

The battle at Vitoria, June 21, 1813, came after the disastrous invasion of Russia, when the Emperor was reeling and striking out with the desperation of a losing gambler. Following his headlong course to destruction, Thiers speaks of his injustice in blaming his officers, of his mistreatment of Joseph, who was abler than Napoleon recognized, and of his premonitions (XVI, 135 ff.). Much of this, which accompanies Thiers' discussion of Vitoria, Hardy used here and there in characterizing the Emperor. For the battle itself (III, 2, i, ii, and iii), which led to Wellington's promotion and to extravagant celebrations in London, he took most from Napier, some apparently from H. B. Robinson's *Memoirs of Lieutenant-General Sir Thomas Picton* (1835), in two volumes, and more than usual from unidentifiable sources, perhaps including oral ones. In Napier he left a book-mark by the map (V, 108–109) and, having underlined *fifteenth hussars* (V, 121), he noted, "W. Young (of Sturminster Newton) was here in this reg't," and again, on the next page, "W. Young." In his text itself he included "Sergeant Young," and in a footnote identified him as "Thomas" Young, who died in 1853. It is doubtful that he came to know much about Young, but, steeped as he was in the atmosphere of his subject, he was concerned to give the authentic, if antiquarian detail.

Militarily the battle offers variety in that Wellington takes the offensive, though not until his men have had at least a day of rest. What Thiers describes as a seesaw affair is simplified by Hardy into a steady progess.[84]

In the narrative of the action there is one new touch. Helping Wellington in the melee at the center is "loud-voiced Picton, in an old blue coat and round hat, swearing as he goes." Since in his account of Picton at Waterloo, Hardy seems to have drawn on Robinson, he probably did so here. Picton was a legendary hero. He had so defied Government as to be accused in Parliament; he had at first annoyed Wellington by his independence as an officer; he was a soldier's soldier, from whom oaths were the highest compliment; he had, moreover, rushed from England to fight at Waterloo. For all this he was to have a monument in St. Paul's. Robinson does not describe his clothes at Vitoria, but he speaks of his restiveness while awaiting orders, and then of his "encouraging them [the Third], according to the words of an amusing writer, with the bland appelation of 'Come on, ye rascals! —come on, ye fighting villains'" (II, 197). No matter what Hardy might think of the folly of war, he could respect Picton.

The battle proper being over, there is the usual sad aftermath. Hardy mentions what he could have recorded after every battle, the depredations of night preyers, who roamed the field stealing and, when it served their convenience, killing; the terror of the women; and the release from discipline to mere concern for self. Here this last takes the form of breaking open Joseph's treasure chests and destroying old masterpieces which he is belatedly trying to carry away. So heroism having for a moment reached its height, moral inertia brings men careening to an equal depth.

[84] Napier speaks of Spanish and Portuguese forces; Hardy uses the sole term "English."

After Vitoria the French were generally on the defensive in Spain. Hardy's scene, III, 3, vi, again on French soil—"The Pyrenees. Near the River Nivelle"—takes place November 10, 1813, after the near annihilation of Napoleon's army at Leipzig, and it represents one of the last efforts of French forces in the west. Hardy needed to narrate events succeeding Leipzig, but he was interested in showing the amenities that existed between opposing officers and, perhaps more, in giving what amounts to a choral commentary on the collapse of French morale. Since the comment is presented through the dialogue of mortals rather than of Spirits, the scene offers artistic variety.

Napier's account (V, 368–384) indicates a hard-fought, prolonged battle. He writes that Wellington "directed superior numbers with superior skill." Hardy marked Napier's passage on Clausel's plan of battle and also "the French fled to the different bridges over the Nivelle and the signal redoubt was left to its fate." He apparently interpreted this remark in the light of what he found in his chief source, cited in his rough draft: "[Nov 10. 13] [*sic*] See Well$^{n's}$ Dispatches XI for exact place." In his stage direction he put, "The battle of . . . has just been fought." One can only infer that, at least when he began the scene, he did not have the *Dispatches* beside him and was depending on recall. The passage on which he drew appears to be a postscript to a letter to General Sir John Hope, dated November 11. Wellington writes:

> The Colonel who was taken yesterday dined with me. He was at first very melancholy, and would not speak; but he was afterwards more communicative. Having been asked where the Emperor's head quarters were, he answered, "*Nulle part; il n'y a point de quartier général, et point d'armée.*" I understand here that it is positively true that the army is entirely destroyed.[85]

Hardy may have done violence to the specific incident, as the French had fought with persistence. But he knew that ultimately morale was fundamental, and so he made the most of the clue Wellington's letter gave him. Whether or not the words of his own French Commandant fit the given battle, they did fit the war:

[85] *The Dispatches*, XI, 275. Hardy reads:

> There are no French headquarters now, my lord,
> For there is no French army! France's fame
> Is fouled. And how, then, could we fight to-day
> With our hearts in our shoes!

Alas, my lord,
'Twas more than flesh and blood could do, to fight
After such paralyzing tidings came.
More life may trickle out of men through thought
Than through a gaping wound.

The last two lines merely restated what Hardy had been saying from
The Return to *Jude*.

The final scene in the western campaign (III, 4, v) is at Bayonne,
April 28, 1814, the very day Napoleon embarked for Elba. The
tricolour comes down the flagstaff and a "mildewed and dingy" white
flag replaces it. There is some shouting and marching, and then "the
scene shuts." So, too, closes the campaign. Many of its principals,
named in lists of officers or otherwise identified in the battles, will no
longer perform the urging of the Will. The others, with some new-
comers, will return at Ligny, Quatre-Bras, and Waterloo.

THE AUSTRO-GERMAN TRAGICOMEDY, 1805–1809

The career of Napoleon between 1805 and 1815 may lack the exact
proportions of an ideal five-act tragedy, but for so extended a series of
historical actions it comes singularly close. The first years were marked
by more success than failure, the setbacks being at Trafalgar, in the
Peninsula, and wherever else the influence of the British navy and
British diplomacy served to annoy. The peak of good fortune in battle
occurred early, at Austerlitz; but the acme of the Emperor's confidence
came years later when, at last within the territory of Russia, he
envisioned a glorious triumph awaiting him in Moscow. There followed swiftly a concatenation of disasters, climaxed by the defeat at
Leipzig. What should have been the concluding scene, the journey to
Elba, was to serve the function of anticipation, as in a stage play, of
what was still to come. From what would seem to be the lowest point
to which a protagonist could fall, the Emperor was to rise, as if super-
naturally chosen, in one final act of defiance, only to succumb to
unequivocal defeat.

As Thiers unfolds the pattern of events it is the career of a genius
who should have accomplished wonderful deeds for France, but who
lost his initial vision when he forgot his role as servant of his country
and made it instead his tool. At times Thiers' history reads almost as if
the author were contemporary with events and wondering how all will

end. Though he sometimes chides his protagonist, he tries to maintain sympathy long after the reader has begun to protest. It is evident, however, that, as he becomes more and more immersed, his pre-occupation leads him to see more clearly into the nature of what he is describing. Finally he will break forth in impassioned eloquence as he sees *hubris* take irrevocable possession of his man.

In the campaigns in central and eastern Europe before the first abdication Thiers was to offer Hardy both historical fact and literary inspiration. The essential difference in Hardy's tone would spring from the fact that, as he began his own pursuit of the Emperor across the battle-scarred landscape of Europe, Hardy saw the young dynast as father to the dynast he was to become, and both as the subjects—and agents—of the Will. The events of 1805–1809 in central Europe—from Ulm to Wagram—are part of the rising action of the drama.

Following Thiers in I, 3, i and ii—"Boulogne. The Château at Pont-de-Briques" and "The Frontiers of Upper Austria and Bavaria" —and drawing also on Capefigue and possibly Gifford in I, 3, iii— "Boulogne. The St. Omer Road"—Hardy mapped out Napoleon's strategy for destroying the Austrian armies and then the Russian. Always concerned with the colour of events, he took his clues for scene iii from a passage in Capefigue: "l'aigle des régiments, sur les drapeaux déployés, fut-elle saluée par des milliers d'acclamations, et le *Chant du Départ* fut entonné par les belles troupes . . . ." [86] To this he added the traditional "Vive l'Empereur" and, as a reminder of the long sequence that had led up to the present, "babble of repeating the days of Italy, Egypt, Marengo, and Hohenlinden."

Pertinent to the interpretation Hardy was to give of the campaign ahead were certain passages he marked in Capefigue and Lanfrey. In the former he singled out a description of the division of the Boulogne army into five corps, which Capefigue followed with characterizations of Soult, Davout, Ney, Lannes, and Murat (V, 305–306). In Lanfrey's anti-Napoleonic narrative Hardy came across Napoleon's words upon leaving for the Rhine, words which Lanfrey had italicized: "*Je gémis du sang qu'il va en coûter à l'Europe.*" And he marked the ironic line which followed: "Pendant qu'il gémissait sur cette cruelle

---

[86] *L'Europe Pendant le Consulat*, V, 305. Thiers' account in *Histoire du Consulat* begins VI, 18; Gifford's *History of the Wars*, I, 457. The original of part of Napoleon's orders for bringing his armies together for the attack on Ulm is the Bulletin de la grande armée, October 6, 1805, *Oeuvres*, III, 425–426.

extrémité ..." (III, 317). Two pages later he marked and in part underlined Lanfrey's summation on Napoleon's appeal to his soldiers:

> Pour la France, Napoléon était devenu un despote redouté, une majesté, une sorte de souverain de l'ancien régime; pour ses soldats il était resté le Bonaparte de l'armée d'Italie. Ils retrouvèrent avec ivresse le langage et les allures familières de leur ancien général. C'étaient des soldats, mais des soldats qui se souvenaient d'avoir été des citoyens; ils servaient son despotisme, mais ils avaient été formés par la liberté, ils étaient malgré tout les fils de la Révolution. Napoléon était moins leur maître que leur favori; *il était leur ouvrage*: il n'était pas à leurs yeux un souverain, mais une sorte de tribun militaire.

The contrast between the orderliness in Napoleon's plans for surprising General Mack and the confusion at the Austrian headquarters is emphasized by Thiers. Before the actual attack on Ulm the Austrians had lost in minor skirmishes, and Hardy put a bookmark at the page describing the "perplexitées du général Mack après le combat de Haslach." Thiers writes that, from his ignorance of where the French were, Mack "était tombé dans un désordre d'esprit facile à concevoir" (VI, 107). In part from the summary Thiers gives, Hardy built up his description of the setting (I, 4, ii—"Before the City of Ulm") and then dramatized the conflict of opinion among the military staff (I, 4, iii—"Ulm. Within the City"). Thiers emphasizes the fact that Mack did not wish to divide his troops, as recommended by the Archduke Ferdinand and others, and that he finally yielded to the extent of sending Jellachich to Memmingen and Riesc to the heights of Elchingen (VI, 108–109). Thiers regarded this division of the army as fatal. Instead of unmistakably pointing out Mack's error, Hardy has his reversal seem almost like a local tactical deployment, and then he resorts to the weak device of having an unidentified officer comment, "Disjunction seems of all expedients worst * * *." This was to be one of a very few examples of Hardy's failing to heighten what he found in his sources.

The dumb show in I, 4, iv—"Before Ulm. The Same Day"— also falls short. This is Hardy's first description of a battle, and he had not determined what could be done with narration. Ending his account with the coming of twilight, he missed good opportunities. To emphasize the ferocity of the fighting he has Ney "recede, re-advance, halt," and then remain for a while in confusion before he takes the Michaelsberg. Thiers, in contrast, presents what was to become the distinguishing characteristic of Ney. When Dumas gives him Napoleon's command to delay, he replies, "La gloire ne se partage pas," and pushes on (VI, 119). In Thiers, we have the Ney of Hardy's later scenes, including Waterloo. Also Hardy has Napoleon voluntarily move to a safer position when a bomb lands near. In Thiers, when a battery showers *mitraille* on the Imperial group, Lannes pulls Napoleon's horse away. The incident could have provided irony when Hardy came to the reported disillusionment of Lannes as he lay dying at Aspern. Finally, Hardy's allusion to compassionate Nature is arbitrary and unconvincing. The monastery and bridge "wear a desolated look, and the stream, which is swollen by the rainfall and rasped by the storm, seems wanly to sympathize."

In the capitulation scene, I, 4, v—"The Same. The Michaelsberg"— Hardy dramatizes the humiliation of the Austrian forces which occurred three days later, October 20, 1805. His source this time was Gifford, whose version differs in phrasing from that of Thiers. Hardy changed the order and ornamented Napoleon's language, but he borrowed without hesitation whatever would fit into his blank verse.

Gifford writes: "Gentlemen, your master wages an unjust war: I tell you plainly I know not for what I am fighting ..." (I, 462). Hardy expands this:

> Listen, I pray you, Generals gathered here.
> I tell you frankly that I know not why
> Your master wages this wild war with me.
> I know not what he seeks by such injustice * * * .

Gifford's "you are no longer a power" becomes "You are no more a European power." Gifford writes: "At a single word 200,000 volunteers crowd to my standard, and in six weeks become good soldiers; whereas, your recruits only march from compulsion, and do not become good soldiers till after several years."

In Hardy we find:

> Two hundred thousand volunteers, right fit,
> Will join my standards at a single nod,
> And in six weeks prove soldiers to the bone,
> While your recruits, compulsion's scavengings,
> Scarce weld to warriors after toilsome years.

Gifford reads: "I desire nothing further upon the continent; I want ships, colonies, and commerce, and it is as much your interest as mine that I should have them." Hardy interpolates an animadversion upon England:

> But I want nothing on this Continent:
> The English only are my enemies.
> Ships, colonies, and commerce I desire,
> Yea, therewith to advantage you as me.

Gifford says, "All states must have an end." Hardy found that the words fitted without change in his iambic pentameter.

If Hardy proceeded here as the rough draft shows him doing later, he broke up Gifford's passage and copied the parts in his manuscript, then composed his own verse form between the lines. Where, then, is his originality? It is not in Napoleon's own words, but in what comes after. Neither Gifford nor Thiers does more than record the scene, but Hardy saw it not merely as an example of man's arrogant degradation of his fellowmen, but as a vain illusion of power. Thirty thousand men, according to Gifford, laid down their arms before the neo-Roman conqueror, and according to Napoleon's eighth bulletin the filing past continued from 2:00 P.M. until 7:00.[87] But, with perhaps an echo of *The Rubáiyát*, Hardy subjects the perpetrator of such cruel vanity to evaluation by the Spirit of the Years, who sees not the moment, but the eons:

> So let him speak, the while we clearly sight him
> Moved like a figure on a lantern-slide.
> Which, much amazing uninitiate eyes,
> The all-compelling crystal pane but drags
> Whither the showman wills.

Thus the momentary triumph takes its petty place within the universal. But the suffering of the defeated is another matter. Though it be but of a moment's duration, it partakes of an essence which is limited neither in place nor in time, and so we have the cry of the Spirit of the Pities:

> But O, the intolerable antilogy
> Of making figments feel!

Such sentiments are not to be found in Gifford; they stem from *The Return*, and *Tess*, and *Jude*.

After mingling with his troops Napoleon returned to his tent to await "l'aurore d'une journée qui devait être l'une des plus grandes de

[87] *Oeuvres*, III, 447.

sa vie, l'une des plus grandes de l'histoire" (VI, 301). Thiers is, of course, writing of the battle of Austerlitz, December 2, 1805, where the breaking through of the sun to dispel the fog became for the Emperor an omen to which he was to refer in later years—the famous "sun of Austerlitz."

Since writing about Ulm, Hardy had described the battle of Trafalgar, and he came to the field of Austerlitz willing to trust his imagination. For his five scenes (I, 6, i–v) he used a few details not traceable to any specific place in the histories. For Napoleon's anti-English sentiments he could find, as usual, special evidence in passages he had marked here and there in Lanfrey—though Thiers is not wanting. The interchange of courtesies between Napoleon and the conquered Francis is closest to Capefigue.[88] The rest is from Thiers. But with what he had before him Hardy improvised freely. Even in Napoleon's proclamation to his troops on the eve of battle (I, 6, i) he appears to have rethought Thiers' sentences instead of merely translating them into verse. "Ce sont ces mêmes bataillons que vous avez battus à Hollabrunn, et que depuis vous avez constamment poursuivis jusqu'ici"—so reads the original (VI, 299). Hardy's language, though stilted, befits the tone of a proclamation, and it is more graphic:

> Are not these the self-same bands
> You met and swept aside at Hollabrünn,
> And whose retreating forms, dismayed to flight,
> Your feet pursued along the trackways here?

Thiers indicates the Emperor's outburst against England when the news came from Trafalgar. Hardy puts it, "These water-rats may paddle in their salt slush * * * ." Caught up in his linguistic improvisation, he went even further than his critics could tolerate in such a line as "His projects they unknow, his grin unsee!"

For the arguments that represent the muddle in the Russian headquarters (I, 6, ii) Hardy used Thiers' footnote quoting the manuscript of Langeron.[89] He himself noted how well Langeron fared in his own

[88] "'Je suis fâché,' dit Napoléon, 'de vous recevoir ainsi; mais depuis deux mois je n'ai pas d'autre palais.' François II lui répondit avec son accent un peu allemand: 'Vous en tirez si bon parti, que vous devez en être content'" (*L'Europe Pendant le Consulat*, V, 447).

[89] Emma Clifford has noted that a few details not in Langeron's account are in *War and Peace*. "*War and Peace* and *The Dynasts*," *Modern Philology*, LIV, No. 1 (1956), 41–42.

report. Wherever he had occasion to look at original memoirs he would have found similar examples. In using here the English version of Thiers, Hardy proved the willing victim of a strange error in the translation. In the French, anticipating an attack, Langeron says, "Il a éteint ses feux, on entend beaucoup de bruit dans son camp" (VI, 303). The English (VI, 160) ends, "and not a sound is heard in his camp." This translation makes no sense. Hardy, however, assumed its accuracy and gave the sentence to Weirother, who cannot conceive of an attack, and in his mistaken trust he tossed in an additional line for verisimilitude:

> His fires are dark; all sounds have ceased that way
> Save voice of owl or mongrel wintering there.

Coming from Weirother, this does amusingly make sense.

Through all the action and dialogue in the five scenes on Austerlitz, Hardy emphasized the military shrewdness and the barbarism of Napoleon. In all this, including the firing on the ice to drown two thousand fugitives, he followed Thiers, but with his own twist. He alone speaks of the Emperor's "vulpine smile" as he orders the massacre.

And in the midst of the slaughter Hardy gives two pages to his Spirits to tell what the dither is all about. First he renders visible his sensation of the Will: "the scene becomes anatomized and the living masses of humanity transparent. The controlling Immanent Will appears therein, as a brain-like network of currents and ejections, twitching, interpenetrating, entangling, and thrusting hither and thither the human forms" (I, 6, iii). Then the Ironic Spirits have their say. Reminding the Pities that they are mere youngsters—having sprung into being where men "moan / Against a ruling not their own"—they recall the world process. For eons before Austerlitz, Years and the Ironic Spirits have

> Heard laughters at the ruthless dooms
> Which tortured to the eternal glooms
> Quick, quivering hearts in hecatombs.

These lines, too, are part of Hardy's historical substance. If the Immanent Will is by the nature of things inconceivable, Hardy, nevertheless, could feel its presence in the world of Nature and in man's doings. The picture he tries to give represents but one perspective. It is as suggestive, however, and, indeed, as plausible as many another.

And it was not an arbitrary creation. Hardy's reason might coerce things into a pattern, but the essence of his supernatural world was the creation of his poet's imagination.

When the intricate negotiations were completed after Austerlitz, Napoleon was at the height of his career, though not of his ambition. He had broken the coalition and dictated his own terms for central Europe. Capefigue (VI, 76) remarks that he was now "plus monarchique, plus hardi." Thiers comments that he was now secure as emperor, that there was nothing to fear except the inconstancy of fortune and the weakness of the human spirit, "qui quelquefois supporte le malheur sans faillir, rarement la prospérité sans commettre de grandes fautes" (VI, 569).

To illustrate the popular response to victory and to report miscellaneous information Hardy wrote a most uneven scene (I, 6, vii— "Paris. A Street Leading to the Tuileries"). The date was January 26, 1806; the occasion, Napoleon's return to Paris. To build up the significance of recent events Hardy employed as one narrator a woman of the streets who is almost preternatural in her percipience and as another the Spirit of Rumour, who, disguised as a mortal, is even more eerie than when he appeared in London to spread rumours at a party. The result is self-conscious and laboured writing. The historical news reported contains one strange error. Napoleon had affianced the young Stéphanie Beauharnais to the Prince of Baden. Hardy is loosely correct in saying that she "stands as daughter" to Napoleon, but he adds a hint of scandal—"Some say as more." This can only represent an inexplicable confusion with Hortense's reputed relations with her stepfather brother-in-law.

Between the battles of Austerlitz and Jena, an interval of ten months, Napoleon and Talleyrand were busy trying to gain favourable alliances everywhere. December 26, France signed a treaty with Austria and made the electors of Bavaria and Württemberg kings. January 14, 1806, Eugene married the daughter of the King of Bavaria. July 17 brought the Confederation of the Rhine, intended to separate Bavaria, Württemberg, Baden, and lesser states from their German kinsmen. During the summer and early fall fruitless negotiations were carried on with England, an initial condition being that Russia not be a party; these finally broke off September 26. Meanwhile, July 30, France secretly signed a treaty with Russia's emissary, but, influenced by England, Alexander refused to ratify it. Meanwhile, too, England was briefly at war with Prussia and captured Prussian merchantmen. Prussia was also negotiating with France, seeking advantage at the expense of England; then, when her efforts appeared futile, she hoped for support from England in resistance to France.

In II, 1, ii—"The Route between London and Paris"—as we have noticed, Hardy tried to cover the part played by Fox in seeking peace. In II, 1, iii—"The Streets of Berlin"—he supplied other bits of the canvas. As usual, however, in scenes where citizens comment on the state of affairs, he was handicapped by his dual purpose of trying to tell at the same time what had happened and what was the feeling of the people who had no part in shaping events but were affected by them. In any of the histories he would have found criticism of the devious role of Prussia. Gifford, for example, writes that Prussia had been "as perfidious, as unprincipled in her ambition as France; . . . but after selling her honour and reputation, she had been defrauded of the price" (I, 511). In Hardy, however, we do not find any evidence of this. We do learn that Frederick William is an ineffectual king and that Prussia is living in a sentimental memory of past glory, in no way prepared for going to war against the military machine of France.

Hardy, however, is sympathetic to Prussia. Pities and Years offer the commentaries in a scene that might well have inspired the keenest barbs of the Spirit Ironic. Taking his cue from reports of marching and singing in the Berlin streets and of the enthusiastic allegiance to the beautiful Queen Louisa, Hardy, too, became chivalric. Prussia is doomed, and its military parades are indeed quixotic in this age of Napoleon. Nevertheless, a lovely queen at the head of a regiment is a thrilling sight. It has about it a mystic aura which Hardy refused to let irony destroy. The sardonic Spirit could wait till the Queen left to join her husband after the debacle of Jena, when he would again speak words of chill reality:

> So the Will plays at flux and reflux still.
> This monarchy, one-half whose pedestal
> Is built of Polish bones, has bones home-made!
> Let the fair woman bear it. Poland did (II, 1, v).

The scene in the Berlin streets is any time shortly before September 24, 1806. Between then and June 19, 1807, when Napoleon was to arrive at Tilsit to dictate a peace to Alexander and the Prussian monarchs, there were a number of battles. Hardy had, perforce, to choose among them and give to each that he chose a decisiveness which it did not by itself possess. October 14, occurred the Battle of Auër-stadt-Jena (Hardy's spelling); November 6–7, that of Lübeck; February 7, the terrible slaughter at Preussisch-Eylau; during the early summer, the siege of Danzig; and June 14, another slaughter at Friedland. Meanwhile, there were various minor conflicts. Hardy described some of the tactics of the battle of Jena, which was actually a route, and then used hearsay technique to emphasize the brave, though futile resistance at Auërstadt. Later he used a flash back to summarize Eylau and Friedland. In so compressing he could not depict the real nature of the war. But, as always, he was concerned primarily with incidents that would illuminate the human spectacle.

In Napoleon's own bulletin, as Lanfrey noted, he played up the Jena portion of the October 14 battle, presumably because he directed it, though Davout faced larger numbers and harder fighting at Auërstadt. In limiting himself to the actual fighting at Jena, the poet had to omit the phenomenal exertions and ingenuity—most fully described in Alison (X, 330)—by which the French blasted away obstacles and pulled their cannon up the steep hillside to gain advantage in terrain. He also misrepresented the facts in crediting Bernadotte equally with Davout in defeating the Duke of Brunswick's forces at Auërstadt, though, according to Thiers (VII, 150), his soldiers had not fired a shot.

But his own interest was not primarily in Napoleon's success. After telling of the immediate devastation at Jena, he turned to the heroism in defeat at Auërstadt, where the Duke was fatally wounded and even the King fought valiantly. The account by Thiers is far the most extensive, and Hardy built upon the clues it offered. The Duke had had a presentiment of catastrophe which Hardy turns into a premonition of his own death. Thiers calls him "hésitant dans le conseil, jamais au feu" (VII, 139). Hardy negligently does him injustice in his attempt to play up the contrast: "Reed in council, rock in fire" (II, 1, iv). Thiers records Moellendorf's wish not to survive; Hardy reads:

> The gallant Moellendorf, in flushed despair,
> Swore he would not survive; and, pressing on,
> He, too, was slaughtered.

The description of Jena attests to the tactical skill of Napoleon; the reports from Auërstadt bring us glimpses of individual men, self-forgetfully heroic. For Thiers the evaluation of the battle at Jena was a simple matter. Depicting the flight of the Prussians amidst vast slaughter he finds inspiration in "la gloire": "Scènes terribles, dont l'aspect serait intolérable, si le génie, si l'héroïsme déployés, n'en rachetaient l'horreur, et si la gloire, cette lumière qui embellit tout, ne venait les envelopper de ses rayons éblouissants!" (VII, 127). Hardy could respect such sentiments, even as he admired their outstanding exemplar, Ney. But he himself found a nobler expression of heroism. The Duke and Moellendorf had been heroic because they had accepted their fates as mortal men.

It was two weeks later that Napoleon came to Berlin. Thiers remarks that even the vanquished admired the triumphal entry:

> C'était pour la première fois qu'il lui arrivait d'entrer en triomphateur, comme Alexandre ou César, dans une capitale conquise.... Mais aujourd'hui, soit orgueil d'avoir terrassé une armée réputée invincible, soit désir de frapper l'Europe par un spectacle éclatant, soit aussi l'ivresse de la victoire montant à sa tête plus haut que de coutume, il choisit le 28 au matin pour faire dans Berlin une entrée triomphale (VII, 174).

Thiers reports that the aristocracy had fled, but that the rich bourgeoisie were at the windows: "Les femmes . . . semblaient avides du spectacle qui était sous leurs yeux: quelques-unes laissaient couler des larmes . . . ."[90] Hardy, of course, read other sources, too,[91] but in bringing Napoleon into Berlin he drew mainly on Thiers' extensive account. Thiers, along with others, speaks of the Emperor's appropriating relics from the Sans-Souci Palace and of the bulletins he dispatched to Paris. Hardy gives the natural displeasure of the Berlin ladies at the despoiling and the "loud scurrility" in the bulletins "against a queen who cannot make reprise!"[92]

In telescoping events in II, 1, vi, Hardy faced technical problems.

[90] Hardy reads, "some in tears."

[91] For example, in having the Ironic Spirits stress Napoleon's hatred of England he drew from a general comment by Coquelle, *Napoléon et l'Angleterre* (291): "L'échec des préparatifs de descente, la défaite de Trafalgar surtout sont des blessures qui ne se cicatrisent jamais." As noted by Rutland, this became:

> The wane of his armaments ill-advised,
> At Trafalgár, to a force despised,
> Was a wound which never has cicatrized.

[92] "les sarcasmes les plus virulents contre les reines qui se mêlaient des affaires d'État . . . ," *Histoire du Consulat*, VII, 176.

He wanted to give additional facts about the battle, to describe the immediate aftermath, to bring Napoleon to Berlin, and to summarize the Berlin Decree, which was pronounced November 25, almost a month after the triumphal entrance. While doing all this he also wanted to let his imagination play with the reaction of the Prussians themselves and so to tell his story as it appeared to them. Thiers' reference to the ladies at the windows gave him the hint for having ladies overlook a street where they could see returnees from the battlefield (II, 1, v) and then, from the same vantage, observe the contrasting scene of October 28. The device was convenient, but unfortunately Hardy made a slip. Actually he made two, the first trivial but possibly responsible for the second. In II, 1, vi, a lady has Napoleon at Potsdam "yesterday," whereas Thiers explicitly puts him there on the twenty-sixth and at Charlottenburg on the twenty-seventh. This, of course, would make a difference as to his path in entering Berlin.

In scene v, horsemen come along the Potsdamer-Strasse and turn into the Leipziger-Strasse to a "public place" overlooked by the window where the ladies are.[93] In scene vi—"The Same"—Napoleon's "procession passes along the front until it reaches the entrance to the Royal Palace." In the very paragraph from which Hardy had borrowed, Thiers gives the route as "la longue et vaste rue de Berlin, qui conduit de la porte de Charlottenbourg au palais des rois de Prusse." This is, of course, not the Potsdamer-Strasse, but Unter den Linden. The lapse in geography is irrelevant to the substance of the scene and could be forgotten if we were not following the steps of a man who wanted to know the precise location of the ballroom at Brussels and who altered his manuscript more than once to tell exactly where a given corps was stationed as a battle opened.

Hardy's own apology in a letter, October 12, 1922, is interesting because it justifies a method he had a perfect right to use and yet does not justify the scene in question. In answer to a query from General J. H. Morgan, he wrote:

> I cannot for my life recall where I obtained the idea of N's entry into Berlin by the Potsdamer-strasse, though I don't think I should have written it without authority. However, you have to remember that the events generally in *The Dynasts* had to be pulled together into dramatic scenes, to show themselves to the mental eye of the reader as a picture viewed

[93] Since Leipzig Platz is at the intersection, it best corresponds to Hardy's "place."

from one point; and hence it was sometimes necessary to see round corners, down crooked streets, and to shift buildings nearer each other than in reality (as Turner did in his landscapes); and it may possibly happen that I gave "A Public Place" in Berlin these convenient facilities without much ceremony.[94]

Actually, since the room in scene v could just as well have overlooked Unter den Linden, no dramatic license was necessary. A simpler explanation would appear to take us back to "yesterday." Hardy probably had forgotten that Napoleon had moved on from Potsdam to Charlottenburg, and so brought him northeastward, well south of the actual route.

"'Ce spectacle,' s'écriait Napoléon, 'est fait pour inspirer aux princes l'amour de la paix, et l'horreur de la guerre!'" (VII, 394)—and Thiers adds that the Emperor was sincere at the moment he spoke. The spectacle was the Battle of Preussisch-Eylau, February 7, 1807. Since Jena there had been a succession of lesser encounters and great suffering on both sides. France had pushed far to the northeast and now was fought to a draw by superior Russian forces. Thiers gives the dead and wounded as forty thousand, mainly Russian, and Hardy accepts his figures. Alison (X, 153) says the battle was conducted "under circumstances of unexampled horror," and Hardy's four verses capture that horror. The days that followed were hardly less terrible. March 1, Napoleon wrote to Joseph of the destitution of his army, which, nevertheless, continued to fight. After remarking that everyone else had been ill, he ended his letter, "pour moi je ne me suis jamais trouvé plus fort, et j'ai engraissé."[95]

May 24, Danzig yielded after a barbarous siege. Then, on June 14, at Friedland, a short distance from Preussisch-Eylau, the Emperor soundly defeated the Russians, and, as Alison noted (X, 307) in words borrowed by Hardy, the event "dissolved the great confederacy" formed by Pitt. Meanwhile, Napoleon dictated yet more repressive measures for France, "voulant non-seulement agir, mais penser pour tout le monde."[96] Meanwhile, too, the Russian armies had endured starvation, and stragglers from both armies had become marauders, their morale exhausted, their existence reduced to mere concern for survival. Hardy could not put all this into a scene primarily on a

[94] *The Later Years*, p. 228.
[95] Thiers, *Histoire du Consulat*, VII, 417.
[96] *Ibid.*, 431.

different matter, but he captured its tone in II, 1, vii—"Tilsit and the River Niemen." Through choruses of the Years and the Pities he told of the two battles in long alliterative lines whose plaintive rhythm reads like a dirge.

But he did not start his scene with the horror. The occasion is one of improvised splendour, in which the defeated Alexander is to be patronized as if an ally and the hapless Queen of Prussia is to be the object of gallantry. So we begin with a spectacle of courtly elegance as the Emperor, who "looks well, but is growing fat," is the gracious host on a raft in the Niemen. Only then is the death's-head placed before us. In the rest of the scene and the next, as Europe is carved into delicious morsels and a rose is bestowed upon a lovely young queen, we cannot forget what the banqueting has cost.

Napoleon took up his residence at Tilsit, June 19, an armistice was established June 21, the Emperor and Alexander met on the raft June 25,[97] and the negotiations ended with a treaty July 7 between the two and another July 9 between Napoleon and Frederick William. Frederick was sometimes blunt, Alexander was courtly, Napoleon was gracious but unyielding, and the Queen epitomized beauty in distress. Much of what happened, apart from the treaties, was, of course, hearsay; and Hardy was free to invent. He also employed license in putting into two scenes events from several days. For what did not concern the Queen he has little that is not stated or implied in Thiers. Sometimes, as in "Why are we at war?" he made no change.[98] Again Thiers, in translation, gives us, "Between you and me . . . there must be no third person" (VII, 339–340). Hardy puts it, "Between us two, henceforth, must stand no third." Once, in having Napoleon hint of a marriage with Alexander's sister, he interpolated information from other occasions.

Knowing that English spies were at Tilsit, Hardy enlivened his narration of prosaic negotiations by using two as spokesmen—and characteristically he added a footnote giving their probable identity. Then follows a somewhat stilted dialogue of the two emperors, not inappropriate for a diplomatic exchange. But Hardy was saving for his climax, which would pit tearful charm against middle-aged prudence.

In Thiers he could find a summary and in the other histories somewhat more, but it would appear that he went to the original source, the

[97] Hardy writes, "It is the day after midsummer."
[98] *Histoire du Consulat*, VII, 628; English version, VII, 337.

Memorial of Las Cases, who had the story from the ex-Emperor himself. Obviously Napoleon had remembered with fondness the temptation which had proved so winsome at Tilsit, and his biographer probably heightened what he was given. Hardy merely rearranged and heightened further. Las Cases, for example, writes:

> "Prussia," she exclaimed, "had been blindfolded with respect to her power;—she had dared to contend with a hero . . .; she was deservedly punished for it. The glory of the great Frederic, his memory, and his inheritance had puffed up the pride of Prussia, and had caused her ruin" (II, part iv, 213).

Hardy is more metaphorical:

> Prussia was blind in blazoning her power
> Against the Mage of Earth! . . .
> The embers of great Frederick's deeds inflamed her:
> His glories swelled her to her ruining.
> Too well has she been punished!

The most famous incident was the giving of a rose. As Las Cases narrates the anecdote—

> An instant before dinner Napoleon took a very beautiful rose from a flower stand, which he presented to the Queen. She at first expressed by the motion of her hand a kind of prepared refusal; but suddenly recollecting herself, she said, *Yes, but at least with Magdeburg.* The Emperor replied, "But . . . [*sic*] I shall observe to your Majesty, that it is I who present, and you, who are about to receive it."

Hardy has the presentation as the Queen is ready to leave, and he sharpened Napoleon's reply:

> It is for you to take what I can give.
> And I give this—no more.

After their last dinner together Napoleon took the Queen to the middle of the staircase. Las Cases continues:

> She squeezed his hand, and said with a kind of tenderness, "Is it possible, that after having had the honour of being so near to the hero of the century and of history, he will not leave me the power and satisfaction of being enabled to assure him, that he has attached me to him for life?"— "Madam," replied the Emperor in a serious tone, "I am to be pitied; it is the result of my unhappy stars."

Hardy made the Queen's words more coquettish and at the same time more plaintive, and he expanded the Emperor's reply to five lines. He must have taken the reference to the stars as devoid of sentimental self-glorification, for the Spirit of the Years comments:

> He spoke thus at the Bridge of Lodi. Strange,
> He's of the few in Europe who discern
> The working of the Will.

Having put the weeping Queen in her carriage, the Emperor boasts to Talleyrand that he had "a good mind" to kiss her thoroughly and "agree to all she wanted."

Hardy makes no comment, but strange relationships are suggested. Though she is a sophisticated coquette, the Queen's abasement is as great as Tess's before Angel or Alec, and Napoleon is as self-righteous as Angel, as libertine as Alec. Yet what is it that Louisa wants in pleading vainly not to be bereft of Magdeburg. It is not the welfare of its citizens so much as her own personal happiness. At the moment it is two human individuals that are before us, one cautiously practical, the other passionately unhappy. But both happen also to be dynasts, and, because of such as they, scores of thousands have died within a year, and that by no means the bloodiest of the age.

Two years separated the peace at Tilsit and the Battle of Wagram, July 5–6, 1809. In Hardy's narrative the interim is represented by Vimiero, August 21, 1808, Coruña, January 16, 1809, and such bits and pieces as he could work into dialogue summaries of events elsewhere. September 8, 1808, Napoleon had obtained a new treaty, not mentioned by Hardy, with Prussia. But before the end of the year Austria had armed, and on January 6 the Emperor left Astorga for Paris to prepare for war. This Hardy covered in II, 3, ii. Hostilities with Austria began April 9. April 20–24 there were continuous battles, including Echmühl and Ratisbon, and on May 3 the devastation of Ebersberg. May 11–12 Vienna was bombarded and forced to capitulate. May 20, Napoleon established a bridge on the island of Inder-Lobau. The following two days brought the indecisive Battle of Aspern-Essling, where Lannes was killed; and after further skirmishes came Wagram.

In II, 3, v—"Vienna. A Café in the Stephans-Platz"—and II, 4, i—"A Road out of Vienna"—Hardy tried to give some notion of the events between Coruña and early May. Using his now established device of having mortals do the work of the Spirit of Rumours, he let Austrian citizens and an Englishman, in scene v, complete unfinished news about Coruña and further defend Moore, mention—for future use—the young Maria's hatred of France, indicate the failure to gain Russian support—to become ironic at Borodino—praise England for having never wavered in hostility to Napoleon, and indicate the warlike spirit and preparations in Vienna. The style is undistinguished, and only by implication are there serious overtones. Bands are playing and the scene ends with dancing to a patriotic waltz in the confidence of assured victory. Hardy does not comment, but certainly the eagerness of "hot volunteers" and the joy of the dance suggest the hypnotic yielding of the individual will to the Will that impels the multitude.

Scene II, 4, i has to take place between May 3, as Ebersberg is mentioned, and the eleventh, as Vienna has not yet been attacked. The Empress calls the defeat at Echmühl fatal, and an officer is arbitrarily introduced to describe the massacre at Ebersberg and the approach of the French to Vienna. The livelier part of the scene, the gossip of the young archduchess and her youngish stepmother about the prospective marriage of Napoleon to Anne of Russia, is essentially fiction. The conversation has its motif, of course, in history, which also contrasted the young Maria Louisa with the mature Josephine. But the girl in *The Dynasts* who hopes that the prophecy will come true that Napoleon will "die this year at Cologne, in an inn called 'The Red Crab,'" and who calls him a "bourgeois Corsican" and the Empress-mother of Russia a "pompous old thing" is a country lass from a Wessex novel who happens to have been reared at the Austrian court.

Maria is leaving Vienna and Hardy implies its imminent fall; but even so, in II, 4, ii we are unprepared to find ourselves at the island of Lobau in the Danube, a few miles from Essling. There were two reasons why Wagram should outrank the battles of late April and those at Ebersberg and Essling. One was the tactical novelty; the other, the consequences. For days Napoleon had prepared boats, rafts, and sections of floating bridges; and during the night of July 4–5 he was able to move men, horses, and guns to the river bank as if on a schedule, despite torrential rains and enemy resistance. In the two-day battle he suffered reverses; and, as he subsequently lamented, because many of his troops were young, he did not dare to risk a model wheeling manoeuvre—giving way on one flank to spin the enemy around. But with an army of 150,000 or more he managed a flanking motion while holding in the center and on the other flank. July 11, after pursuing the remnants of the Austrian army, he achieved an advantageous armistice which ended the Austrian campaign of 1809.

To sort out Hardy's borrowings in II, 4, ii and iii is impossible. In general he accords with Thiers, but with exceptions in detail, and he is not very close to any other history. Having given the troop movement in dumb show, he compressed two days of battle into one and resorted to the awkward device of reporting from the vantage of the Emperor Francis and his staff, some distance away. Though he draws on messengers, there is not only undue looking around corners, but a constriction of what was in reality a huge canvas. Moreover, the words catch nothing of the sensations of the combatants and, unlike choruses by the Spirits, they fail to universalize the meaning of the tragic event. Except for the concluding lines by Francis, they are rather commonplace expressions of hope, surprise, and finally dejection. Unfortunately, too, Hardy's dramatic structure, as sometimes elsewhere, did not permit him to follow the pursuit and to indicate the significance of the armistice. Instead, he abruptly closed the scene and turned to Talavera. In short, in *The Dynasts* Wagram is misrepresented as an isolated action with no special political significance; and, perhaps even more disturbing, though there is massive killing, the story has little true poetry, no special human touches, nothing that contributes pointedly to Hardy's theme on the ways of the unconscious Will.

Very different, as we have noticed, are the two succeeding scenes at Talavera, dominated by the Spirits. Different, too, is Hardy's last scene on the campaign in the east in 1809. Here, II, 4, viii—"Walcheren"—the prose has a poetic tone and the verse brings new connotations to the theme.

An English army debarked onto the marshland at Walcheren, July 30, 1809, and the survivors departed September 24. Citing Dodsley's *Annual Register*, Alison speaks of a loss of 7,000 men. Lanfrey alludes to 10,000 suffering from fever, with the number increasing. Thiers gives the highest figures: 12,000 to 15,000 ill in late August, of 44,000 only 24,000 to 25,000 available to go to Anvers, 4,000 dead, and 12,000 able to return to England. There were recriminations in Parliament, and the nation was shocked by the horror. It was not only the loss of life that was a stunning blow; as seen in retrospect the expedition epitomized the most stupid folly. Had fever not stricken the men, the project would have been militarily unwise, and the event proved the lack of foresight of those who were responsible.

For Hardy, Walcheren was, of course, unlike the battle scenes. There was no conflict. Men, some of whom had fought in the Peninsula, had no chance to prove their courage. They merely shivered and burned and died. The subject was consequently fitted for lyric rather than dramatic representation, and it was primarily in the domain overlooked by the Pities. It is the Chorus of the Pities which repeats the words of the dying men, words not as they would actually have been spoken, but as they might have been distilled from thousands of individual lamentations into a ghostly composite in which still-living voices speak as from the grave. Men going into battle may seem automatons, but they still have some apparent choice of action within the predestined whole. At Walcheren action of any meaningful kind is denied:

> We might have fought, and had we died, died well,
> Even if in dynasts' discords not our own ＊＊＊.

The voices insist that these men are more unfortunate than others, and certainly it is this fact that justifies the scene. And yet they are really the voices of all men who stop to think of the futility of human life, for they negate even the semblance of free will. And with no malice whatever the Spirit of the Years denies that any special regrets are justified for the deaths of these thousands of young soldiers:

> —Men pass to dark corruption, at the best,
> Ere I can count five score: these why not now?—
> The Immanent Shaper builds Its beings so
> Whether ye sigh their sighs with them or no!

Hardy does not, of course, mean that Years has the better of an argument. What the aged Spirit says is simple truth. But the wailing lines repeated by the Pities are no less true; and though there may be hope, there is no certainty that the pathetic lot of mankind will ever change.

The lines on Walcheren could stand as a complete poem. Though in the Wars themselves the catastrophe had a causal relationship to other events, Hardy is not concerned with this. The scene is therefore unrelated dramatically to the rest of the epic. As a lyric vision, however, it is an integral part. It has a meaning by itself, but that significance is intensified by its being found in a work of cosmic implications.

Indeed, the scenes which enclose it give it bold relief. It follows the buffoonery of the Prince of Wales as he celebrates in advance the success of the expedition, and it precedes Napoleon's machinations to create a dynastic succession and so, in a way, to make his own personal spirit immortal.

In looking at the events of 1805–1809 in central Europe, Hardy had three choices, and he used all three. Under the eye of eternity, most nearly represented by Years, they are part of a pattern whose beginning is lost in prehistoric times and whose future is unknown. When the poet became emotionally involved, however, in the lot of mankind, he had to choose between irony and pathos.

However neutral the impulsion of the Will, man could be viewed as a desolate creature. In contemplating his predicament, one could find some kind of surcease from pain by discovering matter for laughter. The dynasts were comic manikins. So, too, were the hundreds of thousands who were led by them to destruction, not finally because they were dynasts' slaves, but because they themselves required that dynasts exist. The Spirit Ironic could not laugh effectively at the Will. But he could laugh at Napoleon and Francis and Alexander and at the folly of their subjects. And irony was certainly better than no rational response at all. Without it—or with too much of it—sentimentality would triumph. In the years 1805–1809 in central Europe, as in the Peninsula, the Spirit Ironic had his say.

But finally one came around to the pity of it all. After the railing at the madness of the human zeal to cause quickly the deaths that Nature rendered sooner or later inevitable, one came back to the pathos of the individual mortal spirit, godlike in its apprehensions and capable of sorrow. Ulm and Jena and Wagram and Walcheren, the weeping Louisa and the unnamed widows and orphans were matter finally for tears—tears not even to be dismissed by the paean of hope that would end the play.

An Old Wife and a New: An Interlude

Hardy was later to select and arrange for the stage a number of scenes from *The Dynasts*. His epic itself, despite its length, might be called scenes selected from the careers of dynasts, for many of the activities of Napoleon are slighted or omitted altogether. We learn that he was annoyed by the economic effects of the British blockade, but we are told virtually nothing about his extensive preoccupation with steps to preserve financial stability and raise revenues for his wars. We are told of his ordering public works to symbolize the glory of France or to lull the populace in times of defeat, but nothing of his reorganizing of the governmental administration or even of his machinery for recruiting soldiers. These and other matters which are discussed in Thiers testify to the Emperor's genius and also reveal his increasing enslavement to the forces he alone must direct. When in Paris, he was planning the logistics of campaigns; on the way to battle he would dictate administrative orders to be carried out at home. By the end of 1809 the welfare of France and the perpetuation of his own concepts of government and empire were for Napoleon inseparable. Indispensable for fulfillment of his dreams was an heir. Without an heir the structure would collapse. With a son, even under a regency till he came of age, the glory would somehow outlast his own sojourn on earth and, in a sense, render his spirit immortal. The Emperor could not know what talents a child might have; in history he would have found repeated evidence of reversal from one generation to the next. Contemporary Prussia afforded an example. But still the megalomania grew.

Leaving out the rest, Hardy chose to concentrate on the *idée fixe* itself. He knew the history of Napoleon's domestic life from the time of his marriage to Josephine in 1796, including her coquetries soon after marriage, when her husband was in Italy, and Napoleon's own infidelities in Egypt and after. The latter were numerous enough, but the only one to which Hardy attached importance was the affair with Mme. Walewska, and that because she had borne a son. The climactic events were the divorce and second marriage. In the inevitable cruelty involved in the public humiliation of Josephine for failure to produce an heir Hardy found dramatic substance that fitted his theme. It was the will of one man that brought grief to one woman, and yet, given the poet's world view, Napoleon himself was but an agent of the Will. There was sardonic comedy in the plots to obtain a new wife, who must, of course, be not from the social rank from which Bonaparte had lifted himself as the democratic overthrower of kings, but of royal lineage. There was sheer animal barbarism in the willingness to marry a mere child—the sister of Alexander—who might not be quite ready as yet for procreation, and cynicism in keeping the way open, as a last resort, for an alliance with the house of Saxony. There was a mixture of these and whimsical irony in the Emperor's finally obtaining an eighteen-year-old bride who had been educated to hate him as an enemy and a villain.

For later historians there were three sources of special pertinence for the events immediately preceding the divorce and for the divorce itself. De Bausset, the prefect of the palace, had written of what he saw and heard the evening of November 30, 1809.[99] His account was extensively quoted and is given at length in Capefigue (VIII, 267–269). In his memoirs of Josephine, Memes had fused eyewitness evidence with what he had been told by Josephine and whatever he could glean from other reports, including De Bausset's. Even when describing the anguish of the Empress, Memes tried hard to be sympathetic to the Emperor as well, and his book sometimes reads like an apology. Its chief value for Hardy was that it offered glimpses of the marital difficulties from the beginning. The third source was the *Memoirs of Constant*.[100] As Napoleon's valet, Constant, like Memes, could sometimes report at first hand. He was generally favourable to Napoleon, even when he had to rationalize that great men were not to be judged as common mortals. He knew more than any other commentator of the seduction of "Mme. V——" as he had assisted in arrangements for the Polish lady's assignations with the Emperor. He was also present November 30, though he got part of his story from De Bausset. Both he and Memes were present December 16, when Josephine consented to the divorce.[101]

Capefigue, Thiers, De Bourrienne, and Lévy[102] drew mainly on these three and added their own editorial impressions. There were small discrepancies in fact, and for his convenience Hardy took further liberties. What mattered, however, was the interpretation. While following the historians, Hardy was writing fiction. The first scene, II, 2, vi—"St. Cloud. The Boudoir of Josephine"—is entirely imaginary. The second, II, 5, ii—"Paris. The Tuileries"—and the report of the divorce in II, 5, iv—"London. A Club in St. James's Street"—are concerned with the specific events of November 30 and December 16.

[99] *Mémoires anecdotiques sur l'intérieur du palais.*

[100] French edition, in 4 volumes, Paris, n.d. The British Museum has the 1896 translation by Percy Pinkerton.

[101] A source apparently known by Hardy only at second hand was the *Mémoires* of the Duchesse d'Abrantès.

[102] Arthur Lévy, *Napoléon Intime* (Paris, 1893), in the Memorial Library.

In all three, we may believe, Hardy wished to give true portraits. The problem, however, was how to determine the truth. For Hardy there was finally only one way. His characters brought onto the stage a personal history and their conduct must be consistent with that past. Whether or not he remembered Memes's words on Josephine (27), he was aware that "at every period of her life jealousy appears to have held great sway over her mind." He knew that she had good reason for anxiety, partly because she had heard rumours of her husband's infidelities, partly because among the Bonapartes only Joseph was her friend. As Hardy saw her, she had endured much and her repentance of her own early flirtations left her gentle and pathetic, though by no means spiritless. She was now fighting for the symbol of her self-respect, and she was also in love with her husband. As to Napoleon, the limning of the portrait was less simple. He had certainly been in love with Josephine; Memes gives ample evidence. Yet he had treated women cynically, and he had used political intrigue amounting to coercion to bring Mme. Walewska (Mme. V——) to his bed. As in his dealings with men, he judged women by their loyalty to him, however irresponsible he had been in return. And by now he had reached the point where whatever fitted his schemes was for him a matter of destiny.

How would two such persons act when the will of the man was inflexible and the woman must reluctantly submit? Clym Yeobright was a kindly person, but he had been unable to see with Eustacia's eyes. Angel Clare had felt sorry for Tess, but he had, nonetheless, condemned her. There were events in Hardy's life that led him to believe that, even more than for her own folly, the woman must pay for the egocentrism of her lover. The stronger a man's rational argument, the greater his mission—or the more exalted his ideal of womanhood—the more cruel would be the judgment he pronounced. In his confrontation of Josephine and Napoleon, Hardy saw both the individuals and the generic situation. The latter, as in the novels, was fraught with heartlessness, no matter how tender or regretful the executioner might be. Memes, De Bausset, and Constant supplied the facts, including some of the very words; but the nuances were Hardy's own.

The first scene is on a summer evening after the defeat of Beylen, July 19, 1808, to which Napoleon refers. Hardy brought in the fact that the Emperor liked to play "Catch-me-if-you-can," but with no opportunity to explain that he ordinarily showed partiality to his wife in such games. Instead, he had to present with abrupt suddenness what in reality evolved slowly. This meant having Josephine reproach her husband for the affair with Mme. Walewska after Jena and having Napoleon vulgarly reply that the incident had "proved the fault not mine." Hardy also tucked in some general history and such personal items as Joseph's friendliness to Josephine, the rumour of negotiations for the hand of Alexander's sister, and Napoleon's rankling memory of Josephine's refusal to come to him in Italy. The basis of the scene was historical, but the conversation was imaginary. One feels that in actuality any dialogue between the two in the summer of 1808, more than a year before the divorce, would have been less frank, but Hardy had to prepare in one scene for a painful bluntness in that of November 30, 1809.

Though his words could easily be the rationalization of a sentimentalist, Hardy chose to present seriously Napoleon's defence:

> Come, dwell not gloomily on this cold need
> Of waiving private joy for policy.
> We are but thistle-globes on Heaven's high gales,
> And whither blown, or when, or how, or why,
> Can choose us not at all!

Not, of course, that the poet wanted to minimize the Emperor's egoism; but the last lines, vaguely reminiscent of FitzGerald, were perhaps less Napoleonic than Hardian.

For the November 30 scene De Bausset reported his own part in the action, Constant (III, 192–194) retold De Bausset's story and added details, and Memes drew on De Bausset and on Josephine's own version. In Hardy's opening narration Constant's "held a handkerchief to her lips to repress her sobs" became "patting her eyes with her handkerchief," and his "stood there in a sort of stupor" was the hint for "to sink cowering into a chair like a frightened animal." Hardy added "pushes her aside" and made other minor changes concerning De Bausset's re-entrance and the carrying of Josephine from the room.

But the major alteration is in what he put in his imagined dialogue when the two are alone. Memes quotes Josephine:

He took my hand, placed it upon his heart, gazed upon me for a moment, then pronounced these fearful words—"Josephine! my excellent

Josephine! thou knowest if I have loved thee! To thee—to thee alone do I owe the only moments of happiness which I have enjoyed in this world, Josephine! My destiny overmasters my will. My dearest affections must be silent before the interests of France!" (354–355).

Hardy had scantly drawn on this in the earlier scene. Here he omitted all tenderness, and what he added was cruel, indeed. As we shall note, soon after the divorce Josephine did actually assist in bringing about the marriage with her successor. Since she was acting to please Napoleon, Hardy invented his own version. The Emperor climaxes his brutality as if impelled by a fiend:

> And one thing further still,
> You'll help me in my marriage overtures
> To win the Duchess—Austrian Marie she,—
> Concentring all your force to forward them.

Both Constant and Memes stress Napoleon's immediate grief.[103] Hardy, in contrast, returns him to the scene irritably complaining to Hortense of Josephine's unreasonableness. His two sources report that several days later Eugene conferred with Napoleon and unavailingly requested permission to withdraw from his service to accompany and comfort his mother; Memes adds that Hortense was in accord with her brother. Hardy telescopes time and substitutes Hortense for Eugene. Knowing of the love of his stepdaughter for Napoleon, Hardy obviously found in the shift not only a convenience, but an additional touch of cruelty.

Having in this scene reached an acme of violence, Hardy had to avoid anticlimax in narrating the divorce itself. He resorted to summary after the fact in a club in London, and he gave to his narrator the tone of the Spirit Sinister. Josephine's white muslin gown is from Memes (360), and the rest could as easily come from him as from Constant. But Memes is considerate to both principals and follows the report of the divorce with their weeping together that evening. If Hardy needed support for his bitter version, he could have found it in Lanfrey (III, 539), De Bourrienne (III, 186–187), who quoted Rovigo, or even Thiers. In any event, he altered the portrait of Josephine to fit his own beliefs. The sources reveal that she was tragically stricken and that she gave way to sobs, but that she recovered

[103] Thiers emphasizes Napoleon's sadness then and later, *Histoire du Consulat,* XI, 342 ff.

and in a dignified manner retreated on Hortense's arm. Eugene, on the other hand, was overcome and, upon leaving the room, fell down unconscious. Hardy omits the effect on Eugene, but has Josephine "led off fainting." The revision puts greater shame on Napoleon, but it also unintentionally commits injustice against a woman who had studied conscientiously the art of being a queen.

By the chronological delay in telling of the divorce Hardy placed the two scenes as a frame before and after the Iphigenian sacrifice of the young Maria, for the possession of whose health, youth, and hoped-for procreative capacity Napoleon, with the urging of his countrymen, had created this horrible ado.

The intrigue that ended with Maria Louisa of Austria's becoming Marie Louise, Empress of France, was indeed a comedy of errors played in deadly earnest. Nowhere could Hardy find an authentic account of all the machinations, though each purported to be definitive. In Capefigue (VIII, 333–334) he came upon an anecdote of flirtatious repartee between Mme. Metternich and Napoleon, during which the Emperor asked his companion, "croyez-vous que si je demandais l'archiduchesse Marie Louise, elle voulût de moi et qu'on me la donnât?" Napoleon reportedly insisted that she confer with the Austrian ambassador in Paris, Prince Schwarzenberg, and that she also write her husband. The conversation took place during carnival time, after December 16. Mme. Metternich went to see the ambassador, and both dispatched letters to Vienna.

In II, 5, i—"Paris. A Ballroom in the House of Cambacérès"— Hardy arbitrarily put the exchange of pleasantries before the November 30 incident, thus emphasizing Napoleon's duplicity. And he assumed that the letter to Metternich recounted the vivacious conversation as Capefigue had given it. In his misplaced confidence he added a foot-note: "So Madame Metternich to her husband in reporting this inter-view. But who shall say!" The definitive source was the letter itself, dated January 3, 1810, and printed in the *Memoirs of Prince Metter-nich*.[104] In it Mme. Metternich mentions having recently been flattered by Napoleon, but states that the possibility of his marrying Maria was broached to her by Hortense and Josephine on January 2, at Mal-maison, with Napoleon not present.

Napoleon's own account of the marriage flurry is narrated by O'Meara. It is, of course, complimentary to the Emperor, but it

[104] London: Richard Bentley and Son, 1880–1882, II, 373.

deserves a hearing. According to O'Meara, Napoleon told him at St. Helena that, when a divorce was rumoured,

> the greatest sovereigns of Europe intrigued for an alliance with me. As soon as the Emperor of Austria heard that a new marriage was in agitation, he sent for Narbonne, and expressed his surprise that his family had not been thought of. At this time an union with a princess of Russia or of Saxony was contemplated. The cabinet of Vienna sent instructions on the subject to Prince Schwarzenberg, who was ambassador at Paris. Despatches were also received from the ambassador in Russia, stating the willingness of the Emperor Alexander to offer his sister, the Grand Duchess Anne (II, 370–371).

Hardy could have read a different account in Thiers. After trying to determine what the stage of negotiations with Russia, Saxony, or Austria was at any given time in late 1809, he himself might well have felt like muttering "but who shall say."

The scene is not exclusively in the tone of the Spirits Sinister and Ironic. It is opened with Pities, in the role of a Familiar, eliciting from the Emperor an expression of his haunting sense of mortality. The death of Lannes had singularly impressed Hardy, and the poet chose to make it a symbol of the things that, in his reflective moments, ought to creep forward from the shadowy regions of the Emperor's mind. So now, as he soliloquizes, Napoleon recalls, among other memories,

> The unexpected, lurid death of Lannes—
> Rigid as iron, reaped down like a straw.

When Thiers differed from another historian, Hardy tended to choose his version, but not for what happened in the Austrian Imperial Palace in II, 5, iii; for Thiers says that, far from being afraid of the life before her as Napoleon's spouse, Maria Louisa was joyful (XI, 381–382). Hardy's principal source for the scene as a whole was Capefigue, but he probably also used Méneval, a primary source on Maria's own reaction to the proposed marriage.[105] There is nothing in Hardy demonstrably closer to Méneval—whom Hardy later cited in his rough draft—than to Capefigue, who drew upon him, but the tone is much more Méneval's. In any event, Hardy expanded what he found. In Capefigue, Metternich points out to Francis the political advantages

[105] Méneval, *Napoléon et Marie-Louise. Souvenirs Historiques*, I, 222–223; and *Memoirs to Serve for the History of Napoleon I from 1802 to 1815* (3 vols.; London, 1894), II, 266–267.

of the marriage, and the Emperor replies laconically, "Allez voir ma fille Marie-Louise de ma part; exposez-lui notre situation, et avant d'agir, ayez son consentement" (VIII, 335). Maria consented, though she had "les larmes aux yeux." As Capefigue remarks, "Pouvait-elle faire une autre réponse?" He adds that the pamphlets had represented the invader of Austria as "brusque, grossier, sans galanterie, dur avec les femmes, ne les prenant que comme distractions vulgaires."

Méneval, to whom Maria told her thoughts freely, says that she felt "comme une victime dévouée au Minotaure." When young, the children of Francis had made "la plus noire et la plus rébarbative" of their toy statuettes represent Napoleon, and then "ils la lardaient de coups d'épingles et l'accablaient d'outrages." Hardy has Maria recall the "horrible things" she has uttered, including wishing Napoleon dead. He represents Metternich as a realistic diplomat trying to do best for Austria, but in a few words of soliloquy at the end the statesman becomes the Spirit Sinister:

> Decently done! . . . He slipped out "sacrifice,"
> And scarce could hide his heartache for his girl.
> Well ached it!—But when these things have to be
> It is as well to breast them stoically.

Again, in this scene, there is a special touch. Maria is saddened by the vanishing of "five poor little birds." She is still a girl as she laments their probable freezing. Later it will be the deaths of thousands of French soldiers on the frozen fields of Russia which will shock Marie Louise of France.

It was March 13, 1810, that the royal *cortège* left Vienna. Hardy's description of the procession in II, 5, v—"The Old West Highway out of Vienna"—owes little to the histories; its significance is in the bird's-eye point of view. This is itself a commentary on the world in which a girl whose eyes are still red from weeping will be thrust into the center of terrestrial affairs. The procession is "no more than a file of ants," a "puny concatenation of specks," as it carries its special passenger from a sheltered girlhood to a future of intrigue and tragedy.

In quick change of pace, in the next scene, we find Napoleon at Courcelles, March 28, restively awaiting his eighteen-year-old bride. His arrival in a "plain" carriage seems to be based on De Bourrienne (III, 192), most of the rest could have come from Lévy (207 ff.),

Murat's presence may be from Thiers (XI, 386), and at least one comic detail is from Constant, one of Lévy's sources. As Lévy tells the story,

> Il s'approcha de la voiture de Sa Majesté sans être reconnu; mais l'écuyer ... ouvrit la portière et baissa le marchepied en criant: L'Empereur.
>
> Napoléon se jeta au cou de Marie-Louise, qui n'était nullement pré-parée à cette brusque et galante entrevue, et il ordonna sur-le-champ d'aller en toute hâte vers Compiègne ... (207).

Constant reports Marie's recovery: "Votre portrait n'est pas flatté" (III, 222). Hardy converts "sans être reconnu" into Marie's "Ah, Heaven! Two highwaymen are upon us!" and Constant's five words into "You are so much—better looking than your portraits—that I hardly knew you!" The portraits were the caricatures.

So the Ironic Spirits can break forth into ribald doggerel, winding up:

> She'll bring him a baby,
> As quickly as maybe,
> And that's what he wants her to do,
> Hoo-hoo!
> And that's what he wants her to do!

We are suddenly at Petersburg in the palace of the Empress-mother. For this scene, II, 5, vii, Hardy did not need to sort through the details of Napoleon's negotiations for the hand of Anne, who was still too young for child bearing. Starting with the general situation, he had fun inventing a dialogue between an irate mother and her son. The Empress chides Alexander for failing to bring about a marriage with Napoleon—after she herself has married off Catherine, leaving only Anne. Yet she is horrified at the thought of Anne's becoming the wife of Napoleon. The delaying tactics which she and Alexander pursued in the matter of a possible wedding were the best means of teaching Napoleon a lesson:

> And may such practice rule our centuries through!
> The necks of those who rate themselves our peers
> Are cured of stiffness by its potency.

But it was effrontery in Napoleon not to wait to be taught the lesson. Such delightful logic surpasses that of a Joan Durbeyfield. And to cap all, in an undignified explosion she speaks of Napoleon's "bourgeois quality." Though she admits to being "a Romanoff by marriage merely," yet is she every inch a dynast.

In the next scene—"Paris. The Grand Gallery of the Louvre and the Salon-Carré Adjoining"—we have another reflection on what it is to be a dynast. In the midst of the wedding pomp that second of April, 1810, Pities senses the presence of the "thin and headless ghost" of Marie Antoinette. Despite the formal festivity, Marie speaks of

> A clammy air * * * as from vaults
> Peopled with looming spectres, chilling me * * *.

Napoleon's cry of rage at the absence of several cardinals is reported by Thiers:

> "Comptez-les," avait-il dit à un prélat de sa chappelle; et ayant obtenu la certitude que treize manquaient sur vingt-huit, il s'était écrié à demi-voix, avec une violence dont il n'était pas maître:—"Les sots! ils sont toujours les mêmes! ostensiblement soumis, secrètement factieux! ... [sic] mais ils vont voir ce qu'il en coûte de jouer avec ma puissance!"
> (XII, 60–61)

Thiers adds that immediately after the ceremony the Emperor commanded the arrest and dispersal of the cardinals and the sequestration of their property (XII, 60–61). Hardy gives us the spirit of Napoleon's rage and then telescopes, to read "The factious fools!" His "But they shall flinch for it!" inadequately conveys the rest.

The actual historical event was planned theatrically, as if it were on a huge stage; and the Emperor's unexpected frustration and resort to tyranny were in the tradition of despotic protagonists from the days of Aeschylus to Dryden. Hardy merely added his own chorus of Spirits to make the scene fully Greek.

When word reached St. Helena of the death of the Princess Charlotte, it led Napoleon to reminisce about the nearness to death of Marie at the birth of the King of Rome, March 20, 1811. As O'Meara[106] recorded his recollections—

> After she had been some hours in labour, Dubois, the accoucheur, came to me while I was reclining on the sofa, with great alarm painted on his countenance, and said that the empress was in a state of great danger, that there was a wrong presentation. I asked him if he had ever seen any thing of the kind before. Dubois replied that he had but very rarely, perhaps not one in a thousand, and that it was very afflicting to him that so extraordinary a case should happen with the empress. "Forget," said I,

[106] *Napoleon in Exile.* I have corrected O'Meara's faulty use of quotation marks.

"that she is empress, and treat her as you would the wife of a little shop-keeper in the Rue St. Denis. This is the only favour I ask of you." Dubois then asked, if it were necessary that one should be sacrificed, which should he save, the mother or the child. "The mother certainly," I replied, "it is her right." I then accompanied Dubois to the bed-side, encouraged and tranquillized the empress as much as possible, and held her while the forceps were applied. . . . His birth produced a delirium of joy in the nation (II, 367–368).

In II, 6, iii—"Paris. The Tuileries"—almost twelve months after the wedding, Hardy picked up from elsewhere a few facts for background and he invented a good deal. Apparently, he found it inconvenient to make use of Napoleon's actual holding and encouraging Marie, but the rest of O'Meara's story he followed closely. In the scheme of his epic the scene has more than one implication. There is, of course, tender-ness, which Hardy was willing to grant despite Napoleon's being his ultimate source of information. But there is also egoism, which will out, no matter what. And finally, though it is presented soberly, there is comedy in the conclusion of the scene. Within minutes after his wife has been near death and while the rejoicing is mounting in the streets at the birth of a son, the little shopkeeper is back at his counter dis-cussing the "ban on English trade" and the ill success of his forces in the Peninsula. The Chorus of Ironic Spirits merrily asserts,

> The Will Itself is slave to him, * * *
> And ordered issue as he planned.

And, of course, no one is more enslaved than he.

There is, to be sure, a kind of pleasure in caricaturing the mighty. But the Spirits Ironic are not in the poem to cater to vindictiveness. They are inherent in Hardy's perspective. Life for Hardy was at its best a search for reality. In the quest that which was vanity must, as in Ecclesiastes, be reckoned as such. And so the comic Spirits must have their say.

Horror in the Russian Wastes

January 24, 1812, Napoleon signed an alliance with Prussia for both defensive and offensive co-operation, and March 14 he signed a treaty with Austria. Meanwhile, despite the confidence with which Alexander had accepted terms of peace at Tilsit a few short years before, Napoleon had begun to gather forces for an attack. May 9 he inspected the Grand Army on the Vistula; May 17, the day after the battle of Albuera, he arrived at Dresden; and June 22 he announced a proclamation of war. The next day he crossed the Niemen to begin his plunge toward disaster.

Hardy indicated the growing tension with Russia, though he was unable to trace its complex development. His primary concern, however, was the tragic drama of the invasion itself. Of all the episodes in his ten-year epic this was the only one before the Hundred Days which could have stood by itself as a complete tragedy. Napoleon was to raise a new levy of troops to die in the slaughter at Leipzig before he finally succumbed, but the journey to Moscow and the retreat contained all the elements of Hardy's theme.

Since the histories were written in retrospect, their authors could point out the follies of the Emperor and the significance of what they were about to report. In his copy of Ségur, Hardy marked the comment that, in attacking Russia while engaged in Spain, Napoleon was violating his own precept "de ne jamais entreprendre sur deux points à la fois, mais sur un seul, et toujours en masse." [107] To be sure, he had violated it successfully before. Having recorded the crossing of the Niemen, Thiers concludes Volume XIII: "Nous allons nous engager dans ce douleureux et héroïque récit: la gloire, nous la trouverons à chaque pas: le bonheur, hélas! il y faut renoncer au delà du Niémen."

In his opening scene of Part III—"The Banks of the Niemen. Near Kowno"—Hardy revealed a protagonist experienced from years of campaigning, but himself a creature of the forces he had set in motion. Napoleon could still electrify his soldiers with his display of confidence, but the years had, nonetheless, exacted their toll. He had to believe in his own invincibility, but he was subject to strange sensations that were inconsistent therewith. Though an unconscious Immanent Will should be indifferent to the future, as a poet Hardy had always enter- tained omens, and he was willing to credit Napoleon with suscepti- bility to them, too. Both Ségur and Alison report a sign of bad luck June 23, at the outset of the campaign. Alison writes: "His horse suddenly fell as he approached the shore, and he was precipitated on the sand. Some one exclaimed, 'It is a bad omen—a Roman would have retired'; but, without regarding the augury, he gave orders * * *"

[107] M. Le Lieutenant-Général Comte de Ségur, *Histoire de Napoléon et de la Grande Armée en* 1812 (2 vols.; Paris, 1839), I, 78.

(XV, 282). Ségur, one of Alison's sources, puts it: "On ignore si ce fut lui ou quelqu'un de sa suite qui prononça ces mots" (I, 125–126). Hardy gives the words to Years, who represents an inner voice so real that Napoleon thinks it external:

> Whose voice was that, jarring upon my thought
> So insolently?

This is a determined Macbeth, but one who has sensed the presence of Banquo.

The proclamation that follows is a paraphrase of the bulletin of June 22, translated in Alison.[108] The most salient part reads: "*Fate drags her* [Russia] *on—let her destinies be fulfilled.* Does she imagine we are degenerated? Are we not still the soldiers of Austerlitz?" (XV, 283). Hardy could not improve this reference to both fate and Austerlitz. He merely expanded it:

> Russia is forced on by fatality:
> She cries her destiny must be outwrought,
> Meaning at our expense. Does she then dream
> We are no more the men of Austerlitz,
> With nothing left of our old featfulness?

Napoleon's "we" is, of course, that mystical soldiery which fought in battle after battle, though new bodies replaced the old.

Hardy now had a source perhaps more significant for interpretation than for facts—*War and Peace.*[109] He was not disturbed that the work was fiction. Presumably, it was essentially reliable, and besides, Hardy himself was taking liberties with the facts. In his initial prose version of Napoleon's despondent meditation he noted "[W + P]." The annotation refers to no single passage in Tolstoi, but as Miss Clifford has observed, Hardy marked three of Tolstoi's frequent comments on the relation of individuals and the course of history. In the first the novelist writes:

> For every command that is carried out, there are always enormous numbers that are not carried out... Our false conception that the command preceding the event is the cause of the event, arises from the fact that when an event has taken place, and only those out of a thousand

---

[108] The rough draft manuscript in the Memorial Library begins with this scene. Hardy first quoted and paraphrased Alison in prose, then rewrote the proclamation in verse.

[109] Cf., Emma Clifford, "*War and Peace* and *The Dynasts.*"

commands which are connected with the event are carried out, we forget those which were not carried out because they could not be carried out.[110]

The second passage scorns popular belief in freedom of the will (IV, 348). The third is a dogmatic denial of it:

> For History to regard the Free Will of men as a force able to exert influence upon historical events, that is, as not subject to law, is the same thing as for astronomy to recognize freedom in the movement in the heavenly forces.
> This admission would destroy the possibility of the existence of laws, that is, of any knowledge whatever. . . .
> If a single human action were free, there would be no historical laws, no conception of historical events (IV, 361).

Exactly when Hardy first read in the novel is unknown. It would have confirmed him in views expressed in Parts I and II of *The Dynasts*, but it was especially apposite at the beginning of Part III. Another significant statement was in Ségur's study of Napoleon only a few pages beyond a passage marked by Hardy: "Mais, dans leur grande carrière, les fondateurs d'empires marchent vers leur but, comme le destin, dont ils semblent être les ministres . . ." (I, 87).

When optimistic, Napoleon liked to view himself as one destined to wield a great empire, and there is no historical evidence that at the Niemen he was despondent. But Hardy chose to give him a melancholy in accord with the stumbling of the horse and what Hardy himself knew was to follow. So the Emperor soliloquizes in a way to hint of the beginning, the rise, and the approaching decline of his fortunes:

> That which has worked will work!—Since Lodi Bridge
> The force I then felt move me moves me on
> Whether I will or no; and oftentimes
> Against my better mind . . . . Why am I here?
> —By laws imposed on me inexorably!

There has been no subsidence of the feeling that he is at the center of the Universe. There is, however, a bewilderment that is poetic.

In Hardy's copy of *La Lyre Française* (272–275) is the song of 1709, "Mort et Convoi de l'Invincible Marlbrough." A note at the

[110] *War and Peace*, trans. Nathan H. Dole (4 vols.; London, n.d.), IV, 339. The four-volume set is in the Memorial Library.

back (408) reads: "Not being able to vanquish the Duke of Marlborough, the French avenged themselves by composing upon him the
present song, which soon became as popular in England as it was under
the latitude of Paris. The tune to which the words are sung is the rather
Bacchanalian one of 'We won't go home till morning!'" Hardy
annotated the verses by referring to the note. As the song relates the
wished-for events, Marlborough was to return at Easter, but his lady's
page tells her that he has been carried to his grave by four officers.
One carried his cuirass, one his buckler, one his great sword, and the
fourth nothing. A nightingale now chants above his grave.

The annotation suggests that, despite its popularity generations
earlier, the song was new to Hardy. He could assume, nevertheless, that
Napoleon might have known it, and the opportunity to use such
antiquarian lore was, as always, not to be resisted. Thus he has the
Emperor try to buoy up his depressed spirits by adopting a "saturnine
humour" and humming the lines. It is unlikely that Hardy meant to
symbolize anything by the fact that the song reports its hero "mort et
enterré!" Rather, it was the devil-may-care tune that expressed the
Emperor's fatalism.

When Napoleon begins his meditation the "films or brain-tissues of
the Immanent Will" are visible in the "unnatural light." It is thus that
Hardy implies universality of the emotion. Before he begins to hum,
the light has again become natural, but in taking up the tune from him
the Spirit Sinister gives a new universality—this time in a mocking
tone. Then the figure which seemed to fill the stage as he stood alone is
"diminished to the aspect of a doll," and the scene closes in torrents
of rain.

Hardy's method in the conclusion of his scene is not altogether new.
He had long before made a character stand out against the sky at the
center of the little world bounded by the horizon and then brought
him back to inconspicuousness against the brown waste of the heath.
For the banks of the Niemen one can read Egdon; for the Emperor
Napoleon, any of several natives of Wessex, ambitious yet bewildered,
godlike in aspiration, but fettered by laws imposed inexorably. At the
crossing of the Niemen, Hardy's pity for his vain and foolish
protagonist begins to deepen.

The retreat from Moscow is so famous that the journey to the
heart of Russia has been almost forgotten. Actually, Napoleon lost a
great proportion of his army between the Niemen and his destination.

Thiers considers the Battle of Smolensk-Valoutina, August 17–19, one of the most sanguinary of the century (XIV, 241). There were other encounters, too, before September 7. Hardy chose, however, to focus on the battle fought on that day at Borodino, some seventy miles from Moscow. In III, 1, iv—"The Field of Borodino"—his account is at first closest to that in Thiers, later to Ségur's; but he made the usual alterations for heightening. Thiers writes that, having learned of the defeat at Salamanca, Napoleon announced that on the banks of the Moskowa he would repair "les fautes commises aux Arapyles" (XIV, 318). Hardy followed his source literally: "I'll mend his [Marmont's] faults upon the Arapeile"; and he built up the speech with an attack on England's gold and a wish to "face this Wellington myself!" Napoleon's display of his son's portrait is from Ségur, who writes, "lui même il exposa ce tableau devant sa tente . . ." (I, 351). Hardy achieves irony by having the portrait serve the function of an icon for the soldiers and then letting Napoleon scorn the religious rites of the Russians as an icon is borne among them. In Ségur the Emperor asks Rapp whether he expects victory. Rapp answers, "Sans doute, mais sanglante," and Napoleon replies, "Je le sais" (I, 353). Hardy ends his dialogue:

> Victory;
> But, sire, a bloody one!
> NAPOLÉON
> So I foresee.

The sharpest bitterness is in words that would befit the Spirit Sinister. Napoleon scoffs at the "enginry of Heaven" of the Russian ecclesiastics:

> I am no theologian, but I laugh
> That men can be so grossly logicless,
> When war, defensive or aggressive either,
> Is in its essence Pagan, and opposed
> To the whole gist of Christianity!

Like Angel Clare, Hardy could not subscribe to Article 4, and his Immanent Will was not a Christian God, ancient or modern. Yet, in the note we have quoted, having first objected to Christianity, Hardy inserted "modern." Moreover, he respected Angel's parents for their Christian charity, however inadequate their theology. Here Napoleon is scorning the modern perversion of a faith—a sin of which he himself is guilty, for he has repeatedly employed the machinery of the Church with cynical calculation. He is, of course, a pagan in the Roman sense, an emperor posing as a god.

For scene v—"The Same"—Hardy jotted down as he went the sources on which he was drawing. Since Miss Clifford has noted the parallels, we can give our attention to their significance. Having first quoted almost verbatim Tolstoi's words ending "trying and inhuman *rôle* which was imposed upon him" (III, 277), Hardy tinkered with the wording in the rough draft. Later he made the key revision: "He thinks imposed upon him." By strict definition there has been no wavering from determinism, since thoughts would as readily manifest it as anything else; but there is in spirit a shift, nevertheless, in the suggestion of human illusion.

The next use of Tolstoi is especially interesting. It must be remembered that Tolstoi's reliance on Christian theology was not acceptable to Hardy, but he could give his own meaning to his author's terminology. In the manuscript he had no hesitation in quoting and paraphrasing Tolstoi's "and still that strange affair went on which was accomplished not by the will of men, but by the will of Him who rules men and worlds" (III, 281). He may have felt that he changed the implication by ending with "by the will of Heaven." Yet, Tolstoi's determinism was not derived through the same philosophic reasoning as his own, and so he rewrote the passage completely, in accord with his understanding of Schopenhauer and Hartmann. The revision is important because it describes the condition which must be reversed if the lot of mankind is ever to be meliorated. Presumably when he wrote the new version Hardy had not decided that the epic was to end on a note of hope. But after he had written the words of the Pities he saw no need to revise the speech of Years:

> Thus do the mindless minions of the spell
> In mechanized enchantment sway and show
> A Will that wills above the will of each,
> Yet but the will of all conjunctively;
> A fabric of excitement, web of rage,
> That permeates as one stuff the weltering whole.

What takes place on the battlefield is philosophically not different from what occurs in Wessex or London; it is only intensely manifested. Each soldier in rushing into battle is impelled by the spirit of the entire army and he himself contributes to the impelling force. So the Will itself represents all wills and yet is not a mere accumulation of them. If the mesmeric enslavement to it is ever to cease, a conjunctive effort is requisite. The matter is not simple, for somehow an impulse toward assertion of freedom will have to be born, and from what can it take its birth?

After the words by Years there were still details to be recorded, with the danger of anticlimax. Consequently, Hardy experimented extensively with the last part of his scene and struck out much in the rough draft. He continued to note "Tol" or "W. + P.," though the exact passage in *War and Peace* is not always traceable. Indicative of his drawing on more than one author is "Napoleon / Answers muzzily being half drunk (Al. Tol.)." This line was dropped, but it contributed to "drowsed half-drunken Dictator." Murat's remark that "in this great day he had not recognized the genius of Napoleon" is tagged "Ségur," and is, of course, a translated paraphrase. Hardy then rewrote it in much different verse. Other lines are identified with "Al" or "Th." Without noting his source, Hardy, after a little tinkering, decided on "it is the sun of Austerlitz"—close enough to Ségur's "Voilà le soleil d'Austerlitz" (I, 356), and exactly translating the words in the bulletin of September 12, which he may or may not have seen. From Thiers he first paraphrased in prose, with the label "Th," what he then turned into

> * * * even within that tent no notes of joy
> Throb as at Austerlitz!

There is so much in Hardy's scene as he finally hammered it out that one hesitates to complain. Unfortunately, it still suffers when compared with Ségur and even more when compared with Thiers. The latter's description of the battle is complex and filled with suspense. The conflict is like numerous others, and yet it is unique. Hardy, in his unavoidable simplification, does not fully capture its individuality and its horror. He speaks of wholesale butchery, but hardly conveys a sense of the magnitude. In contrast, before summing up the slaughtered and wounded as 9,000 to 10,000 dead, 20,000 to 21,000 wounded, and 60,000 Russians "hors de combat," Thiers gives us, "Le soleil s'abaissa enfin sur cette scène atroce, sans égale dans les annales humaines . . ." (XIV, 347).

Hardy marked this passage and in his rough draft wrote, "'This terrible scene—without a parallel in the annals of humanity.' *Th.*"

But, presumably in concern for economy, he struck it, and he abridged other lines from Thiers. As often, the individual phrase in Hardy may be as emphatic as any single statement in his source, but accumulation and repetition are essential. Hardy obtains the cumulative effect over a succession of scenes; Thiers achieves it in each scene.

Thiers remarks on the fact that some of the wounded were carried to the ravine for protection "sans distinction de nation" (XIV, 348). It is strange that Hardy did not pick up this proof of the utter exhaustion and of the humaneness for which the exhaustion alone could account. For here, as at the ravine on the field of Talavera, the Will which has impelled men to insane slaughter has forced some of them on to clarity of vision and purification of soul.

The next few days after Borodino were to bring supreme irony. Though he had lost at Salamanca and had been unable to counter England's blockade, Napoleon still held the grandiose dream that from Moscow he would begin issuing orders that would bring England to subjection and even lead to his eventual mastery of the Near East and India. It was natural that he and his soldiers should attribute the most glamourous qualities to the Russian capital and that, when they first caught sight of it, their willing eyes should be amazed. Since the historians knew of the devastation so soon to follow, it was natural, too, that they should emphasize the contrast between the first glimpse and the aftermath. Ségur (II, 6–7) describes the splendour of the city when the sun hits it, and Hardy marked the passage (II, 30–31) in which the soldiers are shown rushing forward "battant les mains" and crying "avec transport: 'Moscou! Moscou!'" Thiers (XIV, 369) remarks in words paraphrased by Hardy that on entering the city Napoleon had entered all the capitals of Europe, London "seule exceptée." He pictures "une ville immense, brillante de mille couleurs ... ville à la fois gothique et byzantine, réalisant tout ce que les contes orientaux racontent des merveilles de l'Asie." Saving the Kremlin for his fairyland climax, he throws away the bridle of his imagination: "A cet aspect magique l'imagination, le sentiment de la gloire, s'exaltant à la fois, les soldats s'écrièrent tous ensemble: Moscou! Moscou!" (XIV, 370–371). Tolstoi dramatizes the Emperor's thoughts of glory: "Here she is—this capital at my feet, awaiting her fate. Where now is Alexander, and what thinks he now?" (III, 349). All the accounts, including Alison's, describe the exodus of the Russian populace and the feverish efforts of the incendiaries, led by Rostopchin.

Hardy first summarized the evacuation and the beginning of Rostop-chin's work, then went back to record Napoleon's initial view of the city. For III, 1, vi—"Moscow"—he had more facts than he could use, and much in the histories and in Tolstoi was based on rumours put together in later years. So he felt free to improvise, singling out the leader of the incendiaries and the defeated Kutúzof. Thiers says that the latter "se cacha en traversant Moscou" (XIV, 367); Hardy has him "surrounded by his lieutenants." In other details, likewise, he does not conform to his sources, but he settles for an impression of confusion and desolation. Thus, when he turns to Napoleon's elation at the opening of scene vii—"The Same. Outside the City"—the reader is struck with the irony. Hardy's impressionistic description of the city is a distillation from all his sources: "splendid panorama * * * curiously grotesque architecture of domes and spires * * * peacock of cities to Western eyes, its roofs twinkling * * * the ancient citadel of the Tsars * * * a centre-piece." Properly noting that Napoleon's forces are now but "one-fourth of those who crossed the Niemen so joyfully," Hardy draws on Tolstoi to conclude the Emperor's illusion of great victory: "*Now* what says Alexander!" [111] Again rising beyond history itself for dramatic intensity, he lets Napoleon promise mercy, "wait the city keys," and issue directions for the orderly occupation of a crowded city.

By now *The Dynasts* has made us aware repeatedly that men have conducted themselves as automatons, that they have done senseless things, that war is a phantasmagoria of unrealities. But certainly we here reach a summit of madness. Hardy takes up the scene two days later, September 16, to pose on the top of the Ivan Tower a "small lone figure." Then, as the scene darkens on the star of destiny, a new "lurid, malignant star" appears, which will soon turn the blackness into day. A graphic picture of the Moscow fire is given by Capefigue (IX, chap. 11), and Hardy put a bookmark at Thiers's account (XIV, 382–383); but, while depending on his sources, Hardy continued to write as of some preternatural manifestation. The role of his con-queror has a sequence reminiscent of Satan's in *Paradise Lost*. In the next scene he will resume his chores as general, but for a little while he is first the world destroyer, exultant in his pride, and then a solitary mortal, whose image vanishes in the flames of Hell.

[111] "Ha! There she is at last. And it was time" translates Ségur, *Histoire de Napoléon* (II, 33): "La voilà . . . . Il était temps."

In scene viii—"The Same. The Interior of the Kremlin"—the nightmare has not yet ended. The Emperor is in peril and the Kremlin itself is about to be set afire. Yet there is a slow return to reality—a reality not unlike that to which the porter opens the gates in *Macbeth*. In the midst of danger there are decisions to be made and work to be done. Again Hardy fused information from several places and extensively modified the details. Thiers speaks of Lariboisière's urging Napoleon to leave, mentions the Russian plans to swing back and cut off supplies, and suggests the tone Hardy gave to the last part of his scene; he remarks that during the fire the Emperor's reflections were "les plus amères, les plus sombres de sa vie" (XIV, 389). From Ségur, Hardy translated, with slight adaptation, "Ce sont eux-mêmes! Quels hommes. Ce sont des Scythes" (II, 49), and Napoleon's complaint: "c'était ce ministre russe, vendu aux Anglais, qui l'avait fomentée. Le perfide y avait entraîné Alexandre et lui!"[112] Ségur also speaks of the powder magazine, the artillery park, the execution of the incendiarist who fired the Kremlin, and the argument of Bessières and Berthier that the army must not head for Petersburg because of the weather and the roads (II, 44 ff.). When Napoleon reached Petrowsky, he said, according to Alison, "This sad event is the presage of a long train of disasters!" (XV, 366). Hardy antedates the Emperor's thoughts:

> I fear that this event
> Marks the beginning of a train of ills.

Not since the crossing of the Niemen has the Spirit Sinister uttered a sound, and the Spirit Ironic has spoken but two lines. In scene viii no Spirits appear at all. Yet it is the two sharp-tongued Intelligences that have directed Hardy's pen. Of course, in the mass exodus of the Moscow citizenry one could find cause for pity. But the focus has been on a horror that is insane.

The three scenes that follow—"The Road from Smolensko into Lithuania," "The Bridge of the Beresina," and "The Open Country between Smorgoni and Wilna"—return us to the realm of the Pities. In the second the only spoken words are by the Pities, and in the third the Spirit Sinister enters merely to comment on Napoleon's desertion of his starving and freezing army.

[112] *Histoire de Napoléon*, II, 156; antedated by Hardy. The rough draft is annotated "(Ségur)."

Alison, Capefigue, Constant, and O'Meara describe the desolation
of the retreat. The most extensive account of the numerous rear-
guard skirmishes is in Thiers. For his own details, however, Hardy
relied mainly on Ségur. The parallels are so numerous that they run
through more than three hundred pages in Ségur, from the evacuation
of Moscow to the end of Volume II. The manuscript revisions which
Hardy made in the three scenes concern us later. But two passages in
the rough draft show the craftsman's immediate response to his source.

In his copy of Ségur, Hardy put a line by

> Plus de soixante mille hommes bien nourris et complètement armés, en
> assaillaient dix-huit mille à demi-nus, mal armés, mourant de faim,
> séparés par une rivière, environnés de marais, enfin embarrassés par plus
> de cinquante mille traîneurs, malades ou blessés, et par une énorme masse
> de bagages   (II, 331).

With a note "(from Ségur)," Hardy translated this almost verbatim,
but having written "60,000," he added, "[say], 50,000." In the text he
further qualified—"forty or fifty thousand" (III, 1, x).

Once the snow had begun to fall, the suffering of the French was
much the same for Hardy's scenes ix and xi. At first he paraphrased in
scene xi Ségur's description of the motley apparel of the soldiers
(II, 304). Then he struck this and incorporated a more precise paraphrase in his revision of scene ix. He also, as before, telescoped events.
The first snowfall and severe cold had come on November 6; Hardy's
"Till floats down one white morsel" in ix is sometime after the army
passed through Smolensk, November 14.

Revising a prose version which emphasized the "unconscious
impetus" supplied by the Will, Hardy represented the demoralized
army—"like a dun-piled caterpillar"—as "moved by some master-
sway." In scene ix and the dumb show of scene x the army and its
hangers-on are almost like sleep walkers, who go through the form of
fighting, making fires, eating, and even, at the expense of scores of
lives, throwing bridges across the Beresina. Then suddenly a bridge
collapses and the walking spectres come to life in a cry of anguish.[113]
Ségur writes that, even before the bridge gave way, November 28,

[113] In describing the crossing and the battle of the Beresina, the writer in
Oeuvres says simply, "Une plume française se refuse à retracer les désastres de ces
deux terribles journées" (in chronological table). A primary source is Bulletin
29, issued December 3 (*Oeuvres*, V, 80 ff.; Capefigue, *L'Europe Pendant le
Consulat*, IX, 439–441).

women had been forced by the crush into the water "avec leurs enfants dans leurs bras, les élevant à mesure qu'elles enfonçaient; déjà submergées, leurs bras raidis les tenaient encore au-dessus d'elles" (II, 336). Hardy paraphrased this first in prose, then in verse, and added:

> Yes, motherhood, sheerly sublime in her last despairing,
> and lighting her darkest declension with limitless love.

Thiers sums up the horror at the bridge: "spectacle atroce bien fait pour rendre odieuse, et à jamais exécrable, cette expédition insensée!" (XIV, 629). As Hardy continues in scene xi to delineate the deaths by two's and three's of the depleted caterpillar he draws more from Ségur than from Thiers for individual facts. But certainly the tone of all three scenes owes much to lines such as these on the crossing of the Beresina.

Having previously defended the Emperor's strategy and tactics, Thiers recognizes that in not providing magazines within the last three-hundred miles of Moscow and in not keeping his depleted forces together Napoleon was guilty of the crudest of blunders. He traces the ineptness, however, to its primary cause, the invasion itself, which revealed "tous les genres d'illusions que le despotisme enivré par le succès puisse se faire!" (XIV, 674). In his choral summary Thiers writes as of a classical tragedy, and his last sentence is of special import:

> Pour être vrai, pour être utile, il ne faut pas rabaisser Napoléon, car c'est abaisser la nature humaine que d'abaisser le génie; il faut le juger, le montrer à l'univers, avec les véritables causes de ses erreurs, le donner en enseignement aux nations, aux chefs d'empire, aux chefs d'armée, en faisant voir ce que devient le génie livré à lui-même, le génie entraîné, égaré par la toute-puissance (XIV, 678–679).

Though, through the Spirit Sinister's quip and the "Mad Soldier's Song," Hardy portrays Napoleon as a deserter, he identifies him with "la nature humaine"; the desperate general is a sleepwalker, driven by the Will, and his tragedy partakes of the universal.

History sometimes offered Hardy incidents of the very kind that he could have used in a novel, perhaps even in a melodramatic romance. One such event was Napoleon's arrival at the Tuileries, near midnight December 18, looking so unlike his regal self that he was at first denied entrance. The documentary evidence on the conversation which ensued between Marie Louise and her husband was so slight that Hardy was free to put into the scene sentiments expressed elsewhere by Napoleon and, through the words of Marie, his own feelings. Indeed, in scene xii—"Paris. The Tuileries"—the Empress is essentially a character of fiction.

Memes quotes Napoleon's "favourite apothegm, 'There is but a single step from the sublime to the ridiculous'" (180). Napoleon left his army December 5, at Smorgoni, and on his way to Paris reached Dresden, December 14. Describing his bitterness as he hurried home to conscript a new army and quell unrest, Thiers reports his conversation at Dresden with Archbishop De Pradt: "Du sublime au ridicule il n'y a qu'un pas, dit-il au prélat ambassadeur, avec un rire contraint, qui prouvait l'excès de son embarras en voulant le cacher, mais aussi la vigueur de son caractère" (XV, 155). Thiers adds that the Emperor continued with Marie "l'espèce de comédie qu'il avait jouée avec tout le monde, et répéta que c'était le froid, le froid seul qui avait causé cette surprenante mésaventure, facile à réparer d'ailleurs . . ." (XV, 158).

Bulletin 29, of December 3,[114] was one of Thiers' sources for Napoleon's blaming all on the weather. Another primary account was that of Las Cases, which begins: "Was I defeated by the efforts of the Russians? No! my failure must be attributed to pure accident, to absolute fatality" (IV, 142). In the English version of Méneval, who used Las Cases, there are minor variations on the lament:

> Was it, however, the efforts only of the Russians which annihilated me? No, it was a capital burned down in spite of the inhabitants, and by means of foreign intrigues; it was a winter, a frost, whose sudden appearance and excessive rigour were phenomenal; it was the false manoeuvres, the countermarches of the Austrian corps, false reports, low intrigues, treachery, stupidity, and many other things, in one word . . . this famous war, this audacious enterprise, were never desired by me; I had no wish to fight. Alexander had no wish to fight either, but once face to face, circumstances drove us one against the other and fatality did the rest (*Memoirs*, III, 94).

In Méneval, Hardy found a few details with which to create the atmosphere of his scene. After dramatizing the surprise encounter, he let Napoleon speak of "all the disasters summed in the bulletin," and then launch into his self-defense, forgetful that he had lost most of

[114] *Ibid.*

his "six hundred thousand" on the way to Moscow. The tone is that of Thiers, and the apothegm is repeated:

> From the sublime to the ridiculous
> There's but a step!—I have been saying it
> All through the leagues of my long journey home—
> And that step has been passed in this affair! . . .
> Yes, briefly, it is quite ridiculous,
> Whichever way you look at it.—Ha-ha!

In the rough draft, with the notation "Méneval," Hardy quoted and paraphrased, beginning "I had no wish to fight"; and while setting down the words he crossed out "fatality" and substituted "the Genius who outshapes my destinies." As Hardy depicts him, only in his reflective moments does Napoleon regard himself as a passive victim of destiny.

Drawing on the often repeated evidence that the Emperor placated the citizens with public works, sometimes ostentatious displays, and that he recognized the magnetism of his own presence, Hardy lets him speak of "daily outings as a family group" and of gilding the dome of the Invalides, thus giving the populace "something / To think about. They'll take to it like children."

Except for a half line by Ironic no Spirits are called upon, but then, none are needed, for Napoleon himself is a Spirit Sinister and Marie has been transformed into the Spirit of the Pities. The very atmosphere lifts the scene from the realm of ordinary events and gives it a quality both mysterious and symbolic. The strange appearance of Napoleon and the clandestine nature of the meeting suggest a rendezvous of an outlaw or even of a ghostly lover with his beloved. Though Hardy does not tell his reader how to interpret the dialogue, it has the universality of tragedy. For the most significant impression left by the midnight affair is the inability of the two human spirits to achieve affinity. Napoleon is not really addressing his wife, but is pleading his case before an imaginary tribunal created by his own conscience. Having donned a mask of cynicism in self-protection, he cannot remove it for Marie. The Empress is equally alone, aware that her cry of compassion for the 600,000 and their mothers does not penetrate the mask. So, on almost the longest night of the year, surrounded by a chill world and embittered men and women, the two stand in the dim light of the room, shadows to each other, each utterly alone, and each a creature of the Will.

The Debacle at Leipzig

Six months after Napoleon's return to Paris the Battle of Vitoria was fought. Meanwhile reinforcements had been enlisted for the war in the east, and various skirmishes had occurred. Hardy took stock of the situation in III, 2, iv. Here, at a fête at Vauxhall Gardens, which was held July 20, 1813, we learn that English gold has been at work on the Continent and that Francis of Austria has shifted from benevolent neutrality by declaring war on his son-in-law. The early dialogue is in a low key, as Hardy recognized the value of a change of tone. The end of the scene, however—with Years and Pities playing the role of Rumours—attempts to imply the seriousness of what is to come. Possibly taking his cue from *Paradise Lost*, where the size of speakers typifies their importance, Hardy somewhat laboriously magnifies the letter of Francis declaring war:

> The object takes a letter's lineaments
> Though swollen to mainsail measure,—magically * * * .

The beginning of III, 3, i—"Leipzig. Napoléon's Quarters in the Reudnitz Suburb"—continues on matters diplomatic, with the Ironic Spirits narrating events initially assigned to the Spirit Sinister. Despite what Hardy was able to tell, however, in the two scenes, there is a great leap from the retreat in December to the battle which is about to take place at Leipzig in mid-October, 1813. The poet could not dramatize the multitude of separate actions through which Napoleon at first kept a foothold and then, within nine months, built a massive army. Nor would he resort to a simple record of what had happened.[115] So it is that we find ourselves hardly prepared for the battle which was to engage more combatants than any other in the Napoleonic Wars.

In his letter to General Morgan, October 12, 1922, in which he admitted his error in using the Potsdamer-Strasse, Hardy continued: "You allude to Leipzig. That battle bothered me much more than Jena or Ulm." The extensive revisions in the rough draft bear out his admission, as whole sections were stricken and others were rewritten.

[115] The most important incidents—January 11, the request was granted to conscript 300,000 recruits; March 4, the French evacuated Berlin; March 22, Blücher and the Russians entered Dresden; May 2, Napoleon routed the Allies at Lützen; May 20 and 21, he defeated them at Bautzen and Würtchen; August 26–27, he won at Dresden; October 7, Marie, as regent, asked the Senate for 280,000 men.

Nowhere could Hardy find an account that was easily paraphrased. Even Thiers, who gives abundant detail, is an uncertain guide. The chronology of events during the fighting on three sides of the city and also some distance away could be determined only vaguely, and the manoeuvres of the various units could not be pieced together to make a coherent pattern. Hardy was, of course, concerned with the dominant impression of the battle and with Napoleon's thoughts. But, before starting to write, he wanted to identify the geography, the names of the officers, and the chronology. Typical of his care was his affixing the dates in Thiers at the tops of pages. Starting at XVI, 547, we find "(15th)," "(16th)," "(end of 16th)," "(17th)," "(17–18)," and "(18th)." Even so, Hardy was not secure, because Thiers occasionally went back to begin a new sequence.

In trying to achieve a simple picture of a complex action Hardy went to various sources, jotting down his references in his manuscript. He was willing to make use of unscholarly works, presumably on the assumption that they would suffer from incompleteness in detail rather than from errors. So it was that he took a passage from Hazlitt's *Life of Napoleon* and also initially drew on the history of the battle by the Reverend George R. Gleig.[116] Hazlitt gives only a cursory survey of the campaign, in which he repeats his naïve praise of Napoleon and brands enemies of the French as tyrants or, if they be Russians, as barbarians. Gleig filled his narrative with platitudes generally unfavourable to Napoleon and with such remarks as "Dresden was in the height of its natural beauty." Hardy also consulted his 1901 copy in four volumes of W. M. Sloane's *Life of Napoleon Bonaparte*. Though Sloane was a professor of history, his report is sketchy and partly dependent on sources Hardy himself was using. In addition to Thiers, to whom Hardy had to turn for the main share of his facts, these were Marmont,[117] who participated in the battle, and Méneval.[118]

For his continuation on British diplomacy at the beginning of III, 3, i, Hardy at first quoted from Sloane (IV, 48–50), then abridged the substance into hexameter couplets, altering "England's" first to "John Bull's," then to "Bull's" to give the right tone of scorn. Hardy was proud of the British soldiers and, as we have seen, he admired

[116] *The Battle of Leipsic*, Part I, and *The Leipsic Campaign*, Part II (London, 1852).

[117] Viese de Marmont, *Mémoires du Duc de Raguse de 1792 à 1841* (9 vols.; Paris, 1857).

[118] *Memoirs to Serve* . . . .

Pitt, who had poured coin into the money bags of England's allies. But his concept of dynastic evil did not exempt Britain; and so Sloane's "Poland's three despoilers thus united in England's pay" became "Poland's three despoilers primed by Bull's gross pay."

To keep his chronology clear Hardy wrote "[14–15 Oct 1813]" after the title of the scene. In what followed, however, he fused materials from different occasions and put into dialogue substance from written orders and other documents. Most of scene i is either from Thiers or represents Hardy's own invention. At times he quoted or paraphrased, with the tag "(Th)" to remind him of his source. Thus he annotated Napoleon's plans to attack Schwarzenberg one day and Blücher the next, the recognition of the French inferiority in numbers, and Napoleon's order to compensate by arranging the men in two lines instead of the usual three.[119] He also, without annotation, drew on Thiers for Napoleon's chiding of Augereau and Murat.

An irrelevant slip suggests the hurry with which Hardy may have gone through his sources. The passage in Marmont is easily misread: "Le 15, dans la journée, des sapeurs, pris deux jours auparavant près de Delitzsch, conduits au quartier général à Halle, et qui s'étaient échappés, m'informèrent de la marche des armées combinées ..." (V, 279). Hardy writes, "Some sappers I have taken captive, sire * * *." Actually, Marmont was not present, but exchanged messages with Napoleon, the latter's orders to traverse Leipzig reaching Marmont the morning of the sixteenth. According to Marmont, also, it was on the night of the twelfth-thirteenth that, in his presence, Napoleon rebuked his subordinates.[120] Hardy's rearrangement of such details was, of course, deliberate.

One function of scene i is to set the conditions for the battle to begin on the sixteenth. Hardy was more interested, however, in foreshadowing the ultimate tragedy and perhaps yet more in contemplating the strange fellowship which war had brought. The Emperor has depended on the loyalty of his generals; yet his language to Augereau and Murat is contemptuous. To sum up the altercation Hardy called on the Spirit Ironic and, after much revision, arrived at

> A seer might say
> This savours of a sad Last-Supper talk
> 'Twixt his disciples and this Christ of war!

[119] *Histoire du Consulat*, XVI, 532–533.
[120] Thiers puts this on the fourteenth, but Marmont was a primary source.

The orders and other letters written by Napoleon rarely compli-
mented his chief subordinates. Again and again he chided, or even
reviled, them for their shortcomings; and the memoirs of some of
them reveal that the accusations rankled. Yet the team was held
together by a self-interest that was inseparable from a belief in "la
gloire." To possess a title one was willing to live in a tent, to endure
exhaustion, and to gamble one's life on a field where generals were
almost as likely to be killed as common soldiers. In a few months
disciples would defect, but by October, 1813, the fellowship had
survived bitter jealousies and staggering defeats. Unlike Thiers, Hardy
had not space to review the paradoxes. But he was capable of flashes
of poetic genius, and certainly the words of the Spirit Ironic are
among his best. The lines could not more aptly remind one of what
could happen in a world purportedly suffused with the spirit of
"Modern Christianity." Yet they imply a mystic kinship that transcends
rationality.

The first day of the battle, October 16, was a seesaw affair, in which
Thiers estimated the killed and wounded at 26,000 to 27,000 French,
40,000 allies (XVI, 573). Hardy tried to sort out the various actions
and, by enumeration, to give an impression of their composite vastness;
but the essence of his scene is in his generalized summary, once again
achieved only after extensive revision. The combatants cease to be
individuals and become "amorphous drifts, clouds, and waves of
conscious atoms, surging and rolling together." There is no mention
of the Will, but the implication is clear. The morning of the sixteenth
a French officer named Maison addressed his men: "Mes enfants, c'est
aujourd'hui la dernière journée de la France; il faut que nous soyons
tous morts ce soir." At the end of the day five-sixths of his men were
dead or wounded and he himself was among the wounded; yet he was
sorry that night had brought a halt.[121] It was unfortunate that Hardy
could not fit Maison's story into his scene, for it was a microcosmic
epitome of what the Spirit Ironic had said, and Maison was but one of
the atoms in the amorphous drifts.

Having summarized the action mainly in dumb shows in scene ii,
Hardy shifted to dialogue in scene iii. His intent was obviously to give
a sense of dramatic immediacy. He had a hard time, however, because
of the mass of detail which he felt obliged to narrate. He finally ended
with a rather arbitrary device. For a quick review of the licking of

[121] *Histoire du Consulat*, XVI, 566.

wounds and regrouping of forces on the seventeenth and the disposition of the armies on the morning of the eighteenth he resorted to
the use of citizen narrators who possess a greater knowledge of what
has occurred than the principals themselves could have had. They are,
in short, nothing more than the Spirit of Rumours in mortal guise.[122]
Then, for the battle itself, which was even more devastating than that
of the sixteenth, he employed a chorus by the Rumours, broken for
variety into semichoruses, with a couplet and Alexandrine to give a
poetic ending to each segment of a prosaic recital.

In the manuscript Hardy adapted freely from Marmont (V, 290)
and more closely from Gleig (227): "The Emperor rode over the
battlefield yesterday—gloom, regret, inaction. Had an interview with
Meerveldt whom he had taken prisoner. Spent the rest of the day in
his tent ... was nerveless, careless Gleig + Marmont." He went to
Thiers to report Napoleon's nocturnal visit to his marshals, but he
also recorded Gleig's version. Finally, he bracketed "At last he
returned to his tent at Stetteritz. Gleig" and "He bivouacked at Probs-
theyda—Th?"[123] All this was eventually reduced to "at Probstheida, /
Where he has bivouacked." So Hardy did not finally retain Gleig's
versions; but that he should ever have used them is interesting, for
there are sharp discrepancies otherwise between Gleig's account and
his own. Having sacrificed his picture of what Marmont had characterized as Napoleon's "insouciance," he decided, for what he kept, to rely
on Thiers. From Thiers (XVI, 586–587) he also took, initially almost
verbatim, the report of the arrival of Schwarzenberg and Bernadotte.

In trying to untangle the incidents Hardy now drew upon Hazlitt.
Giving no source, Hazlitt had written:

> the French were posted on an inner line, nearer to Leipsic, of which
> Probtsheyda was the central point. He himself, stationed on an emimence
> called Thonberg, commanded a prospect of the whole field. The troops
> were drawn up behind the villages; cannon were planted in front and on
> their flanks, and every patch of wooded ground, which afforded the least
> shelter, was filled with riflemen.[124]

[122] Hardy's point of view is shown in his attribution of a passage taken from
Sloane, *Life of Napoleon* (IV, 73) which he crossed out in the rough draft to use
in part elsewhere. It was to be spoken by the "Spirit of" before Hardy decided
to use citizens.

[123] *The Battle of Leipsic*, p. 231; *Histoire du Consulat*, XVI, 594 and 596.

[124] William Hazlitt, *The Life of Napoleon Buonaparte* (London: Chapman and
Hall, 1828), IV, 120.

In his initial version Hardy wrote:

> Out there between Connewitz + Dölitz is the right wing under Murat.
> That's Napoleon's centre at Probstheida, where he bivouacked—Those
> here are his left under Ney—fronting the north between Paunsdorf +
> Gohlis. Here are Poniatowski, Augereau [stricken], Victor, + the rest.
> You see they are really skilfully drawn up behind villages with cannon in
> front of them. And every patch of copse is packed with riflemen. Haz[tt].

Actually the situation and some of the names of generals are from
Sloane, and "where he bivouacked" is from Thiers; but the rest is
from Hazlitt. There is one alteration of consequence in the translation
of the prose into Hardy's final verse form. "Behind villages" became
"within the villages." At some point Hardy decided that Hazlitt had
erred.

The rough draft exhibits the poet's struggles, with rejection of
tantalizing facts, abridgment of others, and rearrangement of the order
of what remained—all because in the histories there were two or more
versions of what Napoleon had done on the night of the sixteenth and
much of the seventeenth. Yet the lines that Hardy did finally preserve
are of a meticulous, pedestrian nature. Though he had long regarded
Leipzig as a famous battle, he knew few of the details when he began
his special research. What he originally knew was adequate for his
ballad "Leipzig," published in *Wessex Poems* in 1898. But now he felt
the need for scholarly precision. Exactly where the French marshals
were stationed and where Napoleon spent the night suddenly took on
pedantic importance, even though Connewitz and Dölitz and Probstheida were mere names for any reader without a map and irrelevant
for a reader supplied with one. Unfortunately, in his preoccupation
with these external, unemotional tags, Hardy forgot the one fact that
mattered most of all, a fact for which he had about as reliable authority
as for anything in his whole account. He should not have stricken his
adaptation of Marmont's reference to the Emperor's insouciance.

For the battle itself on the eighteenth Hardy twice annotated his
manuscript "Th" and twice "Sloane." The first reference to Thiers
seems to cover the numbers in the allied armies, though Hardy's
figures are much smaller than Thiers' (XVI, 598) in so far as they
correspond at all. From Thiers he also took the salvo of two thousand
cannon as night closes in. Employing heightened verse, he sought,
with uneven effect, to convey the magnitude of what his author

(XVI, 607) had called "cette bataille, justement dite *des Géants,* et jusqu'ici la plus grande certainement de tous les siècles."

The second stanza of Semichorus I of Rumours and the end of the chorus are from Sloane's impressionistic summary:

> But magnificent as was the work of all these doughty champions on both sides, it was far surpassed in the center, where during the entire day, under Napoleon's eye, advance and resistance had been desperate. Men fell like grass before the scythe .... The allied troops charged with fixed bayonets, rank after rank, column following column; cannon roared while grape and shrapnel sped to meet the assailants; men said the air was full of human limbs ... in hand-to-hand conflict men shouted, struggled, wrestled, thrust, advanced, and withdrew .... By dusk the heated cannon were almost useless, the muskets entirely so, and, as darkness came down, the survivors fell asleep where they stood, riders in their saddles, horses in their tracks (IV, 74).

This underwent transformation in the rough draft, and it was still more freely played with before it yielded such fruit as "And forms walm, wallow, and slack suddenly." Most significant is Hardy's transmutation of Sloane's last words. In copying, he wrote "tracks (traces?)" He could hardly have been questioning his source; rather, he must have been considering how he could make the image stronger. When he converted the prose into verse the originally motionless soldiers and horses became sleepwalkers:

> The marching remnants drowse amid their talk,
> And worn and harrowed horses slumber as they walk.

So those who all day have been creatures of the Will are now literally somnambulists. But the thirst of the wounded prevails, and the Second Citizen, as agent of the Pities, will "do what mercy may." Once again the Pities have had the last word.

Scenes iv and v—"At the Thonberg Windmill" and "A Street near the Ranstädt Gate"—are undistinguished artistically. Napoleon is forced to retreat, and Hardy has citizens see around corners in order to record by way of dialogue the Emperor's journey through the city, no longer at the head of his forces. Drawing from Méneval (III, 143–144), Hardy referred to the pathetic words of farewell of the dejected King and Queen of Saxony, whose troops had defected.[125] Of more

---

[125] The manuscript is annotated "Men." "... begged him to withdraw ... adjuring him to leave them to their sorrowful fate" became the clumsy "Did beg of him to leave them to their lot."

interest is a different kind of borrowing—the taking of six stanzas, with slight modification, from his own ballad, the last four to describe the disastrous premature blowing up of the bridge on the nineteenth. The ballad itself is at best ordinary, with trite rhymes and artificially achieved meter. It is another indication of Hardy's frugal nature and of his uncertain judgment that he should have mined such verses.

Hardy most certainly recognized the significance of the battle of Leipzig. The magnitude of the slaughter alone justified the space he gave to the terrible days of combat. But he could not as sometimes elsewhere draw forth the lyric essence of the action. He was too immersed in the bog of confused details, and his letter in 1922 suggests that he was by no means satisfied with the scenes even after he had scrapped lines and tried to inject emotion into verse that became a mixture of declamation and poetry. His best lines are those which have nothing to do with particular events, but which accord with his feeling for life. One does not, for example, forget the drowsing marchers and the horses that walk in their sleep.

November 2, Napoleon's main forces recrossed the Rhine. After an excursion to the banks of the Nivelle to review the demoralization of the French in the west, Hardy turned eastward again to lay his first scene of Act 4 on "the upper Rhine," on "the morning of New Year's Day." Though starting a new act, the scene represents the aftermath of the battle of Leipzig. The historical facts consisted of the movement westward of the three allied armies—Russian, Prussian, and Austrian. Hardy distorted the details of history by implying that a military vacuum lay ahead; but, since resistance was only sporadic and short-lived, the impression in his scene is true.

The style is subdued, and the scene purports merely to indicate the progress of the three invading columns as they would be visible from a "vague altitude." What gives significance to the description is the images chosen for illustrative analogy:

> the undulating columns twinkle as if they were scaly serpents. * * * They glide on as if by gravitation, in fluid figures,[126] dictated by the conformation of the country, like water from a burst reservoir; mostly snake-shaped, but occasionally with batrachian and saurian outlines. In spite of the immensity of this human mechanism on its surface, the winter landscape wears an impassive look, as if nothing were happening.

[126] "Protean shapes" in the rough draft.

The snake is obvious enough to connote a column on a winding road; the fluidity indicates the occasional spreading out or even the moving like water through a delta when the terrain permits; and "saurian" befits a wider than serpentine column, ending with a thin tail of carts at the rear. The images were chosen, however, not alone for their pictorial aptness. Napoleon's own armies have flowed across Europe as inevitably as water. It is the nature of armies to flow. Now that there is no consequential resistance in France, the allied armies have nothing to dam their course, and so they, too, must as inevitably move onward. They have no choice. As for the serpent, the toad, and the lizard— whatever cunning they possess is primordial. Whatever purpose they have, it is not of the conscious intellect. And the whole is a "human mechanism" on an impassive earth. No spirit is granted to that mechanism, and yet it continues to move. This is because, though it has not once been mentioned, we feel that present and impelling all is the unconscious Immanent Will.

La Chute

The Duchess d'Abrantès writes, "In one day I heard ten different versions of the manner in which he took leave of the national guard, and confided his wife and child to their protection."[127] Constant (IV, 193), De Bourrienne (III, 327), who was present, and the Duc de Rovigo[128] give variant accounts of Napoleon's farewell; but Hardy appears to have depended mainly on Thiers (XVII, 211 ff.). The address to the guard took place January 24, 1814, and the familial separation the next day. Hardy put both into III, 4, ii—"Paris. The Tuileries." For the address he began with the factual record, but he reworked his materials extensively in the manuscript revisions to catch the spirit of a leader who, though defeated, is contemptuous of his enemies and, to all appearances, still confident of miraculous victory. At one point, in letting the Emperor refer to Marie Louise and the King of Rome as "those dearest in the world to me," Hardy was

[127] The Duchess d'Abrantès (Mme. Junot), *Memoirs of Napoleon, His Court and Family* (New York: Appleton, 1854), II, 442.

[128] Duc de Rovigo [M. Savary], *Mémoires Écrits de sa Main* (Paris, 1828), III, seconde partie, 198–199; probably not read by Hardy, but cited in his sources.

forgetful. On this occasion, as on all others, Napoleon put first of all his love of France.[129]

The ending of the scene, a commentary by the Spirit of the Years, was achieved with much labour and is pure Hardy. The histories, of course, revealed that after the second abdication Marie would become immersed in efforts to save Parma for the King of Rome—in essence, for herself as his mother—and would soon after be drawn into marriage with Neipperg. Without censuring her, Hardy found in her future lot a romantic exemplar of tragedy. Marie has shared in what may well be considered the most profound human experiences. She has nearly died bearing Napoleon's heir; she has seen her husband in times of glory; and now she is with him as he is about to endure martyrdom, betrayed by his officers and humiliated by his country. Possibly with the ultimate sea journey in mind, Hardy concluded the chorus:

> Until his image in her soul will shape
> Dwarfed as a far Colossus on a plain,
> Or figure-head that smalls upon the main.[130]

For Hardy the most poignant of tragic happenings was attrition of the memory of a poignant event.

The succeeding scene—"The Same. The Apartments of the Empress"—is really two. Possibly even more than elsewhere Hardy was at a disadvantage in the first half in fitting together incidents of March 29 and 30, 1814. He had to plunge into a situation which was fully intelligible only if one knew its antecedents. First of all, in order to understand the references to Joseph as Marie's trusted adviser, one should know that, like Josephine, she had suffered slights from the Emperor's sisters and that Joseph alone of the brothers had been kind to her. He should know, too, that, although Napoleon spoke contemptuously of Joseph, the King of Spain was an honourable and sensible man. It would help also to be aware that Talleyrand, Rovigo, and others were plotting against one another on how to make peace with the Allies, even while Napoleon was still trying to block their

---

[129] Rovigo quotes Napoleon: "ce que j'ai au monde de plus cher après la France."

[130] In Thiers, *Histoire du Consulat* (XVII, 212–213), Hardy marked a passage including: "Sa femme pleurait et craignait de ne plus le revoir en effet, sans que les boulets ennemis dussent l'enlever à son affection! On l'eût bien surprise assurément si on lui eût dit que ce mari, actuellement l'objet de toutes ses sollicitudes, mourrait dans une île de l'Océan, prisonnier de l'Europe, et oublié d'elle!"

armies from Paris. And Marie's attitude toward her son becomes more understandable if one has read the Duchess d'Abrantès' portrait of a somewhat indolent mother who found the boy wearisome and welcomed his turning to his nurse, "Mamma 'Quiou." Whether or not Hardy read the Duchess' account, his own portrait concurs.

Despite his lack of space to fill in the background, Hardy managed to write a rather heroic scene. Marie perceives that she is a pawn, doomed to unhappiness. Nevertheless, unlike the historians, Hardy emphasizes the fact that she herself makes the climactic decision. We recall her sorrow when speaking of the scores of thousands who died in Russia. Now, when told that to stay will mean fruitless battle and "wanton waste of life," she determines to go: "And let none try to hinder me again!"[131] In that moment she is indeed a queen. In that same moment, too, she is choosing the side of the Pities at the expense of her husband.

In the succeeding lines Hardy needed only to follow his sources to create a symbolic portrait of the little boy who was already a king. Napoleon's son was a tender-hearted child, not born to rule, but already being educated for the chore. Méneval describes the young king's clinging to the door in his protest against leaving, Las Cases concurs, and Hardy made only slight changes. Yet Hardy's context itself gives implications to "Now papa is away I am the master!" that are not in "puisque papa est absent, c'est moi qui suis le maître." They are the last words uttered in the epic by the boy who, as the son of a dynast, has been valued by his father less for his merits than for his usefulness as a dynastic pawn.

The second part of the scene is low comedy; the Empress's servants are spiritual brothers of the folk who dwell in Wessex. In donning the white cockade they typify the fickle multitude. Again, Hardy's sources record with contempt the agility with which Parisians of all ranks became patriotic adherents to the Bourbons as soon as the handwriting was apparent. The poet merely used his imagination to invent dialogue that would dramatize the baseness. The words are indeed comic as the four servants, trusting to their insignificance as their best insurance, forget the national disaster to think of their own bellies:

[131] Las Cases, *Mémorial de Sainte Hélène* (IV, 161) reports that Napoleon said Marie Louise was following his orders. Méneval (*Napoléon et Marie-Louise. Souvenirs Historiques*, II, 53) says her failure to receive word from Joseph caused her to leave.

"The storm which roots the pine spares the p——s——b——d. * * * Now there will be a nice convenient time for a little good victuals and drink, and likewise pickings, before the Allies arrive, thank Mother Molly!" But the fun is also a choral commentary in which these urban clowns are but avatars of the Spirit Sinister. Thus, the second servant: "Well, well! There's rich colours in this kaleidoscopic world!" To which the third rejoins: "And there's comedy in all things—when they don't concern you. Another glorious time among the many we've had since eighty-nine. We have put our armour [white cockades] on none too soon. The Bourbons for ever!" We know, of course, that some months later they and their ilk will be donning the tricolour again.

As much as any other lines in the epic the dialogue of the servants helps keep a proper perspective. We have witnessed and shall again witness the terrible scenes in which the dynasts have seemed to direct mankind to the slaughter. If we have mitigated our censure of their conduct, we have done so perhaps by blaming some sort of deterministic force, sometimes the Immanent Will itself. Here, in the Tuileries, we are reminded that it is such creatures as these servants who have made dynasts inevitable. They, too, are like a river, moved only by gravitation and running in whichever channel is least resistant. If the Will is ever to be awakened, they will have no part in its enlightenment. Hardy's theme could have been quite simple had it concerned the mere overthrow of a given dynast. But he had really taken all human folly and moral lassitude for his province.

In III, 4, iv—"Fontainebleau. A Room in the Palace"—Hardy telescoped events of April 5–6 and the night of April 11–12. Once again, as his scene opened, he had to give bits of information to indicate what had occurred in a few short days. Then he was ready for the first of his two principal actions, Napoleon's abdication. After a last burst of defiance comes the inescapable resignation. Except for his improvisations Hardy followed Thiers (XVII, 750 ff.), noting in his manuscript "[more in Thiers]." The language in the abdication is merely Thiers' prose turned into verse. The defection of Marmont was the symbol of Napoleon's fall. In actuality, there was ambiguity concerning Marmont's role in the surrender of his soldiers; but Thiers found him guilty, and Hardy made of his desertion a climactic blow. The historian writes: "Puis il parla de Marmont avec chagrin, mais sans amertume.— Je l'avais traité, dit-il, comme mon enfant. . . . Je l'ai créé maréchal et duc, par goût pour sa personne .... Il est le seul homme peut-être dont je n'aie pas soupçonné l'abandon" (XVII, 751). Hardy built this up, while keeping the same melancholy and patient tone. Thiers (752) wrote, "Cette France que je voulais faire si grande, la laisser si petite!" Hardy translated:

> I faint to leave France thus—curtailed, pared down
> From her late spacious borders.

In the classical tradition the scene might properly end in suicide, and by omitting intervening days Hardy was able to approximate the ancient tragic pattern. The mameluke, Roustan, stands in for the Roman servant, only to be misled by an apparent rebuff. Thus far Hardy was writing essentially fiction. In what followed he had at least Alison and Thiers to guide him, but he was still free to invent.

Constant, who was quickly called to his master's presence, left a long account of the attempted suicide.[132] De Bourrienne drew on Constant and also on Baron Fain, who was not present. In a footnote he identified the drug as "not opium alone, but a preparation described by Cabanis" (IV, 69). Las Cases (IV, 163) went back to Fain. Lévy (633–634) drew on Constant and on Caulaincourt, who was also present. And Méneval gave yet another version.[133] As both De Bourrienne and Las Cases remarked, the incident was shrouded in mystery; Napoleon himself blamed illness for his throes.

Hardy certainly recognized the importance of the incident, but he seems to have been willing to rely on Alison and, much more, on Thiers. In fact, instead of using the presumably definitive account by Constant, he makes that valet out to be a knave. There was some authority for this in the later role of Constant, and so in his invented conversation Hardy was free to suit his artistic convenience. He also used his imagination for Napoleon's soliloquy.

The most dramatic gesture was, of course, the taking of the poison. Constant reports that the Emperor had a sachet of leather and black silk which, during campaigns, he wore suspended from his neck and "which I used to keep so carefully for him during the interval between one campaign and another." Alison, though ambiguous, implies that the sachet was still on his person. Hardy put a book ribbon in Alison at the heading "Abortive attempt of Napoleon to poison himself"

---

[132] *Memoirs,* IV, 255–259.
[133] *Napoléon et Marie-Louise. Souvenirs Historiques,* II, 117–118.

(XVIII, 381), and in his manuscript he wrote, "unfastens the breast of his coat (Al), takes out ∗ ∗ ∗." But he marked in Thiers (XVII, 803) "et tirant de son nécessaire la redoutable potion," and parallel with his borrowing from Alison he wrote, "goes to a letter case—unlocks it (Th)." In revising, as so often, he chose to follow Thiers. From Alison, apparently, he borrowed the reference to Cabanis—"Sage Cabanis, you primed me"—and, as on other occasions, made a little knowledge imply a reservoir.

Hardy marked several lines in Thiers and incorporated their essence in his manuscript with marginal acknowledgment. Thiers had, of course, drawn on sources available to Hardy, but the poet was satisfied with his secondary account. He obviously felt that he was hearing the ring of truth in the repeated lament attributed to Napoleon, "Qu'il est difficile de mourir, quand sur le champ de bataille c'est si facile! Ah! que ne suis-je mort à Arcis-sur-Aube!" (XVII, 805). But perhaps the most important lines involved destiny: "Le destin en a décidé, dit-il à M. de Caulaincourt, il faut vivre, et attendre ce que veut de moi la Providence" (806). Hardy lets the sentiment pass as a lament. In the light of the midnight scene in the Tuileries on the return from Moscow and of what the reader would already know lies ahead, it becomes an omen of ill; Providence would always seem to want what Napoleon himself wanted. Even so, his wishes could be impelled by the Will.

The peaceful resignation that ends the scene is drawn from Thiers, but with significant additions. The historian quotes Napoleon: "et puis j'écrirai l'histoire de ce que nous avons fait. . . . [*sic*] Caulaincourt, s'écria-t-il, j'immortaliserai vos noms!" (807). Hardy gives us "our unmatched accomplishments" and "immortalize your names / By linking them with mine." That last phrase has the true Imperial tone.

Historically Hardy's scene, III, 4, v—"Bayonne. The British Camp" —succeeded by about three days scene vi, on the reception of Napoleon at Avignon. Either from ignorance or from artistic concern to represent the passing of time since April 11–12, Hardy reversed the order. Napoleon left Fontainebleau, April 20, and reached Avignon before 6:00 A.M. on the twenty-fifth; he embarked for Elba on the twenty-eighth. The journey subjected him to repeated insults and such threats of violence that a few minutes beyond Avignon he consented to disguise himself and even put on a hat with a white cockade.

The full account is in *Les Cent Jours,*[134] by Capefigue, which gives the versions of Sir Neil Campbell and General Koller and also draws on other eyewitness reports. In his rough draft Hardy wrote the dialogue of the officers and Napoleon in prose. There were minor variants in Capefigue's sources, and Hardy adapted facts for his convenience. The line "Ogre of Corsica! Odious tyrant! Down with Nicholas!" is straight from the history with the order of the epithets reversed. Other lines are close to the original. But again there are additions of consequence.

The dramatizing of the bitterness of the populace, with here and there a dissenting note of pity, gave Hardy an opportunity to put in some more Wessex touches. Thus, in his final version, we have a market woman hoping "by the Virgin, as 'a called herself." The remark owes nothing to Hardy's own refusal to accept miracles. The speaker is supposed to be a Christian, and her lewd cynicism sets the tone of degradation to which the Emperor must submit.

Another stroke that goes beyond Capefigue is in Schuvaloff's plea against violence:

> Cannot you see that merely to ignore him
> Is the worst ignominy to tar him with * * *.

Here we have Hardy's own appraisal of the tragedy that can stem from *hubris*. The old woman's fear that the "villain" may come back is, of course, a reminder of the contrast that will follow. And the final addition insists that, once an emperor, one cannot desert his character. At the nadir of his fortunes Napoleon can still envision triumph. Europe, he admits, is lost, "But Asia waits a man, / And—who can tell?" And so he is sped away, but destined to return. For only destiny could rescue even the strongest of men from so abject a degradation.

During his reminiscences at St. Helena, Napoleon was to speak nostalgically of Josephine, though with an egoist's bias—she would have followed him to Elba. In the days after the divorce he had now and then turned to her, always unmindful of the anguish he had caused. But when he spoke of retirement the night of April 11, he mentioned only his present wife. Keeping to the general tenor of the Emperor's life, Hardy for a time left Josephine in oblivion. Then he suddenly brought her forward to record her death, scarcely a month after the happenings at Avignon. The succession of Napoleon's fall by scene

[134] (Paris, 1841), I, 24 ff., mainly 51–53. The work is in the Memorial Library.

vii—"Malmaison. The Empress Joséphine's Bedchamber"—is like the return of a ghost of the past.

For his description of the bedroom Hardy adapted from Memes (363–364). The latter says that the furniture in the reception room was "covered with needlework, on a ground of white silk, wrought by the empress and her ladies." The bedchamber, in contrast, was "extremely simple, draped only with white muslin, its sole ornament being the gold toilet service." Possibly drawing on another source, or possibly using artistic license, Hardy made the room and the furniture luxurious, with the windows and the bed draped in white silk. Such surroundings befitted the last hours of an empress whose tastes had always been imperial. Memes (395) says that Alexander, as well as Eugene and Hortense, was present. Hardy preferred not to clutter his scene.

Hardy drew from various sources for Josephine's own words. Again he modified the facts.[135] According to Constant (III, 251–252), Mme. Montesquiou had brought the King of Rome to Josephine; Hardy has Napoleon do so. He has the Empress repent her early coquetries and then adds, as if from one of his own novels, her sense of retribution:

> * * * but afterwards
> I grew to be the captive, he the free.
> Always 'tis so: the man wins finally!
> My faults I've ransomed to the bottom sou
> If ever a woman did!

Hardy returned to Memes for the Empress' final words: "I have always desired the happiness of France; I did all in my power to contribute to it; and I can say in truth to all of you now present at my last moments, that the first wife of Napoleon never caused a single tear to flow" (395). Using this convenient translation, Hardy retained some of its very language, heightened parts, and, perhaps guided by his own sense of reality, altered "single" to "needless" tear.

Placed between the hatred and baseness of the scene at Avignon and the royal folly at the London Opera-House, the quiet beauty of Josephine's farewell to life reminds us of the finality against which all must be judged. In the midst of an arid landscape, where men wander madly and forget whither they are bound, come such oases of sanity and peace.

[135] For his concern as to the time of day the revisions in the manuscript are of interest and will be noted.

The Return of a Lucifer

The disaster at Leipzig, the abdication, the despair that prompted suicide, and the personal humiliation—such a sequence was enough for a great tragedy. Yet these were to become submerged in the popular memory of Napoleon because of the fame of Waterloo. Hardy had still before him the challenge to surpass the tragic denouement of 1814 and to build to a greater climax. Once again he had to sacrifice stores of historical fact of pertinence to his theme.

During the ten months that the Emperor was at Elba he had resumed his old course on a miniature scale. The little island had become his kingdom and responded to his creative touch. Far from retiring to write his memoirs, he had begun to reorganize the machinery of government and to initiate a program of public works. Meanwhile, the Allies were involved in bickering and intrigue which revealed the true stature of the leaders of Europe. Hardy omitted the vigorous activity of the Emperor and in his first scene of Act 5—"Elba. The Quay, Porto Ferrajo"—let the Ironic Spirits, in six lines, give the essence of months of battle at the peace table:

> The Congress of Vienna sits
> And war becomes a war of wits,
> Where every Power perpends withal
> Its dues as large, its friends' as small;
> Till Priests of Peace prepare once more
> To fight as they have fought before!

Meanwhile, too, the restiveness in Paris had grown to conspiratorial proportions. The true history could not be written, but the histories did record the rumblings of the populace that prepared for the return of the Corsican Ogre, the tyrant, Nicholas. And so Hardy's Spirits continue in the mocking rhythm of *Hudibras*, but with a cryptic tone:

> In Paris there is discontent;
> Medals are wrought that represent
> One now unnamed. Men whisper, "He
> Who once has been, again will be!"

If Hardy could not tell the whole story in all its engaging detail, he did show himself a master of economy in compressing the essence of ten months into ten short lines.

The Hardy who had written *Desperate Remedies* never lost his interest in sensational adventure. The escape of a royal prisoner at night, amidst an aura of conspiracy and mystery, carried all the excitement of romance.

The three best sources available to Hardy on events of February 26–27, 1815, were Capefigue, Thiers, and Alison, who used Capefigue as one source.[136] Hardy's version is at times at variance with all three. None mention Napoleon's fatness; Hardy inferred it from remarks elsewhere.[137] All put the embarkation at seven o'clock, Hardy at "about eight."[138] Thiers says that only those who remained behind were melancholy; Hardy remarks that the singing of the sailors, too, has a "melancholy cadence." All indicate that it was given out that the flotilla was to attack the Barbary pirates and only some time later was the true destination revealed; Hardy has shouts of "Paris or death!" All report a light southern breeze, with a complete calm ensuing some distance away; Hardy writes, "Not a breeze is there to stir a sail." We may assume that all these modifications were deliberate. The fatness was for Hardy a symptom of Napoleon's decline as a general. The later hour better fitted a nocturnal adventure. Hardy had to telescope incidents of two days or weaken the drama and suspense of the departure. Finally, the cadence of unpremeditated melancholy is an omen, and Hardy was, of course, always attracted to omens.

Probably even more than any other, Act 5 resorts to the device of the traditional novel, having to account for what was going on in various places at about the same time. Later it will take us, as we have seen, to the House of Commons and to Wessex. But first of all we need the effect of Napoleon's escape on certain persons at Vienna.

In scene ii we are in the Imperial Palace. The time is indeterminate, and not all that is presented actually happened on one day, but the

[136] *Les Cent Jours*, I, 135 ff.; *Histoire du Consulat*, XIX, 64 ff.; *History of Europe*, XIX, 253 ff.

[137] Dorsey Gardner quotes a review of Ségur's Memoirs in the *London Quarterly Review* of July, 1875: "Before the end of 1810, when he was in his forty-second year, he had contracted an inconvenient degree of *embonpoint*, and he told M. de Ségur's father that he could not ride the shortest distance without fatigue" (*Quatre Bras, Ligny, and Waterloo* [London, 1882], p. 34). Gardner also quotes from Lt-Gen. Charras' *Histoire de la Campagne de 1815*: "His eye flashed with the same brilliancy; his gaze had the same power; but his heavy, almost obese body, his swollen and pendant cheeks, indicated the arrival of that time of life when a man's physical decline has commenced" (33).

[138] Hardy agrees with *Oeuvres*.

news reached the Congress in early March. Scene iv, at Schönbrunn, is soon after the Declaration of the Allies, which was announced March 13. In his copy of Thiers (XVIII, 548–549), Hardy put a bookmark by the picture of the Congress. The substance of the declaration appeared in many places, including the *Annual Register* for 1815. Much of Hardy's two scenes, however, is from Méneval, who was at Vienna. Méneval himself obviously erred on dates, and so Hardy had grounds for assuming that there was no authentic version. Besides, except for giving a few historical facts, such as the substance of the declaration, Hardy was interested mainly in character studies which could be presented in fiction. His focus was on Marie Louise.

According to Méneval, Marie's grandmother spoke her romantic advice before Napoleon left Elba, and Marie was on horseback when the news reached her of the escape. That evening "il y eut dîner, billard et musique comme à l'ordinaire," but the next day Marie was more emotional and expressed the fear that Napoleon would fail and, in so doing, destroy her hopes of obtaining Parma.[139] Hardy had to rechronicle the spirited words of Maria Carolina to fit them in, and they were too good to be omitted. His rearrangement of the circumstances under which Marie learned the news represented a significant economy. First we see the shock on the faces of the statesmen, and moments later we hear the almost childlike accusation by Alexander, who had held out for Elba, and the retorts of Talleyrand and the King of Prussia. But we also see Marie as a virtual prisoner of the father who, though loving her dearly, treats her as a tool. She may be vain and selfish in her concern for Parma, but she is no more self-interested than those at the conference table, and she is helpless. In presenting to us at the same moment the response of the dynasts and the pathos of the Empress, Hardy succeeds in giving the latter the greater magnitude. Then he shifts from the little pair of worlds in the Imperial Palace to the continent of Europe. No network is laid before us of the Immanent Will and no Spirits appear, but the Countess of Montesquiou becomes a prophet:

> The red god War
> Stalks Europe's plains anew!

In scene iv we have the Declaration dressed up in blank verse; the rest of the scene pertains to Marie Louise. Having written romantic

---

[139] *Napoléon et Marie-Louise. Souvenirs Historiques*, II, 247–248.

stories, Hardy seized upon Maria Carolina's advice related by Méneval:

> Elle ne pouvait retenir son indignation des manoeuvres employées pour arracher sa petite-fille à des liens qui faisaient sa gloire, et pour priver l'Empereur [whom she once hated, but now admired and pitied] de la plus douce consolation qu'il pût recevoir après les immenses sacrifices arrachés à son orgueil. Elle ajoutait que si l'on s'opposait à leur réunion, il fallait que Marie-Louise attachât les draps de son lit à sa fenêtre et s'échappât sous un déguisement. "Voilà," répétait-elle, "ce que je ferais à sa place; car quand on est mariée, c'est pour la vie." Elle venait de prêcher l'exemple en quittant furtivement la Sicile.[140]

The daring spirit of Maria Carolina provides a touchstone, for the contrast with that of the broken Marie is complete. Méneval, who defended Napoleon, also liked and pitied the Empress. For Marie's reply to her grandmother Hardy found his evidence in Méneval's pages, and he certainly intended to vindicate her:

> A puppet I, by force inflexible,
> Was bid to wed Napoléon at a nod,—
>   * * * I kissed the cup,
> Gulped down the inevitable, and married him;
> But none the less I saw myself therein
> The lamb whose innocent flesh was dressed to grace
> The altar of dynastic ritual!—
> Hence Elba flung no duty-call to me,
> Neither does Paris now.

There is one disconcerting note, for which Hardy alone is responsible, and unfortunately it ends the dialogue. Méneval spoke of Neipperg, Marie's chamberlain, as a "mauvais génie" (II, 166), but he also indicated that when Neipperg became her husband he worked hard and ably in Parma, and that it was only after his death that Marie had trouble with her subjects. While treating Neipperg respectfully, Hardy does let Marie remind him that he has been "a trifle swift" in composing her letter renouncing Napoleon. And now, at the end, the salty Maria Carolina is unfairly cynical about her deeply troubled "petite-fille":

> Go, join your Count; he waits you, dear.—Well, well;
> The way the wind blows needs no cock to tell!

[140] *Ibid.*, II, 145. Much the same account is in *Memoirs to Serve . . .* , III, 277.

This is the last we shall hear of Napoleon's wives except for an allusion at Charleroi, where Napoleon remarks cryptically:

> Count Neipperg, whom they have made her chamberlain,
> Interred his wife last spring—is it not so? ＊ ＊ ＊
>   H'm.

Meanwhile the Emperor has begun his triumphal return to Paris. Scene iii—"La Mure, near Grenoble"—is close to Thiers. In Hardy's copy of Volume XIX there are uncut pages, but not for the events of March 7. He placed a bookmark by an engraving of Steuben's "Retour de L'Ile d'Elbe" (102–103), which shows Napoleon in cocked hat and a cloak; one man is embracing his knee, and others are waving their hats and swords. Hardy took his cue from the picture. By omitting the preparation for Napoleon's arrival the poet gave the incident at La Mure an unreservedly heroic tone. Actually, Napoleon had emissaries ahead to determine the tenor of the reception he could expect and to prepare the way; so that he knew that the odds were overwhelmingly in his favour when he stepped forward and invited his former soldiers to shoot. Nevertheless, in Thiers the gesture is a gallant one, and with his greater space, the historian wrings from the scene its full measure of chivalry:

> Soldats du 5ᵉ, s'écrie-t-il, me reconnaissez-vous?—Oui, oui! répondent plusieurs centaines de voix.—Ouvrant alors sa redingote, et découvrant sa poitrine: Quel est celui de vous, ajoute-t-il, qui voudrait tirer sur son empereur?—Transportés à ces derniers mots, artilleurs et fantassins mettent leurs schakos au bout de leurs sabres et de leurs baïonnettes en criant *Vive l'Empereur*! puis rompent leurs rangs, entourent Napoléon, et baisent ses mains en l'appelant leur général, leur empereur, leur père! ... S'adressant alors à Drouot et à Bertrand, Tout est fini, leur dit-il, dans dix jours nous serons aux Tuileries (XIX, 101–102).

Abridging this and other passages, Hardy concluded with an ironic line, spoken joyfully by a grenadier, but foreboding things to come: "We'll march with you to death or victory!"

At Elba, Napoleon could have lived in ease, spending his energies at his own discretion. Ordinary selfishness cannot account for his return to mountainous tasks and certain tribulation. Hardy saw him, however, as a captive of destiny. The Will performed its doings, both through the unrest of the citizens of France and through Napoleon's own habits of thought, from which he could not escape. He was already being hurried on a path that would quickly lead to Charleroi, Ligny, Quatre-Bras, and Waterloo.

Though the scenes in the House of Commons and on Durnover Green imply the passing of time, there is a sudden leap from La Mure in early March to the Belgian frontier in June. Thiers is the best source for untangling events as Napoleon's former generals began returning to the tricolour and sentiment built up to provide an army. Hardy, however, had to omit the evidence of the Emperor's administrative genius in establishing a new government and, within three months, expanding the active military force severalfold.

What Hardy could do was to draw from Thiers, perhaps Gardner, and others to establish his portrait of the Napoleon who was to make a final gambler's throw with the odds against him. Thiers writes that after his initial exhilaration upon returning to Paris the Emperor became gloomy about the future. He tried to dissimulate, but his sadness was apparent to Hortense and other intimate friends. Murat's catastrophe in Italy was "un sinistre présage. . . . il fut saisi d'une profonde pitié et de sombres préoccupations qu'il voulait en vain cacher . . ." (XIX, 529). Thiers emphasizes his melancholy:

> il croyait voir dans l'ensemble de la situation les signes d'une adversité persistante, qui sans ébranler son énergique coeur, attristaient profondément son esprit. Il se plaisait à en disserter sans fin avec ses intimes, et quelquefois, bien qu'accablé de travail, il passait une partie des nuits à s'entretenir du profond changement des choses autour de lui, de la singulière destinée des grands hommes, et en particulier de la sienne, qui avait bien toutes les apparences d'un astre à son déclin (617).

He revisited Malmaison and spoke of Josephine's death as "l'une des plus vives douleurs de cette funeste année 1814." Characteristically he added that Josephine "au moins ne m'aurait jamais abandonné" (619). If we read into his thoughts of the Empress unmitigated egoism, we must agree, nevertheless, with Thiers, as Hardy was able to do, that Napoleon had so completely identified himself with a transcendent destiny that he was more to be pitied than condemned. It is with such a perspective that we must pursue his career as a dynast to its tragic end.

RAGNAROK

For the few days that concluded in the Wood of Bossu, Hardy could benefit from his own study of the terrain at Waterloo and from the impressions of the veterans at Chelsea Hospital. For the depiction of the military tactics, however, he had, once again, to rely on the histories. He had his choice among an abundance, and he had to decide whom to believe on such controversial matters as the roles of Grouchy and Ney and the strategic competence of Napoleon and Wellington. For this last campaign he had one major new text, the 1900 translation by Mann of Houssaye's *1815: Waterloo.*[141]

Except for the quotation from the Declaration, which in the Memorial Library manuscript is annotated "[Ann. Reg. 1815]," Hardy appears to have put together scenes III, 6, i—"The Belgian Frontier"—and III, 6, iii—"Charleroi. Napoléon's Quarters"— primarily from Houssaye and Thiers. The two differ on details, and Hardy sometimes dissents from both. It must be remembered that even the accounts by those who were present were written much later, that they were filled with hearsay, impressions, and imputations as to the motives and judgment of the principals, and that they differed substantially. Where so much was rumour and conjecture, a poet could allow himself some freedom.

In the manuscript, after the title for scene i, Hardy wrote "June 14–15. 1815." As he developed the action he put it all into one long day. The location of Napoleon's forces accords with that in Houssaye (58), the journey to Charleroi with the account in Thiers (XX, 30 ff.), who speaks of the slow progress on narrow roads through thick woods, the seizing of the bridge, and the blowing up of the gates. Napoleon's arrival with the "Sappers of the Guard, the Marines, and the Young Guard" matches Houssaye (65), who mentions the "cheers of the inhabitants," but makes no reference to their being scared. Citing a number of sources, Houssaye describes the Emperor's halt and subsequent exhaustion "near a little public-house called La Belle-Vue":

> He got off his horse, sent for a chair from the Belle-Vue, and sat down by the side of the road. The troops defiled past him. As soon as they saw him, the infantry and the cavalry cheered lustily, the sound of their voices completely deadening the roll of the drums and the shrill calls of the bugles. The enthusiasm bordered on frenzy; soldiers broke from the ranks "to embrace the horse of their Emperor." According to an eye-witness, Napoleon soon fell into a doze and the uproarious cheering was powerless to rouse him (66).

[141] The translation (London: Adam and Charles Black), from the thirty-first edition, is in the Memorial Library.

Houssaye adds that the reported sleeping is probable because "during April and May" the Emperor "was constantly subject to these sudden attacks of drowsiness," and also he had been in the saddle seven or eight hours. Hardy could not bring in the causes, but he used the incident to gain an immediate effect of foreboding and to prepare for a later recurrence of the escape from consciousness—this time to the realm of conscience.

The Declaration has been given in verse by Metternich at Schönbrunn and denounced in the House of Commons by Whitbread. Hardy now reintroduces it to climax his scene. After the cheering and the sleep, the Emperor awakens to read that he is "without the pale of civil and social relations," in short, an outcast, liable not to justice, but to "public vengeance." The shock of discovery is not in Hardy's sources, nor is the physical sensation that follows—"His flesh quivers, and he turns with a start, as if fancying that some one may be about to stab him in the back." Once more Hardy has presented Napoleon suddenly stripped of all the accoutrements of power and isolated as a fragile and lonely man. No witches have taken form before him, and he is pursued by no Eumenides. But he is living in a world that, with all the appearance of reality, is strangely unreal, where the spectral is all, and he is but one of the shadows.

Scene iii—annotated in the manuscript "[June 15–16]"—is one of the least poetic until the very end. The recital of strategy does not give a vivid picture of the military situation. Hardy, as usually, shifts chronology to report Bourmont's desertion and to give some notion of the plan for keeping Wellington and Blücher apart.[142] But he seems indifferent to a matter of considerable importance. As one reads the histories, even when they attempt to justify Napoleon or Wellington, he cannot help recognizing how inadequate was the military reconnaissance. Hardy, however, accepts the ignorance of the enemy's positions as a normal thing, as in Ney's excuse for not taking Quatre-Bras.

Having plodded through the uncongenial historical part, Hardy turned suddenly to the kind of thing that always intrigued him. Like the voice of vengeance comes the reading of a letter signed "The Duke of Enghien." Though Napoleon had caused the execution of hundreds, the death of the Duke had become a symbol of his tyranny, and Hardy has him start up at the name. Once again the Emperor falls asleep, and

[142] Most of the facts are in Thiers, *Histoire du Consulat*, XX, 45 ff., and Houssaye, *1815: Waterloo*, 67 ff.

there pass before him "hundreds of thousands of skeletons and corpses in various stages of decay." There are a few places in the drama where Napoleon is speaking for effect, but Hardy was convinced of his sincerity whenever he alluded to his destined role. Here there can be no question, as it is the sleeping mind that laments:

> Why, why should this reproach be dealt me now?
> Why hold me my own master, if I be
> Ruled by the pitiless Planet of Destiny?

This is, of course, based on no source. It is what Hardy thought Napoleon would by now feel; and Hardy, in his determinism, must accept it, too.

Meanwhile destiny is also taking its course in a ballroom in Brussels. Where precisely did that ballroom stand, and what kind of room was it, after all? In Volume XVII of Alison's *History* in the Memorial Library there are several laid-in clippings of letters to the newspapers. Three— August 25, 1888, to *The Times*; September 5, to the *Daily Telegraph*; and December 10, to *The Times*—are by Sir William Fraser. A letter in *The Times*, September 25, and one in the *Daily Telegraph*, September 26, disagree with Fraser. The author of the second, Louis Mallet, cites as his authority a letter by Lady de Ros, daughter of the Richmonds, and, in his reply of December 10, Fraser insists that the letter proves his point. The key passage reads: "The house had belonged to a coachmaker, and the warehouse, in which he kept his carriages, was converted into a long narrow room, in which the ball took place." In his first letter Fraser had spoken of having visited the room, which had been converted into a granary. But the letter of September 25 cites as authority the sister of Lady de Ros, who identified the place of the ball as "our schoolroom." The following year Fraser published a chaotic book, *Words on Wellington: The Duke —Waterloo—The Ball*. Besides restating his argument on the location, he gave a ten-page list of those who were invited. Hardy read Fraser, and all his own guests appear on Fraser's list in much the same order, which is, in general, by rank.

In a letter of December 6, 1907, to Miss Owen, after he had sent the proof to the printers, Hardy wrote that he had been unconvinced by Fraser's book, "having visited the same hospital, coach-house, etc. myself in 1876."[143] He was no more convinced by Fraser's opponents.

[143] Weber (ed.), *The Letters of Thomas Hardy*, 73–74. Cf., Emma's Diary of a Journey, June 17, 1876.

Now that he had abandoned hope of obtaining authentic information, he wrote: "But I prefer that the site of the room should remain unknown, as it helps the romance of the event—unless, indeed, it could be where Byron puts it—at the Hôtel de Ville, the only place worthy of the occasion."[144]

After some revision Hardy had arrived at a footnote calling the location of the ballroom as elusive as that of "the tomb of Alexander or the hill of Calvary." In the printed text he replaced Alexander's tomb with two legendary places: "but the spot is almost as phantasmal in its elusive mystery as towered Camelot, the palace of Priam, or the hill of Calvary." The association of names has implications as to Hardy's view of Christianity; yet the linking of the room with the other three retains his feeling of its universal significance. Hardy's curiosity may partake of the antiquarian, but it has its origin in the substance of human passion.

Byron had, of course, immortalized the ball in *Childe Harold's Pilgrimage*, and Hardy's scene is at times singularly close to Byron's, both in substance and spirit. While recognizing the similarity in Byron's version and Hardy's, one is aware, too, of a difference. In Byron even the Alexandrines seem to hurry along as destiny proceeds inexorably. In Hardy the motion is no less relentless, but it is sometimes interrupted by quiet choral reflection. Hardy's chief commentator is the host himself, the Duke of Richmond. When his wife wishes that the dancing would stop, he replies:

> Let be; let be;
> Youth comes not twice to fleet mortality!

And, as he is about to draw the window-curtain before the servants put out the lights, he sums up the tragedy of all mankind trapped by a concatenation of events that must lead to woe:

> Well, it is more than bed-time;
> But little sleep for us or any one
> To-night in Brussels!

Hardy had to give not only the tragic sense of the great event, but also some historical facts. Although Captain William Siborne's *The*

[144] Laid in his copy of Siborne's *The Waterloo Campaign 1815* (4th ed.; Westminster, 1895), however, is a clipping of an article "The Waterloo Ball," from the *Illustrated London News*, November, 1926, which returns to the controversy.

Waterloo Campaign 1815 was considered by many to be the best source, Hardy found the kinds of detail he needed in Houssaye.[145] Sometimes he followed his source closely, and sometimes he once again took artistic license. Houssaye records the premonition of Brunswick when Wellington tells him there will be fighting: "Brunswick, through a sort of presentiment, felt the shudder of death. Turning very pale, he sprang up . . ." (83). Hardy develops the omen dramatically.[146] But Houssaye states that Wellington did not yet know that the French had crossed the Sambre; Hardy's first line of dialogue announces the crossing.

There are complex difficulties in the scene and they all stem from one question: Was Wellington caught by surprise and perhaps, at least to some extent, rescued by subordinate officers already in the field with their troops, or was he a patient, calm strategist, abiding his time? The more charitable view can be supported from the record in the Peninsula, especially in the building of the lines of Torrès Védras, and from reports of the actual battle at Waterloo. The documentary support is in Müffling's *Aus meinem Leben,* which Houssaye quotes. As Blücher's liaison officer with the British army, Müffling was a primary, but not necessarily infallible source on Wellington's reasoning. He quotes the Duke: "My troops are on the point of marching. But here in Brussels the partisans of Napoleon are beginning to agitate. We must reassure *our* friends. Therefore let us show ourselves at the Duchess of Richmond's ball, and we will be in the saddle by five to-morrow morning" (82). But there were contrary views, so that Gardner, for example, felt the need to muster the arguments of others to bolster his own in contending that the Allies were not surprised; and even he blamed Wellington for being in Brussels (28 ff.; 53). Houssaye writes that Wellington's orders would have left Brussels exposed, but that fortunately his officers had already acted before receiving them. Indeed, he firmly censures Wellington for his delay, his mistaken orders, and his presence at the ball (84–85).

How does Hardy choose to portray the great general? First he draws on the words of Müffling, giving them a new setting, at the ball itself after the news of the imminent attack has arrived, and in the

---

[145] Hardy's copy of Siborne has a very few marginal lines and annotations; for example, p. 129, "i. e. Q Bras"; p. 149, "3:00"; p. 158, "4:30." The last pages are uncut.

[146] Brunswick's "The rendezvous is Quatre-Bras?" is verbatim from Houssaye.

same passage he has the Duke deplore Napoleon's strategy. In his next speech Wellington admits that the absence of the Austrians and Russians is a misfortune and that he has "an infamous army" and "a damned unpractised staff." We have already noted Roseberry's words: "'our army is composed of the scum of the earth,' said the Duke of Wellington, with more accuracy than gratitude." As for the absence of the two Allies, it was obvious strategy for Napoleon, with a comparatively small force, to strike his enemies while they were still dispersed, instead of letting them gather while building his own army to greater strength. They might have anticipated such a move. Hardy does not depict a paragon, despite his trust in Müffling. In fact, when next the Duke speaks, he admits that he has mistakenly considered the "move on Charleroi" a "feint"; and then, of all things, he has to ask his host for a map. Finally, he confesses with no reservation:

> Napoléon has befooled me,
> By God he has,—gained four-and-twenty hours'
> Good march upon me!

Such is Hardy's portrait, an attempt to give the evidence for and against the Duke. Why not, he must have felt, acknowledge the weight of Houssaye's argument? It was not the General's brilliance that mattered; it was his courage and integrity. Once the fighting would get under way the Duke's elemental bravery would be multiplied by the number of the "scourged and bullied" who stood firm.

Nowhere else is Hardy's sense of relative values shown better than in scene iv—"A Chamber Overlooking a Main Street in Brussels"— at sunrise the morning after the ball. Included, as if in passing, are the tunes played at the dance or now in the street, a matter of some curiosity for Hardy. Given also are the names of brigades, which, like Homer's catalogue, are meant to resound heroically. Hardy once again speaks as from extensive knowledge, giving no hint of his having first written "the Forty-fourth" and, apparently on rechecking his source, found that he had miscopied "Forty-ninth." But the focus of the scene is on an unnamed girl who has lost her heart at the ball. We know little about her, except that she has remained sleepless waiting for her lover to ride by, that she weeps upon hearing "The girl I've left behind me," and that, after the awaited moment, she becomes "hysterical with grief." Who is she? Except that she is of sufficient rank to attend the ball, she might be any of a score of girls in Hardy's lyrics and novels. Or, for that matter, she could have been a younger sister of Andromache.

Before Hardy lay two fierce battles on the sixteenth, at Ligny and Quatre-Bras, the retreat to Waterloo, and the final overthrow. He had to subordinate the first two battles to avoid anticlimax, and also to vary their presentation. His solution was to stress the discussion of strategy in scene v—"The Field of Ligny"—and to call on the Spirits to narrate much of scene vi—"The Field of Quatre-Bras."

Though he may have obtained fragments of information from his copy of Siborne, Thiers, or others, Hardy stays close to Houssaye. His entire two pages of dialogue in scene v use the pattern and now and then the phrasing of the following from Houssaye:

> They could now see the French columns debouching, and with the field-glass could even discern the Emperor in the midst of his staff. It appeared evident they would have to contend with the entire Imperial Army . . . .
> "What do you wish me to do?" said Wellington abruptly in French, for he knew no German. Gneisenau suggested that the Duke should immediately march all his troops behind Brye so as to act as a reserve to the Prussian Army. This plan, based on an incorrect estimate of the redistribution of Napoleon's forces, was opposed by Müffling. He said in substance that the English should manoeuvre so as to outflank the French left wing. "Exactly so," exclaimed Wellington. "I will overthrow all before me on my way to Frasnes, and I will march on Gosselies." Gneisenau objected that this movement would be most eccentric and its success more than doubtful . . . . As the discussion continued for some time, Wellington closed it, saying, "Very well! I will come, if I am not attacked myself" (86–87).

Hardy has incorporated names of places and officers from other pages. He has given Blücher a share in the planning and has taken from Müffling part of his shrewd advice to give it to Wellington. One wonders whether he wanted to add slightly to the Duke's stature, or whether, as with Langeron, he suspected Müffling, Houssaye's source, of retelling the story in a manner most favourable to himself.

When we examine the manuscripts we shall notice how association affected Hardy's phrasing. The borrowing from Houssaye provides an amusing instance. In Hardy the French cry, "En avant"; the Germans, "Vorwärts." Why did the shouts appear precisely here? Well, it happens that at the very point in Houssaye which matches Hardy's action the historian, evidently referring to Blücher, writes,

"Encouraged by the presence of old 'Forwärtz' (Forwards), the soldiers shouted 'Hurrah' again and again . . ." (98). Hardy's scene is not distinctive. Coming after the simple language of the heart-broken girl, the dialogue is artificial and unrealistic. Indeed, the one natural line in it jars in its contrast, as Wellington unexpectedly blurts out, "I will, by God."

A number of separate actions came to be grouped together as the Battle of Quatre-Bras. In his résumé in scene vi Hardy was able to cover only the main tenor while also recapitulating part of the battle at Ligny. He noted the death of Brunswick and the fact that Blücher's horse was shot from under him. Without having space to explain why D'Erlon did not come to Ney's support, he implied that the failure was disastrous; and he singled out one of his gallant Picton's sallies. In all this he was mainly following Houssaye, though he again put a few relevant marks in his copies of Siborne and Thiers, and, for background drew on miscellaneous sources.[147] Like scene v, that at Quatre-Bras serves mainly to anticipate what is to come.

The histories, of course, move directly on to the retreat to Mont Saint-Jean, but Hardy chose to return to Brussels to remind us that battles cast shadows far beyond the battlefields. There are touches in scene vii—"Brussels. The Place Royale"—which suggest documentary origin, and there is a hint of *Vanity Fair*; but the dialogue is essentially fiction. The best is the last few lines, which take us back to another populace, that in Paris about to don the white cockade. Though Napoleon did have supporters in Brussels, the speakers are not among them. They are merely opportunists, who change their allegiance when convenience serves. Once again we are reminded that, if we are to speak of man's inhumanity to man, the dynasts, in their disregard for the common citizen, must be seen in the midst of a populace which is sometimes base. In the apportioning of goodness and evil the Will makes no distinction between those in high places and in low.

The ultimate victory at Waterloo was dependent immediately on

[147] Cf., Houssaye, *1815: Waterloo*, p. 115 ff.; Siborne, *The Waterloo Campaign 1815*, chap. 5; Thiers, *Histoire du Consulat*, XX, 106, which describes the field of Quatre-Bras. Thiers states that before the fighting ceased at Quatre-Bras at 11:00 P.M., June 16, 40,000 men had been sacrificed there and at Ligny (XX, 122). Indicative of Hardy's close dependence on his sources is an incomplete line in the Memorial Library manuscript. Ney's army "finds itself at
where." The poet rechecked his source, probably a passage he had marked in Thiers, p. 106, and inserted "Frasnes."

the courage under fire of the "scum of the earth." But it was dependent, too, on the near miracle of the retreat, in heavy rain, through the muddy fields that separated Quatre-Bras from Mont Saint-Jean. During the retreat there was only sporadic gunfire, but there was exhausting labour, hour after hour. Some of the officers may have been "damned unpractised," but they appear to have exercised good sense. Though they had not lost a battle, they were forced to proceed as if they had, in bringing together the shattered pieces, salvaging what could be moved, and patiently carrying on the unheroic duties which mark any retreat. Again, for his own account of the withdrawal, Hardy relied mainly on Houssaye. In scene viii—"The Road to Waterloo"—he sometimes merely touched up the lines and coerced good prose into straitened verse. Houssaye (144), for example, quotes Wellington: "'Old Blücher,' he said, 'has had a damned good licking and gone back to Wavre, eighteen miles. We must follow his example. I suppose they will say in England we have been thrashed too! I cannot help it!'" The best part of Hardy's revision is "A damned good drubbing." One could wish that he had let Wellington speak more often in his natural soldier's way.

There was much to cover in the retreat of the seventeenth of June, and Hardy can scarcely be blamed for doing it injustice in his concern to avoid anticlimax in the act to come. But one detail, when the destination has been reached, deserved special emphasis, for it was symbolic. The casual reader might easily miss the significance of Hardy's short paragraph: "Fires begin to shine up from the English bivouacs. Camp kettles are slung, and the men pile arms and stand round the blaze to dry themselves. The French opposite lie down like dead men in the dripping green wheat and rye, without supper and without fire." The immediate source is Houssaye, who writes that the French lay in rye "drenched with rain," and that they "were suffering from tortures of hunger." He contrasts their plight with the lesser misery of the English: "The [British] soldiers settled down on ground which was still dry, made themselves comfortable straw beds out of the long stalks of rye which they beat down, and proceeded to light the fires; the commissariat having been well managed, they were able to prepare their meal in peace" (152–153). For the full significance we go back to Alison's quotation of Foy's contrast between the French and the British soldier. To requote, the latter "is not brave at times merely; he is so whenever he has eaten well, drunk well, and slept well. Yet their courage, rather instinctive than acquired, has need of solid nutriment . . . ."

Poor strategy, wretched communications, and ill luck were to play their usual roles at Waterloo; and indifference to death was to be shared equally by red coats and blue. But in British tradition an almost mystic aura was to envelop the battle, as if the souls of the two countries had been brought face to face. Hardy reserved his main evidence for his final act, but certainly he found once again in Houssaye's words a confirmation of what had been so well stated by Foy and so completely accepted by the poet's compatriots. The battle of June 18 was not won on the evening of the seventeenth. But the same prosaic, unglamourous, matter-of-fact attention to the routine of living that had prevailed at Torrès Védras and Salamanca and Vitoria would again prove its genius when men once more took up the routine of dying at Waterloo.

Among the most celebrated passages in the epic is the Chorus of the Years on the coneys, the mole, the snail, the eggs of the lark, the household of the hedgehog, the butterflies, the unripened ears, and the buds of flowers "that will never bloom." The verse is four-foot *terza rima*, a mixture of anapaests and iambs, with heavy alliteration, that must be read with reflective slowness. One of the best images involves a pathetic fallacy and apparent absurdity—"butterflies, sick of the day's long rheum." Hardy wanted to identify Man and Nature in the suffering imposed by cosmic necessity. Given his concept of the Will, the absurdity vanishes, and there is left the irony; for at the moment the coneys and butterflies are the victims of the mad destructiveness of their human comrades, themselves enslaved by the Will.[148]

The choruses of the Pities drive home the human tragedy. It is the Pities that speak of "this harlequinade" and draw the comparison between the buds and the youthful soldiers. When Years interrupts, we are made aware of the long ages that separate 1805 from 1815. The veterans of whom he speaks seem like old men as their aches remind them—and us—of Ind, the Peninsula, Friedland, and Austerlitz.[149] Finally the rain "falls impartially on both the sleeping armies." We are a few short hours from Waterloo.

[148] In his letter of February 20, 1908, to Edward Clodd, Hardy wrote: "What you remind me of—the lyrical account of the fauna of Waterloo field on the eve of the battle—is, curiously enough, the page that struck me, in looking back over the book, as being the most original in it."

[149] In place of Friedland, Hardy first had Wagram. The change made the list geographically more inclusive.

Hardy liked to take his readers high above the earth to see the network of nerves of the Will or the creeping movement of troops. One who does not aspire to his graphic imagery must, in contrast, follow on an earthbound pathway the journey of the poet's imagination. But perhaps we can for a moment stand on a low hillock to survey what lies ahead, and our first concern is, of course, the historical substance on which Hardy drew. As already mentioned, he had been interested for decades in the last day of battle. He had visited the field, studied maps and pictures, talked with Bentley at Chelsea, and, over the years, read in the histories, biographies, and memoirs. There is no means of identifying all the places where he found hints or specific facts. We may be confident that his reading was extensive. It most assuredly included turning the files of newspapers and journals and following antiquarian byways. It involved especially the perusal of the histories. At the same time, we must remember that Hardy was writing a poem rather than a history and that he could not afford to recheck each fact in a multitude of sources. So, in our view, which is neither that of an eagle nor yet that of a coney, we can make some generalizations.

One of the controversial topics that filled pages in the histories, with frequent footnotes citing the most likely authorities, was the assessment of blame. Was it Grouchy or Ney or Napoleon himself who had blundered? Since Hardy appears to have used Las Cases and O'Meara elsewhere, he probably read Napoleon's own version as given by them.[150] He certainly read the numerous arguments in the other works. Siborne was a standard source for later historians. His account provides maps and detailed descriptions of the disposition of the two armies. In his copy of Alison, Hardy made annotations on the battle, one comment implying that Thiers was the more reliable.[151] The references to Picton draw on the original version in Robinson, possibly modified by some chance quotation of Picton's words in a now unidentifiable source. But the two main reservoirs were Thiers and, far more, Houssaye.[152]

Hardy's copy of Thiers has bookmarks and lines in the margin. Here and there he found a useful detail in Thiers that was not in

[150] Las Cases, *Mémorial de Sainte Hélène*, II, Pt. iv, 252–253, and III, Pt. v, 286–310; O'Meara, *Napoleon in Exile*, I, 174 ff., 465.

[151] Alison, *History of Europe*, XIX, 349, annotated "Ney without orders. (See Thiers)."

[152] The major part is from Houssaye, *1815: Waterloo*, pp. 178–244. Houssaye also has maps which show the distribution of most, but not all, the units.

Houssaye. In running parallel chronologies, he tended to follow Houssaye page by page on the action first in the French and then in the British camp, but he also drew on items pages removed from the immediate account. At the same time, his frugality manifested itself. When Thiers or Houssaye had put something in words that Hardy liked, he used them. Thus he was both the seer, far above his sources, surveying a great battle as a manifestation of the Will, and a poet mining the factual stuff of history for authentic detail.

Because the whole of Act 7 had to be seen as a unit, Hardy's problem was much more complex than in the earlier battle scenes. The use of Houssaye alone represents extensive reorganizing of what he found. We do not possess the rough draft of Act 7; the Memorial Library manuscript is a copy.[153] But we may suppose that Hardy first blocked out his major divisions with concern for chronology and that he then fitted in the details, drawn mainly from Houssaye. When he preferred a phrasing in Thiers he inserted it. When he was discussing things exclusively English, as on Ponsonby and De Lancey, he went elsewhere for greater precision than he could find in either, and for Picton he turned again to Robinson.

At its simplest Hardy's task approached a scissors-and-paste enterprise. But what resulted was much more than a synthesis. Houssaye was at times eloquent, and Thiers, as always, tried to impart a sense of the sublime. Nevertheless, the final act of *The Dynasts* is peculiarly the creation of a sensitive, compassionate poet trying to find his way through a cosmic wilderness of doubt.

Hardy begins his drama of June 18 with an aerial view that makes soldiers the size of ants; then, without hint of stage directions, he descends to earth to reveal individuals cleaning their crossbelts with pipeclay. The details in the prose narration in scene i are partly from the books—"Veillons au salut de l'Empire," for example, is in Houssaye (183)—and partly from Hardy's general knowledge of the mornings of battles. Then comes his catalogue of the divisions, French and English, in a blank verse chant by the semichoruses of Rumours. This is the longest of all the catalogues, with a liberal sprinkling of allitera-

---

[153] Hereafter the Memorial Library manuscript of Acts 6 and 7 and the After Scene, which is a copy of an earlier version, will be referred to as *C* (for copy). The British Museum manuscript, which, as the final manuscript, represents a revision of *C*, will be designated *B*. The rough draft of III, 1–4 will be abbreviated with *R*. For a description of the manuscripts see chap. 5.

tion and a feverish tempo. Except as a given reader might know of
Bylandt, Pack, Halkett, Ompteda, or anyone else, their names build
an effect only through their number and Hardy's tone. The one name
that he could count on for stirring his reader's emotions was Picton,
and so he refers twice to him.

In scene ii—"The French Position"—Hardy found it convenient
once again to alter chronology. In the manuscript he recorded the time
as "1–1:30–2:30." But as this was his first opportunity to introduce
Napoleon in dialogue, he picked up details from his conversation at
8:00 A.M. The description of the Emperor surrounded by his generals
is in Houssaye, but Hardy's version most precisely matches Thiers
(XX, 194). Although almost all the rest is in Houssaye (177–192),
the most vivid part of the scene is adapted from Robinson.

In his action between 1:00 and 2:00 P.M., Hardy draws on Napoleon's
intent at 11:00 A.M. to pierce the center (Houssaye, 186). Then he
quotes from the early morning discussion the odds of ninety to ten
(177), and continues to adapt from Houssaye. The latter writes that
Napoleon rebuked Soult: "'Because you have been beaten by Wellington, you consider him a great general. And now I tell you that
Wellington is a bad general, that the English are bad troops, and that
this affair is nothing more serious than eating one's breakfast.' 'I
earnestly hope so,' said Soult" (178). The words are, of course,
conjectural, their source being Soult's aide-de-camp. But as the
Emperor had just completed breakfast, the homely comparison sounds
authentic. By altering the time of day Hardy lost their aptness, but he
held doggedly to the image itself:

> You have been beaten by this Wellington,
> And so you think him great. But let me teach you
> Wellington is no foe to reckon with.
> His army, too, is poor. This clash to-day
> Is not more serious for our seasoned files
> Than breakfasting.

Hardy's dramatization of Houssaye is typified in the speeches
concerning the troops on St. Lambert's Chapel Hill. Houssaye writes:

> At a distance of about two leagues to the north-east, he perceived what
> appeared to be a black cloud emerging from the woods of Chapelle-
> Saint-Lambert. . . . He consulted with the officers around him. . . . Some
> officers contended that there were no troops there at all, but only a clump
> of trees or the shadow of a cloud; others saw a marching column, even

discerned French uniforms or Prussian uniforms. Soult said he could
plainly distinguish a numerous body of troops which had piled arms.[154]

Hardy takes from this its essence, adds the image "darkly crawling,
slug-like shape," and transforms "clump of trees" into a thing of life
and beauty in the midst of impending death:

> It seems a wood.
> Trees don bold outlines in their new-leafed pride.

His dialogue ends with "piled arms."

A few pages later (195), Houssaye gives us "Travers' cuirassiers and
d'Erlon's skirmishers appeared to dominate the crest of the plateau,
and the bulk of the infantry was following them closely behind."
Hardy merely rephrased this for his alliterative blank verse and made
Napoleon his narrator:

> Travers and d'Erlon dominate the crest,
> And further strength of foot is following close.

Elsewhere, too, Hardy freely used key phrases from his source, sometimes putting into one sentence pieces borrowed from two or three.

Hardy, to reiterate, was not a historian, and he was only moderately
graphic in representing the tactics of a battle. Indeed, it is doubtful
how clear a picture a reader gets if he does not have Siborne's or
Houssaye's maps before him. And once again, such names as the
Twenty-eighth or Ninety-fifth could individually mean little, as the poet
himself got them, not from tradition, but from the printed page.
But Hardy was a poet, and in the midst of tragic folly he cherished
manifestations of the greatness of the human spirit. One of his finest
symbols was Ney; the other was Picton, the gallant fatalist. A striking
contrast to Wellington, whom he sometimes annoyed, Picton was an
impatient soldier who seemed to live to fight. His language was whole-
somely profane—a point on which Wellington would not quarrel—
and his contempt for his own life was infectious. Before leaving for
the campaign "he had a presentiment that it would be his last"; and
he remarked to a friend, "When you hear of my death, you will hear of
a bloody day."[155] Of his death Robinson writes:

[154] *1815: Waterloo*, p. 190. Houssaye cites Napoleon, *Memoirs to Serve for
French History in 1815*, 137, *et al.*

[155] H. B. Robinson, *Memoirs of Lieutenant-General Sir Thomas Picton*
(2 vols.; London, 1835), II, 337, 339.

With the exhilarating cry of "Charge! Hurra! hurra!" he placed himself at their head, and led them forward. . . . He was looking along his gallant line, waving them on with his sword, when a ball struck him on the temple, and he fell back upon his horse—dead. Captain Tyler, seeing him fall, immediately dismounted and ran to his assistance; with the aid of a soldier he lifted him off his horse; but all assistance was vain—the noble spirit was fled.

The rush of war had passed on, the contending hosts had met, and none could be idle at such a moment. Tyler, therefore, placed the body of his lamented friend and general beneath a tree . . . and he rode forward to report to Sir James Kempt the loss which the army had sustained. That general, as senior officer, immediately assumed the command of the division; but Picton's intrepid example had done its work (360–361).

With hints from other pages in Robinson, Hardy, in the manuscript, had Picton call out, "What the hell care I— / Come on." In revising the lines for the text he decided to make them stronger and so inserted, in words that sound authentic enough except for their alliteration, "Is my curst carcass worth a moment's mind?" As for the "intrepid example," Hardy confirmed it in the charge that followed Picton's death. But he was still not done. In a veiled allusion to the accusations that had for a while besmirched Picton's honour—accusations which he had *not* endured stoically—Wellington, in scene iv, pronounces his epitaph:

> He was as grim a devil as ever lived,
> And roughish-mouthed withal. But never a man
> More stout in fight, more stoical in blame!

And Tyler quotes his prophecy of a "bloody day." The reader may easily miss the special quality of Wellington's praise; for the charge has continued rashly, "Sheer to the French lines," and has resulted in disaster. Wellington's own soldiership is the antithesis of Picton's, as he concludes, "Valour unballasted but lands its freight / On the enemy's shore." So, coming from the General, the praise is high indeed.[156]

Scene iii—"Saint Lambert's Chapel Hill"—prepares for the climactic arrival of Blücher, but its immediate value lies in its shifting our

---

[156] The monument to Picton in St. Paul's was erected by vote of Parliament. Moore's verses, quoted by Robinson, helped to immortalize the hero:

> Such fate, gallant Picton! was thine when the few
> Who survived thee in fight
> Won the day by the light
> That thy deeds shed around Waterloo!

perspective. We have been engrossed with the fever of battle which engenders brief displays of nearly superhuman effort. Now we see men engaged in the prosaic routine of endeavouring to come to the slaughter. The gun wheels of the Prussians are sunk in the mud in the valley of the Lasne, "and the men, already tired by marching since five in the morning, seem inclined to leave the guns where they are." But exhorted by Blücher and reminded by the "thunder from Waterloo," they finally free the guns and struggle on. There is no mention of the Will; reference to it would amount to tautology.

Scene iv—"The English Position"—is enlivened by Wellington's epitaph for Picton, the portrait of the General himself, the tribute to Ney, and reflections by the Spirits. But we may notice first some more pedestrian matters.

For his own guidance in manuscript *C*, Hardy put in brackets, after the title, "3–4:30," but again he could not hold to so restricted a time length. When he first listed the officers with Wellington, he included Cole. Before the final revision he evidently checked further and so omitted him. A little later he bracketed Egerton and Bridgman; in manuscript *B* he was able to settle on the latter. At first, on learning that Hill was not killed, Wellington said, "We must be thankful." In revising, Hardy remembered his theme: "Praise Fate for thinking better of that frown." At first Ney "opens his supreme onslaught." Sorting out the confused chronology, Hardy came up with "intensifies his onslaught." Years originally speaks of the "clockwork of the Will!" But Hardy never really felt its nature to be so mechanical; and, re-sensing the emotion he was describing, he saw the Will as a "whirl-wind." At first Pities asks, "Why should men's many-valued virtues take / So barbarous a groove!" But "virtues" mixed up the philosophy; and, not merely for the sake of alliteration, Hardy corrected the word to "motions." And, demonstrating the thoroughness with which he refelt the action during revision, the admonition of a Voice to wait "till their hoofs beat / Before you on this ridge" was transformed from the audial to a visual image, "till their whole height / Shows up above the ridge."

As before, Hardy sometimes varied little from his sources. Houssaye wrote, "The Brunswickers advanced to the support of Maitland's guards, the Mitchell and Adam brigades crossed the road to Nivelles to establish themselves above Hougoumont ..." (205). Hardy only modified the syntax of what he used. Sometimes he changed an image.

Houssaye (206) says that the English bullets rebounded from the French cuirasses "with the sound of hail on a roof of slates"; Hardy has them "snap like stones on windowpanes." Sometimes the poet added his own interpretation of an action. Houssaye quotes from Kennedy, aide-de-camp to General Alten:

> To our surprise, we soon saw that it [Ney's charge] was the prelude to an attack of cavalry upon a grand scale. Such an attack we had fully anticipated would take place at some period of the day; but we had no idea that it would be made upon our line standing in its regular order of battle, and that line as yet unshaken by any previous attack by infantry.[157]

Hardy refurbished this, giving the first part to Uxbridge, the rest to Wellington. On the way to his final version he at first called the rash charge a "madcap cruel enterprise." But the term was too light, too sporting, and so he replaced it with the unreserved pronouncement "madman's."

It was here that Hardy encountered the major question, that of Ney's culpability. He had put a bookmark in Thiers at a long footnote on the subject (XX, 231–234); and Houssaye had a series of notes, the consensus of his authorities being that the order to charge had been given by Napoleon as part of his total design, but that it had been carried out prematurely.[158] Hardy stretched probability ruthlessly to put in his own verdict. The English officer Somerset is endowed with knowledge suitable at the moment only for the French officers or Rumours:

> We have just heard that Ney embarked on it
> Without an order, ere its aptness riped.

To which Wellington rejoins for Hardy:

> It may be so: he's rash. And yet I doubt.
> I know Napoléon. If the onset fail
> It will be Ney's; if it succeed he'll claim it!

It is Ney who is most prominent in the scene. Even Pities is almost carried away with admiration of his charge:

> Behold the gorgeous coming of those horse,
> Accoutred in kaleidoscopic hues
> That would persuade us war has beauty in it!

[157] *1815: Waterloo*, p. 205, from Kennedy's *Notes on the Battle of Waterloo*, 114–115.

[158] *1815: Waterloo*, Notes to Book III, chap. 4.

And Hardy has Wellington praise Ney with wonder that transcends the horror and raises war to a fine and gallant art:

> The finest cavalry commander, he,
> That wears a foreign plume; ay, probably
> The whole world through!

Having put these words in the General's mouth, however, Hardy could not refrain from going beyond the action of his drama to let the Spirit Ironic remark that, when sentenced to execution, Ney would receive no help from his great admirer. But it is Pities who most accurately delineates Ney: "Simple and single-souled lieutenant he."

It is, nonetheless, the British virtue that ends the scene, with Wellington curbing his soldiers' desire to charge:

> They shall have at 'em later on.
> At present keep them firm.

And so the patience that built Torrès Védras prevails. Gazing at those fortifications, the French officer Loison had compared them to Wellington himself—"like him, heavy, slow, laborious, sure."

Hardy had discovered that the shift from one manifestation of horror to another may set both in relief. This is the effect of his turning suddenly, in scene v, to Wessex-type folk in the women's camp. Here we have not only the pathos of the loss of husbands, but the sense of death and dying as they are experienced, not in the hurly-burly that blots out normal reality, but with time for reflection. One woman, before she faints, says, "'twas worse than opening innerds at a pig-killing!"

Hardy was thinking in Wessex sentiment as he wrote this scene, which is almost wholly original. In manuscript *C* he identified the dead soldier as "one of the Thirty ninth"; and he brought in, with footnote identification, Samuel Clark of Dorset.[159] The colloquial language conveys the homely sadness. Perhaps the one sentence which most lingers in the reader's memory is the simple stage direction "Behind lies a woman who has just given birth to a child, which a second woman is holding."

Except for the opening lines, scene vi is concerned again with Ney's premature charge, and the source is primarily Houssaye. On the

---

[159] Indicative of Hardy's methods is the manuscript skeleton of the note: "Samuel Clark of the . . . . . Born . . . . died . . . . Buried at West Stafford, Dorset." He was later able to establish the dates, but evidently not the regiment.

debouching of the Prussians, Hardy merely transformed the prose of his source into blank verse. Thus "fury" in Houssaye's account of Ney's assault gave him "furiously." Occasionally he heightened what he found. When Heymès asked for more men, Napoleon replied, "Troops! . . . where do you expect me to get them? Do you expect me to make them?" (218). In Hardy this became:

> Infantry! Where the sacred God thinks he
> I can find infantry for him! Forsooth,
> Does he expect me to create them—eh?

The best part of the scene, however, is Napoleon's opening soliloquy, as he wakes from "momentary sleep." As we have noted, the death of Lannes bore heavily upon him. Ten volumes before his account of Waterloo, Thiers reported that though the dying general did not speak words of reproach, his Emperor's own conscience probably did —"se disant certainement à lui-même ce que le héros mourant ne lui avait pas dit, car le génie qui a commis des fautes est son juge le plus sévère" (X, 334). As his epic neared its close Hardy needed hints that would take his reader back and remind him of the unity of the action. So he let Napoleon experience a dream that was very much like a vision:

> A horrible dream has gripped me—horrible!
> I saw before me Lannes—just as he looked
> That day at Aspern: mutilated, bleeding!
> "What—blood again?" he said to me. "Still blood?"

The words are reminiscent of *Macbeth* and of antique tragedy. Indeed, the pattern of Napoleon's thoughts in the scene is close to that of Macbeth's. For, despite the horror, the Emperor cannot suffer total remorse and reverse his direction. He can only immerse himself in the action which he is powerless to stop and try to exorcise all discordant images and sensations. He is in the hands of fate, and, when Hardy revised his manuscript, he let Napoleon himself perceive that truth. It was in revising that the poet had the Emperor complete his dictation of orders with the words:

> Further than this
> None but the Gods can scheme!

Napoleon's gods are theologically not the same as the Will. But Hardy's implication is clear.

In scene vii—"The English Position"—Hardy sought to build suspense as both armies neared exhaustion and it was doubtful which would collapse first. The coming of Blücher in scene viii was to bring the final rout. In the two scenes Hardy had to present much factual detail, and manuscript *C* reveals that he had a hard struggle. In revising, he corrected errors—thus "a quarter past seven" became "a quarter past eight"—and made precise what was at first indefinite; but most of all he tried to enliven the style and to improve the consistency in his philosophic point of view.

Except for details that may owe their origin to any of several sources and for four or five that most accord with Thiers,[160] the substance was wrung from Houssaye, with somewhat more rearrangement than before.[161]

In his description of Ney's charges and of his heroism Thiers surpasses his usual eloquence, and he brings his history of Napoleon's military career to its close with a succession of apostrophes that are like the final chorus of a classical tragedy. Hardy recognized the artistic challenge inherent in the nature of an epic and called in the Spirits to set the tone. Scene vii begins with a reminder that both Napoleon and Wellington are subjects of the Will. Once again the Will is anatomized, and the soldiers' faces "wear the expression of those of people in a dream." The focus is unmistakably upon the epic theme.

In scene viii it is the Spirits Ironic and Sinister who pronounce Napoleon's damnation for his desperate lie—that the Prussian troops in the distance are Grouchy's. In his recollections of conversations at St. Helena, O'Meara (I, 174) says that he asked Napoleon "if he had not believed for some time that the Prussians who had shewn themselves, were a part of Grouchy's corps." The former Emperor replied, "Certainly; and I can now scarcely comprehend why it was a Prussian division and not that of Grouchy." In Houssaye's sources there was a difference of opinion, as his notes reveal. But Hardy chose to find the Emperor liable. Ironic reports that Ney "holds indignantly that such a feint / Is not war-worthy." And Sinister continues:

[160] E.g., "en potence," added in the text; Ney's "My friends, see how a Marshal of France can die!"; Rullière's concealing an eagle under his coat; and Napoleon's being "involved none knows where in the crowd of fugitives." *Histoire du Consulat*, XX, 246, 250, 251.

[161] Almost all is from pp. 217–239, but one passage is from p. 289, and hints as to interpretation appear to have come from other pages.

> Excellent Emperor!
> He tops all human greatness; in that he
> To lesser grounds of greatness adds the prime,
> Of being without a conscience.

The liability, of course, is within Hardy's system. Ironic has mentioned Napoleon's own argument—"That he is choiceless." The Emperor's reasoning presupposes the necessity of his winning, and he cannot conceive of choosing to accept defeat. In Hardy's cosmic framework he has not the power to choose. Nonetheless, though an agent of the Will, he is, in Hardy's thinking, damned. For, as we shall have occasion again to remind ourselves, in the After Scene, it is conceivable that the Will can be awakened, and to such a belief Napoleon has offered a determined and unenlightened "Nay!"

Even in these two scenes, only a few pages away from the close of his historical evidence, Hardy was a poet first and then a philosopher. His words sprang into his mind as he sensed the situation he was trying to imagine. Only afterward did he make them consistent. Fearful that Wellington will be killed, Hill asks, "what commands / Have you to leave me, should fate will it so?" This is proper language for a soldier. But in the final revision Hill became a better Hardy spokesman with "should fate shape it so?" When the Spirits again talk about the "Immanent Unrecking," in manuscript *C*, Pities asks, "Why wills the Will so senseless-shaped a thing?" In *B* "wills" became "bids." But either verb might suggest recking, and Hardy ended with "prompts." As the French debacle is about to conclude, Years, in the manuscripts, says, "Let the last Willwork of the show be bared." Since Hardy had been giving vignettes from history as if in an exhibition, in the text he changed the image to "last pictures of the Play."

It was fitting for Years to end the scene with a reminder that, though the names will be changed, the course of the World will continue as he has always known it to be:

> So hath the Urging Immanence [162] used to-day
> Its inadvertent might to field this fray;
> And Europe's wormy dynasties rerobe
> Themselves in their old gilt, to dazzle anew the globe!

So, in a general sense, things will go on as before. The world's great age will not have begun anew; only the names of folk will change.

[162] Hardy first wrote "Necessitation."

But what of the individual case? For that Hardy turned to one sole example, Napoleon himself. The final scene—"The Wood of Bossu"—makes of the fallen Emperor the tragic exemplar of the fate of mankind. Only at the beginning of the scene did Hardy go to the historians, and even then he made a notable change. He needed transition from the melee to a state of reflective solitude. According to Houssaye (274 ff.), Napoleon was accompanied by certain of his generals as he entered the wood sometime after 1:00 A.M., and during the subsequent retreat he was still trying to function as a military commander. Hardy changed the hour to midnight. At first he had Napoleon talk with his officers before dismissing them, but he added a query "? Better Nap. discovered alone. His retrosp[tive]." So he took the Emperor's first speech, which provided the transition, and made it part of a soliloquy broken only by promptings of the Spirits during his fitful drowsing. Napoleon starts to speak as a general, but at once becomes a morally isolated man.

The scene underwent extensive revisions as Hardy tried to make each phrase worthy of what had gone before. Certain of these are so important for the theme that we need to consider them here. They reveal that here, at the very end of his historical matter, Hardy still had to concentrate to maintain his point of view and his feeling for the substance of his poem.

In *C* Years' first speech begins

> "Sic diis immortalibus placet,"
> As mortals used to say.

In *B* Hardy added the translation, "Thus is it pleasing to the immortal gods." The passage concludes:

> Thus, to this last,
> The Will in thee has moved thee, Bonaparte,
> As we say now.

It is probable that in offering the translation Hardy wanted to imply that into the nineteenth century men still found the old sentiment adequate, translating it into their own tongue. He welcomed the age-old version as poetically true. He would not change the feeling, but would give it a new origin metaphysically.

Another revision corrects a strange inappropriateness in *C*. Napoleon has responded to Years:

> Yes, 'tis true, I have ever known
> Felt ever since the fight of Lodi Bridge
> That such a Will I passively obeyed!

To this Ironic replies: "Pardy, I care nothing for these high doctrines, + can only put the case in a common way. So I ask ye, Boney: has all this been worth while?" The tone would have been proper for Ironic in other circumstances, for not only Wessex citizens but British statesmen spoke of "Boney." But Hardy was writing the final pages of a world tragedy. So he put in the manuscript the warning: "To be altered." In the blank verse revision in *B, Boney* gave place to an allusion to Aeschylus—*Ajaccian Bonaparte.*

In Napoleon's long speech Hardy had many troubles. In both manuscripts there is an anachronism: "Yes, a good death, to have died at Waterloo." Napoleon had not yet had time to name the battle, and when he did, he insisted on "Mont Saint Jean." Hardy finally caught the slip and in the text wrote "yonder field."

Perhaps recalling Napoleon's previous recoveries from dejection, Hardy, in *C,* let him still dream of a dynasty:

> My only course
> To make good showance to posterity
> Is, that my son should follow on the throne;
> And how shape that! . . . . This is my darkest hour.
> Great men are meteors planned to burn themselves
> To light the earth, This is my darkest hour.

Hardy must have come to recognize that, however true to Napoleon's probable thoughts, the hope for a dynasty was discordant with the finale of his tragedy. So in *B* he changed the tense: "Was to implant my line upon the throne." And "darkest hour" might leave an opening for a brighter future. At its first appearance Hardy replaced it with "if now extinction nears?" In *C* itself he had offered an alternate reading for "planned to burn themselves," and, accepting it, he arrived at:

> Great men are meteors that consume themselves
> To light the earth. This is my burnt-out hour.

These should have been the Emperor's last words. But Hardy had said much of England's role as Nemesis, and he could not refrain from alluding to it once again, even expanding in the revision Napoleon's cry of bitterness.

Finally, the very last lines were obstinate and had to be trimmed and coerced in retrospection. In *C*, Years calls such men as Bonaparte "but instruments + means of Earth's unfolding." The phrasing could be defended, but it might suggest conscious purpose; and so it finally became "but incidents and grooves * * * ." In *C*, Years continues:

> The brazen poker that but stirs the fire
> Because it must . . . . Accept the title late
> Accorded thee—Commander in-chief of Skulls
> First Gravedigger of the World.

Does one need further evidence of the poet's instinctive feeling? Though only an instrument, the man who has led hundreds of thousands to their deaths stands sentenced as if he had proceeded by his own free will. It was thus Hardy really saw and felt what he had been telling. But it was out of character for Years to censure individuals; he was only the recorder of the life of men from the beginning of time. And so, in *B* Hardy struck all beyond "must." Only the Pities could lament. They would speak their piece in the After Scene.

SOMEWHERE ABOVE OLYMPUS

The terrestrial show is ended; the light of the magic lantern has been put out. We are alone with the spectral commentators, who resume their arguments about what they have seen. And what have they learned since they spoke together before the light was lit? In one sense, nothing new. Yet they have refined their insights and, if the spectacle has meant anything at all, they have the substance of life as the evidence for what they aver. So much we can say as we think of the Fore Scene and the After Scene in the framework of the play. More interesting is how Hardy himself saw his philosophic theme as he wrote both scenes, several years apart. So we turn first to the Fore Scene and to the Preface, which defined the perspective.

In the Preface, dated September, 1903, and written after the composition of Part I, Hardy asserted that his Spirits were not intended to defend any new system of philosophy or theology. In a passage in *B* not included in the printed text he wrote:

> Nevertheless the phantasmal Intelligences here delineated will, without much forcing, be found to lend themselves as readily to the Predestinarianism of the Theologian as to the Determinism of the Scientist, should

any gentle reader so require. As already stated, the writer has no dogma herein either to enforce or to deny.

His identification of the principal Intelligences is equally undogmatic. Drawing upon Schlegel, as we have noted, in a passage which he retained, he wrote that one group only, "that of the Pities, approximates to 'the Universal Sympathy of human nature—the spectator idealized' of the Greek Chorus; it is impressionable and inconsistent in its views, which sway hither and thither as wrought on by events." Certainly the Spirit and the Chorus of the Pities are poetic rather than philosophic spectators. Hardy continued, "Another group approximates to the passionless Insight of the Ages." This group was, of course, the Spirit and the Chorus of the Years. Although life and the Cosmos may be viewed from several points of vantage, Years ought not to "sway" in presenting his philosophy.

The problem which Hardy faced at the beginning was an exacting one. In a short poem he could be a Hebrew speaking to an Old Testament God, or a disillusioned Christian addressing a Christian Deity. He was much at home as a pagan talking to plural gods or even as an animist. A given poem might be trite, but at least, once the metaphoric pattern had been determined, it could be consistent. In all such poems the deity is finite, and, however indifferent to human feeling, it thinks in human terms. It is rarely benevolent, often malevolent, and most commonly indifferent, hence in effect evil in its failure to care for the things it has created. But now, in starting upon his epic drama, Hardy was trying to talk about the indefinable and to do so with somewhat foreign tools of thought. The very word "Will" as a translation of Schopenhauer's and Hartmann's concepts was capable of variant interpretations. A finite cognitive deity could will. Why should not an unconscious force be said to do so? Why should it not be "purposive"? By all his habits of thought since childhood Hardy must allow it purpose, even if mankind were but a momentary phenomenon in Cosmic history.

When he began the Fore Scene, Hardy was still inclined to think in his old ways. And when he tried to describe the workings of the Will he did not know with certainty what metaphors to use. Impersonality could be suggested by the image of a machine, but this did not allow for change except in a recurring order. A botanical metaphor permitted growth and decay. Or, if conceived spatially, the Will might be like something within a cloud, with endless manifestations as the cloud altered in form. Or it might be like a network of nerves reaching to every particle of matter and every sensation of animate life.

Metaphorical consistency persisted in eluding Hardy, and a number of his revisions of the Fore Scene, made after he had completed what he evidently thought was the final version of Part I are concerned with improving the harmony. In the manuscript version[163] of his first speech in the Fore Scene, Years describes the "patterns" in the "artistries" of the Immanent Will as having been "planned by rapt aesthetic rote." Hardy later realized that "planned" was inconsistent with the concept of an unconscious Will, and so he substituted "wrought." In the manuscript Pities calls the Will "this ageless, mighty, brooding, nescient Thing." With a little freedom in defining "brooding, nescient," the description gives one a feeling of the presence of the Will. Hardy revised the line, however, to "This viewless, voiceless Turner of the Wheel." In a sense the revision narrows the concept of the Will by implying mechanical inevitability in the turning; but in the metaphor of the lantern it may also connote the presentation of an unending sequence of pictures whose relationship to one another is purely fortuitous. In the manuscript, in the General Chorus of Intelligences, we find "the PRIME, that willed ere Being was." In the text Hardy altered "Being" to "wareness." He had evidently decided that the Prime must be coexistent with what we think of as the created World rather than something that existed first. The "wareness" with which he was concerned was primarily human consciousness, though in Schopenhauer's system it would be found even in inanimate Nature. The shift permits the final hope for change expressed by the Pities, which could not be justified if the Prime had existence anterior to all else.

Here we find Hardy confronting the issue of the coexistence of Necessity and Free Will. Pities will persist in believing that human effort can count for something in Cosmic evolution. Years will stress Necessity, but not rule out Free Will.

Thus, in Necessitarian terms, Years speaks of "Its clock-like laws" and of

> These flesh-hinged mannikins Its hand upwinds
> To click-clack off Its preadjusted laws.

In the same vein, again using the metaphor of puppetry, Years predicts, "You'll mark the twitchings of this Bonaparte * * * ."

[163] This is the British Museum manuscript, i.e., *B*.

More appropriate for Years are lines—still Necessitarian—that accord with those in the poem "The Sleep-Worker." Contradicting Pities, he retorts:

> Nay. In the Foretime, even to the germ of Being,
> Nothing appears of shape to indicate
> That cognizance has marshalled things terrene,
> Or will (such is my thinking) in my span.
> Rather they show that, like a knitter drowsed,
> Whose fingers play in skilled unmindfulness,
> The Will has woven with an absent heed
> Since life first was; and ever will so weave.

But Hardy could not let Years alone speak for him. Indeed, the very sentiment he denies is to be reasserted by Pities in that final paean of hope. The earlier passage by Pities reads:

> Meet is it, none the less,
> To bear in thought that though Its consciousness
> May be estranged, engrossed afar, or sealed,
> Sublunar shocks may wake Its watch anon?

And we find this interchange in lines which at first were all given to Pities:

> They are shapes that bleed, mere mannikins or no,
> And each has parcel in the total Will.
>   SPIRIT OF THE YEARS
> Which overrides them as the whole its parts
> In other entities.

By implication the parts might conceivably modify the whole. Such an event would be an incontrovertible manifestation of free will. And Years allows for the possibility of such freedom. After he has called Napoleon a puppet, he ends his speech:

> So may ye judge Earth's jackaclocks to be
> Not fugled by one Will, but function-free.

And he reiterates: "Deem yet man's deeds self-done."

So, at the outset, Hardy set the pattern for his interpretation of the human predicament. As an explorer in philosophy he wanted consistency, and, so far as he could, he obtained it. As a poet, however, he could not let Determinism or any other rational system fetter his sensibility or deny the truths presented by his imagination. And he was above all a poet.

In tracing his pathway through the Napoleonic era we have been repeatedly reminded of the tension. It is inherent in his theme. Whenever he was about to lose himself in an historical incident, he called on one of the Intelligences, sometimes through a mortal spokesman, to restate the theme. In Act I, as we have seen, he drew heavily upon them to keep clear his perspective. He did so again in the last lines in the Wood of Bossu—with his double metaphor, the one botanical on "Earth's unfolding," the other the simple Necessitarian portrait of man as the "brazen rod that stirs the fire / Because it must."

In the After Scene, once more in the Overworld, we have a dialogue of Years and Pities, with an interjection by the Spirit Ironic. The revisions show that Hardy was still having difficulty with his philosophic metaphors even as when he began the Fore Scene hundreds of pages before. In *C*, Years's opening line has alternative readings— the pertinent one, "Thus works the Immanent Will on Its designs." In *B* this became "Thus weaves the Great Foresightless Its designs." The succeeding lines are in the imagery of weaving, but Hardy again rewrote his beginning: "Thus doth the Great Foresightless mechanize." If "mechanize" connotes anything, it is changelessness, and the deletion of "designs" eliminates even the suggestion of purpose. So we are here firmly in the bonds of a purposeless Necessity.

A little later, in *C*, Pities remarks:

> Men gained cognition with the Flux of Time
> And wherefore not the Force that fashioned them * * * .

This, like the original passage in the Fore Scene, places the Force before Being, and, in *B*, Hardy corrected the line to "Force informing them." The lines are, of course, a wishful denial of eternal Necessity.

In *C* a semichorus of the Pities sings:

> Though time do not as yet explain
> Why Being cries to Thee in vain * * * .

"Being" had to give way to "Suffering." In an unreservedly Schopenhaurian concept "Being" might serve, but Hardy did not really allow feeling to all created things. "Suffering" was adequate to include all animate Nature, whether conscious or not.

In *C* a semichorus ends hopefully:

> That milding consciousness stands nigh
> This welter, and will fructify.

In *B* "milding" becomes "mild-eyed" and the second line is rewritten in its final form. In the printed text the first line is significantly reconceived to give the verses:

> We hold that Thy unscanted scope
> Affords a food for final Hope,
> That mild-eyed Prescience ponders nigh
> Life's loom to lull it by-and-by.

The optimism of "fructify" is obvious. The Will may become conscious even as a plant gives fruit. The revised "Prescience" is very different in connotation from "consciousness," and "lull" is certainly intended to be ambiguous. One lulls a child by making its sensations pleasant—but also by annihilating its consciousness. And so in the alternative connotation we are back with Schopenhauer, far removed from "fructify."

In *C* another semichorus ends with alternative lines:

> To what tune dances the Immense?
> [or] What fruit matures in the Immense? [*sic*] [164]

In *B* Hardy again rejected the image of fruit.

In *C* the Spirit Ironic ends his speech by asking whether the show is

> an illusion of the gods (The Will,
> To wit) some brooded purpose to fulfil?

This held its place in the later manuscript version, though it was in a language not suitable for Ironic and quite out of accord with Hardy's perspective. In the text he did not necessarily eliminate purpose, but at least he denied it in any meaning relevant to the future of mankind: "To wit) some hocus pocus to fulfil?"

In both manuscripts the last semichorus pleads for surcease from suffering for all "Whom It quickens"; if this cannot be achieved, "let them wither, and the races Earth abjure." Possibly the final form is not different in intent, but it is more emphatic:

> Should It never
> Curb or cure
> Aught whatever
> Those endure
> Whom It quickens, let them darkle to extinction swift and sure.

[164] Cf., *supra*, p. 113.

Even the very last line underwent a significant change. Both manuscripts read: "Consciousness the Will expanding, till It fashion all things fair!" If the Will consisted of the whole, of which man and other beings were parts, "expanding" was, at best, a confusing image. It finally yielded to "informing," which, in so far as the ineffable can be suggested, is a proper term. It takes us back to the earlier revision: "And wherefore not the Force informing them?" The pair of lines thus finally make the whole impel the parts, but, at the same time, they offer the hope that the consciousness in the parts may enlighten the whole.

Have we been merely playing a game of semantics, which could be pronounced irrelevant by a sophisticated metaphysician? Or are we dealing with something that took its origin in the very springs of Hardy's existence? Certainly, in unfolding before us a long record of human history, interpreted imaginatively, Hardy was telling us that, despite any inconsistencies which still remained and which he could not philosophically resolve, he was seeing life the best he knew how. Though during the First World War he was to say that he would now probably no longer end his poem with a hint of amelioration,[165] he never altered the last line. Indeed, its burden of implication was inherent in his very being and was compatible with his most poignant melancholy.

The necessitarian conditions would always exist. Gravity would continue, and the seasons would alternate irrevocably. Death would come, and for the individual it would be final. But it was conceivable that, even while occupied with necessitarian things, the imagination might still break free and, in its freedom, achieve a vision of a reality where Necessity was irrelevant. It had presumably done so with Aeschylus, Wordsworth, Keats, Schopenhauer, and others, and perhaps most assuredly with Hardy's favourite poet, Shelley.

Had it not done so at times for Nelson, for Lannes and Ney, at rare moments for Napoleon and Pitt, and perhaps even for a Wessex soldier dying at Vitoria or Waterloo? And so, in the Overworld, surveying the destiny of mankind, the Pities have the final word.

[165] *The Later Years*, p. 165.

CHAPTER FIVE

The Text from Rough Draft to Book

When Part I of *The Dynasts* appeared, the reviewers expressed a natural bewilderment.[1] Since it was only a fragment of the projected work, they hesitated to speak of the architectonics and concentrated on the diction and imagery. They deplored most the artificiality and the crabbedness of the phrasing. As we have observed, Hardy admitted that the poem was faulty, in fact, that its defects were obvious, and he regretted that preoccupation with them had blinded his readers to what he hoped was of merit.[2] Significantly, however, the complaints had no effect on his style as he continued with Parts II and III. He was confident as to his intent and persisted in it. At the same time, he knew that whenever he reread his lines he altered them, in short, that they could never be brought to perfection.

But the alterations did not consist of polishing. The stone with which Hardy was building was as rugged as that from the Dorset quarries. He did not want to smooth it till it had lost its character, but to retain the quality which it had brought with it from the earth. The reader could object that the syntax was arbitrary, the diction unnatural, and the rhythms cacophonous; but Hardy could not alter his habits. He might call Shelley his favourite poet, revere the lines of Keats, and, at one point or another, manifest his indebtedness to both and to Swinburne and others, but he could not cease to be Thomas Hardy, a Wessex countryman brought up with respect for local folkways and given to the re-examination of his own personal experience in the light of ancient tragedy.

He was not an eccentric genius, but he knew that genius itself is, first of all, a matter of imagination and that a poet's originality consists in the individuality of his imagination. Indeed, to judge from his own practice in revising, the weaknesses which disturbed him were not at all the oddities which for his contemporary critics made him obtuse,

[1] Reviews of the Poetry, in the Memorial Library.
[2] Letter to Newbolt, March 13, 1904.

but the occasional lapses into the traditional or commonplace. When he was at his best, the images forced themselves on his consciousness pell-mell, incongruously, defiant of logic; and if, having set them down on paper, he later struck them, the reason was usually that new images, fresher and more intense, had come into his imagined cosmos and demanded to be preserved. When imagination flagged, he became wordy and his rhythms were mechanical. When he recognized the uninspired verses on the page before him, he could only hope that, giving his fancy its rein once again, he would come forth with something unique. It might sound arbitrary or uncouth; but here and there, hopefully, a grotesque irony, a flash of eloquence, or a naïve expression of simple pathos would shock the reader into a poetic awareness of reality.

Unlike Hardy the architect, who had spent some time restoring fine old churches with nineteenth-century Gothic, Hardy as epic dramatist was both master builder and stonemason—sometimes concerned with the proportions of pillars and arches, sometimes with the fit of the casements and the snugness of the slates. We have implicitly dealt with the edifice as a whole, and we must return to it to study its lights and shadows and its mood. But we can get a clearer notion of the poet's craft if we first explore with him the shaping and fitting with which he was preoccupied from one day to the next. And so we turn to the manuscripts.

In the Memorial Library there are six sheaves. The first four, in Hardy's handwriting and labeled by him "rough draft," give the original form of Part III, Acts 1–4. The paper is of mediocre quality and the pages are so extensively revised that some passages are almost illegible. Sheaves five and six represent a copy, not by Hardy, of a now-lost first draft, with numerous revisions in Hardy's own hand, of Part III, Acts 6–7 and the After Scene. In the British Museum is a three-volume manuscript of the entire drama, on excellent paper, with further occasional revisions, representing the last stage before the printed text. Where it parallels them it differs extensively from both the rough draft and the copy. The printed version, in turn, shows additional hundreds of revisions before Hardy was willing to abandon the poem to its fate. Two further alterations for the sake of philosophic harmony were made in editions subsequent to 1910.[3]

[3] For convenience, as in chap. 4, *R* represents the rough draft of Part III, Acts 1–4; *C*, the copy of Acts 6–7; *B*, the British Museum manuscript; *T*, the printed text.

The British Museum manuscript of Parts I and II, of course, represents earlier work than the Memorial Library manuscripts. The rough draft, on the other hand, gives us the most inclusive evidence of Hardy's methods of composition. Certain kinds of revision are peculiar to it, the most obvious being the conversion of the prose raw materials into verse; for again and again Hardy first recorded his historical substance in prose, sometimes, as we have noted, quoting or paraphrasing his source. Other kinds are common to the rough draft, the copy, the British Museum manuscript, and the printed text. Despite his having eliminated philosophical inconsistencies, for example, as he revised Part I, Hardy confronted new ones in rereading Part II, and he accumulated additional discrepancies as he struggled with Part III, even in the very last scene.

As one collates the manuscripts and the text he finds himself in the presence of a matter-of-fact man who might have joined the country characters in *Under the Greenwood Tree*, *A Pair of Blue Eyes*, or *The Return of the Native* in trying to establish the precise time or circumstance of an incident whose time and place do not greatly matter. On every page he is reminded that Hardy was obsessed with alliteration. Again and again he is aware of unevenness, with artificial, colourless rhetoric cheek by jowl with graphic imagery. But if he is reminded of the unpoetic, he also has his rewards. For he is tracing the pilgrimage of an imagination capable of magnificent sweep and, at the same time, attuned to nuances; and in the midst of the thousands of details he perceives the architectonic skill of an epic dramatist with a feeling for variety, suspense, and climax.

We can begin with matters pedestrian—minutiae of a quasi-scholarly nature, but not irrelevant to the reduction of history to poetry. An immediate problem for Hardy was the identification of his cast of characters. In three or four instances he struck actual names and substituted " officers," possibly because in the given scene he decided to emphasize his principals, possibly because he was not sure of his accuracy. But normally he wanted names for verisimilitude. True, there are many officers who are in no way individualized in the epic, but even for the historically ignorant reader a name carries authority and a sense of immediacy. And if one has a name, his title must be correct. Finally, if he is prominent in the text, he must not be overlooked in the list of characters. So in his cast for Part I, Hardy omitted Count Munster in *T* and identified Daru, Murat, Decrès, Mack, and Kutúzof. For Part III he changed Alten from a general to a count, and, having second thoughts as to a suitable rank for an officer of the Fifteenth Hussars, promoted him from corporal to sergeant. In *R*, III, 1, iv, he bracketed "General" with "Colonel," awaiting confirmation of De Bausset's rank as general. Corporal Young of Sturminster Newton, III, 2, i, was promoted, in *B*, to sergeant. Unable, however, to decide the date of his birth, bracketed as 1788 and 1798, Hardy abandoned the item in his footnote. For antiquarian reasons he would have preferred the birth date. In *R*, III, 2, iv, he wanted a name for the attendant of the Princess of Wales, but had to settle for "Lady Glenberrie (?)." By *B* he had it correct as "Glenbervie." In *R*, III, 5, ii, he identified Colonel Campbell as English, but on reflection made him British. In *C* and *B*, III, 6, ii, Wellington speaks to Pack and Kempt, among others; in *T* they are replaced by Hill and Clinton.

The problem of scenic accuracy was perhaps more disquieting. In *R*, III, 1, i, Hardy knew how to characterize a wood on the Niemen, but he evidently had to discover later that what he called the Pilwisky was the Wilkowsky cited in a note from Tolstoi a few pages further on. In *B*, I, 4, v, the surrender of the Austrians after Ulm is finally "hidden by clouds." On rechecking, Hardy found "haze" more appropriate. At Trafalgar, *T*, I, 5, i, he added "folds of smoke." At Jena, *B*, II, 1, iv, the French have their backs "to the dawn." In *T* Hardy persisted with "Day has just dawned through a grey October haze"; but Thiers emphasizes the fog, and Hardy compromised with "backs to the nebulous light." Near Astorga, *B*, II, 3, i, the mud is at first "nearly knee deep," then "nearly ankle deep"; in *T* it is "half knee-deep." At Lobau, *B*, II, 4, ii, the Austrians look eastward; in *T* the map is righted with "southward."

These were matters of historical accuracy. There are many revisions that display Hardy's concern for scenic point of view. He seldom forgot that he was presenting a play as if on a Cosmic stage; and, having placed himself at a given vantage, he wanted his furniture correct. Thus, the Austrian army which, in *B*, I, 3, ii, is in the foreground, is removed in *T* to "mid-distance." In *B*, II, 2, i, Pampeluna and San Sebastian are "at this end" of the scene, in *T* "at the front." "To the left" of the Palace where Godoy is trapped, *B*, II, 2, ii, was too vague a location for the wall to be used in the Queen's escape; Hardy clarified the action with "on the flank." As the British fleet crosses toward Spain, Hardy remained unsatisfied with the fact that the first group is "vanishing behind Cape Mondego" and the second has "come out from Plymouth Sound." He meticulously added, *T*, II, 2, v, that the first was "to the right," the second "in the midst." In the same scene he gave away his machinery, in *B*, with "the soldiery are discernible by the fancy." In *T* they are "indefinitely discernible"—a variation of the looking around corners. Near Astorga the French dragoons first enter "some way back." This gave place to "at the back," and then, simply because accuracy is a virtue, in *T*, to "left-back."

At Wagram, *B*, II, 4, iii, the plateau first rises on the left, but Hardy corrected in the manuscript to "middle-left," and made the sun rise, not "over it," but "On the extreme left." At Albuera, *T*, II, 6, iv, he discovered that, without guidance, the reader might see the little stream flowing in the wrong direction, and so he had it come "from the distance on the right." Thinking undramatically, Hardy put the ford of the Tormes, *R*, III, 1, ii, "about two miles east of the city," but he promptly eliminated the discrepancy with "near the foreground." At Elba, *B*, III, 5, i, the port is initially "toward the western horn of the concave," but where is the reader? To place him properly, after "western" Hardy tucked in "(right-hand)." He was naturally most eager to have his topography clear at Waterloo, and so in *T*, III, 7, iii, he added "To the left of the scene, towards Waterloo, is a valley."

Time was also a most vexing problem. For his own convenience Hardy frequently inserted in *R* the date and occasionally the hour after the title of his scene. In accounts of battles there were inevitable discrepancies among his sources. Sometimes he made a choice; again he compromised with such approximations as midafternoon. For clarity in *T*, I, 2, v, he added "of the same summer," and in *T*, II, 6, iv, "in the same spring." In *T*, II, 6, iii, on Marie Louise's accouchement, he decided that the earliness of the hour was important and added "The time is before dawn." In *R*, III, 3, vi, where Wellington talks with the French officer prisoners, Hardy, as we have already noticed, was still uncertain about the occasion. So he wrote, "The battle of . . . . has just been fought." On rechecking before *B*, he filled in with "the Nivelle." In *B* he also added "Evening." The scene was almost entirely imaginary, but whatever historical authenticity it had in the vague reference in the *Dispatches* must be rendered absolute. In inventing dialogue for III, 4, vii, Hardy could take some freedoms, but the death of Josephine was of such importance in tradition that he could not risk a demonstrable error. Consequently, we find, in *R*, "It is four in the afternoon, Madame." Then, inserted above are "ten" and "morning." "Ten" is next replaced by "eleven." Finally "ten" is dotted for reinstatement. So we must conclude that three separate sessions of revision were involved, with rechecking of sources for the most probable time. Hardy would have been chagrined to receive a corrective letter from some antiquarian who was an authority on such matters.

A source of great concern was attire. In B, I, 4, ii, Napoleon is wearing "a gray great-coat"; in T, his "familiar blue-grey overcoat." Once he had corrected his error as to the precise shade, Hardy did not hesitate to treat the coat familiarly. Three scenes later, in T, Hardy struck "gray," leaving "shabby greatcoat," and in the same sentence he converted Napoleon's "slouched hat" to a "plain turned-up" one. At Waterloo, in C, III, 7, i, Wellington wears "white doeskin breeches"; in B, "light pantaloons." In C and B, III, 7, v, a dead soldier has a uniform with green facings; in T they have become buff. Many such details could have been omitted with substantial saving of effort, but Hardy appreciated the value of sensory clues for enlivening his action, and so he was willing to go back to the illustrations, paintings, or historical texts for verification.

The examples we have noticed seldom required extensive revisualizing of a scene. On the other hand, revisions of the action usually did. The simplest are the insertion of such stage directions as, in T, I, 1, iii, "(Ironical Opposition cheers)"; in T, I, 2, ii, "He [Villeneuve] gazes listlessly, and resumes his broodings"; and, in T, I, 4, iii, "in argument," to leave no mistake about the dissension in the Austrian headquarters before Ulm. More dramatic is the awarding, in T, I, 1, i, to the third passenger a pair of pistols to unpack and repack, thus marking the rise and subsidence of his comic wrath. Sometimes the mood is changed, as when the Austrian army, in B, I, 3, ii, creeps "noiselessly," but, in T, "dully."

More striking revisions show a new approach to an action. In I, 5, vi, where Villeneuve commits suicide, letting the despondent man write a letter to his wife was an afterthought which, in T, necessitated writing materials and the sealing and addressing of the missive. It was a happy inspiration which intensified the poignancy of the scene. In his account of Godoy, II, 2, ii, as we saw, Hardy was virtually creating fiction, as his sources gave only a few details. The expansion of the stage directions is toward traditional melodrama. In B, Godoy goes to a "private door." In T he goes to a "jib-door concealed by sham book-shelves, presses the spring of it * * *"; and his wife then sits down "with her back against the jib-door." In *B*, II, 3, iii, Hardy was again inventing fiction as a straggler remarks that, when Moore was hit, he "remembered the way to the rear." In *T*, Hardy spotted the colourlessness of the line and sent the soldier "over this wall." A notation in *R*, III, 1, iii, is indicative of Hardy's technical problems. Wellington is about to begin the battle of Salamanca, and Hardy has him eat while walking and talking. He also raised a query for later meditation—"[If W^n sleeps, it must be here]."

These are but a few of the numerous alterations that are more historical than poetic and yet were inspired by a concern for artistic verisimilitude. They remind us that before Hardy set down a detail which needed no later correction he must have gone through the same careful sorting of facts to pick out those which would most illuminate and best fit together.

When Hardy determined to employ spectral personages, he evidently had in mind for them four major functions. They could help with narration, discuss the manifestations of the Immanent Will, and point up both the absurdity and the pathos of mankind. But he discovered that subtle distinctions were necessary and that the borderlines were often obscure. Once again, experience provided no sure guide, for he continued to struggle in Part III in the designation of his spokesmen, and the final text is not always consistent.

In Hardy's first conception of the cast, Recording Angels would relate in heightened manner what otherwise would have appeared in prose narration; the Spirit and Chorus of the Years would tolerate no sentimentality in reminding us that thus impelleth the Will; the Spirit and Chorus of the Pities would comment on things pathetic; and the Spirits Ironic and Sinister would find delectation in the absurd. For occasional chores there would be Minor Spirits, Spirit Messengers, and the Shade of the Earth. Such was his cast for *B*, Part I. In time he discovered that he needed a spirit who could mingle with earthlings both to record happenings and to spread news; and so, in revising *B*, he evolved the Spirit and Chorus of Rumours, whose role was not clearly separable from that of Recording Angels or of Spirit Messengers.

Most ambiguous were the provinces of the Spirits Ironic and Sinister. The latter, while at liberty to speak in the manner of Satan, must in his negative way perform a constructive function. In *Tess of the D'Urbervilles* Hardy had remarked, "No man can be a cynic and live"; and

Sinister could not represent irresponsible, indiscriminate denial. Just how, then, should he be distinguished from Ironic, who had right enough to be bitter? Of more consequence was the overlapping by implication of the moods of Pities and Years. To record the workings of an unconscious Will that had led to human suffering was to convey emotion; and the insistence by Years that human pain was irrelevant to the Will intensified the poignancy. And though a simple, naïve lament was clearly in the province of the Pities, what of a paean that also commented on the nature of the Will?

In the light of the reassignment of speeches in R^4 or from R or C to B, we may suppose that there were many similar alterations from the first draft of Parts I and II to B; and it is significant that further reassignments were made in all three parts from B to T. We can only sample the total. In Part I, as we have observed, Rumour—or Rumours—was an afterthought, and in T speeches were bestowed upon him that were taken from Pities, Earth, and Ironic, as well as from Phantom Messenger and Recording Angels. The passage shifted from Pities in the Fore Scene is prophetic of Trafalgar; but it is weighted more toward simple narration than pathos. In I, 1, iii, the reassigned passage is more complex. Hardy first gave it to Earth, who is most akin to Pities, for in his metaphysics, as we have seen, Earth and mankind both suffer, the difference being that Earth is as aged as Years and Pities is the youngest Spirit. The speech, already cited reads:

> There may react on things
> Some influence from these [men], indefinitely,
> And even on That, whose outcome we all are.

By implication Earth is saying that the efforts of the members of Parliament, by affecting the Will, can affect her. Now, despite his metaphysics Hardy never attempted to grapple with such a theory. So the designation was inappropriate. The words were most suited to Pities, for whom *we* would less pointedly include Earth; but in the dialogue Pities has expressed disappointment with the Parliamentary bickering. Rumour provided the best alternative.

In I, 6, vii, the Spirit Ironic initially talked with a "street-woman." The repartee was in character, but his commending the woman on

---

[4] In a very few instances in R the name of one spirit may have been cancelled and another inserted before Hardy wrote the speech that followed. In most, however, the revision is tucked in.

being more charitable than some "who would not name thee with their white-washed tongues" had a touch of compassion. Rumour was the proper Spirit to talk with the woman about recent gossip and he could also display humaneness. In III, 1, iii, Hardy gave to Rumour what was in *R* a prose continuation of historical narration and to Pities a lament transformed from prose initially assigned to Rumour. In *T*, III, 3, iv, he took from Rumour to give to Pities lines from the poem "Leipzig." In *R*, III, 3, v, on the hypocrisy that will greet Napoleon's first collapse, Hardy bracketed Rumours without filling in the alternative. In *B* he gave the lines to Years. Finally, in *T*, he recognized belatedly that they were unequivocally suited to the Ironic Spirits.

In *B*, I, 1, vi, Hardy reassigned a slightly ribald passage from Sinister to Ironic, only to reverse his judgment in *T*. The usual pattern was to bestow on Ironic lines stripped from Sinister that were more witty than contemptuous.[5] But the distinction between the two Spirits remained shadowy.

The most significant revisions involve the province of the Pities. In *T*, Fore Scene, Hardy took from the youngest Spirit to give to Years a general comment on the Will in return for a broken commentary reassigned in *B* to Pities on "this terrestrial tragedy * * * this earth-tragedy." In *B*, I, 2, ii, he replaced "Recording Angel reading" with "Villeneuve (writing)." What the melancholy Admiral writes is under the aegis of the Pities, and so in *T* Hardy identified the human avatar with the aerial personage by shifting from "A minor Intelligence" to Pities the introductory lines on the hopelessness of his position. In I, 5, iv, we find a delicate discrimination. In *B*, Years has been philosophizing to Pities on the nature of the Will and the undesigned origin of human consciousness, which he calls

> needed not
> In the economy of Vitality,
> Which might have ever kept a sealed cognition
> As doth the Will Itself.

The lines fitted Years except that man's cognition was the cause of his sorrows; by giving the lines to Pities Hardy converted them into a lament.

[5] In *B*, Fore Scene, "Nay comedy"; *B*, II, 3, i, "Quaint poesy, and real romance of war!"; from *R* to *B*, III, 3, i, four couplets on the success of "Bull's" bribery of Napoleon's foes.

In *B*, I, 6, iii, after the Ironic Spirits have cried out against the senselessness of Austerlitz and its like, Years rebukes them for distressing the Pities. In revising, Hardy gave to the Shade of the Earth "Pain not their young compassions by such lore." From Years the line would inevitably sound ironic. Spoken by Pities' fellow sufferer, it is quite simply poignant.

Some striking reassignments are from Rumours to Pities. At the end of *B*, II, 4, vii, and in all of viii, Hardy was depicting the horrors of Walcheren. Apparently because narration was involved, he gave some forty-five lines to Rumours. On rereading the manuscript he realized that only the Pities should utter these verses of unmitigated pathos. At the end of III, 1, v, on the battle of Borodino, Hardy made a similar change from *R* to *B*. Dying men are blaspheming, and maimed horses are "tearing round / In maddening pangs." Yet it was only after reflection that Hardy saw his spokesman aright. In the next scene he first used prose narration to tell of Rostopchin's preparing to set fire to Moscow. When he revised this to verse he tucked in "Spirit of the [Pities?]." This time the case was not so clear between Rumours and Pities, but Hardy kept the designation.[6]

The perplexities we have been examining probably stem from the fact that, once he started on a line of thought, Hardy became so immersed that he followed where his imagination and convictions led him and only afterward perceived that he had shifted from his initial direction or mood. His most natural drift, of course, was toward the Pities.

Together with the assigning of the appropriate speaker was the problem of maintaining consistency in the philosophic terminology which the Spirits should use. We have already studied examples in the Fore Scene, the final pages of the drama proper, and the After Scene. Others are scattered through all three parts. The revisions are relevant not only to the philosophy, but to the craft. That there were inconsistencies at the beginning and that some were never corrected is further evidence that Hardy imagined and felt his subject first and only then tried to reduce it to order. In short poems he could express now one feeling, now another. With equal validity God could be purposive, indifferent, seemingly malevolent, or unconscious. But in *The Dynasts*, Hardy was artistically committed to an attitude toward the Immanent Will, and in his revisions he tried to reconcile discrepancies.

[6] Years and Rumour continue the narrative.

In *B*, I, 6, viii, the Chorus speaks of the "evolving Will." Hardy, of course, conceived of such a possibility, as "informing" of the Will would cause it to change; but the epithet was unequivocal in its assurance. So, in the manuscript, Hardy revised to "all-urging Will." In *B*, II, 5, vi, the Ironic Spirits address Years as "Dear Father Kronos." But absolute identification with Kronos does mischief to the nature of Years, and, in *T*, Hardy resigned his attempt at equating ancient and modern to write "Showman Years." In *B*, II, 6, vi, Years remarks, "But as the Immanent Will may arbitrate." Hardy changed "Will" to "Mode," but still missed the false note in "arbitrate." In *T* he revised substantially: "But as the unweeting Urger may bestead!" After teasing his thought in *R*, III, 1, i, Hardy ended with the Will moving men to its "inexplicable purpose." In *B* he caught his slip and changed "purpose" to "artistries," a term morally neutral. And as mentioned, Hardy had trouble till the very end. Even after the poem had been printed he changed the activity of the "unweeting Mind," in I, 5, iv, from "purposive" to "processive"; and in II, 2, iii, he altered "purposive, unmotived, dominant Thing" to "mutative * * * ."[7]

If the revision of such words as "evolving" and "purposive" represented primarily a rational effort, certain alterations were acts of imagination. Though the Will was immaterial, its functioning must be connoted, and concrete images were essential. In the Fore Scene, in *B*, Years tries to describe the Will as manifested in its workings:

> These are the Prime Volitions,—fibrils, veins,
> Will-tissues, nerves, + pulses of the Cause,
> That through Earth's life and substance ramify.

The branching of the nerves was to remain one of Hardy's images; but here, on revisualizing, he decided that the pulsation of the life force should dominate, and so, in *T*, he ended, "That heave throughout the Earth's compositure." In *B*, I, 1, vi, Years tells Pities:

> Let me then once again
> Show to thy sceptic eye the very nerves
> And sinews of this all-informing Power.

In *T* he shows Pities

[7] Cf., Amiya Chakravarty, "*The Dynasts*" *and the Post-War Age in Poetry* (London: Oxford University Press, 1938), pp. 38 and 47.

>   the very streams
> And currents of this all-inhering Power.

Where either image would fit, the poet in each instance replaced an essentially static anatomical description with an image of motion, and he replaced a possible connotation of intelligence implied by a nervous system with a not necessarily purposive impulsion.

In Hardy's system the impulse of the Will must, of course, work through Napoleon, and, in II, 1, viii, Hardy lets him rationalize his firmness to the Queen of Prussia by speaking of "some force within me" that controls his actions, as well as "my star." In III, 6, iii, however, he revised a similar expression to accord with what a man really wants to believe about himself. For Hardy knew, as his short poems sometimes demonstrate, that a man does not wish to think of himself as expressing a tragic power. If successful, he prefers to believe that, because of his merits, he has been singled out by the gods for glory; if he fails, he wants no part in the blame. In *C* and *B*, after the horror of his vision of skeletons on battlefields, Napoleon protests the injustice of the vision in words consistent with Hardy's philosophy:

>   Why hold me my own master, if I be
>   Ruled by the Spirit of Destiny in me?

But "in me" was psychologically false, and Hardy removed Destiny to its proper place in Napoleon's thought—"Ruled by the pitiless Planet of Destiny?"

On occasion Hardy was inclined to put his own thoughts into another's words. In *B*, I, 5, vi, where Villeneuve commits suicide, the Admiral utters a lament couched in philosophic terms. Hardy must have recognized that it was more the language of the poet himself than of Villeneuve, for in *T* he struck almost all. Again, in *B*, II, 3, iii, the dying Moore says:

>   And others have been treated worse than I
>   By Him who holds us in His hollowed hand!

But Hardy had no evidence that Moore would believe in a malevolent God. So, in *T*, he made him an orthodox Christian by correcting "treated worse" to "chastened more."

In *B*, II, 5, ii, a servant, speaking after the cruelty of Napoleon to Josephine, is the Spirit Ironic in human form. He finds the situation "droll" and continues, "Well, God is a great philosopher, if you take him right." In the manuscript Hardy revised this with a Catholic twist: "Well, Holy Mary * * * her right." Such an attack on the symbol of mercy turned the servant into the Spirit Sinister. But the gratuitous sneer was false, and in *T* Hardy hit upon a version that actually accorded with his own view: "Well, Father Time is a great philosopher, if you take him right." His feelings, however, about Christianity refused to be put down entirely. In commenting on the religious service that grants the Emperor the crown of Lombardy, I, 1, vi, Years speaks of "a local cult, called Christianity." And as we have noticed, speaking in his own name in the revision of his footnote, in III, 6, ii, Hardy linked Calvary with the mythical abodes of King Arthur and King Priam.

If Hardy had been trying only to work out a theoretical system, the task would have been impossible, for even Schopenhauer and Hart-mann were compelled to make assumptions as profound as the con-clusions they reached through logic. His own chore was greater because of the extra dimension with which he had to work. To delineate one quality of human experience he had to slight or even sacrifice another, and there was no end to the making of choices. If "purposive," for example, had been totally false, he would hardly have used it in the beginning. Yet its replacement, "mutative," is also incomplete. The poet could but symbolize the tenor of life, and in steering from Charybdis he inevitably came nearer to Scylla.

Naturally, most of the thousands of revisions are concerned with the elimination of commonplace or unimaginative phrasing or with taking adequate lines and surcharging them with emotion. Here and there the meter limped or the pronunciation of a word was distorted. Thus what was, in *B*, I, 1, vi, "I cannot own such phantasmatics real" became, in *T*, "I cannot own the weird phantasma real." Again, "The French broke through Aderklaa, alas," in *B*, II, 4, iii, became, in *T*, "The French in fierce fume broke through Aderklaa." Some-times tautology was stricken, as in *B*, I, 1, vi—"visibly manifests." Flat terms that had survived *B* came out in *T*. Thus, in I, 4, i, "the dark" gave way to "thick night." An astonishing number of filler syllables were replaced, though too many remain. We find, for example, in *B*, II, 2, iii, "To solder any Treaties," in *T* "To clinch and solder Treaties"; in *C* and *B* III, 6, iii (Ney to Napoleon) "Give me another opportunity," in *T* "Give me one rich last opportunity."

Passages lacking in colour could sometimes be enlivened with a dialect word or an image fitted to the speaker's occupation. In *B*, I, 2, v, Mrs. Cantle, frightened by her husband's bravado, asks, "Why didn't a man of no glory content me!" In *T* she wishes for a husband of no "sprawl." On the quarter-deck of the "Victory," *B*, I, 5, ii, Captain Hardy pleads with Nelson not to risk his life:

> My lord, each common creature of the earth,
> Dock-labourer, longshoreman, + waif, + stray
> Sees it as policy to guard his life * * * .

In *T*, Hardy remembered his speaker's calling:

> My lord, each humblest sojourner on the seas,
> Dock-labourer, lame longshore-man, bowed bargee * * * .

Yet, even while seeking the quaint or striving for verisimilitude Hardy perceived now and then that he had sacrificed the essential for the superficial. His second deserter in *B*, II, 3, ii, near Astorga, is comic, to be sure, and so Hardy had him, at first, speak of "this bullet I gnaws." But the man is chewing the bullet to "squench my hunger," and Hardy eventually averted undue distraction from the pathos with "chaw." Though his common soldiers swear, Hardy allowed them only sparing profanity and always with a poetic flavour. In revising, he also stripped Wellington of several oaths. Swearing, if too frequent, would obscure the soldiers' melancholy or the high seriousness of the General.

The usual revision is, of course, in the direction of greater concreteness. In *B*, II, 3, i, a deserter's reference to "good drink" was promptly individualized with "old-fashioned tipple." In *B*, II, 1, i, the traitor Gevrillière tells Fox, "I readily go wherever you appoint." Perceiving the dullness of such a line, Hardy reworked it in *B* and again in *T*, toe end with a totally new concept—"Though my far bones bleach whit on austral shores!" In *B*, II, 3, ii, accusing Austria, Napoleon says, "Ah this means war." After two revisions this commonplace became "Ah,—swords to cross." In *C* and *B*, III, 6, vi, at Quatre-Bras, Rumour speaks of the Brunswick bands "that border the plantation of Bossu." In *T* the line has taken on character—"That hug the tangled tree-clumps of Bossu."

The most significant changes heighten the emotional tone. In a few instances a rearrangement of lines built toward a climax. At Trafalgar, in *B*, I, 5, iv, the cruel comedy about the naked woman interrupted the drama of the last moments of Nelson. In *T*, Hardy put this and other matters earlier to leave the pathos unbroken.

Often the substitution of a word or two transformed the mood. In *B*, Fore Scene, Years calls the cloud "sunbeam-silvered," then "sunbeam-burnished." In *T* it is "sunbeam-smitten." In *B*, II, 4, iii, Napoleon is called "victory-spoilt," in *T* "victory-gorged." In *R*, III, 1, xi, Kutúzof speaks of the cold and adds that the Russians will be stumbling "over their stiff shapes." In *B* the dead French soldiers have become "frost-baked meats." In *R*, III, 4, iv, after his unsuccessful attempt at suicide, Napoleon laments how easy it is, by contrast, to die on the "smoking battlefield." In *B* the arena is the "passionate battle-plain."

Frequently Hardy added phrases or sentences to emphasize physical or mental suffering or the sense of Cosmic melancholy. In *B*, I, 5, iv, his lines from Sophocles on the gods read:

> Such gross injustice to their own creation
> Is their pronounced disgrace.

The second line, in *T*, became

> Burdens the time with mournfulness for us,
> And for themselves with shame.

A few lines later Pities' "Yea, yea, yea / Your hasty judgments stay" became, in *T*, Years's

> Nay, Nay, nay:
> Your hasty judgments stay,
> Until the topmost cyme
> Have crowned the last entablature of Time.

After Napoleon has taken poison, in *R*, III, 4, iv, Hardy patched up the prose to scan—"It is but Bonaparte who has so failed. ¶ By no means the French people."[8] In *B* the lines became:

> Yet is it but Napoléon who has failed.
> The pale pathetic peoples still plod on
> Through hoodwinkings to light.

To intensify the horror at Waterloo, in III, 7, vii, Hardy added, in *T*, an entire speech for the Spirit Sinister:

> One needs must be a ghost
> To move here in the midst 'twixt host and host!
> Their balls scream brisk and breezy tunes through me
> As I were an organ-stop. It's merry so;
> What damage mortal flesh must undergo!

[8] ¶ was Hardy's symbol for a new line.

As one remembers that for every such revision Hardy had to revisualize and refeel his subject, one has some awareness of the mental anguish the poet himself had to undergo.

Many of the revisions are not individually distinctive, but the total effect is very much so, indeed. Even in his slightest ballads Hardy managed to assert his personal identity. And whether, in *The Dynasts,* he was carried by the Muse into ethereal realms or whether he trudged along on a dusty plain, he was determined to have an adventure peculiarly his own.

The most obvious stylistic manifestation is in the alliteration. Hardy was influenced, of course, by others, including Swinburne, and by the example of old ballads, but he was not a mere imitator. He tended to associate words alliteratively even in prose. Often when he replaced one word with another, with no resultant alliteration in his line, the replacement, nevertheless alliterated with the original word. In the factual prose narration there is more alliteration than chance would bring. The most elementary conversion of prose to verse, in *R*, commonly involved its addition. In subsequent revisions there were a few instances where, to achieve novel phrasing, Hardy sacrificed his device, but there are hundreds of examples to the contrary. Sometimes one alliterative combination replaced another.

In quick reading we are struck with the mechanical aspect of the practice. But we must remember that Hardy heard his rhythms in slow, meditative cadences; so that he could find pleasure, without monotony, whenever the first consonants of syllables were the same, whatever letter came after. Thus, in I, 1, iii, "Whence an untactical torpid despondency" became, in *T*, "Whence the grey glooms of a ghost-eyed despondency." In the Parliamentary debates Hardy was seldom above the dusty plain, and reviewers objected to the factitious declamation. Certainly, Bathurst's original line, in *B*, in the above scene—"A finer scheme of military defense"—is more natural than the version in *T*—"A finer trick to trounce intrusive foes." Yet, if one reads the latter slowly, rising to the end of the second foot and then falling away, with stress on "foes," the alliteration is no longer obtrusive; it becomes, indeed, as subdued as the iambic beat itself. So with such a line as Tomline's in *B*, I, 6, viii, where Hardy gave up the alliteration of "When winds of rumour breathed the word across" for that of "When tongues of rumour twanged the word across." If one drawls "twanged," the repetition of the *t* sound goes almost, yet not quite unnoticed. Or take the line by Pities, originally, in *B*, II, 1, ii, "My hope for Europe's craved tranquillity." In the manuscript Hardy gave up the alliteration for "sweet reposefulness." In *T* he came back strong with "reason-wrought repose." Yet the stress on "pose" softens the effect.

A strongly alliterative semichorus, in *B*, II, 2, v, speaks of the guns "wheeled heavily / To bear their bulk along." No method of reading could subdue the *b*'s. In the manuscript Hardy shifted to "roll the roads * * *" and, in *T*, perhaps for vowel variation, to "roll the routes along." The poet had regained his ear. The account, in *B*, II, 4, v, of the fraternizing of the exhausted fighters at Talavera, first went:

> They fall to grasping hands across the rill,
> Sealing their oneness as poor humankind.

In the revision in the manuscript Hardy achieved both a familiar tone and alliteration with "They get to grasping * * *" and both alliteration and greater pathos with "Sealing their sameness as earth's sojourners." Comparable examples can be found on many pages.

Yet we must not suppose that the poet never nodded. In II, 4, i, the matter-of-fact line, in *B*, "So Marshal Lannes comes first upon Vienna" is not improved in *T*—"So Marshal Lannes swings swiftly on Vienna." And it is impossible to forgive Hardy a line by the Recording Angel, in III, 6, vi, at Quatre-Bras. In *C* he wrote, "The English break, till Picton to the rescue * * *." This was still good enough in *B*. But in *T* Hardy fired a salvo of *p*'s: "The English broke, till Picton prompt to prop them * * *."

Whatever the number of his failures, Hardy was always searching for the distinctive in imagery and phrasing. At the same time, he was also confronted with problems of economy and proportion. In the margins in *R* are notations questioning whether to omit certain passages or to expand others—e.g., III, 2, iii, "[Embody some of above descr?]"; III, 4, iv, "omit if too long"; III, 4, viii, "may be omitted if too long." Here and there are dashes to be filled in, showing that Hardy was first testing his rhythm or even his rhyme—e.g., *R*, III, 1, x, for ten-foot lines:

> Their yell of mortal agony— — — — —above the gale
> — — — — — — — — — — — — — —prevail.

Usually the fragmentary lines were discarded, but the architect's sketch had served its purpose in giving direction to the replacement.

Commonly Hardy bracketed words, lines, or entire passages for future choice. Either version sacrificed something of the total concept, and the question became which of the many qualities most needed to be preserved.

Many revisions involve unusual words, such as "uncreation" or "smalling" or eccentric use of standard words. Since in the final text there are scores of examples, one need only browse for a page or two to see that Hardy was employing whatever startling means would imprint his meaning or sharpen his image.

As we have noticed, even for verse passages Hardy repeatedly set his thoughts down first in prose. Next he might either rewrite substantially or tinker hardly more than enough to get iambic meter. In the latter event, he would eventually hear his lines in new cadences and usually bring forth a passage very different from the primitive transitional stage. We cannot take time to examine all the variations. But lines in the first scene of Part III will illustrate what often took place. Napoleon is addressing his soldiers as they are about to invade Russia. First the prose, with Hardy's own dots and brackets:[9]

> Soldiers! war has begun again. The last ended at Friedland + at Tilsit . . . . At Tilsit Russia swore an eternal allegiance with France + war against England. To-day she violates her oaths: she will not give any explanation of her strange conduct till the French eagles have recrossed the Rhine [+ left our allies at her discretion] Russia is led on by fatality: her destiny must accomplish itself [She says] Does she then believe us degenerates—that we are no more the soldiers of Austerlitz?

The lines are close to Hardy's source, but they approach poetry as he comes toward his climax. This time his initial revision goes well beyond mere tinkering to achieve considerable regrouping of his thoughts. In the manuscript it appears as prose with ¶'s in pencil to mark line divisions:

> Soldiers! wild war is to the fore again. ¶The — — — alliance Russia swore ¶At Tilsit for the English realm's undoing ¶Is violate beyond refurbishing (all vampery. ¶And she un[taciturn] + unashamed. ¶Russia is led on by fatality. ¶She says her destiny must be outwrought.
> [Does she then reckon us degenerates {No more the warriors / With nothing left in us of Austerlitz?]

The brackets show where Hardy was least satisfied. Except for a minor

---

[9] A colon in the manuscript represents either itself or a semicolon.

detail he finally got everything worked out for B, and ended with the
following in T:

> Soldiers, wild war is on the board again;
> The lifetime-long alliance Russia swore
> At Tilsit, for the English realm's undoing,
> Is violate beyond refurbishment,
> And she intractable and unashamed.
> Russia is forced on by fatality:
> She cries her destiny must be outwrought,
> Meaning at our expense. Does she then dream
> We are no more the men of Austerlitz,
> With nothing left of our old featfulness?

Though the changes in the first lines are minor, the climax has been
virtually rewritten.

Sometimes it was a problem in rhythm that concerned Hardy.
Thus, from C to T in the extensively reworked choruses of III, 6,
viii, "And the forms all so foreign to hill, plain, + tree" lost two
syllables—"And the forms so foreign to field and tree"—and therewith increased the emphasis on what remained. At times Hardy played
with various line lengths, with differences of tone, before settling on the
one that best caught his mood. Frequently he shifted parts around.
Thus, another heavily revised passage, in R, III, 3, i, had Ironic speak
of the "sad Last-Supper talk / Between this Christ of War and his
disciples." In the manuscript Hardy improved the order with an
alternative line—"'Twixt his disciples + this Christ of war!" The
latter held.

Sometimes the poet went after better concrete detail. In R, III, 1,
vii, for example, Davout views Moscow from a distance:

$$\text{How vast a host of churches} \begin{cases} \text{prod} \\ \text{pricks the sky!} \\ \text{breaks} \end{cases}$$

In B this becomes "How huge a heap of church tops prick the sky!"
But the verb was misleading for Russian churches, and, more important, Hardy wished to convey the traditional glamour of Moscow, a
beauty soon to be destroyed by fire. So, in T, we read "What scores
of bulbous church-tops gild the sky!"

Hardy's attention to detail and his problem in making choices appears strikingly in the song "Budmouth Dears," which ends III, 2, i. One line in *R* first went "Will the broidered blue pelisse again attract the muslin gown?" "Escort" replaced "attract," and then gave way for "* * * pelisse yet glow beside the muslin gown?" Then "pelisse" yielded to "broidered jacket glow again * * * ." Finally, Hardy arrived at "Will the gay sling jacket glow again beside the muslin gown?" Still unsatisfied, in *B* he tried "smart" for "gay" and momentarily "against" for "beside." In *T* he returned to "gay." As for "pelisse," he recaptured it in his footnote.

Even a seemingly casual remark in prose might exact critical attention. In *R*, III, 4, vi, a postillion speaks of Murat's having been born "in Cahors, out in Perigord, a little dormant place." Above "little," Hardy added "poor," and he jotted down four alternatives for "dormant," two above, two below the line—"ragged," "weakling," "simple," "crumbling." In *B* he at first chose "weakling." But it would not do; and so, for a French speaker, he finally had to call on dialect—"a poor little whindling place."

Usually more than one issue faced Hardy in a single line. Thus, drawing on Houssaye, in *C*, III, 7, ii, for conjecture on whether the distant object is Grouchy's troops or a wood, he quoted a marshal: "Trees don strange outlines at their leafing time." In *B* he tried for a new quality, ending with "Trees don bold outlines in their pride of leafage." Presumably he so read the new version that it did not appear to limp. But in *T* he obtained both the quality and a valid rhythm— "Trees don bold outlines in their new-leafed pride."

Sometimes he was struggling with the image, the rhythm, and the vowels to secure a strangeness of tone, as in the "Mad Soldier's Song," in III, 1, xi, during the retreat from Moscow. One line, in *R*, first read, "We are hard as stones, being only bones." Hardy tried and rejected "cold" for "hard" and "bags of" for "only." Then he replaced "hard as stones" with "grinning crones." For "grinning" he tried and abandoned the alliterative "conscript." In *B* he returned to "bags" with "We are grinning crones—thin bags of bones."

It was through such fitting of his quarried rock that Hardy fashioned his edifice. But there were, of course, too, the inspirations that owed nothing to the craft. It is in these that we have the essence of years of thought and feeling. Their tenor may take us back to Sophocles, but for a student of Thomas Hardy, poet of Wessex, they have a special ring. Such a personal touch is in a simple line by Josephine. In *B*, II,

2, vi, Hardy wrote, "Yet much is wise in foolishly forgetting," an ambiguous statement in its context. In the final text the forsaken Queen speaks in character, but at the same time for the poet: "Yet all joy is but sorrow waived awhile."

Sergeant Young, who "once walked with a girl * * * for some weeks," only to lose her to a tallow chandler's dipper, concludes his melancholy reminiscence, in *R*, III, 2, i, "I was a good deal upset about it at the time." In *B*, like Josephine, he adds for Hardy, "But one gets over things!" The irony is subtle and poignant. Neither Sergeant Young nor Hardy quite got over things. The soldier remembered a song, and Hardy wrote many other verses about just such things. The natural tendency is toward forgetting, and it is the loss of memories that decays the spirit. The attempt to revive and cherish is an effort to partake of immortality. But it means the recall of joy in the midst of its absence; and the very struggle to relive the precious moments reminds one that man is a fettered god, doomed to an existence where all joy is but sorrow waived awhile.

In organizing the abundance of historical fact into acts and scenes, and in mastering his images and rhythms, the poet was never forgetful of the informing principle and the architectonics of his work. His theme was always before him, with all its tragic intensity. There had to be a fusion of thought and feeling, and the structure itself must make use of the varied resources of imagery and meter. By the nature of art most must be omitted, but what was set down should symbolize the mortal predicament. So Hardy employed token summaries and vignettes for the interstices and chose for dramatization scenes that were rich in implication. His technical problem was to maintain unity in essentials and at the same time to represent the manifold variety of their expression.

Each battle scene, consequently, partakes of the universal in its preoccupation with determinism and free will, with human heroism and defeat; yet each possesses its uniqueness, and each portrait, whether of a dynast or of an unknown man or woman, has its own peculiar lineaments. Hardy's men are of the race of men, and yet they are strangely set apart in their individual natures and destinies. The human tragedy is manifested in day-long bloodlettings, where men and horses are but a confused mass of mortality. But when singled out, each soldier takes on specific identity, and the pathos is born afresh in a given heart with each tragic event.

Queen Louisa of Prussia plays her role as dynast, but she weeps with personal grief for the loss of Magdeburg. "The girl I left behind me" has a generic theme, but the girl at Brussels on the morning of Waterloo gives it a fresh reality in a grief that is hers alone. The stragglers are mere impedimenta, but each dies pronouncing his own verdict on existence. Pitt and Fox have subordinated their private cares to exalted principles, yet each senses the futility of his personal efforts. In the midst of his fellow sailors, bent on a common cause, Nelson carries his own private burden of melancholy. Ney is the symbol of the true warrior, yet he is entranced in his own world of illusion. Josephine and Marie Louise are alike pawns, but the human vanity of each gives its own nuance to her pathetic fate. And the old King's madness at Windsor mirrors that of the world he has forgotten, yet represents the ultimate loneliness of one frail man.

Finally, there is the strange enigma—the Emperor. In earlier centuries he might have been interpreted as a man driven by his own daemon. But neither a concept of daemons, nor of *hubris*, nor even of the Immanent Will can do more than provide an abstract indication of his bewildering and bewildered genius. Despite all that he does and says, despite his blasphemy and his hellish nightmares, he is not a mere creature of evil. For, more than those of others, his visions are exalted, and he carries the burden of responsibility imposed upon him by his suffering compatriots. Each of the characters casts a shadow larger than himself, as all contribute to the theme. Napoleon, in the multiplicity of his cruelties and follies, his heroism, and even his idealism, casts the longest shadow of all. We feel that we see, at least to some extent, the three dimensions of the others. But the chief dynast is inscrutable. In the midst of his drama of existence Hardy managed to give each of his characters a symbolic role, and always he took care that the archdynast was an actual or felt presence as a captive and vicegerent of the Will.

Informing all the scenes are the strange powers that seem to govern human destiny. Each force could be given a Greek or Roman name and treated with a pretense of familiarity. But they, too, are for Hardy illusory manifestations of the Immanent Will. So, in the diversity of action, mood, and thought, we are ever reminded of the unity.

The ten-year period itself is a symbol, framed by scenes in the Overworld. Its shadow is the aeons of human struggle and human pain. We begin with a question that cannot be answered and we return to it at the end. The last line is, of course, not really final. Hardy came to doubt its truth. And yet, though until his death he could have stricken it for another, he did not. It was neither to be proved nor to be disproved by logic, no matter what the system of one's metaphysics. Artistically, however, it was an assertion of the validity of the poet's work. An epic should begin *in medias res* and should have a progression toward an end. The conclusion should remind the reader of where he began his journey, and also of how far he has come. For Hardy this meant that what had gone before should justify a new note at the end. He had wrestled valiantly and he felt that the pageant he had reviewed did justify the words of the Pities. And so the spirit of the poet and the logic of his art led to the same culmination—the tentative, qualified cry of hope as Hardy brought his last great work to a close.

Hardy's novels had infused the spirit of Aeschylus into a few square miles of Wessex. With the inspiration of Thiers and the help of Houssaye and the others, *The Dynasts* brought Greek and modern concepts of tragedy to an epoch of human history. The artistic task was the poet's most ambitious and exacting. What he paid in emotional strain we can only surmise. It might seem that he was imposing upon himself a gratuitous burden. But Hardy had lived through intense personal experiences, and he had come to accept as part of his own spiritual existence the potential suffering of humanity. To forget such experiences or to fail to transmute them into art would have been to deny nourishment to his very spirit. He wrote *The Dynasts* because he could not and would not "get over things."

If we were to remove from Hardy's epic drama all the discourse of the Spirits and the reflective commentaries by the mortals, we should have left a narrative in which people struggle amidst complexities which they cannot understand. Except for those whose destinies are prescribed by the dynasts, they might seem to be free agents, responsible for the devastation which they bring to themselves and others. We could become absorbed in their adventures, participate in the suspense, and feel compassion even as we feel it in daily life. The protagonists would be dramatically present before us, and they would typify the variety of tragic experience. We should, however, find nothing more distinctive than in the weakest of Hardy's novels, where the plot is tragic enough. It is the poetic overtones that give greatness to the finer prose works, and it is the lyric quality which finally distinguishes *The Dynasts*. It is never long absent in the prose conversations of the common soldiers and Wessex countrymen, and it even breaks through here and there in the Parliamentary debates.

Giving a tone to the lyric commentaries is the poet's sense, reiterated by the Spirit of the Years and his ghostly associates, that, even when man seems most to rejoice in his freedom, he is subservient to an incomprehensible spirit which impels him to acts of evil and of heroism and destines him to tragedy which is sometimes ignoble, but also sometimes exquisitely beautiful. It is the lyricism which shocks us into seeing in a new way. What we see is a world that is familiar, yet spectrally strange. It is a very real world, historically verifiable. Yet it is far more the personal creation of a post-Darwinian student of philosophy who was steeped in the great works of literature, beginning with Lucretius, Sophocles, Ecclesiastes, and the Book of Job.

APPENDIX

The Views of Others

THE PHILOSOPHY

Most Hardy criticism focuses on the novels and the short poems.[1] When it discusses ideas, it is inevitably concerned with the antinomy of determinism and free will. Although they vary in emphasis on the seriousness of Hardy's determinism, critics usually find in the conflict the origin of his force as a poet: determinism brings little sadness if one thinks of the generations of human life; it offers only pathos when one thinks of the individual.

One of the most important early studies is Helen Garwood's *Thomas Hardy: An Illustration of the Philosophy of Schopenhauer* (Philadelphia: John Winston, 1911). After noting resemblances to the views of Schopenhauer and Hartmann, Miss Garwood remarks, "But in *The Dynasts* [unlike the novels] we have a set of puppets who are wound up . . . determinism worked out into a system like that of *The Dynasts* has gone beyond the point of vital interest" (80). (Hardy put a few marks in his copy.) In the same year F. A. Hedgcock in *Thomas Hardy Penseur et Artiste: Essai de Critique* (Paris: Librairie Hachette), writes, "Une seule qualité caractérise la Volonté Immanente: l'activité, l'effort pour l'effort, l'éternel devenir sans but apparent. . . . le seul espoir [for men] d'une amélioration de leur sort réside dans un progrès de cette essence vers la conscience complète, vers la sympathie avec ses créatures et vers la moralité. Et quelquefois M. Hardy semble prêt à croire avec Renan, que Dieu n'est pas encore, mais qu'il sera un jour" (383–385). Hedgcock finds Hardy a pessimist because he looks at man as an individual rather than at the universe "en son ensemble" (396).

Herbert B. Grimsditch, *Character and Environment in the Novels of Thomas Hardy* (London: Witherby, 1925), contrasts the philosopher and the artist who sees "the human side. . . . Both [good and evil] are due to the workings of the Will, but man has somehow

[1] The material included in this Appendix is supplemental to the footnotes.

313

become percipient, feeling the love of good and the hatred of evil, while remaining a pawn in the game; hence 'the intolerable antilogy of making figments feel' [in *The Dynasts*]. Here the philosopher becomes at variance with the simple man, who feels within him, as all men feel, that the individual *can* will many of his deeds, that he *can* choose between good and evil, true and false. And out of this clash between a determinism arrived at by logical processes and freedom felt as a deeply rooted innate belief arises Hardy's tragic apprehension of the world. The irony of the situation is that man's every action is performed under the urge of this belief in his freedom, which is nothing but an illusion" (24).

Robert Shafer, *Christianity and Naturalism: Essays in Criticism, Second Series* (New Haven: Yale University Press, 1926) credits Hardy with integrity, but blames him for allowing insufficient scope for the human will. He concludes, "His naturalistic philosophy has conspired to reinforce a native tendency, so that he has steadfastly, even truculently remained blind to life's higher values" (280). Joseph Mainsard, "La Pensée de Thomas Hardy: Études," *Revue Catholique*, CXCI (1927), objects that Hardy makes creatures parts of the Will, yet in total greater than the Will itself. In the conflict between his reason and his feeling, Hardy is constrained "à prononcer en dépit de son athéisme et de ses blasphèmes des prières [in the sense of pity and charity] véritablement chrétiennes" (461). G. R. Elliott, *The Cycle of Modern Poetry* (Princeton: Princeton University Press, 1929), gives an impressionistic response to *The Dynasts*. Though praising the poem, he continues, "Hardy's main idea, the Immanent Will, is confused and stagnant. Mainly it is an hypostasis of his own sense of pity for mankind. However, it is made up of various elements: it is indebted to the Christian Jehovah and to the Shadowy Something of peasants, to Greek mythology and to nineteenth-century naturalism. But it is neither as human as a god, nor as surging as desire, nor as austere as fate" (105).

Bonamy Dobrée, *The Lamp and the Lute* (London: Oxford University Press, 1929), sees the Will as evil: "Man suffers, man struggles; Christianity gave him reasons for the suffering and the struggle, and made them worth while; but when a man comes no longer to believe in Christianity, the sufferings to which he is subjected seem only the work of some maleficent, or faintly sardonic, indifferent demon, informing the universe. To Hardy this sort of terror seemed a completely modern product ..." (25). Louise De Ridder-Barzun in *Le Pessimisme de Thomas Hardy* (Brussels: University of Brussels, 1932), sums up, "S'il souffre, c'est de voir le monde réglé par un déterminisme impacable et l'humanité déchirée par tant d'instincts contradictoires" (187). Lionel Stevenson, *Darwin among the Poets* (Chicago: University of Chicago Press, 1932), indicates the contradictory sentiments in Hardy. As for the determinism, he concludes, "In spite of the metaphysical terms, such as 'Immanent Will,' and paradoxes, such as 'purposive yet superconscious,' Hardy's interpretation abides more closely to the Darwinian theory than does that of any of his poetic contemporaries. By denying purpose to the creative force, he nullified the great nineteenth-century confidence in progress" (284). But coming to the last lines of *The Dynasts*, Stevenson remarks that the "concept of the Will's awakening ... joins hands with Meredith's creed of the 'sighting brain' which must be extended into an attribute of all human beings" (296).

Joseph Warren Beach, *The Concept of Nature in Nineteenth-Century Poetry* (New York: Macmillan, 1936), calls the Immanent Will "nothing more than a metaphysical convenience,—a term for expressing the unity and pattern of existing things." It is "no more than the sum total of all the activity in the universe" (518, 520). The emotional implications of Hardy's determinism are stressed by Lascelles Abercrombie in "Thomas Hardy's 'The Dynasts,'" *Proceedings of the Royal Institution of Great Britain* XXIX, (1937): "And the tragic thing is, that human nature has, by some meaningless accident, become endowed with that self-consciousness that will not accept, though it cannot deny, its uselessness; and, what is even worse, has somehow become capable of *pain*, that monstrous irrelevance" (461). Speaking in theoretical terms, Amiya Chakravarty, *The Dynasts and the Post-War Age in Poetry* (London: Oxford University Press, 1938), interprets the last lines: "... Nature herself will become more and more cognizant as human consciousness impinges on Nature and there is a closer correspondence between the two; a correspondence, in fact, which will tend to become more and more a coherence" (76).

R. P. Blackmur, "The Shorter Poems of Thomas Hardy," *Southern Review*, VI (Summer, 1940), would cut the Gordian knot with one sweeping simplification: "Hardy is the great example of a sensitivity violated by ideas; and perhaps the unique example, since Swift, of a sensibility great enough—locked enough in life—to survive the viola-tion" (48). Howard Baker, "Hardy's Poetic Certitude," *Southern Review*, VI (Summer, 1940), defends the philosophy: "Still its bleak inflexibility constitutes its peculiar value: it stiffened and consolidated a mind that otherwise would have been extremely tender and diffuse" (54).

David Cecil, *Hardy the Novelist* (London: Constable, 1942), considers the last lines of *The Dynasts* the momentary representation of a "whimsical fancy . . . a sporadic flash" (24). Annette B. Hopkins, "*The Dynasts* and the Course of History," *The South Atlantic Quarterly*, XLIV (October, 1945), defines the Will as "the God-within-man that drives him to follow his will rather than his reason. This is the Ultimate Irrationality that explains the age-long tragedy of life" (434). John Laird, *Philosophical Incursions into English Literature* (Cambridge, England: University Press, 1946) rejects the meta-physics: "The Whole is said to 'override' its parts, to admit the parts, it would seem, as constituent entities, but to deny their constituent operation, a doctrine which is not good physics, not good logic, not good sense." The interjections of the Pities "are not much more than sentimental bleats" (193).

John Holloway, *The Victorian Age: Studies in Argument* (London: Macmillan, 1953), finds all aspects of Nature "integrated, however obscurely, into a system of rigid and undeviating law" (252). Richard Church, "Thomas Hardy as Revealed in *The Dynasts*," *Études Anglaises*, VII, (1954) sees the interest in the poem as residing in human aspiration: "But the whole tendency of *The Dynasts* . . . is to strive to reveal something beyond the pre-determinism" (77). Mark Van Doren, "The Poems of Thomas Hardy," *Four Poets on Hardy* (Baltimore: Johns Hopkins Press, 1959), feels that the philosophy is artistically constraining, but adds, "The bitterness of the world did not forbid him to embrace it: a poor thing, but his own" (103).

Samuel Hynes, *The Pattern of Hardy's Poetry* (Chapel Hill: University of North Carolina Press, 1961), discovers excellence when the poet defies the philosopher: "Hampered by a philosophy which he only partly understood and could only partly assimilate, he took, no doubt unconsciously, the poetic course—he reduced philosophy (at least in his best poems) to the folk level of belief, to superstition, to a sense of the impenetrable, contradictory mysteries of existence . . . it is this antinomial tension between his thought and his feelings that gives his verse its characteristic pattern and its integrity, and which gives order, though a minimal order, to the chaos of experience" (41, 45).

Harold Orel, *Thomas Hardy's Epic-Drama: A Study of the Dynasts* (Lawrence: University of Kansas Press, 1963), contrasts Hardy and Milton: "Pessimism is at the core of Hardy's singularly strong-minded awareness of the impossibility of bringing intact Milton and the Miltonic dream to the modern world, a nihilism which negates three essential features of the Christian epic, God, Man ennobled, with God's aid, and the possibility of Man's ascension to God" (85).

J. O. Bailey, *Thomas Hardy and the Cosmic Mind: A New Reading of "The Dynasts"* (Chapel Hill: University of North Carolina Press, 1956), has been quoted in Chapter I. Like Orel's, his thorough and careful analysis should be read in its entirety.

The metaphysics underlying the interpretation of one scholar is frequently inharmonious with that of another; and Hardy would certainly have protested that several oversimplify his thought. Yet, even as a novel was, for him, not an argument but an impression, so he would have had to acknowledge the validity of the impressions which his works, including *The Dynasts*, left upon his appreciative critics.

THE ART

Criticism of the art of *The Dynasts* has been incidental to discussion of Hardy's art in general. It may be grouped under perspective, structure, and style. The effect of the spectral representation is commonly noted. George L. Harper, "Hardy, Hudson, Housman," *Scribner's Magazine*, LXXVIII (August, 1925), remarks that, like *The Divine Comedy*, the poem manifests "the power of hallucination, the power of seeing things with dreamlike vividness" (152). George R. Elliott, *The Cycle of Modern Poetry*, writes, "The folk and their rulers pass and repass before us in 130 scenes each of which is so clearly drawn as to fascinate the eye, and so swift and insulated as to give us just that sense of unreality which is in the author's heart. The whole is the vivid and naïve architecture of a dream—or of a moving picture" (108). A. J. Waldock, *Thomas Hardy and The Dynasts* (Sidney: privately printed, 1933), observes that we follow the retreat from Quatre-Bras "as if through the lens of a pursuing camera" (18). A comment on the novels by Leo J. Henkin, *Darwinism in the English Novel 1860–1910*

(New York: Corporate Press, 1940) also fits the poem: "Hardy viewed man from both ends of the telescope. . . . It is this ironic contrast of the greatness and littleness of life which gave the tang of bitterness to all of Hardy's novels" (225).

Mark Van Doren, "The Poems of Thomas Hardy," offers strictures. For him *The Dynasts* "does not get close to its people, whom Hardy too convincingly calls automata, cheese-mites, and mackerel. The view he takes of them is from too far away. . . . When we descend into the action—battles, conferences, love passages, riots, and duels—we do not find ourselves among people to whom warmth has even by inadvertence been given" (85–86). The specific items here are puzzling, and the comment suggests a swift perusal.

On the over-all design Arthur Quiller-Couch, *Studies in Literature, First Series* (Cambridge: University Press, 1923), is unreservedly laudatory: "I suppose *The Dynasts* to be the grandest poetic structure planned and raised in England in our time" (95). Henry Reed in "The Making of 'The Dynasts,'" *The Penguin New Writing* (Harmondsworth: Penguin Books, 1943) reminds us of the technical problems: "Hardy's first task was to discern rhythms, turning points, contrasts, climaxes in his huge and inchoate material . . ." (44). J. M. Stedmond, "Hardy's *Dynasts* and the 'Mythical Method,'" *English*, XII (1958), calls the plan Aeschylean: "the three long acts are equivalent to the three plays which make up a trilogy like the *Oresteia*" (3). Harold Orel, *Thomas Hardy's Epic-Drama: A Study of The Dynasts*, remarks, "The triad of years dramatized in Part Third is in some ways as unified as a morality play" (59). He adds, "The miracle of *The Dynasts* is its infinite variety, not its singleness of theme or tone" (61). Sir Archibald Strong, *Four Studies* (Adelaide: F. W. Preece and Sons, 1932), took the trouble to ascertain that there are 298 mortals with speaking parts.

John Pollock, "*The Dynasts*," *Independent Review* IV (October, 1904), is perhaps the most discriminating of Hardy's contemporary critics, who focused mainly on style. Reviewing Part I, he praises the structure and the prose scenes, but, like others, is disturbed by the blank verse: "Much of the diction in the blank verse, and especially in the colloquies of the supernatural personages, is bald and unpoetical, even at times repulsive." Pollock calls the best verse "trenchant rather than . . . musical" (151). Among various critics of the verse, the reviewer for the *Edinburgh Review* ("Mr. Hardy's 'Dynasts,'" 1908), comments that

Hardy "evidently lacks the 'physical' gifts of the poet, the miraculous leaping together of sound and sense which Byron and Shelley show in their best verse at their best moments" (433).

Arthur Quiller-Couch finds the blank verse "often too prosy." Arthur McDowell, *Thomas Hardy: A Critical Study* (London: Faber and Faber, 1931), agrees that blank verse was "an alien medium for Hardy" (182); but even when the subject matter is prosaic, he finds in the verse an emotional effect as of an incantation. John Crowe Ransom, "Honey and Gall," *Southern Review*, VI (Summer, 1940), protests against Hardy's attempt in "the big Shakesperian style"; but, speaking of his poetry in general, he asserts, "No poet has a firmer sense of the function of a meter ..." (12). E. A. Horsman, "The Language of *The Dynasts*," *The Durham University Journal*, XLI (December, 1948), calls the diction sometimes "merely factitious"; but he continues, "in memory the poetry, crackling and unmusical though it is, forms by its very dissonances an image of a world view which awakens neither joy nor reverence, an image, too, of the mingled contempt and compassion of a man who feels himself to be more moral than the powers commanding him" (16).

As for Hardy's own view of the blank verse, Henry W. Nevinson, *Thomas Hardy* (London: Allen and Unwin, 1941), says that, when he visited the poet in 1906, Hardy "thought he was right in turning Parliamentary Debates into verse when the argument was high, as in one of Pitt's last speeches" (17). And for such credence as the reader may want to give it is Ford Madox Ford's reminiscence (*Portraits from Life* [New York: Houghton Mifflin, 1936]), of Hardy's once talking "after sufficient pressing—by the hour about *The Dynasts*, going over page after page minutely in a nook on the beach, explaining why he had used here heroics, here Alcaics or Sapphics or ballad forms or forms invented by himself ..." (106).

Bibliography

The Dynasts

The Memorial Library Manuscripts
    Part III, Acts 1–4—four sheaves in Hardy's handwriting.
    Part III, Acts 6–7 and After Scene—two sheaves in another hand, revised
    by Hardy.
The British Museum Manuscript
    Parts I, II, III, in separate volumes—fair copies, with revisions.
The Printed Text
    The Dynasts: An Epic-Drama of the War with Napoleon. London:
    Macmillan and Company, 1958.
    "*The Dynasts": The Prologue and Epilogue.* Prepared for the production,
    November 25, 1914, by Granville Barker. Privately printed (copy in the
    British Museum).
    "Preface for a French Translation of *The Dynasts*," *La Revue Nouvelle*
    (Janvier–Février, 1928), 40–41. Typed copy in the Memorial Library.
Purdy, Richard L. *Thomas Hardy: a Bibliographical Study.* London:
    Oxford University Press, 1954.

The Memorial Library Notebooks

Book of Observations.
British Museum Notes taken for "Trumpet Major" + other works of time
    of Geo III in (1878–1879–), Volumes I, III (no II).
Correspondence with Edward Wright.
Literary Notes, Volumes I, II.
Memoranda of Customs, Dates +c, Volumes I, II.
Personal.
Reviews of the Poetry (clippings).
Hardy, Emma. Diary of a Journey to Holland, the Rhine, Black Forest +c,
    1876.
————. Italy 1887 Switz^d 1897.

Autobiography and Printed Correspondence

Hardy, Florence. *The Early Life of Thomas Hardy, 1840–1891.* New York:
    The Macmillan Company, 1928.

————. *The Later Years of Thomas Hardy, 1892–1928.* New York: The Macmillan Company, 1930.

Notes on "The Dynasts," in Four Letters to Edward Clodd. Edinburgh: The Dunedin Press, 1929.

The Letters of Thomas Hardy. Edited by Carl J. Weber. Waterville: Colby College Press, 1954.

The Sales Catalogues

A Catalogue of the Library of Thomas Hardy. For an auction May 26, 1938, by Hodgson and Company (copy in the Memorial Library).

Catalogue of Books from Hardy's Library. For sale, by the Export Book Company, July, 1938 (copy in the Memorial Library).

The Historical Sources

Works in the Memorial Library

Alison, Archibald. *History of Europe from the Commencement of the French Revolution in 1789 to the Restoration of the Bourbons in 1815.* 20 vols. London: Blackwood and Sons, 1847–1848.

Antommarchi, F. *Mémoires du Docteur.* 2 vols. Paris: Barrois, 1825.

Capefigue, Jean B. H. R. *Les Cent Jours.* 2 vols. Paris: Langlois et Leclercq, 1841.

————. *L'Europe Pendant le Consulat et l'Empire de Napoléon.* 10 vols. Paris: 1840.

Gruyer, Paul. *Napoléon Roi de L'Ile d'Elbe.* Paris: Hachette, 1906.

Houssaye, Henry. *1815: Waterloo.* Translated by Émile Mann, from 31st edition. London: Adam and Charles Black, 1900.

Lanfrey, P. *Histoire de Napoléon Ier.* 5 vols. Paris: Charpentier, 1876.

Lévy, Arthur. *Napoléon Intime.* Paris: Librairie Plon, 1893.

Napier, Sir W. F. P. *History of the War in the Peninsula and in the South of France, from the Year 1807 to the Year 1814.* 6 vols. (Reprint) London: Warne, 1892.

Roseberry, Lord. *Pitt.* London: Macmillan and Company, 1892.

Ségur, M. Le Lieutenant-Général Comte de. *Histoire de Napoléon et de la Grande Armée en 1812.* 2 vols. Paris: Houdaille, 1839.

Siborne, William. *The Waterloo Campaign 1815.* 4th ed. Westminster: Constable, 1895.

Sloane, W. M. *Life of Napoleon Bonaparte.* 4 vols. London: Macmillan, 1901.

Thiers, L. A. *Histoire du Consulat et de l'Empire.* 20 vols. Paris: Paulin, 1847–1862. (Hardy also owned the translation, in part by D. F. Campbell, in 20 volumes. London: Henry Colburn, 1845–1862.)

Tolstoi, Leo. *War and Peace.* Translated by Nathan H. Dole. 4 vols. London: Scott, n. d.

Works Formerly in Hardy's Library

Gifford, C. H. *History of the Wars Occasioned by the French Revolution, from the Commencement of Hostilities in 1792, to the End of the Year 1816.* 2 vols. London: Lewis, 1817.

Hazlitt, William. *The Life of Napoleon Buonaparte.* 3 vols. 1887.

Works not in the Memorial Library

The Annual Register, or a View of the History, Politics, and Literature for the Year 1815. London: Baldwin, Cradock, and Joy, 1916.

Beatty, William. *Authentic Narrative of the Death of Lord Nelson with the Circumstances Preceding, Attending, and Subsequent to That Event.* London: Cadell and Davies, 1807.

Brenton, Edward P. *The Naval History of Great Britain from the Year 1783 to 1836.* 2 vols. Rev. ed. London: Colburn, 1837.

Constant (L. C. Wairy). *Memoirs of Constant.* 4 vols. London: Nichols, 1896.

Coquelle, P. *Napoléon et l'Angleterre, 1803–1813.* Paris: Librairie Plon Plon-Nourrit, 1904.

De Bourrienne, L. A. F. *Memoirs of Napoleon Bonaparte.* 4 vols. Rev. ed. New York: Crowell, 1885.

Fitzgerald, Percy. *The Life of George the Fourth, including His Letters and Opinions with a View of the Men, Manners, and Politics of His Reign.* New York: Harper and Brothers, 1881.

Fraser, Sir William. *Words on Wellington: The Duke—Waterloo—The Ball.* London: Nimmo, 1889.

Gardner, Dorsey. *Quatre Bras, Ligny and Waterloo. A Narrative of the Campaign in Belgium, 1815.* London: Kegan Paul, Trench and Company, 1882.

Gifford, John (pseudonym). *A History of the Political Life of the Right Honourable William Pitt.* 3 vols. London: Cadell and Davies, 1809.

Gleig, George R. *The Battle of Leipsic,* Part I; *The Leipsic Campaign,* Part II. London: Longman, Brown, Green, and Longmans, 1852.

Las Cases, Count M. J. E. *Mémorial de Sainte Hélène. Journal of the Private Life and Conversations of the Emperor Napoleon at Saint Helena.* 4 vols. London: Colburn, 1823.

Memes, John S. *Memoirs of the Empress Josephine.* New York: Harper and Brothers, 1844.

Memoirs of the History of France During the Reign of Napoleon Written at Saint Helena and Published from the Original Manuscripts Corrected by the Emperor. 7 vols. London: Colburn and Bossange, 1822.

Méneval, Baron Claude-François de. *Memoirs to Serve for the History of Napoleon I from 1802 to 1815.* 3 vols. London: Hutchinson, 1894.

———. *Napoléon et Marie-Louise. Souvenirs Historiques de M. Le Baron Méneval, Ancien Secrétaire du Portefeuille de Napoléon Premier Consul et Empereur.* 3 vols. Paris: Librairie d'Amyot, 1843.

Méry, François, J. P. A. *Trafalgar.* Paris: Michel Lévy Frères, 1865.

Moore, James C. *The Life of Lieutenant-General Sir John Moore, K. B.* 2 vols. London: Murray, 1834.

———. *A Narrative of the Campaign of the British Army in Spain, Commanded by His Excellency Lieut-Gen. Sir John Moore, K. B.* 2nd ed. London: Johnson, 1809.

Oeuvres de Napoléon Bonaparte. 5 vols. Paris: Panckoucke, 1821.

O'Meara, Barry E. *Napoleon in Exile; or, A Voice from St. Helena. The Opinions and Reflections of Napoleon on the Most Important Events of His Life and Government in His Own Words.* 2 vols. London: Simpkin and Marshall, 1822.

Parliamentary Debates. Edited by Cobbett and Hansard. Vols. III, XVI, XXX. London: Brettell.

The Speeches of the Right Honourable William Pitt in the House of Commons. 4 vols. London: Longman, Hurst, Rees, and Orme, 1806.

Robinson, H. B. *Memoirs of Lieutenant-General Sir Thomas Picton.* 2 vols. London: Bentley, 1835.

Speeches of the Late Right Honourable Richard Brinsley Sheridan. 5 vols. London: Martin, 1816.

Southey, Robert. *The Life of Nelson.* New York: Harper and Brothers, 1871. (Hardy may have used the 1814 edition.)

Stanhope, Earl. *Life of the Right Honourable William Pitt.* 3 vols. London: Murray, 1879.

The Dispatches of Field Marshal the Duke of Wellington During His Various Campaigns in India, Denmark, Portugal, Spain, the Low Countries, and France, from 1799 to 1818. Compiled by Gurwood. 13 vols. London: Murray, 1838.

Speeches in Parliament of the Right Honourable William Windham. 3 vols. London: Longman, Hurst, Orme, Brown, 1812.

Works of Primary Importance Cited in Hardy's Sources

Chesney, Lt. Col. Charles C. *Waterloo Lectures: A Study of the Campaign of 1815.* 2nd. ed. London: Longmans, Green, 1869.

Elliott, George. *The Life of the Most Noble Arthur Duke of Wellington.* 2nd ed. London: Sherwood, Nefly, and Jones, 1816.

Memoirs of Don Manuel de Godoy, Prince of the Peace. London: Bentley, 1836.

Jomini, Baron. *Life of Napoleon.* London: Trübner, 1864.

Junot, Madame, the Duchess D'Abrantès. *Memoirs of Napoleon, His Court and Family.* Vol. II. New York: Appleton, 1854.

Marmont, Viese de. *Mémoires du Duc de Raguse de 1792 à 1841.* 9 vols. Paris: Perrotin, 1857.

Mélito, Count Miot de. *Memoirs.* 2 vols. London: Low, Marston, Searle, and Rivington, 1881.

Memoirs of Prince Metternich. 5 vols. London: Bentley and Son, 1880–1882.

Savary, A. J. M. R. *Mémoires Écrits de sa Main pour Servir à l'Histoire de l'Empereur Napoléon.* 4 vols. Paris, 1828.

A Sketch of the Battle of Waterloo to Which Are Added Despatches of Field-Marshal the Duke of Wellington; Field-Marshal Prince Blücher; and Reflections on the Battles of Ligny and Waterloo by General Müffling. Brussels: Gérard, 1845.

Index

NOTE: Hardy's spellings of proper names have been retained.